李知宇　宫　齐　范毅方◎编著

非文学
翻译读本

Non-Literary Translation:
Selected Readings

中国·广州

图书在版编目（CIP）数据

非文学翻译读本/李知宇，宫齐，范毅方编著．—广州：暨南大学出版社，2018.12
ISBN 978-7-5668-2496-7

Ⅰ.①非…　Ⅱ.①李…②宫…③范…　Ⅲ.①英语—翻译—教材　Ⅳ.①H315.9

中国版本图书馆CIP数据核字（2018）第209681号

非文学翻译读本
FEI WENXUE FANYI DUBEN
编著者：李知宇　宫　齐　范毅方

出 版 人：徐义雄
责任编辑：姚晓莉
责任校对：苏　洁
责任印制：汤慧君　周一丹

出版发行：暨南大学出版社（510630）
电　　话：总编室（8620）85221601
营销部（8620）85225284　85228291　85228292（邮购）
传　　真：（8620）85221583（办公室）　85223774（营销部）
网　　址：http://www.jnupress.com
排　　版：广州市天河星辰文化发展部照排中心
印　　刷：佛山市浩文彩色印刷有限公司
开　　本：787mm×1092mm　1/16
印　　张：15
字　　数：350千
版　　次：2018年12月第1版
印　　次：2018年12月第1次
定　　价：48.00元

前 言

2007 年国务院学位委员会批准暨南大学设置翻译硕士专业学位，旨在培养高层次、应用型、专业化的翻译人才。根据全国翻译硕士专业学位教育指导委员会的指导性培养方案，专业方向必修课（笔译方向）的应用翻译和文学翻译各占 4 个学分，但选修课则明显倾向应用翻译——科技翻译、商务翻译、传媒翻译等，应用翻译的重要性和显著性可见一斑。

《非文学翻译读本》的几位编者长期进行非文学类文本的翻译和写作，积累了一些英汉/汉英译文或论文，编辑成册，希望能对攻读翻译硕士专业学位的学生有所裨益。

本书选录两篇翻译研究的开山之作为理论篇，即卡萨格兰德（Casagrande）1954 年发表的论文《翻译的目的》（*The Ends of Translation*）和霍尔姆斯（Holmes）的《翻译的“名”与“实”》（*The Name and the Nature of Translation Studies*）。本书所选均为编者们近年来的作品——典型的英译汉（摘译）和汉译英对照文本，可作为广大翻译专业的学生和对英语写作与翻译感兴趣的读者的阅读和分析材料。

本书的编写受到了暨南大学外国语学院研究生院的大力支持，在此，表示衷心的感谢！同时，感谢程薇、何梓健、李瑞宁三位研究生对第三部分所做的回译工作，感谢暨南大学出版社姚晓莉编辑和苏洁校对对本书的出版付出的辛勤劳动！

由于编写时间仓促，个人能力有限，其中难免有一些疏漏之处，望读者批评指正！

编　者

2018 年 6 月

目　录

前　言 …………………………………………………………………… 1

第一章　概　述

引　言 …………………………………………………………………… 2

Selected Reading 1　The Ends of Translation …………………… Joseph B. Casagrande　3

翻译的目的 ……………………………… 李知宇　何梓健译　9

Selected Reading 2　The Name and the Nature of Translation Studies … James Holmes　14

翻译的“名”与“实” …………………… 李知宇　何梓健译　24

第二章　摘　译

Selected Reading 1　Translation as Intercultural Communication ………… David Katan　32

作为跨文化交际的翻译 …………………… 宫　齐　陈慕羽译　50

Selected Reading 2　Higher Education and Europe After 1992:

The Framework ……………………………… Ladislav Cerych　60

1992 年后的高等教育与欧洲 ………………………… 宫　齐译　73

Selected Reading 3　Toward a History of Modern Sociolinguistics …… Konrad Koerner　77

现代社会语言学史 ……………………………………… 宫　齐译　86

Selected Reading 4　On the Developing History of Psycholinguistics ……… J. F. Kess　91

心理语言学的发展史 …………………………………… 宫　齐译　107

Selected Reading 5　Ecolinguistics: State of the Art 1998 ………………… Alwin Fill　114

当代生态语言学的研究现状 ……………… 范俊军　宫　齐译　125

第三章　学术论文汉译英

Selected Reading 1　步态中的最小作用量原理 …………………………… 范毅方等　134

Least-Action Principle in Gait ………… Translated by Zhiyu Li　138

Selected Reading 2　非病理性扁平足和高弓足的自然步态 ………………… 范毅方等　145

Natural Gaits of the Non-Pathological Flat

Foot and High-Arched Foot …………… Translated by Zhiyu Li　149

Selected Reading 3　骨组织最优化原则 …………………………………… 范毅方等　157

Optimal Principle of Bone Structure …… Translated by Zhiyu Li　162

Selected Reading 4　骨表面地图化技术 …………………………… 范毅方等　173
Bone Surface Mapping Method ………… Translated by Zhiyu Li　180
Selected Reading 5　基于步行足底冲量检测肌肉骨骼衰老及损伤的筛选方法 …………………………… 范毅方等　191
Screening Method Based on Walking Plantar Impulse for Detecting Musculoskeletal Senescence and Injury ……………………………… Translated by Zhiyu Li　201
Selected Reading 6　站立足印迹诊断方法 …………………………… 范毅方等　216
Standing Footprint Diagnostic Method … Translated by Zhiyu Li　223

第一章

概　述

引　言

德国翻译理论家冉佩尔特（Jumpelt）称二十世纪为“翻译时代”，因为全球的翻译活动和翻译研究发生了巨大的变化。二十一世纪的数字时代则见证了翻译活动的普及——各种类型的翻译活动数量激增，翻译题材包罗万象，翻译文本类型日益繁多。翻译活动也由于对其研究的广泛和深入而逐渐成为一个学科领域。

翻译活动覆盖各个学科领域，从宗教、文学和科学著作延伸至技术、贸易、时事宣传、广告等，这带来了翻译文本的多样性——从书籍到文章、合同、条约、法令、告示、广告、处方、食谱、信函、报告、公文等①。

时至今日，译界对文本的分类尚未达成共识，但大部分文本是依据文本的主题或文本的功能来分类的。根据主题分类的有卡萨格兰德（Casagrande）的四分法——语用翻译（pragmatic），美学—诗歌翻译（aesthetic-poetic），人种学翻译（ethnographic）和语言学翻译（linguistic）②，罗姆（Hieronymus）的二分法——圣经翻译类（biblical）与非圣经翻译类（non-biblical）等；根据文本功能分类的有赖斯（Reiss）的四分法——信息型（informative）、表情型（expressive）、操作型（operative）和视听媒体类型（audiomedial）③。

尽管学者们对文学和非文学翻译的划分颇感忐忑④，但非文学翻译（non-literary translation）已经是一个大的分类，且有许多同义词——专业翻译（specialized translation）、应用翻译或者实用翻译（pragmatic translation），且渐入佳境，目前不仅是翻译硕士的必修课，相关的专著、论文也颇丰。

“非”虽然有不入主流之嫌疑，但也有宽泛的涵盖内容，即文学翻译之外的文本统统归属于非文学翻译。目前，非文学翻译尚无被学界广泛接受的定义。但在迪里索（Delisle）等编著的《翻译研究关键词》一书中，“实用文本”（pragmatic text）就与“非文学文本”近义，即“任何总体上具有实时、短期用途，旨在传递具普遍性或某领域特有的一些信息而美学效果只起次要作用的文本”。目前世界上90%的翻译可以归入实用文本之列。⑤

本书以关于翻译的目的、翻译研究的学科性质和研究范围的经典之作为开篇。

---

① NEWMARK P. A textbook of translation［M］. New York: Prentice Hall, 1988.

② CASAGRANDE J B. The ends of translation［J］. International journal of American linguistics, 1954, 20（4）.

③ REIB K. Möglichkeiten und Grenzen der Übersetzungskritik［M］. Muich: Max Hueber, 1971.

④ BAKER M. Translation studies (Vol. 4)［M］. London: Routledge, 2009.

⑤ 迪里索，利加恩克，科米尔. 翻译研究关键词［M］. 孙艺风，仲伟合，编译. 北京：外语教学与研究出版社，2004.

Selected Reading 1

The Ends of Translation

Joseph B. Casagrande

1. In this paper we are concerned with the ends of translation in a two-fold sense. First, we shall consider the purpose of the translator in making the translation and, second, we shall discuss the end-product of translation, particularly the problem of the equivalence of messages in the languages in question.

2. While the intent of the translator in every instance is probably to translate the text or utterance as accurately as possible, his purpose in undertaking his task as well as the nature of the material with which he deals may vary. Differences in purpose and material may affect both the character of the end-product and the process of translating itself. Moreover, the nature of the material may influence, or even determine the purpose. However, we shall address ourselves here primarily to the translator's aim and discuss differences in the material and in the translating process only incidentally.

Although there are undoubtedly others, four major aims will be discussed below in some detail. These are tentatively designated PRAGMATIC, AESTHETIC-POETIC, LINGUISTIC, and ETHNOGRAPHIC aims. The same material approached with these various goals in mind may yield different translations, but given the translator's aim they may nevertheless be equally valid.

2.1 In pragmatic translation, the purpose is essentially to translate a message as efficiently and as accurately as possible. The emphasis is on the content of the message as such rather than on its aesthetic form, grammatical form or the cultural context, all of which are subsidiary to the practical, matter-of-fact goal. Instructions, explanations, directions (such as those given in several languages on dress patterns or packaged goods), scientific treatises, government documents and communiques lend themselves quite naturally to pragmatic translation, but myths and tales, literary works or folklore may be similarly treated.

2.2 If, on the other hand, the translator's purpose is aesthetic-poetic, while content obviously is not ignored, express consideration is given to the literary or aesthetic form of the message in both languages. Parenthetically, however, it may be noted that the aesthetic form of the original is all too frequently sacrificed to the prevailing literary mode—witness many versions in both poetry and prose of the works of certain Greek and Roman poets.

Of the several aims, the aesthetic-poetic is the most difficult of realization and the most demanding of the translator's art and skills. He is subject to the twin constraints of form and meaning, and if the translator is sensitive to the demands of his task, maintaining proper balance between the two may be the source of no little anguish. Marianne Moore has testified to this in connection with her labors on a recent translation of *The Fables of LaFontaine*.

The elements of poetic or aesthetic expression—rime, meter, imagery, metaphor, onomatopoeia, style and the like—as well as the particular form into which the work is cast, are precisely those aspects of language which are most resistant to translation. In large measure these elements partake of the unique qualities of the individual language (and, one might add, the culture) with which they are inextricably intermingled. Thus, to attempt to translate James Joyce's *Finnegan's Wake* into Navaho would be patently absurd. For to bring about the wedding of expressive form and substance in such a manner that a translation truly reflects the original, whether it be Dante's *Divine Comedy*, a Navaho chant, or magical formulae of the Dobuans or Trobrianders, is no small accomplishment. Assuredly, the French epigrammatist had an aesthetic aim in mind when he said, "traduire c'est à trahir".

2.3 Ethnographic translation is concerned primarily with the explication, either in annotation or in the translation itself, of the cultural context of the message in the source language. A secondary goal is the specification and explanation of differences in meaning between apparently equivalent elements of messages in the two languages, particularly with those differences that may be masked by other forms of translation. It may be noted that the overall purpose of ethnographic translation is closely akin to that of ethnolinguistics.

The writer recalls a Plains Indian poem or war song quoted with visible emotion by Ralph Linton in an anthropology class a good many years ago:

The bleached skulls of young men
Lie in the new grasses of spring.
With strong white teeth they grin
At death and the riding sun.
How beautiful they are to behold!

Translation of this poem into what might pass for free verse may satisfy an aesthetic-poetic aim, yet its full significance is lost unless one understands the value placed upon warfare by the Plains Indians and the prestige accorded the young warrior for whom to be killed in combat with a hated enemy was truly to die a glorious death. But ethnographic translation is not limited to placing a message within its broader cultural context; it also figures in a finer-grained approach. In the process of transcoding one is frequently called upon to supply supposedly equivalent terms for traits that are analogous rather than identical in the two cultures. While in most contexts the meaning will not be materially affected by this translator's fiction, in others the difference between, say, "poison" (potassium cyanide) and "poison" (a compound of human exuviae and innocuous herbs) may be crucial, and its specification becomes important.

A similar problem is encountered when dealing with generalizing concepts if there are no equivalent terms that encompass the same range of phenomena. For example, "reptile" in English subsumes a variety of animals that are differently categorized in numerous other languages.

Another problem, which like the above is common to all forms of translation, is faced when dealing with words which cannot be satisfactorily translated by a single word or, in some cases, by a circumlocutory phrase. For example, the German word Schadenfreude has no English equivalent, but may perhaps be adequately translated by the phrase "pleasure in another's misfortune". However, the Comanche word puha, which refers roughly to the "supernatural" or to "powers emanating from the supernatural which may be bestowed upon an individual", cannot be easily paraphrased in English. An extended commentary would be required to translate this concept in a manner consistent with an ethnographic aim. The reader will have little difficulty in supplying additional examples.

2.4 The essential aim in linguistic translation, whatever the ultimate form the translation may take, is to identify and assign equivalent meanings to the constituent morphemes of the source language. Interest centers on structural or grammatical form. Linguistic translation thus involves a kind of comparative linguistic anatomy well exemplified in Voegelin's analytic approach in his paper elsewhere in this issue on multiple stage translation, wherein he makes explicit steps in the process of translation which other translators having somewhat different aims do not specify.

When the aim is primarily linguistic, the resulting translation is frequently in the form commonly designated "literal" or "interlinear", as compared with a so-called "free" translation. Morphemes, words, or larger segments (which may consist of metaphorical or idiomatic expressions) are often sequentially translated into their nearest equivalents, thus preserving the original word order and, presumably, the flavor of the original message. This procedure of course serves a legitimate linguistic purpose. However, the writer is of the opinion that it may result in a kind of pseudo-translation which can be as misleading as an overly free translation. For example, the lay reader may gain serious misconceptions about the language in question, especially if it is that of a preliterate people, when he inevitably compares such a translation with his own language, say, English. Certainly an utterance that is in accordance with good usage in the original language deserves to be translated into equally acceptable form in the second language. Moreover, some of the statements about the habitual modes of thought or the world view of a people made on the basis of inferences from language by such writers as

Lee and Whorf appear to the writer to be derived from half-translations, or to stem from a preoccupation with what one might call "grammatical meaning".

In actual practice the four aims of translation identified and briefly discussed in the foregoing paragraphs occur in a mixed rather than a pure form. It is primarily a matter of the translator's emphasis rather than of his exclusive attention to a single purpose. In pragmatic translation emphasis falls on the content of the message and the transfer of information as such; in aesthetic-poetic translation the concern is with aesthetic form and the communication of expressive or affective elements of the message; the ethnographic aim is to elucidate differences in cultural context and in meaning; and in linguistic translation attention is paid primarily to structural or grammatical form.

Ethnographic and linguistic translations, as the terms suggest, reflect in part the more narrowly technical interests of the translator—the former of anthropologists and the latter of linguists. Their approach to the material to be translated is in large measure dictated by these interests, while that of the translator having a pragmatic or aesthetic-poetic purpose is probably determined in greater measure by the nature of the material itself.

3. The point was made in the first section of this paper that the same material approached with different aims may yield somewhat variant translations. Nevertheless, within such limits as may be imposed by any given aim, there is a common desire to achieve an accurate translation. It may also be observed that aesthetic-poetic, ethnographic, and linguistic translations are in a sense all embroideries upon this essentially pragmatic goal. There then remains in the final portion of this paper to consider the general problem of translation equivalence.

Briefly stated, the task of the translator is to decode a message presented in one code, which we may designate code A (or FL), and encode that message in a second code, code B (or TL), so that the two messages are equivalent, or more accurately, approximately equivalent. Perfect equivalence, in the sense that the messages evoke identical responses in the speakers of the two languages, is probably impossible of attainment except perhaps in brief pragmatic messages. To achieve absolute equivalence in this process of transcoding presupposes an identity of cultural or socially shared experience between the two speech communities. Unless one subscribes to the view that two groups can have identical cultures yet speak different languages, this state of affairs is a virtual contradiction in terms. It seems to the writer that many of the more subtle problems of translation are obscured or glossed over by the fact that most translations with which we are familiar are from FL Indo-European to TL Indo-European, whose speakers share in large measure a common cultural heritage.

The attitudes and values, the experience and tradition of a people, inevitably become involved in the freight of meaning carried by a language. In effect, one does not translate LANGUAGES, one translates CULTURES. Ethnography may, in fact, be thought of as a form of translation. That it is possible to translate one language into another at all attests to the universalities in culture, to common vicissitudes of human life, and to the like capabilities of men throughout the earth, as well as to the inherent nature of language and the character of the communication process itself; and, a cynic might add, to the arrogance of the translator.

It follows from the above that the ideal translator should, among other qualifications, be equally proficient in the languages concerned, and that he be BICULTURAL as well as BILINGUAL. Although their scholarship may be impeccable and their spiritual homes indeed be in the civilizations of antiquity, translators of the classics or of other documents in noncontemporary languages must necessarily work with the disadvantage of not having had direct contact with a living language and a living culture.

In spite of the various difficulties standing in the way of translation that we have thus far discussed in this paper, the fact remains that information is effectively communicated across language barriers—intentions of speakers expressed in one language are capable of being expressed in another language so that they are comprehended and appreciated. If there is a loss of information in this process of switching codes, it must be remembered that much information is also lost in messages transmitted between members of the same speech community, particularly if they belong to different subcultures or status groups.

3.1 When the intentions of a speaker encoded in a message in language A are commensurate with the significance of the message for the hearer when transcoded into language B, we have FUNCTIONAL EQUIVALENCE and the foregoing may be taken as an operational definition of translation equivalence. However, functional equivalence like absolute equivalence ap-pears to be a goal which in actual practice is only infrequently achieved.

3.2 The correspondence between messages purportedly the same in two languages is in most cases probably a matter of degree. Following the definition given above, it may be possible to arrive at a measure of the degree of correspondence between similar messages. For example, a set of directions, selected so that readily observable actions would be required to carry them out, might be presented to matched groups of monolingual speakers and the differences in their performance compared. In such an experiment, it would of course also be important to note differences in performance within the two groups of speakers.

Appropriate tests, such as the semantic differential developed by Charles E. Osgood and his students at the University of Illinois, might also be devised to determine the degree of correspondence between nonpragmatical utterances in which connotative meaning figures to a greater degree. One might hypothesize that the degree of correspondence between translated messages will vary inversely with the amount of connotative meaning or associational loading of the constituent words in the messages. Stated differently, one might predict greater disparity between messages at the aesthetic-poetic end of the scale than at the pragmatic end.

The problem of message equivalence may also be approached from the point of view of the translator without reference to his audience. If there is consensus or a high level of agreement among a number of competent translators on a single version, one might assume that it is an accurate translation. Consensus is, after all, the ultimate arbiter of linguistic usage.

3.3 Back-translation affords another test of internal consistency. In this process a message in code A is translated into code B by one person, then retranslated into code A by another person and the retranslated message compared with the original. If there are discrepancies between the two versions in code A, they are presumably diagnostic of trouble-points in the process of transcoding. Certain of these discrepancies, however, may be due to the use of al-ternative forms which do not necessarily affect the import of the message.

3.4 Various changes which may yield interesting experimental results may be rung upon the device of back-translation. Two of these, mentioned in Voegelin's paper on multiple stage translation, are what might be designated SERIAL TRANSLATION and PARALLEL TRANSLATION. In the former a message in code A is translated successively into codes B, C, D, etc. and if desired, back into code A. Serial translation, as Voegelin suggests in his paper, has frequently been used by anthropologists working with monolingual informants in such places as West Africa, Mexico or South America, and using interpreters bilingual in the native language and in French, Spanish, or Portuguese. There are, of course, obvious hazards in such a procedure and extra precautions must be taken to check texts or ethnographic materials obtained in this fashion.

Parallel translation involves the translation of one language into two or more related languages, say, English into Comanche, Shoshone, and Southern Paiute. Comparison of the translations in the several target languages may reveal significant and systematic differences in the way English is handled at both the grammatical and semantic levels. For example, English tenses may be differently construed and English meanings variously interpreted in the several related languages.

In this paper undue emphasis has perhaps been placed on obstacles in the path of accurate and facile translation. However, translation is not a mere mechanical process which when once set in train proceeds by identical stages from diverse beginnings to identical ends. Equivalent words, phrases or constructions are not ready at hand and ripe for the plucking. Whatever the purpose with which the task is approached, translation is a creative process which in all but its simplest forms presents a real challenge to him who would undertake it.

翻译的目的

［美］约瑟夫·B. 卡萨格兰德
李知宇　何梓健译

一、引言

本文将就翻译目的展开两方面的讨论：译者进行翻译的目的为何？译文最终将发挥何种作用？尤其涉及上述语言信息对等问题时该如何处理。

二、翻译的目的

译者的意图无一不是把文本或话语转换成另一种语言，越准确越好。但其目的及所处理的语言材料的性质会有所差别。这种差别也许会影响最终译文甚至翻译过程本身，再者，语言材料的特性也会影响，甚至决定翻译的目的。然而，本文在此主要论及译者的目的、语言材料之间的差别，以及翻译过程的巨细。

无疑，在本文作论之前已有其他相关文献对翻译的目的有所提及，下文也将就翻译目的的四个主要方面详细展开，分别为：语用翻译、美学—诗歌翻译、人种学翻译、语言学翻译。即使是同一语言材料，只要目的相异，所得的译文也会不同，但考虑到译者自身的目的，上述这些目的也并不一定能达到相等的效果。

1. 语用翻译

语用翻译的目的即尽可能把信息有效而准确地翻译出来，强调内容大于审美、语法形式或文化语境，因此三者皆以实际效果为目的。比如介绍、说明、指引（这些文本通常在服装样式或包装商品上出现，且附有好几种语言版本）、科学专著、政府文件及联合公告，这些材料自然都需要运用到语用翻译；而对于神话传说、文学作品、民间故事等文学性较强的文本也可以采用相似的手段。

2. 美学—诗歌翻译

另外，如果译者以美学—诗歌翻译为目的，加之材料的内容十分突出，那么译入语、译出语和文本的文学、美学形式就能够对应起来。但要注意的是，源文本的审美形式往往要让位于普遍的文学模式。古希腊罗马诗人的作品存有多个译本就是最好的例子。

在这几个目的中，美学—诗歌翻译最难实现，对译者的造诣和技巧要求也是最高的，他必须为形与意两者服务。如果他对翻译任务足够敏感，形意之间达到平衡也不成问题。玛丽安·摩尔在《拉方丹寓言》的翻译中就证明了这点。

凡诗性或美学的语言都涵盖了几个元素：韵、律、意象、隐喻、拟声、文体，以及生成译文的形式，所有这些正是翻译最难处理的部分。很大程度上，这些元素都体现出某种语言的不同特质（或者说这就是文化的多样性），这是一个必然的结果。若是将詹姆斯·乔伊斯的《芬尼根的守灵夜》翻译成纳瓦霍语，显然会词不达意，错漏百出。要是把表达形式与内容结合起来，使译文真实反映出原文的意思，那么不论是《神曲》这样的鸿篇巨制，还是土著人稀奇古怪的表达，最后的成果必然十分瞩目。无疑，玛丽安·摩尔在说“翻译就是背叛”时，头脑中就已浮现出一幅美丽的画面了。

3. 人种学翻译

人种学翻译首先要关注的是对源语言信息的文化语境的阐释，无论是注释还是翻译本身。两种语言信息元素之间虽然能达到对等，但其含义也会存在差异，特别是那些可能被其他翻译形式掩盖的差异，于是，第二个目标就是要对这些差异做一番解释说明。我们注意到，人种学的整体目的与民族语言学的目的密切相关。

在此，笔者回顾了拉尔夫·林顿多年前在人类学课上引用的平原印第安诗歌或战歌：

年轻战士的白骨
正安躺在暖春的新绿中。
他们的牙齿白皙而有力，
无论是死亡凛冽，还是高挂暖阳
他们都付之一笑。

虽然这个被视为自由诗体的翻译也能满足美学—诗歌翻译的目的，但它的意义已全然消失，除非人们能够明白平原印第安人的战争价值和年轻战士们的威望与仇敌浴血奋战，死得光荣。

但人种学翻译并不仅限于在宏观的文化背景下传播信息，也体现在微观层面的方法上。在语言转换的过程中，译者经常有义务为两个文化提供相应的术语，这些术语不一定要完全一致，可以是意义类似。大多数情况下，译者的这种加工行为并不会对其意义产生什么重大影响。但其他词语之间的差异却甚为重要，比如说“毒物”（氰化钾）与“毒药”（人造毒素和无毒草药的化合物），有必要对两者进行额外的区分。

如果没有涵盖相同现象的对应词的话，我们在处理泛化概念时也会遇到类似的问题。例如，英文中的“爬行动物”就包含着许多其他语言中不同分类的动物。

当遇到的词语不能用单个词或委婉表达翻译时，就出现了另一个问题，这也是所有翻译都会碰到的问题。例如，德语单词 Schadenfreude 没有英文的同义词，但也可能用“幸灾乐祸”来达到充分翻译。然而，（印第安）科曼奇语中的 puha 大概指的是“超自然的”，或是“可以被赋予某个人的超自然力量”，这意义过于独特，不能轻易改写。我们需要进行进一步解释才能符合人种学翻译目的。这样一来，读者可以轻而易举地提供更多例子。

4. **语言学翻译**

无论翻译的最终形式如何，语言学翻译的基本目的都在于识别和赋予源语言语素对等的含义，重心在结构或语法形式。因此，语言学翻译其实与比较语言结构相关，沃格林有关多层次翻译的文献中提到的分析方法就是很好的例证。他明确指出了怀有不同目的的译者都没有指出的翻译步骤。

当翻译的目的主要围绕语言学的时候，与所谓的“意译”相比，最终得出的翻译通常只能是“直译”或“逐字翻译”。语素、单词或篇幅较大的语篇（可能包含隐喻或惯用语）通常依次译成与其意义最相近的对应词，从而保留了原词的词序，也许还能保持原始信息的意义。这个过程当然是为合理的语言目的服务的，然而，笔者则认为它可能会导致伪翻译，也会像过度意译一样具有误导性。特别对于那些生活在还没形成文字系统的地区的人而言，难免会将这种翻译与他自己的语言（比如英语）进行比较，那么就可能会对语言产生严重的误解。当然，能够符合源语言用法，并得到良好运用的表达方式值得被翻译成第二语言为大众所接受。此外，作家李和沃尔夫推断，部分关于习惯性思维或世界观的言论似乎是由半机器翻译衍生出来的，也有说来源于早期的所谓“语法意义”。

在翻译实践中，上述简要讨论的四个翻译目的通常会错综出现，一般不会“一枝独秀”。译者不会只专注于单一目的。总而言之，语用翻译侧重信息的内容和转换；美学—诗歌翻译则放眼于审美形式、表达或情感元素的交际效果；人种学翻译则旨在阐释文化语境和意义之间的区别；语言学翻译主要关注结构或语法形式。

人种学翻译和语言学翻译，顾名思义，反映出译者对某个领域的兴趣——前者切合人类学，后者切合语言学。他们采用的翻译方法很大程度上取决于这些兴趣。相反，怀有语用学或美学—诗歌翻译目的的译者很可能是因为语言材料本身的特性使然。

三、翻译对等

本文的第一节已经指出，对于同一语言材料，可有形形色色的目的，由此得出的翻译也不尽相同。不管是何种目的，总有其局限性，不能一言以蔽之，但最终总会推向一个共同的意图：实现翻译的准确无误。同时，我们也发现，美学—诗歌翻译、人种学翻译以及语言学翻译三者不过是分支，是修饰，终究还是要归到实际运用的目标中去。那么，我们需要讨论的就剩下翻译对等的问题了。

如果说源文本是一段密码，那么译者的任务是解码其中的信息，我们可以指定该段密码为代码 A（或 FL，即源语），并以第二个代码 B（或 TL，即目标语）对该消息进行编码，从而使两段信息达到对等，更准确地说应该是近似对等。在两种语言的话语者之间，信息在某种程度上能引起相同的回应，但绝对对等是不可能实现的，在简短的语用信息中也许还有机会“昙花一现”。若要在解码的过程中实现绝对的对等，除非在两个语言区之间存在文化认同或社会共享经验，这与两个语言区文化相同但语言不同的事实显然是矛盾的。笔者认为，我们耳熟能详的翻译其实都是从印欧语系的源语译成印欧语系的目标语，以此为母语的人其实都生活在同一文化中，继承着同一份文化遗产，正因如此，翻译中一些更加微妙、更加需要注意的问题却被掩盖了。

人们的态度、价值观、经验以及传统都会受一种语言所带来的意义的影响。实际上，人们翻译的不是语言，而是文化。而人种学翻译就被视为其中的一种翻译形式。将一种语言翻译成另一种语言证明了文化的普遍性，证明了人类生活的共同变迁，证明了全世界人类的能力，证明了语言的固有本质和交际过程本身的特质；一些愤世嫉俗的人可能会认为：这还证实了译者嚣张的态度。

从上述分析可以看出，理想的译者应该能够熟练掌握对应的语言，并且要了解双语文化、具备双语能力。他们的学术能力也许无可挑剔，他们的精神的确继承了各种文明，但专注于典籍与其他非当代语言文本翻译的译者必须面对一个事实：他们不可能直接接触到现用的语言、鲜活的文化。

本文讨论的翻译方式至今仍存在各种难点，但事实上，信息仍能突破语言障碍，实现有效交流——也就是，一种语言说话者的意图能够通过另一种语言表达出来，最终让人们理解并领会他们所言。如果在“转码”的过程中出现信息丢失，那么其在同一语言社区成员之间的传递中也会失去大量信息，如果他们从属于不同的子文化或处于不同状态组中则尤其容易丢失。

1. 功能对等的定义

在一段信息中，说话者的意图以 A 语言“编码”，当转换成 B 语言时，听者接收到的信息与 A 语言的效果相称，那么我们称之为功能对等，也就是翻译对等的实用定义。然而，功能对等跟绝对对等一样，在翻译实践中鲜有出现。

2. 对等的度

两种语言之间的对应关系在大多数情况下可能是度的问题。按照上面给出的定义，可以得出相似信息之间的对应程度。例如，设置一个语言行为观察组，在另一个匹配组中对单个说话者进行操作，并对比其表现的差异。当然，记录下两组说话者表现的差异也十分关键。

另外也可以适当设计类似的测试，如查尔斯·E. 奥斯古德及其在伊利诺伊大学的学生开发的语义差异测试。这些方法可以确定非语言话语之间的对应程度，其中含义对应程度最大。我们可以假设翻译信息之间的对应程度与信息中组成词的含义或关联负载量成反比。换句话说，估计以美学—诗歌为目的的翻译，其译文与原文的差别要远大于语用翻译。

我们也可以从译者的角度来看待信息对等的问题，不用以受众为参考对象。在译者有足够能力胜任的前提下，对于同一个译文，如果能达成一致认可，那么这就是准确的翻译。毕竟，共识才是语言使用的最终评判标准。

3. 回译

回译的存在，为文本的内部一致性提供了证据。在此过程中，代码 A 中的信息由一个人转换为代码 B，然后由另一个人重新转换为代码 A。将重新传送的信息与原始代码相比较，如果代码 A 中的两个版本之间存在差异，那么它们可能是在代码转换过程中出现了问题。虽然当中的某些差异可能是由词语的替代形式造成的，但这并不影响信息的传递。

4. 连续翻译与平行翻译

使用回译策略可能会发生很多变化，这些变化可能会产生有趣的实验结果。其中两个结果即为沃格林在关于多重翻译的论文中提到的连续翻译和平行翻译。连续翻译的代码 A 中的信息被连续地转换为代码 B、C、D 等，如果有需要的话，可以再次转换为代码 A。正如沃格林在文中所建议的，连续翻译往往适用于与单一语言使用者一起工作的人类学家，这类人群一般在西非、墨西哥或南美等，而负责翻译的一般为双语使用者，他们除母语之外还能说法语、西班牙语或葡萄牙语。当然，在此过程中也有明显的风险，最后的译文是否准确尚是未知之数，因此必须采取措施来核查以回译得出的文本或人种学材料。

平行翻译，亦即将一种语言翻译成两种或多种语言，例如将英语翻译成科曼奇语、肖松尼语和南派尤特语（三者皆为印第安族语）。对几种目标语的翻译进行对比分析，也许能揭示英语在语法和语义层面上处理方式的系统性差异。例如，人们对英语时态可能有不同的架构，英文的含义在几种相关的语言中也有不同的解释。

本文也许过分突出了准确、简单翻译的难点所在。然而，翻译不是一个机械的过程，以为同一个阶段有不同的出发点，最终只会落到同一个目的上。只能说我们对于对等词、短语或结构的准备尚有不足，技巧尚不成熟。无论翻译任务的目的是什么，翻译都是一个创造的过程，对于承担任务的译者来说，除了最简单的项目之外，每每都是真正的挑战。

Selected Reading 2

The Name and the Nature of Translation Studies

James Holmes

"Science", Michael Mulkay points out, "tends to proceed by means of discovery of new areas of ignorance." The process by which this takes place has been fairly well defined by the sociologists of science and research. As a new problem or set of problems comes into view in the world of learning, there is an influx of researches from adjacent areas, bringing with them the paradigms and models that have proved fruitful in their own fields. These paradigms and models are then brought to bear on the new problem, with one of two results. In some situations the problem proves amenable to explicitation, analysis, explication, and at least partial solution within the bounds of one of the paradigms or models, and in that case it is annexed as a legitimate branch of an established field of study. In other situations the paradigms or models fail to produce sufficient results, and researches become aware that new methods are needed to approach the problem.

In this second type of situation, the result is a tension between researches investigating the new problem and colleagues in their former fields, and this tension can gradually lead to the establishment of new channels of communication and the development of what has been called "a new disciplinary utopia", that is, a new sense of a shared interest in a common set of problems, approaches, and objectives on the part of a new grouping of researches. As W. O. Hagstrom has indicated, these two steps, the establishment of communication channels and the development of a disciplinary utopia, "make it possible for scientists to identify with the emerging discipline and to claim legitimacy for their point of view when appealing to university bodies or groups in the larger society."

Though there are no doubt a few scholars who would object, particularly among the linguists, it would seem to me clear that in regard to the complex of problems clustered round the phenomenon of translating and translations, the second situation now applies. After centuries of incidental and desultory attention from a scattering of authors, philologians, and literary scholars, plus here and there a theologian or an idiosyncratic linguist, the subject of translation has enjoyed a marked and constant increase in interest on the part of scholars in recent years, with the Second World War as kind of turning point. As the interest has solidified and expanded, more and more scholars have moved into the field, particularly from the adjacent fields of linguistics, linguistics philosophy, and literary studies, but also from such seemingly more remote disciplines as information theory, logic, and mathematics, each of them carrying with him paradigms, quasi-paradigms, models, and methodologies that he felt could be brought to bear on this new problem.

At first glance, the resultant situation today would appear to be one of great confusion, with no consensus regarding the types of models to be tested, the kind of methods to be applied, to varieties of terminology to be used. More than that, there is not even like-mindedness about the contours of the field, the programs set, the discipline as such. Indeed, scholars are not so much as agreed on the very name of the new field.

Nevertheless, beneath the superficial level, there are a number of indications that for the field of research focusing on the problems translating and translations Hagstrom's disciplinary utopia is taking shape. If this is salutary development (and I believe that it is), it follows that it is worthwhile to further the development by consciously turning our attention to matters that are serving to impede it.

One of these impediments is the lack of appropriate channels of communication. For scholars and researchers in the field, but channels that do exist still tend to run via the older disciplines (with their attendant norms in regard to models, methods, and terminology), sold that papers on the subject of translation are dispersed over periodicals in a wide variety of scholarly fields and journals for practising translators. It is clear that there is a need for other communication channels, cutting across the traditional disciplines to reach all scholars working in the field, from whatever background.

But I should like to focus our attention on the other impediments to the development of a disciplinary utopia. The first of these, the lesser of the two in importance, is the seemingly trivial matter of a name for this field of research. It would not be wise to continue referring to the discipline by its subject matter as has been done at this conference, for the map, as the General Semanticists constantly remind us, is not the territory, and failure to distinguish the two can only further confusion.

Through the years, diverse terms have been used in writings dealing with translating and translations, and one can find references in English to "the art" or "the craft" of translation, but also to the "principles" of translation, the "fundamentals" or the "philosophy". Similar terms recur in French and German. In some cases the choice of term reflects the attitude, point of approach, or background of the writer; in other it has been determined by the fashion of the moment in the scholarly terminology.

There have been a few attempts to create more "learned" terms, most of them with the highly active suffix -ology. Roger Goffin, for instance, has suggested the designation "translatology" in English, and either its cognate or traductologie in French. But since the -ology suffix derives from Greek, purists reject a contamination of this kind, all the Late

Latin in the case of *translatio* or Renaissance French in that of *traduction*. Yet Greek alone offers no way out, for "metaphorology" "metaphaseology", or "metaphastics" would hardly be of aid to us in making our subject clear even to university bodies, let alone to other "groups in the larger society". Such other terms as "translatistics" or "translitics", both of which have been suggested, would be more readily understood, but hardly more acceptable.

Two further, less classically constructed terms have come to the fore in recent years. One of these began its life in a longer form, "the theory of translating" or "the theory of translation" (and its corresponding forms: "theorie des Übersetzens" "théorie de la traduction"). In English (and in German) it has since gone the way of many such terms, and is now usually compressed into "translation theory" (*Übersetzungstheorie*). It has been a productive designation, and can be even more so in future, but only if it is restricted to its proper meaning. For, as I hope to make clear in the course of this paper, there is much valuable study and research being done in the discipline, and a need for much more to be done, that does not, strictly speaking, fall within the scope of theory formation.

The second term is one that has, to all intents and purposes, won the field in German as a designation for the entire discipline. This is the term *Übersetzungswissenschaft*, constructed to form a parallel to *Sprachwissenschaft*, *Literaturwissenschaft*, and many other *Wissenschaften*. In French, the comparable designation, "science de la traduction", has also gained ground, as have parallel terms in various other languages.

One of the first to use parallel sounding term in English was Eugene Nida, who in 1964 chose to entitle his theoretical handbook *Towards a Science of Translating*. It should be noted, though, that Nida did not intend the phrase as a name for the entire field of study, but only for one aspect of the process of translating as such. Others, most of them not native speakers of English, have been more bold, advocating the term "science of translation" (or "translation science") as the appropriate designation for this emerging discipline as a whole. Two years ago this recurrent suggestion was followed by something like canonization of the term when Bausch, Klegraf, and Wilss took the decision to make it the main title to their analytical bibliography of the entire field.

It was a decision that I, for one, regret. It is not that I object to the term *Übersetzungswissenschaft*, for there are few if any valid arguments against that designation for the subject in German. The problem is not that the discipline is not a *Wissenschaft*, but that not all *Wissenschaft* can properly be called science. Just as no one today would take issue with the terms Sprachwissenschaft and Literaturwissenschaft, while more than a few would question whether linguistics has yet reached a stage of precision, formalization, and paradigm formation such that it can properly be described as a science, and while practically everyone would agree that literary studies are not, and in the foreseeable future will not be, a science in any true sense of the English word, in the same way I question whether we can with any justification use designation for the study of translating and translations that places it in the company of mathematics, physics, and chemistry, or even biology, rather than that of sociology, history, and philosophy—or for that matter of literary studies.

There is, however, another term that is active in English in the naming of new disciplines. This is the word "studies". Indeed, for disciplines that within the old distinction of the universities tend to fall under the humanities or arts rather than the sciences as fields of learning, the word would seem to be almost as active in English as the word Wissenschaft in German. One need only think of Russian studies, American studies, Commonwealth studies, population studies, communications studies. True, the word raises a few new complications, among them the fact that it is difficult to derive an adjectival form. Nevertheless, the designation "translation studies" would seem to be the most appropriate of all those available in English, in its adoption as the standard term for the discipline as a whole would remove a fair amount of confusion and misunderstanding. I shall set the example by making use of it in the rest of this paper.

A greater impediment than the lack of a generally accepted name in the way of the development of translation studies is the lack of any general consensus as to the scope and structure of the discipline. What constitutes the field of translation studies? A few would say it coincides with comparative (or contrastive) terminological and lexicographical studies; several look upon it as practically identical with comparative or contrastive theory. But surely it is different, if not always distinct, from the case of emerging disciplines, there has as yet been little meta-reflection on the nature of translation studies as such—at least that has made its way into print and to my attention. One of the few cases that I have found is that of Werner Koller, who has given the following delineation of the subject, "Übersetzungswissenschaft ist zu verstehen als Zusammenfassung und Überbegriff für alle Forschungsbemühungen, die von Phãnomenen 'Übersetzen' und 'Übersetzung' ausgehen oder auf diese Phãnomenen zielen." (Translation studies is to be understood as a collective and inclusive designation for all research activities taking the phenomena of translating and translation as their basis or focus)

From this delineation it follows that translation studies is, as no one I suppose would deny, an empirical discipline. Such disciplines, it has often been pointed out, have two major objectives, which Carl G. Hempel has phrased as "to describe particular phenomena in the world of our experience and to establish general principles by means of which they can be explained and predicted". As a field of pure research—that is to say, research pursued for its own sake, quite apart from any direct practical application outside its own terrain—translation studies thus has two main objectives: ① to describe the phenomena of translating and translation(s) as they manifest themselves in the world of our experience, and ②to establish general principles by means of which these phenomena can be explained to and predicted. The two branches of pure translation studies concerning themselves with these objectives can be *designated descriptive translation studies* (DTS) or *translation description* (TD) and *theoretical translation studies* (ThTS) or *translation theory* (TTh).

Of these two, it is perhaps appropriate to give force consideration to *descriptive translation studies*, as the branch of the discipline which constantly maintains the closest contact with the empirical phenomena under study. There would seem to be three major kinds of research in DTS, which may be distinguished by their focus as product-oriented, function-oriented, and process-oriented.

Product-oriented DTS, that area of research which describes existing translations, has traditionally been an important area of academic research in translation studies. The starting point for this type of study is the description of individual translations, or text-focused translation description. A second phase is that all comparative translation description, image comparative and analyses are made of various languages. Such individual and comparative descriptions provide the materials for surveys of larger corpuses of translations, for instance, those made within a specific period, language, and/or text are discourse type. In practice the corpus has usually been restricted in all three ways: seventeenth-century literary translations into French, or medieval English Bible translations. But such descriptive surveys can also be larger in scope, diachronic as well as (approximately) synchronic, and one of the eventual goals of product-oriented DTS might possibly be a general history of translations—however ambitious such a goal may sound at this time.

Function-oriented DTS is not interested in the description of translations in themselves, but in the description of their function in the recipient social-cultural situation: it is a study of contexts rather than texts. Pursuing such questions as which texts were (and, often as important, were not) translated at certain time in a certain place, and what influences were exerted in consequence, this area of research is one that has attracted less concentrated attention than the area just mentioned, though it is often introduced as a kind of sub-theme or counter-theme in histories of translations and literary histories. Greater emphasis on it could lead to the development of a field of translation sociology (or—less felicitous but more accurate, since it is a legitimate area of translation studies as well as also sociology—socio-translation studies).

Process-oriented DTS concerns itself with the process or act of translation itself. The problem of what exactly takes place in the "little black box" of the translator's "mind" as he creates a new, more or less matching text in another language has been the subject of much speculation on the part of translation's theorists, but there has been very little attempt at systematic investigation of this process on their laboratory conditions. Admittedly, the process is an unusually complex one, one which, if I. A. Richards is correct, "may very probably be the most complex type of event yet produced in the evolution of the cosmos." But psychologists have developed highly sophisticated methods for analysing and describing other complex mental process, and it is to be hoped that in the future this problem, too, will be given closer attention from a leading to an area of study that might be called in translation psychology or psycho-translation studies.

The other main branch of pure translation studies, *theoretical translation studies or translation theory*, is, as its name implies, not interest in describing existing translations, observed translation functions, or experimentally determined translating process, but in using the results of descriptive translation studies, in combination with the information available from related fields and disciplines, to evolve principles, theories, and models which will serve to explain and predict what translating and translations are and will be.

The ultimate goal of the translation theorist in the broad sense must undoubtedly be to develop a full, inclusive theory accommodating so many elements that I can serve to explain and predict all phenomena falling within the terrain of translating and translation, to the exclusion of all phenomena falling outside it. It hardly needs to be pointed out that a *general translation theory* in such a true sense of the term, if indeed it is achievable, will necessarily be highly formalized and, however the scholar may strive after economy, also highly complex.

Most of the theories that have been produced to date are in reality little more than prolegomena to such a general translation theory. A good share of them, in fact, are not actually theories at all, in any scholarly sense of the term, but an array of axioms, postulates, and hypotheses that are so formulated as to be both too inclusive (covering also non-translatory acts and non-translations) and too exclusive (shutting out some translatory acts and some works generally recognized as translations).

Others, though they too may bear the designation of "general" translation theories (frequently preceded by the scholar's protectively cautions "towards") are in fact not general theories, but partial or specific in their scope, dealing with only one or a few of the various aspects of translation theory as a whole. It is in this area of partial theories that the most significant advances have been made in recent years, and in fact it will probably be necessary for a great deal of further research to be conducted in them before we can even begin to think about arriving at true general theory in this sense I have just outlined. *Partial translation theories* are specified in a number of ways. I would suggest, though, that they can be grouped together into six main kinds.

First of all, there are translation theories that I have called, with a somewhat unorthodox extension of the term, *medium-restricted translation theories*, according to the medium that is used. Medium-restricted translation theories can be further subdivided into theories of translation as performed by humans (human translation), as performed by computers (machine translation), and performed by the two in conjunction (mixed or machine-aided translation). Human translation breaks down into (and restricted theories or "theories" have been developed for) oral translation or interpreting (with the further distinction between consecutive and simultaneous) and written translation. Numerous examples of valuable research into machine and machine-aided translation are no doubt familiar to us all, and perhaps also several into oral human translation. That examples of medium-restricted theories of written translation do not come to mind so easily is largely owing to the fact that their authors have the tendency to present them in the guise of unmarked or general theories.

Second, there are theories that are area-restricted. *Area-restricted theories* can be of two closely related kinds, restricted as to the languages involved or, which is usually not quite the same, and occasionally hardly at all, as to the cultures involved. In both cases, language restriction and culture restriction, the degree of actual limitation can vary. Theories are feasible for translation between, say, French and German (language-pair restricted theories) as opposed to translation within Slavic languages (language-group restricted theories) or from Romance languages to Germanic languages (language-group pair restricted theories). Similarly, theories might at least hypothetically be developed for translation within Swiss culture (one-culture restricted), or for translation between Swiss and Belgian cultures (cultural-pair restricted), as opposed to translation within Western Europe (cultural-group restricted) or between languages reflecting a pre-technological culture and the languages of contemporary Western culture (cultural-group pair restricted). Language-restricted theories have close affinities with the work being done in comparative linguistics and stylistics (though it must always be remembered that a language-pair translation grammar must be a different thing from a contrastive grammar developed for the purpose of language acquisition). In the field of culture-restrict theories there has been little detailed research, though culture restrictions, by being confused with language restrictions, sometimes get introduced into language-restricted theories, where they are out of place in all but those rare case where culture and language boundaries coincide in both the source and target situations. It is moreover no doubt true that some aspects of theories that are presented as general in reality pertain only to the Western cultural area.

Third, there are *rank-restricted theories*, that is to say, theories that deal with discourse or texts as wholes, but concern themselves with lower linguistic ranks or levels. Traditionally, a great deal of writing on translation was concerned almost entirely with the rank of the word, and the word and the word group are still the ranks at which much terminologically-oriented thinking about scientific and technological translation takes place. Most linguistically-oriented research, on the other hand, has until very recently taken the sentence as its upper rank limit, largely ignoring the macro-structural aspects of entire texts as translation problems. The clearly discernible trend away from sentential linguistics in the direction of textual linguistics will, it is to be hoped, encourage linguistically-oriented theorists to move beyond sentence-restricted translation theories to more complex task of developing text-rank (more "rank-free") theories.

Fourth, there are *text-type* (or discourse-type) *restricted theories*, dealing with the problem of translating specific types are genres of lingual messages. Authors and literary scholars have long concerned themselves with the problems intrinsic to translating literary texts or genres of literary texts; theologians, similarly, have devoted much attention to questions of how to translate Bible and other sacred works. In recent years some effort has been made to develop specific theory for the translation of scientific texts. All these studies break down, however, because we still lack anything like a formal theory of message, text, or discourse types. Both Bühlers theory of types of communication, as further developed by the Prague structuralists, and the definitions of language varieties arrived at by linguists particularly of the British school provides material for criteria in defining text types that would lend themselves to operationalization more aptly than the inconsistent and mutually contradictory definitions or traditional genre theories. On the other hand, the traditional theories cannot be ignored, for they continue to play a large part in creating the expectation criteria of translation readers. Also requiring study is the important question of text type skewing or shifting in translation.

Fifth, there are *time-restricted theories*, which fall into two types: theories regarding the translation of contemporary texts from an older period. Again there would seem to be a tendency to present one of the theories, that having to do with contemporary texts, in the guise of general theory; the other, the theory of what can perhaps best be called cross-temporal translation, is a matter that has led to much disagreement, particularly among literarily oriented theorists, but to few generally valid conclusions.

Finally, there are *problem-restricted theories*, theories which confine themselves to one or more specific problems within the entire area of general translation theory, problems that can range from such broad and basic questions as the limits of variance and invariance in translation or the nature of translation equivalence (or, as I should prefer to call it, translation matching) to such more specific to matters as the translation of metaphors or of proper names.

It should be noted that theories can frequently be restricted in more than one way. Contrastive linguists interested in translation, for instance, will probably produce theories that are not only language-restricted but rank- and time-restricted, having to do with translation between specific pairs of contemporary temporal dialects at sentence rank. The theories of literary scholars, similarly, usually are restricted as to medium and text type, and generally also as to culture group; they normally have to do with written texts within the (extended) Western literary tradition. This does not necessarily reduce the worth of such partial theories, for even a theoretical study restricted in every way—say a theory of the manner in which subordinate clauses in contemporary German novels should be translated into written English—can have implications for the more general theory towards which scholars must surely work. It would be wise, though, not to lose sight of such a truly general theory, and wiser still not to succumb to the delusion that a body of restrict theories—for instance, a complex of language-restricted theories of how to translate sentences—can be an adequate substitute for it.

After it this rapid overview of the two main branches of pure research in translation studies, I should like to turn to that branch of the discipline which is, in Bacon's words, "of use" rather than "of light": applied translation studies.

In this discipline, as in so many others, the first thing that comes to mind when one considers the implications that extend beyond the limits of the discipline itself is that of teaching. Actually, the teaching of translating is of two types which need to be carefully distinguished. In the one case, translating has been used for centuries as a technique in foreign-language teaching and test of foreign-language acquisition. I shall return to this type in a moment. In the second case, a more recent phenomenon, translating is taught in schools and courses to train professional translators. This second situation, that of *translator training*, has raised a number of questions that fairly cry for answers: questions that have stood the primarily with teaching methods, testing techniques, and curriculum planning. It is obvious that the search for well-founded, reliable answers to these questions contributes a major area (and for the time being, at least, the major area) of research in applied translation studies.

A second, closely related area has to do with the needs for translation aids, both for use in translator training and to meet requirements of the practising translator. The needs are many and various, but fall largely into two classes: ①lexicographical and terminological aids and ②grammars. Both these classes of aids have traditionally been provided by scholars in other, related disciplines, and it could hardly be argued that work on them should be taken over *in toto* as areas of applied translation studies. But lexicographical aids often fall far short of translation needs, and contrastive grammars developed for language-acquisition purposes are not really an adequate substitute for variety-marked translation-matching grammars. There would seem to be a need for scholars in applied translation studies to clarify and define the specific requirements that aids of these kinds should fulfil if they are to meet the needs of practising and prospective translators, and to work together with lexicologists and contrastive linguists in developing them.

A third area of applied translation studies is that of translation policy. The task of the translation scholar in this area is to render informed advice to others in defining the place and role of translators, translating, and translation in society at large: such questions, for instance, as determining the social and economic position of the translator is and should be, or (and here I return to the point raised above) what part is translating should play in the teaching and learning of foreign languages. In regard to that last policy question, since it should hardly be the task of translation studies to abet the use of translating in places where it is dysfunctional, it would seem to me that priority should be given to extensive and rigorous research to assess the efficacy of translating as a technique and testing method in language learning. The chance that it is not efficacious would appear to be so great that in this case it would seem imperative for program research to be preceded by policy research.

A fourth, quite different area of applied translation studies in that of *translation criticism*. The level of such criticism is today still frequently very low, and in many countries still quite uninfluenced by developments within the field of translation studies. Doubtless the activities of translation interpretation and evaluation will always elude the grasp of objective analysis to some extent, and so continue to reflect the intuitive, impressionist attitudes and stances of the critic. But closer contact between translation scholars and translation critics could do a great deal to reduce the intuitive element to a more acceptable level.

After this brief survey of the main branches of translation studies, there are two further points that I should like to make. The first is this: in what has preceded, descriptive, theoretical, and applied translation studies have been presented as three fairly distinct branches of the entire discipline, and the order of presentation might be taken to suggest that their import for one another is unidirectional, translation description supplying the basic data upon which translation theory is to be built, and the two of them providing the scholarly findings which are to be put to use in applied translation studies. In reality, of course, the relation is a dialectical one, which each of the three branches supplying materials for the other two, and making use of the findings which they in turn provide it. Translation theory, for instance, cannot do without the solid, specific data yielded by research in descriptive and applied translation studies, while on the other hand one cannot even begin to work in one of the other two fields without having at least and intuitive theoretical hypothesis as one's starting point. In view of this dialectical relationship, it follows that, though the needs of a given moment may vary, attention to all three branches is required if the discipline is to grow and flourish.

The second point is that, in each of the three branches of translation studies, there are two further dimensions that I have not mentioned, dimensions, but of translation studies itself. One of these dimensions is historical: there is a field of the history of translation theory, in which some valuable work has been done, but also one of the history of translation description and of applied translation studies (largely a history of translation teaching and translator training) both of which are fairly well virgin territory. Likewise there is a dimension that might be called the methodological or meta-theoretical, concerning itself with problems of what methods and models can best be used in research in the various branches of the discipline (how translation theories, for instance, can be formed for greatest validity, or what analytic methods can best be used to achieve the most objective and meaningful descriptive results), but also devoting its attention to such basic issues as what the discipline itself comprises.

This paper has made a few excursions into the first of these two dimensions, but all in all it is meant to be a contribution to the second. It does not ask above all for agreement. Translation studies has reached a stage where it is time to examine the subject itself. Let the meta-discussion begin.

翻译的"名"与"实"[①]

[美] 詹姆斯·霍尔姆斯

李知宇　何梓健译

迈克尔·马尔凯（Michael Mulkay）曾指出："科学的发展，依靠的是发现未知领域。"社会学家对此已经有全面而准确的解释了。但翻译是学术界的一个新问题（或者说是一系列的问题），相关领域的济济学者们无不举出了一个个精彩的范例和模型，并各自有所建树。而这些范例和模型则继续被挖掘出新的问题，并出现了两种截然不同的情况。在第一种情况下，这个新问题与显化、分析和阐明方法，以及上述范例、模型当中的界限息息相关，如此一来，它即可成为某一既成学科中的合理分支。在第二种情况下，这些"范式"难以得出有效的结果，于是便需要研究出新的方法进一步解决问题。

在第二种假设中，那无效的结果事实上是研究旧领域的人员不适应当前的新方法所产生的矛盾，虽说如此，它却能促成新的沟通途径，创造一个所谓"学科乌托邦"的观念——它对研究中的同一个问题，采取的同一套方法以及面向的对象都能共享资源、共受利弊。哈格斯特朗（W. O. Hagstrom）曾阐述：这两种现象"让科学家能够辨明新生学科的区别，并能在更广泛的社会中向大学机构宣传时定义其正确的观点"。

无疑，会有少部分学者对此持反对意见，语言学家们更是异议蜂起。于我而言，在翻译领域也有类似的情况，与第二种假设如出一辙。数百年来，作家、语言学家、文学家，以及世界各地的神学家和研究特种语言的人们都陆续关注这个问题。"二战"结束后，其热度更是一路攀升，范围愈发广泛，越来越多的学者也将目光转移到翻译中来。有来自语言学、语言哲学及文学范畴的学者，也有来自信息论、逻辑学、数学等看似瓜葛甚少的学者，每一个人都有各自的范例、标准、模型和方法论，并且都认为能催生出值得探讨的新问题。

乍一看，当下这种有因必有果的情形反而会让人迷糊，对于需要推敲的模型、那些需要应用的方法、要用何种专业名词等一系列的问题，都尚未有一致的定论。不仅如此，人们对于翻译的领域规划和学科分类更缺乏"同理心"，实际上，学者们对于翻译的"名"更是不敢苟同。

然而，还是有证据证实，哈格斯特朗所谓的"学科乌托邦"正渐成气候——关注翻译的研究日益兴盛。假如这是一个良好的态势（我认为它是），那么它就有发展的价值，我们要自觉地把阻碍因素排除。

其中一种阻碍因素即缺乏合适的沟通途径。对于翻译学者和研究人员而言，他们

① 成书于1972年8月，本篇为其第二次出版时的版本。

会有“喜旧厌新”的可能（因为在旧的学科机制中，模型、方法以及术语中既有的框架相对都比现时的有帮助），他们会为从业译者将有关翻译问题投放到各领域的期刊和杂志中。显然，我们需要其他的沟通渠道，从传统的学科切入各行各业的翻译研究者的工作中去。

但我真正想论及的是“学科乌托邦”的阻碍因素。首先就是翻译的“名”。它似乎是相对次要而零碎的一个话题；正如普通语义学家们一直提到的：既然是已经谈过的主题就没必要再详细展开了，毕竟偏不概全。但如果不能清楚区分“名”与“实”，反倒会让人摸不着头脑。

这些年来，翻译论著中运用到的术语可谓琳琅满目。人们可以在英语中找到翻译的“术”与“技”，也能寻得它的“规”、它的“道”。甚至在法语、德语中也存在类似的术语。术语的选择在某种程度上体现出作者的态度、方法以及背景；宏观来说，这也是学术语言逐渐广泛的一种必然结果。

人们曾尝试创设更多的学术词汇，当中大部分都含有后缀 -ology。罗杰·戈芬（Roger Goffin）就曾用“translatology”以及其同源词，甚至法语单词 traductologie 来定义“翻译学”。但那些信仰正统语言的群体则持反对态度，他们认为——无论是源于希腊语的 -ology，源于晚期拉丁语的 translatio，还是源于文艺复兴时期的法语 traduction，都会玷污纯正的“翻译”之名。但单从“××学”这种词来看，别无他法，只能选择希腊语源了，不然连大学机构这些堪称学术中心的地方也分不清“隐喻学”中的 metaphorology、metaphaseology 和 metaphastics 到底是不是同一词汇，更别提进入了广泛语言社会后的其他衍生词汇了。比如“translatistics”和“translitics”两个词都曾被纳入“翻译”的定义列表中，虽为人所熟知，却难广而受之。

近年来，还有另外两个不太经典的造术语渐露头角，其中一个为短语“the theory of translating”或“the theory of translation”（德语为 theorie des Übersetzens，法语为 théorie de la traduction），类似的词在英语中不胜枚举，最终去粗取精，浓缩成“translation theory”。只要对应词义不变，就会是个简约而高效的结构，以后也会是。因为翻译学中已经有足够多的研究为这个定义佐证了，以后也许还需要更多，但严格来说并不属于理论的大框架，这也是本文希望阐明的内容。

另外一个术语，实际上已经成为代言整个翻译学的德语版本——Übersetzungswissenschaft[①]，取自形近词 Sprachwissenschaft、Literaturwissenschaft 以及许许多多的 Wissenschaften 后缀。而在法语中，“science de la traduction”这个表达亦已有普及，相信在其他语言中也有对等的词汇。

尤金·奈达是在翻译中使用 science of translating 的第一批学者之一，早在 1964 年他就将这个词嵌入了其著作《迈向翻译科学》（*Towards a Science of Translating*）的标题中。然而应该强调的是，奈达并没有用“翻译科学”定义整个翻译学领域的意思，他

① 由于缺乏一个普遍的范式，学者往往倾向于把这个术语的含义限制在这个学科的某部分，实际上，“翻译理论”这个名词不那么具有代表性。

认为这只是翻译过程的一部分而已。而有些学者虽是非英语母语人士，却来得更加直接，提议“science of translation（或 translation science）”干脆成为这个新兴学科的代名词。就在两年前（1970 年），鲍施（Bausch）、克拉格夫（Klegraf）和威尔斯（Wilss）决定把 Übersetzungswissenschaft 作为其翻译学分析论著中的主题，这个备受热议的关键词随即被奉为金科玉律。

可惜的是，这是个让我后悔的决定。并不是说我不认同 Übersetzungswissenschaft，只不过这三位学者对这个德语名词的效度论证还少之又少。并非说翻译不是一个 Wissenschaft（学科），但不是所有的学科都可以成为“科学”。正如今时今日，人们都不屑于争论 Sprachwissenschaft（语言学）和 Literaturwissenschaft（文学）的定义了，却有不少人质疑 linguistics 这个词的结构、构词范式是否已经精确到足够成为一门科学的“品牌”；反之，“文学”是众所周知进不了“科学”这个殿堂的，在不久的未来也不可能成为英语词汇中真正意义上的科学。有鉴于此，我心里不禁浮现出一个疑问：翻译研究是否能够与数学、物理、化学、生物等这类自然科学并行，而不是依存于社会学、历史、哲学和文学等人文学科？

在翻译的“名”的层面，还有一个十分活跃的术语值得我们留意——“studies”。以往，大学倾向于将它纳入人文或艺术学科范畴，一如德语的 Wissenschaft 般频繁出现——只要想想那些什么“俄罗斯学”“美国学”“联邦学”“人口学”“交际学”就可见一斑了。不过，这个词也不乏疑难，难以衍生形容词就是其一。翻来覆去，“translation studies”似乎是最合适的定义了，复数代表的是多个学派、多种研究，这样也许就能消除人们对于“翻译学”的误解了。本文将承接这个定义展开讨论。

在翻译学（translation studies）的发展过程中，缺少大家都认可的定义是个很大的障碍。但比这更严重的是，大家对这个学科的研究范围和框架没有达成普遍的共识。到底什么才是翻译学的研究内容呢？有人说它与对比术语或词典编纂学的研究内容一致，有的则认为它与对比理论的研究内容完全一致。当然，翻译跟众多新兴学科是有所不同的（虽然界限不总是那么明显），对于翻译学本质的二次思考还很少，但幸好至少它已成为白纸黑字的论文，让我关注到它的重要性。这里要提到一个人：德国语言学家沃纳·科勒（Werner Koller），他是这样描述的：“翻译学即一个以各种翻译现象为基础或关注重点的包容性学科。”（Übersetzungswissenschaft ist zu verstehen als Zusammenfassung und Überbegriff für alle Forschungsbemühungen, die von Phãnomenen ‘Übersetzen’ und ‘Übersetzung’ ausgehen oder auf diese Phãnomenen zielen）

由此可知，翻译学就是一门经验性学科（我认为没人会否认之）。卡尔·G. 亨普尔（Carl G. Hempel）指出，这类学科一般有两大目标：①描述人类所理解的世界上的特有现象；②建立可解释、可预测这些现象的总则。[①] 如此说来，作为一门纯理论研究，翻译学的目的也有二：①描述人类所理解的所有翻译现象；②建立可以解释、预

① HEMPE G G. Fundamentals of concept formation in empirical science [M]. Chicago: University of Chicago Press, 1967, p. 1.

测这些翻译现象的总则。这两个分支便衍生出两种不同的流派——描述性翻译学(descriptive translation studies，DTS)，或称翻译描述（translation description，TD)，以及理论翻译学（theoretical translation studies，ThTS)，或称翻译理论（translation theory，TTh)。

此两者中，描述性翻译学可能更适合作为这门与经验现象密切相关的学科的“招牌”。当中有三个主要的研究类型，根据其重点不同，可划分为：结果主导型、功能主导型及过程主导型。

结果主导型 DTS 主要描述既有的翻译现象，一向被视为翻译学中学术研究的重头戏。首先是对单一翻译现象或以文本为中心的描述，再就是皆由各种语言构成的有对比翻译描述、图像对比和分析。这样的单一或对比的描述为翻译语料库提供了更广泛的材料——在特定时期、用特定语言或/和采用特定文本产出的译本就属于语篇型语料。这种语料库中却有两种特殊文本受到局限：17 世纪文学作品法译本，以及中世纪圣经的英译本。但它触及的范围其实可以更大，可以是历时或共时性的，不管当下的一个翻译目标多么有针对性，多么宏大，结果主导型 DTS 的任何一个最终目标都非常多元，有可能成为翻译的一部通史。

功能主导型 DTS 的重心并不在于对翻译本身的描述，而在于对目的语受众的社会—文化功能的描述；研究范畴已经从文本深化到语境了。虽说功能主导型 DTS 也是翻译和文学史上的一个分支（或对题)，但它对人们在何时何地、对于何种文本进行翻译，结果如何这些值得探究的问题，都尽量绕开。如果学人们对其深入剖析，那么对于翻译社会学（translation sociology）也是大有裨益的［既是翻译学，又属于社会学，或称为社会翻译学（socio-translation studies)］。

过程主导型 DTS 关注翻译的过程或行为。译者在用目的语输出文本时，有机会产生一个全新的、与原文存在或多或少对等内容的作品，而译者头脑中的这个“小黑匣”究竟藏着些什么奥秘，翻译理论家们已经做了颇多的猜测，但即使创设了实验环境，他们往往也很难进行系统有序的调查。翻译的过程固然非常复杂，甚至连英国著名的文学批判家艾弗·阿姆斯特朗·瑞查斯也认为：“这样的过程很可能是整个宇宙演化中最复杂难料的活动了。”[①] 然而，有心理学家开发出了一套高度专业化的方法，以分析描述其他更为复杂的心理活动，有望在不久的将来从心理学的方向入手解析翻译行为，由此可称之为翻译心理学（translation psychology)，或心理翻译学（psycho-translation studies)。

翻译理论研究的另一个主要分支则独立于前述三者，既不牵涉既有的翻译、观察所得的翻译功能，也不插手实验所得的翻译活动。它能做的，是联合相关学科现有的信息，合理利用描述性翻译学的结果，进而使既成的原则、理论和模型更上一层楼，以解释现在，并预测以后翻译的走向。

广义上，翻译理论家的终极目标无疑是发展出一个充实而多元，又可以解释预测

① RICHARDS I A. Studies in Chinese thought［M］. Chicago：University of Chicago Press，1953，pp. 247 – 262.

所有翻译现象的理论，并排除一切在此领域外的现象。假若存在这么一个“翻译总论”，可以达到真正意义上的合理合规，那它必然是高度形式化的，无论学者们怎么想方设法简而约之，它始终也是十分复杂的。

时至今日所得出的大多数理论其实不过是这个总论当中的“绪论”而已，且从严格意义上说，很大的部分还不成理论，只是依书直说的一堆格言、假设，既过于宽泛（包含非翻译行为以及非翻译产品），又过于排外（排除了某些翻译行为，以及通常被视为译作的部分作品）。

还有一部分理论或许也被冠以“总”或“概”这个名衔［出于保守，学者们都会在前面加一个 towards（对于、关于）］，却只有很少内容真正属于这个范围，涉及翻译理论的只有一个或几个方面。不过回看近年来，能够依靠些许理论就取得不俗成绩的也只有这个领域了。事实上，在我们考虑要不要实现真正的“总论”之前，需要以大量的研究作为基础。即便是局部的理论都能以各种方式呈现，不过我认为主要有以下六种类别：

第一种，我用了一个比较非正式的术语来定义，叫“媒介翻译学”。它可以细分为人工翻译、机器翻译和人机翻译（或称机器辅助翻译）。而人工翻译又可划分成口译（交替传译、同声传译）与笔译。关于机器翻译和人机翻译的珍贵研究成果数量可观（口译可能也在其列），更是我们耳熟能详的内容，反观笔译的媒介理论不能深入人心，则是由于该种理论的作者往往会用一些“默默无闻”的，或一般化的理论做幌子呈现在各种著作中。

第二种为区域翻译，分为两种：因语言局限性导致（程度高低总会稍有不同，但偶尔对翻译也毫不影响）；或因文化差异导致。两者的实际限制因素会有参差，比如在引入理论的语言方面，法德二语（语言对狭义论）会好处理些，而斯拉夫语（语言群体狭义论）或由罗曼语演化成的日耳曼语（语言群体对狭义论）则显得有些困难。无独有偶，在瑞士文化域中（单一文化）或瑞士—比利时文化（文化对）中也有发展区域翻译的可能。相对而言，西欧（文化群体），或在反映技术革命前以及当代西方文化（文化群体对）之间的语言当中的翻译就浅薄点。语言局限性理论也常常出现在语言学和文体学的研究成果中，可见其联系之紧密（虽然必须谨记语言对翻译语法与语言习得完全不同）。虽然文化差异常被混淆成语言差异，有时还被纳入其理论中，但实际上两者完全不同，只有在文化—语言交汇在源语和目的语的情况下才发挥作用，因此，到头来，关于文化的狭义理论并没有太多翔实的记载，有些方面更只适用于西方的文化区域。

第三种为层面翻译，亦即针对语篇或文本整体的理论，却往往把两者置于语言层面的下级。一般而言，人们会以为翻译的大部分论著都是有关词汇、词组层面的，而且会频繁出现聚焦“术语”的科技翻译。不过很多语言学的研究也是在近些年才转阵到句子层面上的，大大忽略了“文本”这个翻译中的宏观结构。如果以文本为导向，句子语言学将得到明晰的区分，更有望促进语言学者超越句子层面的翻译理论，到达文本层面（或者说练就不受层面限制的能力）。

第四种为文本类型（或语篇类型）翻译，重点在特定语言信息类型的转换。作家及文学家群体一直都想得到翻译文学作品的真谛，而神学家也在寻找翻译《圣经》和其他圣典的方法。最近学术界研究出了一套科技文本的翻译理论，却以失败告终，因为我们仍缺乏有效而规范的信息、文本或语篇理论。无论是布莱尔（Bühler）的交际类型理论（后被布拉格结构学派进一步完善），还是英国学派语言学家创建的语言种类论，无一不为界定文本类型的标准提供了充足的素材，使之相比以往那些前后矛盾的定义更加具备操作的可能性。另外，我们也绝不能把传统的理论抛诸脑后，这些成绩将继续在为目标语读者创设新标准方面扮演着重要的角色，同时，研究性学习也是翻译中的一个关键的议题，值得我们深思。

第五种为时间翻译，划分为两类：①古文今译（大概与当代文本的关系会密切点）；②跨时翻译。这种划分惹来颇多争议，文学理论家对此更不以为然，但至少还能得出些有用的结论。这两类有可能再次以“总论”的衣装出现，只会呈现其一。

最后一种为专题翻译，只限于“总论”当中的一个或多个特定问题，既宽泛又基础。对于翻译中出现变异或不变的界限，或文本中比喻或专有名词的翻译对等（我更喜欢称其为翻译匹配）的性质都需要考虑。

需要指出的是，理论的侧重点不止一个。那些研究翻译的对比语言学家就是一个很好的例子，他们可能同时创设出语言差异型、层面型以及时间型理论，多与句子层面的特定现代方言对有关。而文学家采纳的通常都是媒介和文本类型翻译理论，顺理成章地也会指向文化群体的分类——一般在西方文学传统的书面文本上做文章。即便如此繁杂分散，也不一定影响理论的价值，比方说德语现代小说中的从句要译成英语，必定牵涉其源理论，并有一定的影响。我们千万不能忽视“总论”这个根本，更不能因为侧重理论数量大，而尽信其“正确性”。比如，当前存在一大批指导如何翻译句子的语言差异型论著，充其量只是一个比较好的参照和替代品而已。

在快速浏览过纯翻译研究的两个主要分支后，我将就分支展开讨论。用培根的话说就是“论实用”而非“论领悟”，换言之即应用翻译学。①

钻研翻译学与钻研其他学科一样，当说到其外延的应用，第一个浮现在脑海中的就是“教学”。事实上，翻译教学分为两类，需要我们认真区分。一方面，作为一种技能，翻译在外语教学和外语习得测试方面已经有数百年的历史了，后面我将提到这部分内容。另一方面，翻译已经被搬到学校里、课堂上，为培养一批又一批的专业译者而做出贡献。而后者俨然引起了不少亟待回答的疑问：教学的基本方法是什么？测试方法以及课程设置又是怎样的？这些都得详解。显然，最终要到应用翻译学的主要研究领域去（暂时可以说是“主要”）找理据充足的答案。

第二个因素是翻译工具，虽为次要，但其有助于译者培训，亦为满足从业译者的要求提供参考，所谓的翻译工具数量大、内容多样，大体上能分为两个门类：①词典

① 培根的区分实际上不是广义上的两类论调，而是实验：“用途实验”与“领悟实验”。参见 Pit Corder 在 1972 年哥本哈根应用语言学大会全体会议上发表的论文。

编纂及术语工具；②语法。此二者传统上都是由其他相关学科的学者提供的，往往难以全面涵盖应用翻译学。词典编纂工具时常达不到翻译的需求，以语言习得为主的对比语法亦未能真正应对实际翻译中多样的语法情况。看来应用翻译学者们需要厘清某些特殊的要求，并给之以定义，好让现在的从业译者，以及未来的译者都能成竹在胸，让他们与词汇学家和对比语言学家携手合作，共促应用翻译的长足发展。

应用翻译的第三个因素是翻译策略。主攻这方面的学者旨在向他人提出有效而合理的意见，给译者和翻译活动最明晰的社会定位。例如：决定译者社会经济地位的不是别的，就是（在此要再引用上述的内容）翻译在教学和外语学习当中的作用。对于最后一个策略问题，因为翻译研究的任务不该关注“不可译性”，所以我认为要优先进行广泛而谨慎的评估——作为语言学习的一种技术和测试方法，翻译的可行性到底在哪里？但要知道，这样的调查结果事与愿违的可能性很高，在这种情况下，有必要在策略剖析之前未雨绸缪，进行理论解构。

第四个因素为翻译批评。时至今日，该学科批判的水平仍然较低，在许多国家，翻译研究发展的影响力微乎其微。无疑，翻译解释和评价的活动总会在一定程度上脱离客观，反映出批判者的主观意识、主观印象、态度和立场。不过幸好学者和批评家之间的关系足够紧密，足以把直觉、主观因素降低至可接受的程度。

在对翻译研究的主要分支进行简要分析后，我仍有两点要阐明。首先，前述的描述性、理论性以及应用性的翻译学被冠以翻译学科的“三足”，且其顺序表明三者属于单向渗透：翻译描述提供基础数据，而翻译理论则建立在这些数据之上，进而产出的学术成果落到应用中。事实上，这是个辩证关系，三个环节中，任一环都会为其余的提供材料，并利用其所得结果继续推进、供给，如此反复。比方说，描述性和应用性研究能够得出具体而可靠的数据，翻译理论与其唇齿相依；另外，如果没有最起码的、直观的理论假设作为出发点，继续在其余两个环节中运作更是不可能的事。由此看出，翻译需求可能会因时而异，但如果这个学科要发展壮大，这“三足”还是必要的突破口。

在这三个分支中，还有两个属于翻译学本身的维度值得一提。从历史维度看，翻译理论史中已经流传着不少值得借鉴的研究，都是关于翻译描述和翻译应用的精粹（主要为教学及译者培训），这两者是等待开拓的“新大陆”。从方法论（或称元理论）的维度看，要考虑何种方法和模型最适合用于研究各学科的分支问题（例如：如何构筑翻译理论使之效能最大化？用什么分析法来达到最客观、最有意义的描述结果），还要聚焦于学科本身构成的基本问题上。

显然，本文对翻译理论史的几点观察所得，已承接了翻译方法的现状，或者说充实了其理论框架。然而，翻译研究已经踏入了自我检视的阶段，亦即所谓的“元讨论”，只有这样才能让这个学科长盛不衰。

第二章

摘译

Selected Reading 1

Translation as Intercultural Communication

David Katan

1. Introduction

It was E. T. Hall (1959) who coined the term "intercultural communication" (Rogers et al. 2002). In working with US departmental administrators and Native Americans, he noticed that misunderstanding arose not through language but through other, "silent" "hidden" or "unconscious" yet patterned factors. In short, cultural differences. Bennett (1998: 3) explains that the fundamental premise of "the intercultural communication approach" is that "cultures are different in their languages, behaviour patterns, and values. So, an attempt to use (monocultural) self as a predictor of shared assumptions and responses to messages is unlikely to work" —because the response, in our case to a translation, will be ethnocentric.

That translation is "an act of communication" (Blum-Kulka 1986/2004: 291, emphasis in the original) has been a given since Steiner (1975/1998: 49), but not all agree about the existence or relevance of cultural differences in translation. There are three interrelated problem areas.

The first area of controversy is in the definition of culture itself. By 1952, Kroeber and Klockhohn had recorded 165 definitions, and today lobbies are still vying for authority over the meaning of "one of the two or three most complicated words in the English language" (Williams 1976/1983: 87, also in Jenks 1993: 1).

Originally, culture was simple. It referred exclusively to the humanist ideal of what was civilized in a developed society (the education system, the arts, architecture). Then a second meaning, the way of life of a people, took place alongside. Emphasis at the time was very much on "primitive" cultures and tribal practices. With the development of sociology and cultural studies, a third meaning has emerged, related to forces in society or ideology.

Hence, also, the way culture is acquired varies according to theory. For the humanists, culture is technically learnt through explicit instruction. Anthropologists believe that culture may be learned through formal or unconscious parenting, socialization or other inculcation through long-term contact with others. It then becomes unconsciously shared amongst the group (cf. Chesterman's *Memes of Translation* 1997a). In sociology and cultural studies, culture is a site of conflict for authority or power. When it is acquired, it is through the subliminal and enforced norms of, for example, capitalist and colonialist action.

Second, there is a fairly clear historical division between those who perceive language and culture as two distinct entities, and those who view language as culture. In the first case, translation is seen as a universalist encoding-decoding linguistic activity, transferring meaning from the SL to the TL, using what Reddy (1973/1993) called the "conduit metaphor of language transference". Here, culture and any cultural differences can be carried by the language without significant loss. Others, such as Nida (2002: 29), believe that "the context actually provides more distinction of meaning than the term being analysed". Hence, meaning is not "carried" by the language but is negotiated between readers from within their own contexts of culture. Each readership is hence bound to receive the text according to their own expectations, and translation is necessarily a relativist form of "manipulation" (Hermans 1985), "mediation" (Katan 1999) or "refraction" (Lefevere 1982/2004) between two different linguacultures (Agar 1994).

Third, and closely related to both the above is the importance of "the culture filter" in translation.

2. The Culture Filter

House (1977, 1981), Hervey and Higgins (1992) and Katan (1993) talk in terms of a "culture filter" or "cultural filter". Katan (1999) discusses four perception filters, based on neurolinguistic programming (NLP) theory, each of which is varyingly responsible for orienting or modelling our own perception, interpretation and evaluation of (to use Goffman 1974) "what it is that is going on". The filters are: "physiological" "culture" "individual" and "language".

All the filters function in the same way through modelling. A model is a (usually) useful way of simplifying and making sense of something which is complex, such as "reality". All models, according to Bandler and Grinder (1975), make use of three principles: deletion, distortion and generalization. In the case of human modelling we cannot perceive all of "what it is that is going on" (deletion); we tend to focus selectively or fit what we see to what we know, expect, or what attracts our attention (distortion); and we tend to fill details in from our own model or level out salient differences (generalization), to make the resulting "map of the world" useful.

Hence, cultural filters (for Katan) are one of the four particular, but related, ways in which groups organize their shared (limited, distorted and stereotypical) perception of the world. This follows Goodenough's (1957/1964: 36) definition of culture as "an organization… It is the form of things that people have in mind, their model of perceiving, relating, and otherwise interpreting them". For House (2006: 349), on the other hand, "a cultural filter is a means of capturing cognitive and socio-cultural differences" to be applied by translators, which for Katan is more closely related to the translator's capacity to mediate.

To what extent one filter prevails over another in translation is then the third area of controversy. With "the cultural turn" (Lefevere and Bassnett 1990: 1), and Bassnett's proclaiming (1980/2002: 23) that "the translator treats the text in isolation from the culture at his peril", the culture filter appeared to take the central stage. However, for Newmark (in Schaffner and Kelly-Holmes 1995: 80) there is "an over-emphasis on going from one culture to another (due to) universal issues that go beyond culture. They're sometimes dressed in cultural clothes, but that's as far as it goes". His views coincide with many professionals (Katan 2009). Others, again, believe that the filter should operate selectively. House (2006: 347), herself states that the "cultural filter" should be "inserted" only for certain text types, such as tourist information books and computer manuals. For Nida (1964: 130), on the other hand, the degree of intervention depends less on the text type itself than on the cultural and linguistic distance or gap between the languages concerned.

3. Culture as a System of Frames

There are three related ideas which can help clarify the apparently contradictory views of culture: context (ing), frames and logical typing.

3.1 Context (ing)

We have already mentioned Nida's view of the crucial importance of context. Yet, as others have noted, context is not always important. In fact, a phone book, an invoice and an instruction leaflet hardly need any context for the full meaning to be understood or to be translated. Yet what Hall (1983: 61) noted was that at all times, and in any communication, there is a process of "contexting", whereby interlocutors negotiate how much of the meaning is to be retrieved from the context, how much of the context is shared, and if not shared: "It can be seen, as context is lost, information must be added if meaning is to remain constant." For Hall, this constituted "membership"; relevance theory operates on the same principle. Also, even with regard to instructions, what is relevant cannot be assumed to be universal (see Katan 1999/2004).

"Context" is a convenient if fuzzy term, first applied to translation by an anthropologist Malinowski, whose treatise, though focusing on "primitive" cultures, is still relevant today. He studied the inhabitants of the Trobriand Islands and their language, and noted that he would have to make a number of changes in translating their Kiriwinian conversations into English. He used the following literal translation as an example: "We run front-wood ourselves; we paddle in place; we turn we see companion ours. He runs rear-wood behind their sea-arm Pilolu." Malinowski realized that he would need to add a commentary for an outsider reader to make explicit the layers of meaning that would be implicit for the Trobrianders, what Geertz would later call a "thick description". In translation studies, this has now become popularised by Appiah (1993/2004) and Hermans (2003) as "thick translation". First, a reader would need not only lexico-grammatical help to follow the story, but also "to be informed about the situation in which ... words were spoken" (Malinowski 1923/1938: 301), the "context of situation". A version for outsiders might have sounded something like this:

In crossing the sea-arm of Pilolu (between the Trobriands and the Amphletts), our canoe sailed ahead of the others. When nearing the shore we began to paddle. We looked back and saw our companions still far behind, still on the sea-arm of Pilolu.

The extract now makes sense; and with more of the context, the extract may be viewed as part of a story that a Trobriander is telling while sitting round with a group of eager listeners, recounting the end of a day's fishing trip.

However, to fully understand "what it is that is going on" the reader would need to be aware "that language is essentially rooted in the reality of culture ... the broader contexts of verbal utterance" (Malinowski 1923/1938: 305), which Malinowski later called the "context of culture" (1935/1967: 18; cf. Halliday and Hasan 1989: 47). Malinowski noted the use of two words in particular: "front-wood", which contained "a specific emotional tinge only comprehensible against a background of their tribal ceremonial life, commerce and enterprise", as in "top-of-the-range leading canoe"; and "paddle", which here signals the fact that the sail is lowered as shallow water is reached. It now becomes clear that we are witnessing a triumphal recount of a fishing expedition which finished in a race to the shore and which by now is all but over.

Many scholars have since discussed and classified the context of situation, in particular Halliday and Hasan (and see also House 1997). But as Halliday and Hasan (1989: 47) themselves point out, very little had been done in terms of developing the context of culture, which we will now discuss.

3.2 Logical typing

The anthropologist Bateson (1972: 289) noted that context, if it were to remain a useful concept, must be subject to what he called "logical typing": "Either we must discard the notion of 'context', or we retain this notion and, with it, accept the hierarchic series—stimulus, context of stimulus, context of context of stimulus, etc." By logical typing he meant that each context represents a "type" (such as the different context types of "situation" and "culture"), and each "type" frames, or logically informs, the next in a hierarchy of (often paradoxical) types. Goffman (1974) in *Frame Analysis*, explains that a frame tells us "What it is that is going on here." Each frame contains its own reality in much the same way as an area of black and white stripes on a white wall may be called a painting when framed. The labelling of the frame (e. g. "Night and Day") affects our interpretation. If we then frame the whole exhibition as "Reflections on Prison" we change perspective, and understand more of what it is that is going on (according to the exhibition organizer).

We can now move back to the competing definitions of culture and present them as essential parts of a unified model of culture or rather a system of frames which compete in their influence over what, when, how and why we translate.

3. 3 The logical levels of culture

The levels themselves are based on aspects of NLP logical level theory (e. g. Dilts 1990; O'Connor 2001: 28 – 32) and the anthropological "iceberg model", popularized in Hall's "triad of culture" (1959/1990). The logical levels serve to introduce one dimension of the system, dividing aspects of culture (the iceberg) into what is visible (above the waterline), semi-visible and invisible (Fig. 1). The frames below the water line are progressively more hidden but also progressively closer to our unquestioned assumptions about the world and our own (cultural) identities. A further, sociological dimension may be described as operating on the iceberg itself.

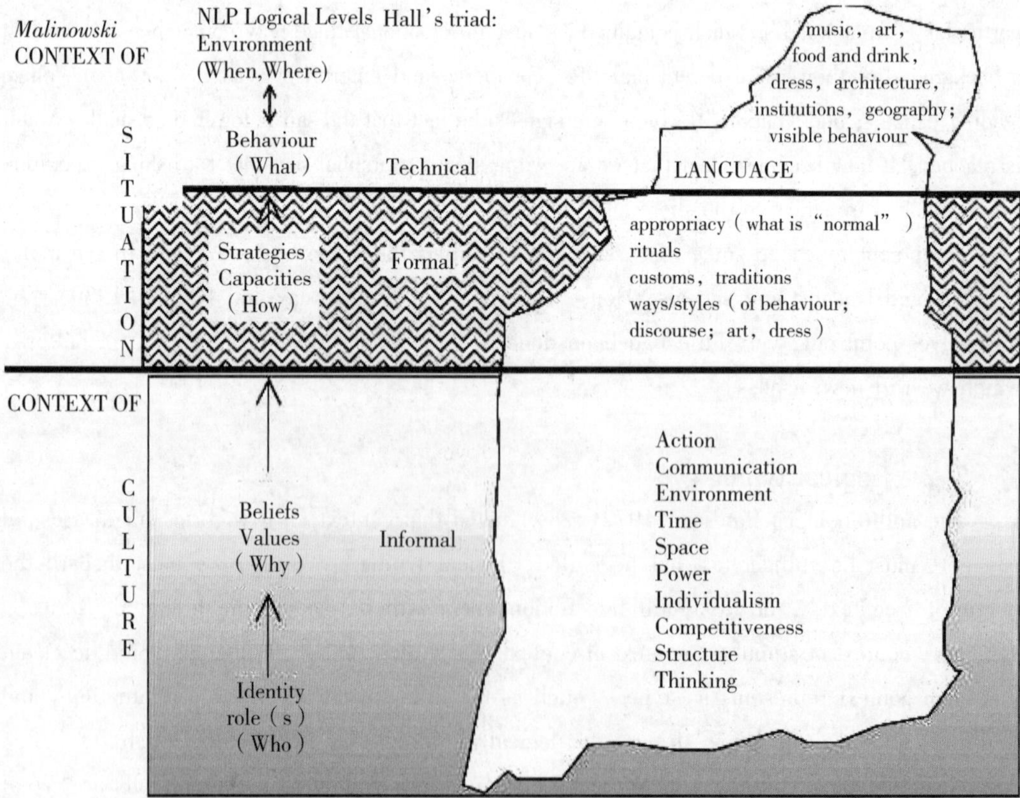

Fig. 1 The iceberg representation of culture (adapted from Katan 1999/2004: 43)

The extent to which a translator should intervene (i. e., interpret and manipulate rather than operate a purely linguistic transfer) will be in accordance with beliefs about which frame (s) most influence translation. Translation scholars tend to focus on the more hidden levels, while practitioners are more concerned with what is visible on the surface (Katan 2009).

4. Technical Culture: Shared Encyclopaedic Knowledge

The first cultural frame is at the tip of the iceberg and coincides with the humanist concept of culture. The focus is on the text, dressed (adapting Newmark) in its best civilized clothes of a particular culture. At this "technical" level the language signs have a clear WYSIWYG (what you see is what you get) referential function, and any associated hidden values are universal. The task of the translator at this level is to transfer the terms and concepts in the source text abroad with minimum loss (from literature and philosophical ideas to software manuals), so that "what you get" in the source text is equivalent to "what you get" in the target text. As long as the two cultures "have reached a comparable degree of development", there is no reason why meaning, reader response and uptake should not be universal (Seleskovich in Newmark, 1988: 6; see also Wilss 1982: 48).

This is what Newmark (1981: 184 – 185) called "the cultural value" of translation, and indeed is embedded in the bylaws (2007) of the International Federation of Translators (Fédération Internationale des Traducteurs, FIT): "to assist in the spreading of culture throughout the world". The chapter headings in *Translators Through History* (Delisle and Woodsworth 1995) give us an idea of what is involved: the invention of alphabets and the writing of dictionaries; the development of national languages and literatures, and the spread of religions and cultural values. Depending on the asymmetries of power, spreading the new terms and concepts might be perceived as enlightenment, "the white man's burden", an affront, the wielding of hegemony or a much-valued addition to intellectual debate.

4.1 Culturemes

However, the main concern of translators intervening at this level is the text itself and the translation of "culture-bound" terms, for example "culturemes": formalized, socially and juridically embedded phenomena that exist in a particular form or function in only one of the two cultures being compared (Nord 2000: 214). These "cultural categories" (Newmark, 1988: 95, after Nida) cover a wide array of semantic fields: from geography and traditions to institutions and technologies. Scholars since Vinay and Darbelnet (1958/1995) have offered a plethora of strategies to compensate for the lack of cultúreme equivalence. Kwiecinski (2001: 157) has summarized these into four groups: "exoticising procedures" "rich explicatory procedures" "recognised exoticisation" and "assimilative procedures". See also Pederson's

(2008: 103) clear overview of "Extralinguistic Culture-Bound Reference Transfer Strategies" in subtitling.

"Exoticising procedures" allow the foreign term into the target language (falafel, macho, Weltanschauung, burka). For Newmark (e.g., 1988: 82), this procedure offers local colour and atmosphere, though this approach has been criticized by Berman (1985/2004: 286), who claims that making a text "more authentic" (the inverted commas are his) insidiously emphasizes and exoticizes a certain stereotype. Clearly, we need to be aware of the difference between the utility of the resources available for a translator and the slavish use of any one irrespective of context or translation purpose.

The second grouping is "rich explicatory procedures". The aim is to slide in an extra term or two which will cue readers to enough of the context, often through a local analogy, to guide them towards a more equivalent cognition. Two of the many possible procedures are the use of explanatory brackets, such as "Knesset (the Israeli Parliament)", or through adjectivizing the source term, as in "hot cotechino sausage". Newmark, amongst others (e.g., Nida 1975), suggests the need here for componential analysis to analyse the semantic properties, connotations or culture-bound components of terms in the SL and the TL.

When, where and how to explicate depends on the translator's acute sensitivity to reader uptake. The following *Harry Potter* translation into French by Ménard is a good example of a translator's balanced membershipping decisions:

Viewers as far apart as Kent, Yorkshire and Dundee have been phoning in (Rowling 1997a: 12)

Des téléspectateurs qui habitent dans des régions aussi éloignées les unes des autres que le Kent, le Yorkshire et la côte est de l'Ecosse m'ont téléphone (*Rowling* 1997*b*: 11)

[Viewers who live in regions as distant from one other as Kent, Yorkshire and the east coast of Scotland have phoned me]

The third grouping is "recognized exoticism". Some well-known geographical and personal names and titles have "accepted translations" according to language: Geneva (English) is Genève (French), Genf (German) or Ginevra (Italian), not to be confused with Genova, which is Italian for the English Genoa. The Italian painter Tiziano Vecelli changes to Titian only in English; Charlemagne (French) is Karl der Groβe (German), Carlo Magno (Italian) and either Charlemagne or Charles the Great (English); and La Gioconda (Italian) is the Mona Lisa. There are more exceptions than rules concerning exoticism, and "recognition" is not only debatable but also ever changing. Thirty years ago the English used to holiday in Apulia while Italians went to Nuova York. Today they go to Puglia or New York. Americans, however, still prefer Apulia. So the translator will always need to check how recognized the exoticism is.

Finally, "assimilative" procedures transform text from the original into close functionally equivalent target terms, or it is even deleted if not considered central. So, *premier ministre* and *presidente del gobierno* are French and Spanish cultural equivalents of prime minister, even though their powers and responsibilities are not exactly the same. And the same goes for equivalent idioms. As Nida and Taber note (1969 1974: 4) "white as egret's feathers" may be as effective as "white as snow" as long as "snow" is not a leitmotif in itself in the target language. Alternatively, a translator can decide to "reduce to sense", which would reduce the evocative power of the simile to a more prosaic description, as in very, very white. The fact, though, that partial or even complete equivalents exist does not in itself mean that assimilation or domestication is the best translation strategy. Like all the other procedures above, they form part of the resources available from which a translator may choose.

4.2 Allusions

While still at the level of shared context, we move away from the "seeing" part of WYSIWYG to more context-based communication, such as Leppihalme's "key-phrase allusions", which include clichés and proverbs (e.g., Apparently taxis all turn into pumpkins at midnight). She proposes "a metacultural capacity" (1997: 20), one that is able to comprehend "the extralinguistic knowledge of the source language culture" and which can also "take into account the expectations and background knowledge of potential TT readers". In fact, Akira Mizuno (in Kondo and Tebble, 1997), a practising broadcast interpreter in Japan, states that translation of popular culture presents one of the greatest challenges to Japanese broadcasters. He gives a list of some recurring American favourites which have caused him the most difficulty to translate for his Japanese audience. These include, for example, "superman" "the tooth fairy" and "Kilroy was here".

Not all allusions have such clear exophoric and exportable referents, but rather carry with them "cultural baggage", opening up frames or schemata more specifically related to what is appropriate or valued in a particular culture, which we shall look at now.

5. Formal Culture: Functionalist, Appropriate Practices

Hall's second, "formal" level of culture is part of the anthropological definition, usually described in terms of what is normal or appropriate. This floats under the visible part of the iceberg because appropriacy and normality are rarely formally taught. They are more fuzzy concepts and only come to our notice when they are absent or performed maladroitly. As Agar (2006: 5) explains: "Culture becomes visible only when differences appear." Many translation scholars have taken up Bhabha's (1994) *Location of Culture* as the space "in between" as a stock metaphor for translation (e.g., Wolff 2000; but see Tymoczko 2003:

186 – 187 for a criticism) .

Vermeer's own definition, based on the first part of Goodenough's (1957/1964: 36), belongs to this level: "Culture consists of everything one needs to know, master and feel, in order to assess where members of a society are behaving acceptably or deviantly in their various roles" (in Snell-Hornby 2006: 55) . According to Snell-Hornby, it is also accepted by German-speaking translators as "the standard" . Intervention at this level focuses on the skopos of the translation (Vermeer), and tailoring the translation according to reception in the target culture.

At this level of culture, linguistically we are no longer able to point to universal features that change label, or to culturemes that may require technical explication, but, as Sapir (1929/1958: 214) emphasized, "distinct worlds" . So, cultures, here, are plural, and texts require mediating rather than conduit translation. Though Leppihalme restricts the term "culture bumps" to "the allusion (which) may remain unclear or puzzling" (1997: 4), the "bump" can apply to any communication problem. It was coined by Archer (1986) as a mild form of "culture shock", which has been defined as the "emotional reactions to the disorientation that occurs when one is immersed in an unfamiliar culture and is deprived of familiar cues" (Paige 1993: 2) .

Two examples below demonstrate the real-world problem bumps of transferring "normal practice" with the conduit approach. A 1996 fax, written in English from a firm in Pakistan to a well-known Italian fashion house with the intent of becoming a supplier, began as follows:

Attn: [name and department]

I made samples for you in 1994 *for the summer and we had received orders for about* 20, 000 *blouses to be shipped in* 1995 *but due to a plague in our country these orders were cancelled by you. The contact was made by* (*full name and full address*) .

This is not "the normal" way to write a business letter of introduction in English. The introductory statement is too direct, personal and accusatory. Bentahila (2004) reports on a study of university students (Tetouan, Morocco) who used a similar more personal and emotive style to write a letter of application for study grants in the UK. Optimum relevance clearly comes from another local norm: 96 percent, for example, expressed a desire to pursue personal ambitions (e. g. , "I don't exaggerate if I say that it is my dream") .

Clearly, texts with a persuasive function, as above, must be manipulated if they are to function persuasively in the target culture. As Nida (1997: 37) puts it: "Many translators believe that if they take care of the words and grammar, the discourse will take care of itself, but this concept results from an insufficient understanding of the role of discourse structures in interlingual communication." He continues by noting that it is the "intelligent secretaries in

North America" who know how to delete overtly complimentary statements from Latins, and to add appropriate expressions of greeting and friendship from their North American bosses. Otherwise Latinos will think that American businessmen will be reluctant to do business with Latinos Who appear to be too flattering and insincere.

The fact that he does not mention translators is striking but belies a fundamental issue: who actually acts as a cultural mediator? The "translator", paradoxically, does not have the freedom a secretary has to facilitate communication, due both to domestic fidelity-to-the-text norms and to the (limiting) beliefs that professional translators themselves have about their role.

Pragmatically speaking, a target reader is bound within an "environmental bubble" (Cohen 1972: 177; Katan 2001) of his or her own normality, or model of the world, and in general can only have at most a technical understanding of another culture. If there is understanding of the formal level of culture, it will usually be an ethnocentric one (Bennett 1993, 1998; Katan 2001). As Chesterman (1997a: 54) informs us: "Norm flouters threaten normality, produce difference and are quickly ostracized or punished."

Useful technically oriented communication preference models are now becoming available, thanks to the study of contrastive rhetoric (Connor 1996). These can help in the mediation between culture specific accepted practices (e. g., German/English, House 2003b: 31; Italian/English, Katan, 1999/2004: 261 - 262); see also Ventola (2000); Candlin and Gotti (2004).

As noted above regarding Nida's comment, translation norms dictate the extent to which these models can be put into practice. Also, as descriptive translation studies have shown (Chesterman 1993; Toury 1995; Pym et al. 2008 amongst others), the rules and conventions guiding appropriate translation decisions are domestic rather than universal. They govern all translation practice, from decisions regarding which texts are acceptable or accepted for translation, to the type of translation and assimilation/compensation strategies to employ, and to the criteria by which a translation is judged.

6. Informal Culture: Cognitive Systems and Values

Hall's third level of culture he terms "informal" or "out-of-awareness" because it is not normally accessible to the conscious brain for meta-cognitive comment, while, as we have seen, the formal level can be technically analysed and modelled. At the informal level, there are no formal guides to practice but instead unquestioned core values and beliefs, or stories about self and the world. As such, culture, inculcated, for example, though family, school and the media, becomes a relatively fixed internal representation of reality, Bourdieu's "habitus", which then both guides and constrains an individual's orientation in the real world.

Psychological anthropology defines culture in terms of a *Weltanschauung*: a shared model, map or view of the perceivable world (Korzybski 1933/1958); "mental programming" (Hofstede 2001); "the form of things that people have in their mind" (Goodenough 1957/1964: 36), which orients individual and community ways of perceiving and doing things. These are "core, primary ethical values" (Chesterman 1997a: 149) and guide formal culture choices. Wierzbicka (1992: 63) gives an example of a Russian core value dusa lacking in "the universe of Anglo-Saxon culture". The repetition of the term in Vasily Grossman's (1980) novel *Zizn'i sud'ba* (*Life and Fate*) is an essential feature of the ST. Yet the "faithful translation (soul) leads to an oddness for the target text reader". Wierzbicka's advice is to use other partial synonyms and/or eliminate some of the references to duša altogether.

However, not all interculturally-aware translation scholars agree with this form of active distortion of the form. For Venuti (1998a), the main issue is exactly the opposite: the loss of the foreign and an over-domestication, pandering to Anglo value systems. House, herself, warns against actively manipulating the culture filter for written language, particularly literature, as, in her view, the ST text form has its own "worth" (and here mediators would agree); and also because "context cannot be regarded in translation as dynamic" (2006: 343).

Nevertheless, readers at this level of culture will evaluate the use of language (behaviour) not so much in terms of "oddness" of style but through attributing features of personality (identity) according to their own value system. The universal modelling filter here not only distorts the meaning of behaviour but also generalizes in terms of "type". So, limited information about "the other" easily slips into generalized negative stereotyping regarding type of person. The following text from Italo Calvino's *L'avventura di una Moglie* (*The Adventure of a Wife*) (1993: 116) provides a good example (see Katan 2002). Stefania, the well-mannered wife, has just walked into "a bar" for the very first time and goes up to the counter. Her very first move is to make the following bold request (highlighted):

Un ristretto, doppio, caldissimo, - *disse al cameriere.*
"**A concentrated, double, very hot**", she said to the barman.

Initially, this foreignized translation will leave the Anglophone reader bewildered, as none of the words directly cue "coffee". More serious is the fact that we have a projected directive, which the English language and cultural filters are likely to distort into a flouting of negative politeness norms; and Stefania's unassuming behaviour (for an Italian addressee) is likely to be "typed" as "brazen" or "rude".

Katan (2002) suggests a number of mediating strategies, including couching the projecting directive within an explicit request frame, thus leaving the politeness to the context so that there is no distortion of the target text within the projection. This will allow the readers (and, in reality, the barman too) to add the politeness from their own expectancy frame:

She asked the barman for an espresso, "*thick*, *double and really hot*".

This solution allows the readers to glimpse, from the safety of their own environmental bubble, something of the foreignness of Italian directness in projected requests—without distorting the illocutionary intent. The choice of the foreignizing "thick, double", rather than the domestic "large, strong", takes the reader away from the domestic towards the look, feel, taste and aroma of an espresso. In so doing the reader is likely to experience a richer perlocutionary effect, and will have begun to learn something new.

At this level of culture, no word is entirely denotative. Hence, even seemingly technical words can have "cultural baggage" attached to them according to readership. Bassnett (1980/2002: 18 - 19, 28 - 29), for example, notes how global products, such as butter, whisky and martini, can change status and connotation once translated or transferred to a new readership, due to culture-bound practice differences. Diaz-Guerrero and Szalay (1991), furthermore, show how the same term can be associated with almost polar-opposite values and beliefs. Their free-association experiment demonstrated that Americans related United States to patriotism and government while Mexicans associated Estados Unidos with exploitation and wealth. As Allen (2000: 17), taking his cue from Bakhtin, puts it: "Meaning ... is unique, to the extent that it belongs to the linguistic interaction of specific individuals or groups within specific social contexts."

In monocultural communication, this "uniqueness" does not usually require clarification of the performative, as Leech points out (1983: 174 - 175, 325). Intercultural communication mediators, on the other hand, will always need to consider how anchored the intended meaning is to its "specific social context" and hence value system; and also how clear it is to the target reader that the meaning is framed within a different model of the world. The humble chrysanthemum, for example, has little specific connotation within the Anglo cultures, but strong symbolic meaning in most of the rest of the world. It is often the "flower of the dead". So a text which states "these autumn classic chrysanthemums will make for a warm, wonderful feeling any time", taken from an American catalogue, will need to have the speech act framed with a performative, which answers the question: According to whom/which context? e. g., "In America ..." "As they say ..." (See also Katan 1999/2004: 145 - 148).

Finally, the original writer's individual stance is also likely to be distorted or simply deleted in translation through lack of astute membershipping of the target reader. As Dillon (1992: 39 - 40) notes, insider and outsider reading will be very different because:

Insiders have large funds of special information about other relevant claims, received opinion, and previous positions of the writer, in addition, they have an interest in the matter under discussion: they themselves have positions against which they test the argument...they are in a position to evaluate what is said in terms of what is alluded to, obliquely touched on, or even unsaid.

7. Cultural Grammars

Ethnographers have talked about the creation of a "cultural grammar" (see Duranti 1997: 27), which Wierzbicka (1996: 527) describes as "a set of subconscious rules that shape a people's ways of thinking, feeling, speaking, and interacting".

The values and beliefs that form the basis of the subconscious rules can be teased out in two particular ways, emically and etically. Wierzbicka's emic ethnographic approach (e.g., 1996, 2006) is to spell out subjective beliefs about appropriacy using semantic universals to provide "cultural scripts". The "universals" contain a strictly limited use of language, free of cultural baggage, such as the adjectives "good" and "bad". Table 1 is an example of her analysis of the difference between the "vague, undefined" Japanese "self-effacement" and Anglo "self-enhancement".

Table 1 Japanese "self-effacement" and Anglo "self-enhancement" scripts①

Japanese "self-effacement" script	Anglo "self-enhancement" script
It is good to often think something like this: "I did something bad I often do things like this Not everyone does things like this Other people don't often do things like this"	It is good to often think something like this: "I did something very good I can do things like this Not everyone can do things like this Other people don't often do things like this"

Alternatively, either through ethnographic fieldwork or through extensive questionnaire research, attempts have been made to distil the subjective scripts into etic classifications to model the basic orientations, such as "self-effacement". Kroeber and Klockhuhn (1952) were the first to introduce value orientations, suggesting that there were a limited number of responses to universal human needs or problems and that cultures tended to prefer one response over another (for a summary see Katan 1999/2004).

E. T. Hall (1976/1989), for example, through his "contexting theory", distinguished between a culture's preference to communicate in a WYSIWYG way ("low context") or through more context-based channels ("high context"). This general cline of preference helps to clarify the relative values of verbal/written contracts across cultures (Hampden-Turner

① Source: Adapted from Wierzbicka (1996: 537).

and Trompenaars 1983: 123 – 124), website design differences (Wurtz 2005), the relative importance and detail of public signs (e. g., the "Caution HOT!" take-away coffee cups—a necessity in low-context communication cultures) and, indeed, the Anglo concern for clarity in translation (Katan 1999/2004: 234).

In a study of insurance brochures offered by banks in Britain and Italy, Katan (2006) analysed the frequency of words that logically indicate orientation alternatives, as outlined by Hofstede (1991, 2001). The frequency of terms, appertaining for example, to "security/sicurezza" and to "comfort/tranquillita" was significantly different, as were the use of time markers and interrogatives/declaratives, to the extent that "basically it would seem that the British reader is being sold an independent and comfortable life, whereas the Italian reader is being sold security and certainty" (Katan 2006: 69).

See also Mooij's (2004b) work on advertising, and Manca (forthcoming) for a corpus-driven perspective.

8. Outside the Iceberg: Societal Power Relations

Sociologists and cultural studies scholars focus on the influence of culture at the level of society, institutions and prevailing ideologies. Culture, here, is the result of the "pressures that social structures apply to social action" (Jenks 1993: 25). These pressures mould, manipulate or conflict with the individual but shared models of the world discussed above.

There are two other fundamental differences compared to the pure anthropological model. First, individuals (and texts) cannot be assigned to "a culture". This is seen as "essentialist" (Green in Bhabha 1994: 4). Also, Verschueren (2003: 7) believes that "any attempt to compare cultures" is "risky", and believes that Hofstede's "decontextualize(d) idealised parameters of variability" are "a particularly deplorable example". Wierzbicka (2006: 24) agrees, stating "there is no common, no set list of categories invented by the researcher and then 'applied' to various human groups". Instead individuals will have many cultural provenances. Within this frame of culture, the idea of a "useful simplified model of reality", with neat ready-made classifications, begins to fall apart. Cultures are seen to be variously privileged or suppressed, and individuals will negotiate a position within a set of complex cultural systems jockeying for power. Within translation studies, scholars drawing on polysystem theory (e. g., Even-Zohar 1990/2004), postcolonial theory (e. g., Bassnett and Trivedi 1999) and narrative theory (e. g., Baker 2006) all share this assumption.

Secondly, the system in which the translator works is itself under question (as is the validity of cultural relativity). At this level, translators intervene between competing (and unequal) power systems, no longer to facilitate but to take sides, aware that texts (and they themselves) are carriers of ideologies (Hatim and Mason 1997: 147). The decision to translate Salmon Rushdie's *The Satanic Verses* (1988) or *Did Six Million Really Die?* (Harwood 1977) are clear cases in point. The translator at this level is no longer a disassociated mediator but is conscious of being "an ethical agent of social change" (Tymoczko 2003: 181), or "an activist" involved in re-narrating the world (Baker 2006). In a similar vein, Venuti, for example, rails against *The Translator's Invisibility* (Venuti 1995/2008), preferring to let the reader come into direct contact with the difference of "the other". This stance, as he says, "stems partly from a political agenda ... an opposition to the global hegemony of English" (Venuti 1998a: 10), a hegemony that communicates and normalizes specific (e. g., capitalist, colonial) cultural values.

Intervention at this level obviously raises many ethical questions, but there is also clearly a fine practical line between a successful foreignized translation which resists the domestic generic conventions to introduce a new way of writing or way of thinking, and an unread translation because "even breaches of canonical storylines have to be effected within circumscribed, normative plots (i. e., formal culture) if they are to be intelligible at all" (Baker 2006: 98). Also, many scholars confuse the utility of etic classifications designed to encourage mindshifting out of an ethnocentric mindset with mindless stereotyping, the opposite of what translation as intercultural communication represents.

Ultimately, though, culture has to be understood not only as a set of levels or frames but as an integrated system, in a constant state of flux, through which textual signals are negotiated and reinterpreted according to context and individual stance.

9. The Cultural Mediator

It is the mediator's task to negotiate the various signals, contexts and stances. According to Taft:

A cultural mediator is a person who facilitates communication, understanding, and action between persons or groups who differ with respect to language and culture. The role of the mediator is performed by interpreting the expressions, intentions, perceptions, and expectations of each cultural group to the other, that is, by establishing and balancing the communication between them. In order to serve as a link in this sense, the mediator must be able to participate to some extent in both cultures. Thus a mediator must be to a certain extent bicultural. (*Taft* 1981: 53)

As Bennett (1993/1998) makes clear, to be bicultural means having passed through a number of developmental stages towards "intercultural sensitivity".

One of the later stages is termed "contextual evaluation", which is at the same competence level as Pym's (2003) definition of translation: "The ability to generate a series of more than one viable TT (and) the ability to select only one viable TT from this series quickly and with justifiable confidence."

To "select", the mediator will need to " 'mindshift' cultural orientation" (Taft 1981: 53); to be able to do this, a mediator needs another point of reference. This is known in NLP as the "third perceptual position" (DeLozier and Grinder, 1987), disassociated from both the contexts of the ST and from those of the virtual TT. From this third position the mediator (informed also by the other stakeholders in the translation process) can "objectively" manipulate the text.

Of course, Hatim and Mason (1997) and Baker (2006), amongst others, are entirely correct to suggest that mediators feed their own (and are fed) knowledge and beliefs into the processing of the texts. However, the beliefs we are principally concerned with here are of a different "type"; not those of a mediator's ideological position but rather beliefs about the (communicative) needs inherent between texts and their readers. Compare the work of Gutt (1991/2000) from a relevance theory perspective.

Table 2 below shows how the various "types" frame each other. It is a logical levels table that asks at each level what it is that is going on within the context of culture and in that particular context of situation.

Table 2 Logical levels table of context of culture and context of situation

Level	What is going on?	Potential differences to be accounted for in the text	Potential differences to be accounted for between cultures
Environment	Where and when is this "going on"? In what context of situation?	Lexicogrammatical resources, genre, intertextual links, specialized language	Physical, political, social environment: period, people, setting, artefacts; culturemes, encyclopaedic knowledge, allusions, culture bumps
Behaviour	What is it that is "going on"? What is to be translated?	Semantics: visible text, locution, cohesion	Visible action/descriptions: (non) verbal behaviour, proxemics
Strategies	How are these things "going on"? How is it to be translated?	Pragmatics: illocutionary intent/force, register, organization of discourse, house rules, individual style, coherence	Communication preferences: development of ideas, spoken/written styles, habits, customs, norms, appropriacy, rules, linguaculture

(to be continued)

Values Beliefs	Why are these things "going on"? What is the purpose of the translation?	Intentions: message, hidden message, assumptions, presuppositions	The hierarchy of preferred value-orientations : beliefs about identity and about what is "right" "standard" or "normal"
Identity	Who is involved in this "going on"? —Original author —Reader (ships) —Commissioner —Translator as copier/manipulator	Actors in the text: personalities, animated subjects	National, ethnic, gender, religious, class, role, individual personality and cultural provenance(s)
Role, mission in society	Is this "going on" coherent with my role/mission and the relevant social forces? How do I need to act with regard to the social forces?	Text as agent of change or status quo: esteem, ethics (of actors), long-term perlocutionary effects	The social forces: power issues, hegemonies, ideologies; moral issues, professional issues

The first two columns delineate the frame at which intervention will take place, directing the mediator through specific questions to the focus at that level. The third and fourth columns consider the (source and target) texts, contexts of culture and situation, and show which aspects of culture are relevant at each level.

To a large extent, the table synthesizes the discussion of the iceberg and the forces acting on it. So, for example, when translating a text, all translators will need to have an idea of the type of text they have to translate and what culture-bound features it may manifest. They will then, at the level of "behaviour", need to account for "what it is that is going on", the sense immanent in the individual sentences. Moving away from technical culture to the formal, the mediator becomes concerned with appropriacy: how the text has been written and how the text operates (or might operate) in the target culture. At the level of "values and beliefs", mediators, taking the third perceptual position, will focus on the out-of-awareness levels of culture: what beliefs and values are implicitly carried by the ST, how these are likely to be filtered by the intended target reader; and what the (likely) intentions of the ST author were compared to the actors involved in the translation. In short, "why are these things going on?"

Hence, at the level of identity we have a variety of actors involved, both within and outside the text, who embody a cluster of values and/or beliefs which will favour a set of text strategies, visible as the text itself, produced within a particular environment. At this level of "identity", the mediator will take into account the needs or requirements of the other actors, such as the ST author, commissioner and intended reader; and last but not least, the mediator's own beliefs about how to mediate.

Finally, the level of "mission" is concerned with the way roles relate to society and how translating affects the status quo, and questions the profession itself. It answers the larger more existential question as to "why" the mediator should decide to accept (or not) a particular commission at a particular time, and what it is that has guided an individual to act as a mediator. This level, too, brings into question the whole system within which power relations, roles, values, strategies and behaviours underpinning intercultural communication are sanctified.

10. Conclusion

To conclude, translation as intercultural communication requires treating the text itself as only one of the cues of meaning. Other, "silent" "hidden" and "unconscious" factors, which when shared may be termed cultural, determine how a text will be understood. In translating, a new text will be created which will be read according to a different map or model of the world, through a series of different set of perception filters. Hence the need to mediate. The translator should be able to model the various worlds, though, for example, the logical levels model, and by switching perceptual positions gain a more complete picture of "what it is that is, could or should be, going on".

作为跨文化交际的翻译[1]

［意］大卫·卡坦[2]

官　齐　陈慕羽译

一、引言

“跨文化交际”这一术语是 E. T. 霍尔（1959）首先提出的。霍尔注意到误解的产生并非源自语言，而是诸如“沉默”“潜藏”或“无意识”等其他模式化（patterned）因素造成的，即来自文化的差异。贝内特（1998：3）解释说“跨文化交际进路”的最根本前提是“各种文化在其语言、行为范式和价值观方面都不尽相同，因此人们很难使用（单个文化）本身来预测对信息的共享假设和反应”，就翻译而言，这类反应往往具有民族中心倾向。

自斯坦纳以来，把翻译作为“交际行为”（布卢姆—库尔卡，1986）的观点已成为一种既定事实，但并非所有的人都认同翻译中存在文化差异或两者相关的看法。他们的分歧主要体现在以下三个方面。

首先，争议表现在对文化本身的定义。最初，文化的概念十分简单，它仅指已发展成熟社会中文明的人文主义理想（如教育体系、艺术、建筑等）；后来再用于指某个民族的生活方式；再后来，随着社会学和文化研究的进步，它便与社会或意识形态的力量相关。然而，文化习得的方式则因理论不同而大相径庭。在人文主义者看来，文化是通过明确的指导习得的。但人类学家却认为，文化可通过正规教育或父母无意识的家教、社会化，抑或长期与他人的接触等渠道获得。于是，文化便成为群体无意识的共享品。其次，在把语言和文化视为截然不同的实体或持语言即是文化观点的人之间也存在着十分清晰的历史分野。前者把翻译看成普遍主义的编码—解码之语言活动，即雷迪所谓的“语言迁移的导管隐喻（conduit metaphor of language transference）”把 SL（第二语言）移译成 TL（目标语）。也有人（如尼达，2002）认为“事实上，与所分析的术语相比较，语境提供了更多的意义区分”。于是，意义不是由语言所“承载”，而是读者根据其自身文化背景协商的结果。最后，与以上两者密切相关的，是翻译中“文化滤器”（culture filter）的重要性。

---

① 为使译文逻辑清晰、重点突出，仅摘译原文重点和关键内容。

② 大卫·卡坦（David Katan），意大利学者，当代著名翻译理论家。

二、文化滤器

卡坦（1999/2004）曾以神经语言程序学（NLP）理论为基础讨论了四种感知滤器，分别负责我们对“一切正在发生的事情”的感知、阐释、评价及对其定向与模化（modelling），它们分别是生理滤器、文化滤器、个体滤器和语言滤器。

这些滤器通过模化均以同样的方式产生作用。根据班德勒和格林德（1975）的说法，所有模化概不外乎三大原则：删除、曲解和概括。以人类模化为例，我们无法识别所有“正在发生的事情”（删除）；而往往有选择性地聚焦或使我们的所见符合我们的期望，或聚焦于吸引我们注意力的东西（曲解），抑或往往按自己的模式去填充细节或填补突显的差异（概括）。

因此，卡坦认为，不同群体通过文化滤器——四种独特但又相互联系的感知世界的方式之一，形成自己对世界的（有限的、曲解的或程式化的）共同认识。这与古迪纳夫（1957/ 1964：36）的观点不谋而合，即把文化定义为“某群体……它是人们心中既定的事物形式，是他们感知、联想及阐释事物的模型”。与之相反，豪斯（2006：349）认为：“文化滤器是捕捉认知及社会文化差异的方式。”卡坦采纳了这观点，认为这与译者的协调能力密切相关。

然而，在翻译过程中一种滤器在多大程度上优于另一种滤器，是争论的第三个问题。伴随“文化转向”，文化滤器议题似乎占据了论争的中心。纽马克认为“有一种过分强调从一种文化到另一种超出文化范围的普遍性问题的趋向。这些问题有时披着文化的外衣，但已远远超出文化”。他的观点与诸多专业人士的看法一致。也有些人认为，应有选择地使用滤器。尼达（1964：130）则认为，其介入程度更多地取决于所涉及语言的文化与语言的距离或差距，而不是文本类型本身。

三、作为框架系统的文化

我们可以用三个相关的概念来阐明针对文化概念有明显矛盾的观点：语境（化）、框架和逻辑类化（typing）。

1. 语境（化）

我们已提到尼达认为语境至关重要的观点。但也有人认为，语境并不总是那么重要。事实上，电话簿、发票和说明书等就无须任何语境帮助也能看懂或译出。霍尔（1983：61）指出，在任何时候和任何交际情景中都存在“语境化”过程。凭借这一过程，说话人商洽从中提取出多少意义及多少语境的共享信息。因为倘若没有共享信息，“我们可知，由于语境的缺失，如果我们要保持意义的连贯，就必须增补信息”。但卡坦（1999/2004）认为，即使就说明文本而言，相关事物不一定被认为是普遍性的。

“语境”是一个便捷但模糊的术语，最初由人类学家马利诺夫斯基首先引入翻译。他在研究特罗布里恩岛（Trobriand）的居民及其语言时，注意到要把他们的基里维纳语对话译成英语需要进行许多改变。他列举了这样的字面翻译：“We run front-wood ourselves; we paddle in place; we turn we see companion ours. He runs rear-wood behind their sea-arm Pilolu!（我们自己划前面的小船；我们在适当地方划桨；我们转头看见了我们的同伴。他在 Pilolu 海湾划后面的小船）马利诺夫斯基注意到，要使外人清楚特罗布里恩岛居民该话语的隐含意义，他需要加以补充说明，后来格尔茨谓之“深度描述”(thick description)。

其中，读者不仅需要词汇和语法知识帮助其了解故事梗概，还需要知晓这些话语使用的情境（马利诺夫斯基，1923/1938：301），即情景语境。给外来者的文本可作如下改译：

在横跨 Pilolu（位于特罗布里恩岛和 Amphletts 之间）海湾时，我们的小船领先于其他船只。快到岸边时，我们开始划桨。我们回头看去，我们的同伴被远远甩在了身后的 Pilolu 海湾。

改过的这段话便有了意义。然而，要想完全明白“正在发生的事情”，读者就需要清楚“语言从根本上讲根植于文化现实……根植于口头言语更广泛的语境”（马利诺夫斯基，1923/1938：305），后来马利诺夫斯基将其称为“文化语境”（1935/1967：18；参见哈利迪和哈桑，1989：47）。

2. 逻辑类化

人类学家贝特森（1972：289）指出，如果语境还将继续作为一个有用概念的话，就必须受其所谓“逻辑类化”的支配。他认为每一种语境都代表一种类型（如“情景”和“文化”），同时每一种“类型”都构成（或在逻辑上预示）了类型等级中的下一类型。戈夫曼（1974）在《框架分析》一书中解释说，框架告诉我们“正在发生的是什么”。每一种框架都包含了其自身现实，就像是在白墙的某个区域把黑白相间的条纹镶嵌在一个画框里便可称为一幅油画一样。为画框贴上标签（如“白天与黑夜”）也会影响我们的阐释。如果我们把整个展览贴上“战争与自由之反思”的标签，我们就改变了视角，并对眼前正在发生的一切（展览组织者认为的）有了更深刻的领悟。

3. 文化的逻辑层次

这些层次本身基于神经语言程序学的逻辑层次理论的某些部分（迪尔茨，1990；奥康纳，2001），以及霍尔的“文化三角”（1959/ 1990）中的人类学“冰山模型”。这些逻辑层次，把文化部分（冰山）划分为可见层（水平面以上）、半可见层和不可见层（图表略）。水平面以下的框架越来越隐蔽，也越来越靠近我们对世界毋庸置疑的假设和我们自身的（文化）身份。

译者介入（指解释和修改而非纯粹的语言迁移）的程度将与那些框架最大限度地影响翻译的观点相契合。翻译研究者通常会更关注隐藏层面，而翻译从业者往往会更注重表面的可见事物。

四、技术文化：共享的百科知识

第一层文化位于冰山顶部，这符合人文主义的文化概念。其重点在于文本披着某种特定文化最优文明的外衣（纽马克语）。在这一“技术”层面，语言符号具有明显的“所见即所得”（WYSIWYG）的指称功能，所有相关的隐含价值都具有普遍意义。在该层面上，译者的任务是以最小缺失把源文本中的术语和概念移译为其他语言，于是读者在源文本中的“所得”即为目标文本中的“所得”。这也就是纽马克（1981）所谓的翻译“文化价值”。

1. 文化素

然而，译者介入这一层面主要关注的是文本本身及“受文化约束”术语的移译，如“文化素”（cultureme）——指以某特定形式存在或仅对两种被比较文化起作用的社会和法律上认同的形式化的内嵌式现象（诺德，2000：214）。这些“文化类型”（纽马克，1988：95）涵盖了大量的语义场：从地理、传统到制度与技术。自20世纪50年代维奈和达贝尔内以后，研究者提供了大量策略来填补文化素对应的缺失。克维钦斯基（2001：157）将其归为四组：异域程式（procedure）、详释程式、认同的异域程式和同化程式。

异域程式允许外国术语进入目标语，如falafel（沙拉三明治）、macho（大丈夫）、Weltanschauung（世界观）、burka（布尔卡）等。尽管贝尔曼（1985/2004：286）对此持批评态度，认为使文本“更加真实”（引号是他本人所加）的背后强调和突出了某种刻板，但纽马克（1988：82）认为，该程式增添了地方色彩和风味。

第二个分类是详释程式。其目的在于引入一两个额外术语给读者提供充足的语境，通常是借助地方性类比来引导读者获取某种较为相同的认知。许多可用的程式指使用“解释性括号”，如以色列议会（Knesset）；或借助形容词化源术语，如热熏猪肉香肠（hot cotechino sausage）。纽马克还建议，这里使用成分分析法来分析源语言和目标语言中术语的语义特性、内涵或受文化约束组成部分的必要性。

何时、何地、根据什么方式来阐释取决于译者对读者领悟敏锐的感知。以下梅纳尔对《哈利·波特》的法文翻译，便是译者对读者身份适当选择的一个范例：

Viewers as far apart as Kent, Yorkshire and Dundee have been phoning in (Rowling 1997a：12) [远在肯特郡、约克郡和敦提的观众都在打电话进来（罗琳，1997a：12)]

Des téléspectateurs qui habitent dans des régions aussi éloignées les unes des autres que le Kent, le Yorkshire et la côte est de l'Ecosse m'ont téléphone (*Rowling* 1997 *b*：11)

[Viewers who live in regions as distant from one other as Kent, Yorkshire and the east coast of Scotland have phoned me] 根据法文的直译是：住在如肯特郡、约克郡和苏格兰东部沿海那样遥远地区的观众给我打来了电话（罗琳，1997b：11)

第三个分类是认同的异域程式。一些著名的地名、人名和头衔称谓都有“公认的翻译”，如英语的日内瓦，法语为 Genève ，德语为 Genf，意大利语为 Ginevra，它不会与意大利语 Genova（指英语的 Genoa，热那亚）相混淆。就异域程式而言，例外多于规则，“认同”不仅有争议出现，而且还在不断变化。30 年前英国人习惯去阿普利亚度假，而意大利人会去新约克。如今他们会到普利亚或纽约，而美国人仍旧着迷于阿普利亚。因此，译者总是需要去审视异域文化被认同的程度。

最后，同化程式把文本从其原文移译为功能近乎等值的目标语。因此，法语的 premier ministre 和西班牙语的 presidente del gobierno 是法语和西班牙语文化中英语 prime minister 的等值语，尽管它们的权势与责任并不完全等值。习语翻译亦如此对应。正如尼达和泰伯曾指出的，white as egret's feathers（像白鹭羽毛一样洁白）和 white as snow（像雪一样洁白）都能产生同样效果。尽管部分乃至完全等值真的存在，其本身也并不意味着同化或归化是最佳的翻译策略。正如以上所说的所有程式，它们只是译者可进行选择的部分可用资源。

2. 典故

尽管目前依旧停留在共享语境层面，我们先搁下 WYSIWYG（所见即所得）话题来关注一下更基于语境的交际，如莱皮哈尔梅提出了“元文化能力”（1997：20），指的是一种能够领会“源语言文化的语言外知识”，也是一种能“考虑潜在目标文本读者期望和背景知识”的能力。事实上，一位日本广播实习口译员（孔多和特伯，1997）曾指出，对流行文化的翻译是日本播音员所面临的最大挑战之一。他列举出反复出现的美国人之诸多最爱，这些都成了他给日本听众翻译的最大难题。其中包括 superman（超人）、the tooth fairy（牙仙子）和 Kilroy① was here（吉劳埃到此一游）等。

并非所有的典故都有如此明确的外所指和内所指，它们自身都带有“文化包袱”（cultural baggage），具有开放的框架或图式，与特定文化中适当或重要的东西更密切相关。

五、正式文化：功能主义，适当行为

霍尔的第二个“正式”文化层通常以何者为正式或适当来描述。它处于冰山可见部分以下，因为适当与正规几乎从未得到正式的传授。它们都是极为模糊的概念。正如阿加（2006：5）解释的那样：“只有当差异显现出来时文化才会变得可见。”

弗米尔以古迪纳夫（1957/1964：36）第一部分为基础的定义属于这一层面：“文化包括个人需要知道、掌握和感受的一切，旨在评价社会成员扮演不同角色的行为是否得体或有所偏离”（斯内尔－霍恩比，2006：55）。斯内尔－霍恩比认为，文化在这一层面的介入以翻译“目的”为核心（弗米尔），并根据目标文化的接受情况来修正翻译。

---

① Kilroy 意为“热爱旅行者”。

在文化的这一层面，我们无法再从语言上指向改变标签的普遍特征或需要技术说明的文化素，我们只能如萨丕尔（1929/ 1958：214）所强调的指出“截然不同的世界”。尽管莱皮哈尔梅把“文化碰撞”（culture bumps）这一术语严格定义为“可能依旧是尚不清楚或疑惑的典故”，但“碰撞”仍可应用于所有交际问题。阿加尔（1986）将其称为“文化冲突”（culture shock）的和缓形式，而文化冲突的定义是“当沉浸于一种陌生文化中而失去了所有熟识的一切时，出现方向迷失的情感反应”（佩奇，1993：2）。

以下两个例子说明了用导管法移译“常态行为”的现实问题。1996 年，一家巴基斯坦公司给著名的意大利时装公司发了一份英文传真，试图成为其供货商，传真是这样开头的：

联系人：（名字和部门）

1994 年我做了几套夏季样品给你们，然后我们接到了 1995 年大约 2 万件女装衬衫的订单。后因我国的瘟疫，这些订单被你们取消了。合同由（全称和完整地址）拟定。

这不是英文商务信件书写的“规范”格式。其中的措辞过于直截了当，过于私人化，含有责备口吻。本塔希拉（2004）报告了一项对大学生使用类似的、带有更浓郁个人色彩和感情风格的笔法填写的英国研究资助申请书（摩洛哥的德土安）的研究。最佳相关性显然来自另一地方性规范：例如 96% 的学生表达了追求个人目标的愿望（如“如果我说那就是我的梦想，我绝无夸大之词”）。

显然，上文提到的带有说服功能的文本，如果想在目标文化中具有同样的说服力，那就必须给予适当加工。正如尼达（1997：37）所言：“许多译者都认同，如果他们对词汇和语法加以精心加工，整个语篇就变得自然流畅，但这种看法对语际交际中的对话语结构缺乏充分的理解。”他接着指出“在北美，那些聪慧的秘书”知道如何删除拉丁语中的溢美之词，并增补来自北美老板的问候与友好的贴切表述。不然拉美人会以为，美国商人并不情愿与他们做生意，因为他们看起来热衷阿谀奉承、虚情假意。

事实是，他并没有提到译者的突显并掩饰了一个根本问题：究竟是谁扮演着文化中介者的角色？悖论是，译者并不具有秘书为改善交流所拥有的自由，因为他们要恪守忠实文本的原则并（受限于）专业译者对自己角色的信念。

但从实用角度来讲，目标读者往往为其自身的常规“环境泡沫”（environmental bubble）（科恩，1972：177；卡坦，2001）或世界模式所束缚，且通常对其他文化充其量也只是技术性的理解。如果这种理解只是形式上的，那么它往往会带有民族中心的倾向。如切斯特曼（1997a：54）所言：“准则的蔑视者威胁着常态，同时制造着隔阂，因此往往很快就会被边缘化或招致惩罚。”

正如上文提到的关于尼达的评论，翻译标准规定了这些模型的实际运用范畴。指导着恰当翻译决策的规则和规约，是具体的而不是普遍的。它们支配着所有翻译实践，从翻译文本可否接受或已接受的定论，到翻译类型及同化和补偿策略的采用，再到评判翻译的标准。

六、非正式文化：认知系统与价值

霍尔的第三个文化层面谓之“非正式”或“无意识”文化层，因为它通常难以进入大脑的意识部分进行元认知评价，正如我们所见，正式文化层从技术上讲可以进行分析和模化。在非正式层面上并不存在所谓正式行为规范，而只有那些既定的核心价值与信念，抑或关于自我和世界的叙述。文化正是以如是的方式反复灌输，尽管家庭、学校和媒介已成为一种相对一成不变的内部表现形式，即布迪厄所谓的“惯习”(habitus)，而这种形式在现实世界里既引导又限制着个人的取向。

心理人类学是依据 Weltanschauung（世界观）来界定文化的：对可感知世界的共享模型、蓝图或认识（科日布斯基，1933/ 1958）；“心理程式”（mental programming）（霍夫施泰德，2001）；“人们在心里所具有的事件形式”（古迪纳夫，1957/1964：36），它们引导着个人和社区的感知及行事方式。它们是“核心且主要的道德价值”（切斯特曼，1997a：149），同时引领着人们的正式文化取向。而“忠实性翻译（心灵）会让目标文本的读者感到怪异”。

然而，并不是所有具有跨文化意识的翻译学者都赞成如此对形式进行主动扭曲。韦努蒂（1998a）认为，关键问题恰恰相反：异国文化的丢失与过分归化在于迎合英国的价值体系。豪斯反对在书面语中主动运用文化滤器，尤其是文学语言，因为在她看来，源文本的文本形式本身具有其自身价值。

然而，在此文化层面上的读者会根据他们自己的价值系统，通过个性（认同）特征的归属对语言使用（行为）进行评价。此处，普遍性模化滤器不仅扭曲了行为的意义，而且使用“类化”进行概括。因此，对于“他者”的受限信息很容易就陷入对人的类型泛化的负面羁绊。以下选自伊塔诺·卡尔维诺的《一位妻子的历险》（*L'avventura di una Moglie*）（1993：116）的内容就是一个很好的例子（卡坦，2002）。其中，斯特凡尼娅这位具有良好教养的太太，第一次走进一间小酒馆时，径直走向柜台。她的第一个举动便是做出以下大胆的请求（黑体字部分）：

> **Un ristretto, doppio, caldissimo**, - *disse al cameriere.*
>
> **“A concentrated, double, very hot”**, she said to the barman.

首先，这种异化翻译会使以英语为母语的读者感到困惑，因为所有词汇都没有“咖啡”的直接暗示。更糟糕的是，我们有投射指令，英语语言和文化滤器很可能会将其曲解为负面礼貌规范的嘲笑，因此，斯特凡尼娅的谦逊举止（对意大利受众来讲）很可能被认为是“厚颜无耻”或“举止粗鲁”的。

卡坦（2002）提出了一系列调整策略，包括让投射指令如同在源语言中一样大胆，把礼貌留给语境，这样在投射中就消除了对目标文本的扭曲。这也就使读者（事实上也可让酒吧侍者）能够往自己的期待框架中增添礼貌的表达：

她向酒吧的侍者要了杯浓咖啡，“浓的、双倍的、热的”。

这种解决方式使读者可以从他们自身环境中窥见预计请求中意大利语的某些直接外来元素而不扭曲其言外意图。选择异化的“浓的、双倍的”，而不是“大的、强的”，这样的翻译选词可把读者从归化译法引到 espresso（浓咖啡）的色香、感觉、品味和芳香上去。如此，读者很可能会体验到更丰富的言后效应。

在文化这一层面，没有哪一个词语完全具有指示意义。因此，根据特定的读者群，即使是看上去专业的词汇也带有“文化包袱”。例如，巴斯尼特（1980/2002）曾指出，诸如黄油、威士忌和马提尼这类全球化产品，一旦翻译或移译给一批新的读者，由于文化制约的实践差异，可以改变其状态和内在含义。迪亚斯－圭罗雷和绍洛伊（1991）进一步指出，同一术语是如何与几乎完全相反的价值和信念发生联系的。他们的自由联想实验表明，美国人把美国（United States）与爱国主义和政府联系在一起，而墨西哥人则把 Estados Unidos（美国）与剥削和财富相联系。阿伦（2000：17）从巴赫京那得到启示，他说：“意义……是独特的，就这一点而言，它应属于具体社会语境中具体个人或群体的语言交际。”

另外，跨文化交际中介者永远都需要考虑想表达的意义是如何锚定“具体的社会语境”及价值体系的，以及它对目标读者的清晰程度，即在世界大相径庭的文化模式中意义是如何被定义的。例如，卑微的菊花在英国文化里没有任何特别内涵，但在世界大多数其他地方却具有强烈的象征意义。它通常是“死亡之花”。如果某篇美国的短文写道：“这些秋日的古典菊花在任何时候都给人以温暖与美好的感觉”，它需要用以施为功能为框架的语言行为来回答这一问题：“根据谁的/哪个语境？”如：“在美国……”“如他们所说……”（见卡坦，1999/2004：145－148）。

最后，由于缺少对目标读者身份的精确定位，原作者的个人观点在翻译中很可能被扭曲或直接删除。如狄龙（1992：39～40）指出的，局内人与局外人大不相同，这是因为：

局内人对其他一些相关的观点、公认的看法和作者原有的立场都拥有许多特定信息，此外，他们对所讨论的问题充满兴趣：他们本身具有检验特定论点的看法……他们能依据暗示、间接涉及甚至是未言明之意做出评判。

七、文化语法

民族志研究者曾谈到过创立“文化语法”（见杜兰蒂，1997：27），维日贝卡（1996：527）将其描述为“一系列塑造某一民族思维、感知、说话与相互交际方式的潜意识规则”。

形成潜意识规则基础的价值观和信念可以从主位（emically）与客位（etically）两

方面加以梳理。维日贝卡的主位人种志研究法（1996，2006）就是通过语义普遍性提供“文化脚本”的方式，清楚地说明有关准确性的主观信仰。这里的“普遍性”包括对语言使用的严格限制，而不受文化包袱约束，如“好”“坏”这类形容词等。下表是其对“模糊不明的”日语“self-effacement”（自我抹消）和英语“self-enhancement”（自我增强）之间差异分析的例子。

日语“自我抹消”与英语“自我增强”之对比①

日语“自我抹消”文本	英语“自我增强”文本
经常这样想事情很好： “我做了坏事 我经常这样做 不是每个人都这样做 其他人很少这样做事”	经常这样想事情很好： “我做了非常好的事情 我可以这样做事 不是所有的人都能这么做 其他人很少这样做事”

另外，已经有许多人把主观脚本渗透到客位分类，用以塑造基本取向，如“自我抹消”（self-effacement）。价值取向是克勒贝尔和克洛克霍恩（1952）最先引入的，他们认为对普遍的人类需求或问题的答案是有限的，不同文化，取向各异。例如，霍尔（1976/ 1989）通过其“语境理论”（contexting theory），区分了以 WYSIWYG（所见即所得）方式交流的文化（低语境，low context）和通过更基于语境渠道（高语境，high context）进行交流的文化取向。这种普遍取向有助于阐明各种文化间口头/书面约定的相关价值观（汉普登－特纳和特龙佩纳尔，1983）、网站设计差异（维尔茨，2005）、公共标示的相对重要性和细节（如标有“小心烫嘴！”的外卖咖啡杯——低语境交际文化的必要标示）。

在对英国和意大利银行所提供的保险手册的研究中，卡坦（2006）分析了霍夫施泰德（1991，2001）所列的从逻辑上表明取向选择的词频。与“security / sicurezza”有关的词频和与“comfort /tranquillita”有关的词频有显著差异，这与时间标志、疑问句或陈述句的使用一样，“看起来似乎向英国读者兜售的是一份独立且舒适的生活，而向意大利读者售出的则是安全和确定”（卡坦，2006：69）。

八、冰山之外：社会权力关系

社会学家和文化研究学者关注的是在社会、体制和主流意识层面上的文化影响力。这里的文化，指的是“社会结构应用于社会行为压力”的产物（詹克斯，1993：25）。这些压力铸就了上文所讨论的个体及其共享的世界模式，或操纵，或与之冲突。

与纯粹的人类学模型相比，还存在两个根本差异。首先，个体（及文本）不能被

---

① 来源：改编自维日贝卡（1996：537）。

指派为“某种文化”。维日贝卡（2006：24）也认为“并不存在什么研究者所发明的同一、确定的类表，并‘适用于’所有族群”。相反，个体会拥有多个文化渊源。在文化框架内，伴有整洁的现成分类的“现实的有效简化模型”这一想法已开始瓦解。文化被认为在不同程度上享有特权或受到限制，个体需在一套为权力而斗争的复杂文化系统中协商来获取位置。在翻译研究中，多系统论（polysystem theory）（埃文-祖海尔，1990/2004）、后殖民论（巴斯尼特和特里维迪，1999）和叙事理论（贝克，2006）的研究者，均认同这一假设。

其次，译者的工作系统本身存在问题。在这一层面上，译者介入了相互竞争的（或不平等的）权力体系，要持某一方的立场，他们知道文本（及文本本身）是意识形态的载体（哈特姆和梅森，1997：147）。译者在这一层面上不再是局外的调解者，而应意识到自己是“社会变化的伦理代言人”（提莫志克，2003：181）或是进行重述世界的“催化剂”（贝克，2006）。同样，韦努蒂反驳了《译者的隐身》（1995/2008），倾向于让读者直接接触“他者”的差异。正如他所言，这一立场“部分源自政治常规……反对全球的英语霸权主义”（韦努蒂，1998a：10），即传播和规范特定（如资本主义、殖民主义）文化价值的霸权。

在这一层面上，介入显然引发了众多伦理问题。

最后，文化不仅应理解为各种层次或框架，也应该理解为一个完整体系，它处于不断变化的状态中，在这种变化中，文本符号根据语境和个人立场得到了协商和重释。

九、文化的中介者

中介者的任务就是去协商各种语符、语境和立场。塔夫脱认为：

> 文化中介者是促进不同语言与文化的个人或群体间交流、理解和行为的人。中介者通过向其他（文化群体）解释其文化群体的表达、意愿、感受和期望来履行自己的角色，即建立和平衡其相互间的交际。在这一意义上，为了起到纽带的作用，中介者必须在某种程度上参与两种文化。因此，中介者必须具有某种程度的二元文化（塔夫脱，1981：53）。

贝内特（1993/1998）清楚解释说，具备二元文化意味着经过许多通往“跨文化敏感性”的发展阶段。

要去“选择”，中介者就需要“转换”文化取向（塔夫脱，1981：53）。有别于源文本的语境和虚拟的目标文本语境，这在神经语言程序学中被称为“第三感知位”（德洛齐耶和格林德，1987）。从第三感知位出发，中介者可以“客观地”处理文本。

哈特姆和梅森（1997）以及贝克（2006）提出，中介者会把自己的知识和信念融入对文本的处理，这是完全正确的。但是，我们这里主要强调的信念不是中介者意识形态的立场，而是关于文本与其读者之间的内在（交际）需求。

Selected Reading 2

Higher Education and Europe After 1992: The Framework

Ladislav Cerych

The present paper aims at providing an overall framework for the discussion of the theme "higher education and Europe after 1992" and at analysing some of the more general issues which underlie this theme. It does not deal with the most immediate and most obvious implications of the Single Internal Market and of the *Single European Act* for higher education, namely the increased transnational student and staff mobility and the mutual recognition of degrees, qualifications and periods of study abroad as already being promoted by the ERASMUS programme in particular. It can indeed be assumed that the implementation of this and other similar programmes will largely be dependent upon, and accompanied by, more fundamental developments in higher education under the impact and in the expectation of post-1992 Europe. This broader view is called for and justified, among other things, through the mere fact that for a long time to come and certainly well beyond 1992, students moving from one country to another will represent a relatively small part of the total student population of the Community. Assuming that within the next three to five years the original goal of ERASMUS is achieved—implying that 10% of all students spend at least one semester at a higher education institution in another Member State—what happens to the remaining 90% is certainly a matter of utmost importance.

Diversity Versus Uniformity: The Underlying Trend

All statements made resolutions and programmes adopted measures taken or solutions proposed within the framework of the European Communities with regard to the development of higher education assume that 1992 and after will not and should not, constitute a factor of uniformity. In all of them, the diversity of higher education systems is considered as a valuable resource which must be safeguarded in full respect for the autonomy of the various institutions and structures. This, of course, could be viewed as a mere *petitio principii* and a postulate whose implementation may, in practice, be counteracted by forces such as those arising from the standardisation of qualifications, of degrees and durations of study, or by what some perceive as a centralised European bureaucracy. However, we are convinced that the trend towards diversity is not just a *petitio principii*. It is rooted in at least two tendencies which are stronger than any potential factors for greater uniformity.

First diversification of higher education of its admission criteria contents, types of degrees awarded, methods of delivery, etc. —has been taking place since the 1960s in most of the European countries, both spontaneously and as a result of deliberate policies. Moreover, in several traditionally centralised countries we have witnessed a trend towards decentralisation and greater institutional autonomy (however imperfect and partial they may still be). Both these developments are unavoidable at the European level as well, and both are powerful factors contributing to diversification.

Secondly the on-going multiplication of transnational contacts through student and staff exchanges joint programmes of study and joint research projects necessarily leads to an increased amount of borrowing and copying, of new ways of doing things compared with established models, producing a wider range of options within each system. These developments are, of course, also occurring on the European level, which also implies that the borrowing comes not from one but from multiple sources, thereby avoiding the danger of a single dominant influence imposing uniformity.

Thus, even if the political will exist to make higher education uniform across countries—which in our opinion is not the case—it would be doomed to fail because of more profound countervailing historical and sociological forces in the development of higher education.

The Nature of Expected Change

Changes which European higher education will or should undergo in the years in the perspective of the Internal Market of 1993 can be considered from a number of different angles. In this respect, a threefold distinction seems useful:

—changes which will be more or less compulsory and/or unavoidable;

—changes which will be facilitated and/or encouraged;

—changes for which the approach of 1992 will represent an exceptional opportunity.

There will be a relatively small number of compulsory changes, i. e., of changes or reforms virtually imposed as a result of directives adopted by the European Communities. It should be remembered that the latter have *stricto sensu* no competence and power in educational or higher education matters. However, a certain number of binding decisions have already existed, and others will undoubtedly become enforceable in the future. They concern primarily the equality of treatment between home country students and those from other Member States of the Community. This obviously affects, in the first place, access conditions and student fees, two rather important aspects of the functioning of higher education systems and institutions even if, for some time to come, the effects of the corresponding directives will be quantitatively rather limited. In the future, it may also be expected that the equality of treatment will apply to the teaching staff in all Member States. In some of them, this has already been the case for quite a long time; in others, where university teachers and teachers in general are part of the civil service, citizenship of the respective country is usually a requirement, at least for a tenured position. This will probably change sooner or later, and this will enlarge the pool of potential candidates and transform significantly the whole process of recruitment to the academic profession. Again, however, the actual quantitative aspects of this change will presumably remain quite limited for a number of years.

Other changes which we might consider to be virtually unavoidable—probably more immediate and also quantitatively more far-reaching will come about as a direct or indirect consequence of the mutual recognition of degrees and qualifications for a certain (steadily increasing) number of professions (see the already adopted directives of 21 December 1988 as well as of the European Community Course Credit Transfer System). The corresponding directives or schemes will almost certainly lead to changes in curriculum development and, presumably, in the duration of studies. From a purely formal and legal point of view, even these changes will not be compulsory. The European Community will not, and cannot, force universities or national authorities to change, shorten or lengthen their courses and organisation of studies. To the extent that such changes are to be considered as unavoidable and hence as virtually compulsory, they will not correspond to a newly imposed model but constitute a diversified response (among countries and among institutions) to a new situation. It is important to note, however, that the respective directives are not based on any elaborate system of equivalences in contents and structures of studies (except, possibly, with regard to duration), but on mutual trust: country X recognises a particular qualification acquired in country Y because the latter gives it accreditation.

Changes which will be facilitated and/or encouraged will be much more numerous than those which may be considered as compulsory or unavoidable. Most of them are, or will be linked to the major Community programmes fostering joint research projects (ESPRIT, RACE, etc.), mobility of researchers (Science Programme), mobility of teaching staff and students (ERASMUS), university/industry co-operation (COMETT), as well as to the Structural Funds and to the new lingua programme. Obviously, Community resources and support available through these programmes are, and will, constitute a powerful incentive for universities to engage in new types of activities. However, as shown in a later section of this paper, the actual amount of these new resources is less important than their political dimension and impact. To participate in one of the ESPRIT projects, in a COMETT UETP or in an ERASMUS ICP is not just a matter of a few additional thousands of ECU, it is also, and often above all, a label, a sign of recognition and credibility. This certainly applies to some countries and institutions more than to others, but the trend is a general one. The most important aspect here is the conditions and criteria linked to this label and recognition. In order to participate in, and to benefit from, the various Community programmes, certain ways of doing things have to be adopted, particular activities promoted, organisational, scientific, curricular or pedagogical measures taken. And this is where the approach of 1992 and Europe after 1992 have the greatest—potential and actual—impact on higher education. Participation in ESPRIT, for example, implies, among other things, meeting very strict quality requirements. A university that is not up to these requirements is almost forced to improve its standards, the qualifications of its staff, its equipment and library, its relations and communications with the outside world. Quality enhancement of at least certain higher educational institutions and systems (presumably of those which need it most) can and may, therefore, represent one of the particularly important effects of European integration.

The third category of change proposed here—*changes for which the approach of* 1992 *represents an exceptional opportunity*—is closely related to the previous one. We think, in particular, of reforms only very indirectly related to 1992 and after, but whose adoption is advocated by using 1992 as a strong supporting political argument to overcome resistance to change. "If we don't reform our institution or system, we shall be irremediably left behind" is a shorthand expression of this argument. This could be true of almost any reform—whether or not related to implications of the Single Internal Market and the *Single European Act*: access conditions, the degree structure, financing, relations between university and non-university higher education or the creation and development of the latter where it does not exist, and so on. More generally, it can be said that 1992 is used to convince opponents of reforms, in short as a catalyst of overall modernisation of higher education. Again, this applies more to some countries and systems than others, and especially, of course, to those particularly resistant to change, and where the major reform movements of the 1960s and 1970s have had little practical effect so far. But this can also apply to certain specific areas of higher education which have not developed significantly, although the respective system as a whole has undergone quite substantial modifications, e. g. , rules governing the appointment of academic staff, the nature of university autonomy or the degree of decentralisation.

The distinction among the three above categories of change might be purely conceptual, although we believe it useful for analytical purposes. Practically, of course, a continuum exists: from 1992, as a factor of imposed change to one of encouraging or facilitating change, and to 1992, as an argument for and catalyst of change. Only experience will show which parts of this continuum will have the most profound and lasting effects, but all of them represent powerful factors for change and have to be taken into account when looking at the future of higher education in general, and when attempting its reform or adaptation to Europe after 1992 in particular.

General Requirements

What are, concretely, the main changes and reforms which higher education will and/or should undergo in the perspective of post-1992 Europe?

Unavoidably and to some extent at least, any answer to this question will be arbitrary and the list of the necessary transformations or desirable developments will be very long. This is so because of considerations raised in the preceding section of this paper: 1992 is also—and sometimes mainly—an opportunity for changes which should occur in any case, with or without 1992, as part of an overall process of modernisation. We would like to highlight here 10 areas which seem to us of particular relevance with respect to both this overall process of change and to conditions posed by the approach of 1992:

(i) changes in contents (curriculum) of higher education;

(ii) development of a global and diversified system of post-secondary education;

(iii) development of institutional autonomy, responsibility and responsiveness;

(iv) development of competitiveness among higher education institutions;

(v) ensuring equality of opportunity in higher education;

(vi) development of higher education's role in continuing education;

(vii) development of higher education/industry co-operation;

(iii) development of the use of modern communication and information technologies in higher education;

(iv) ensuring and developing higher education's contribution to European economic and social cohesion and to regional development;

(v) development of foreign language teaching and learning in higher education

The first three of these 10 general requirements are analysed in other articles in this issue. We can, therefore, be very brief with regard to their discussion here.

Curricular changes are obviously among the most important requirements, both in the perspective of post-1992 and more generally as part of technological, social and cultural development of modern societies. All disciplines are concerned and so is (maybe above all) what is called "general education", i. e., what, more or less, students should acquire as part of their higher education experience (see articles by Messrs Sperna Weiland, Carinci, Gonzalo &Perez and Karle &Kennedy).

Development of a *global differentiated system of post-secondary education* is another key requirement which has to be met. In almost all countries, universities are, by now, only one component or sector of the whole system. Whether this system is called "higher education" "post-secondary education" or "tertiary education" is a matter of terminology and of national usages, but the concept is clear: The multiple roles which the system is expected to play necessitate a multiplicity of institutional types, and this clearly poses problems of relations between secondary and higher education and between the main sectors of higher education, both at the national and at the European levels, of their co-ordination and/or appropriate division of labour among them. And this also poses the problem of the specific tasks of universities within the global system (see the article by Guy Neave).

Developing institutional autonomy, responsibility and responsiveness is clearly at the heart of present and forthcoming developments of European higher education, the essential practical point here being the link between the three components of this requirement (see article by Roger Dillemans).

Developing competitiveness of higher education institutions is closely related to the preceding requirement. Moreover, this is also an almost automatic consequence and implication of the general framework of post-1992 Europe for higher education. Such a framework—a single internal market—means by definition a situation of increased competition. This also applies to higher education institutions, even if traditionally in many countries a will and capacity to compete are not in their true nature. What will be essential is the establishment of conditions allowing this capacity to be developed, while at the same time respecting the recognised rules and values of academic life.

Ensuring equality of opportunity in higher education is, of course, an old goal widely pursued since at least the 1960s. The implementation of this goal was probably less intensive in the course of the past 10 to 12 years, during which issues related to employment of graduates, finance, adjustment to economic and labour market needs and to quality were given higher priority. But developing equality of opportunity—among social and ethnic groups, nationalities, regions, among those with different educational backgrounds, between young people and adults and between the sexes—must remain on the agenda. To implement this very broad concept of equality of opportunity is not an easy task, especially because it has to be pursued together with other no less important goals, and, in particular, with the search for excellence. In this respect, as in many others, a diversified system of higher education is obviously a precondition of any satisfactory solution.

The importance of *continuing education* for the future of Europe in general, and for the achievement of the objectives of the *Single European Act* in particular, does not need to be stressed here. It is recognised in theory by most higher education institutions—although less in practice, while for many universities continuing education activities may still mainly represent an additional source of income.

What should be underlined in this context is the progressive disappearance of a clear dividing line between initial and continuing education: without 1992 Europe, and even more so in the perspective of 1992, universities cannot escape being increasingly involved in continuing education, partly because the latter is becoming more and more an integral part of a global training process in which initial education without continuing education is meaningless, and partly because initial education for one person might often represent continuing education for another and vice versa. In many cases, this still constitutes a postulate rather than an actual policy, which poses some difficult problems given the traditionally lower status of continuing education in universities.

Increased involvement of universities (and of higher education institutions in general) in continuing education implies more than an additional activity or source of income. It has implications for the whole area of curriculum development and structure of studies, and for the relation between general and specialised education as well as for teaching methods and means of knowledge transfer.

The imperative of close *collaboration between higher education and industry* is by now as widely recognised as the need for the development of universities' involvement in continuing education. Again, the rationale for this imperative does not require any elaboration here. Several of the major Community programmes, from ESPRIT to COMETT, and the almost exponential growth of joint university-industry projects in the area of both research and advanced training point in the direction of an irreversible trend.

Many problems, of course, remain: differences and sometimes even conflicts in the basic aims and values of the two sectors; lack of flexibility in university structures (of their capacity to co-operate) and the often-paralysing regulations to which they are subject (for example, regarding the status and career conditions of their teachers and researchers); the often-inadequate grasp of the nature of university work on the part of industry, and especially of small and medium-sized firms, etc. Several mechanisms have been developed, often very successfully, over the past years to overcome these problems: science parks, industrial liaison offices within universities, various types of intermediary bodies, teaching companies and the like. Two important issues remain and their solution will be crucial in the approach towards 1993.

First, a wider involvement of SMEs in university-industry collaboration is urgently required. Many of the above mechanisms for co-operation, as well as the COMETT programme in particular, do already provide very efficient tools towards this objective, but a continuing effort is necessary and new imaginative solutions have to be developed. The regional framework appears to be of special relevance in this connection; sometimes it may be the only way to involve both SMEs and small or less well-known provincial universities.

Secondly, it is in the nature of the university-industry link that it emphasises—or even concerns exclusively—fields such as engineering, business management and pure science. Combined with another trend, namely the sometimes-dramatic decline in the employment value of degrees in certain traditional disciplines in humanities and social sciences, a dangerous imbalance within the university may be developing, and has often already developed. The

OECD speaks of the emergence of a "vulnerable sector", i. e., of an area of teaching and research which not only lacks adequate resources but which tends to be deserted by top quality students and staff. Counteracting this trend, without diminishing their efforts and role as actors in economic and technological progress, is one of the great challenges facing European universities. They and industry have to look actively into measures where their collaboration will also benefit the "vulnerable fields". Moreover, the concept of university-industry cooperation should certainly be enlarged to become a much broader one of closer links between higher education and enterprises—large and small, public and private—both in the manufacturing and the service sectors.

The use of *modern information and communication technologies* in European higher education is still very underdeveloped. In a certain sense, primary and secondary schools in many countries have undergone a more rapid and certainly better coordinated expansion in this area. Hardly any major national schemes along the lines of the French "*Informatique pour tous*", the English and Welsh Microelectronic Education Programme (MEP) or the Dutch Stimulation Plan have been launched and applied to higher education as they have been, mostly in the early 1980s, with respect to lower educational levels. Micro-computers, databases and information networks have, of course, spread rapidly in universities and other institutions, but they are predominantly used in research and administration; rarely as teaching and educational devices. In particular, they have not significantly influenced educational methods, especially not in humanities and social sciences. Yet their potential is considerable in this respect, and its exploitation is urgently required, particularly in the light of the influx of new clienteles for higher education—adults, employed students or students from under-privileged areas or social groups.

It can easily be argued that a greater and more effective use, both in research and teaching, of information and communication technologies constitutes another general challenge to higher education, the meeting of which the approach of 1992 Europe can, and should, stimulate.

A particular case of the use of new information, and especially communications, technologies is *distance higher education.* The British Open University and other distance universities as well as their newly created European association are showing the way, and so do several schemes such as EuroPACE, SATURN and the like. Besides their further development, especially in countries where they do not yet exist or are very weak, what remains to be carried out is a better integration of new institutions and schemes into the overall systems of higher education. What is also necessary is a greater involvement of an increasing number of traditional universities in distance education. The latter is indeed a valuable, and often indispensable, tool of continuing education, as well as of university/industry co-operation. If universities are to be, as advocated above, more and more active in both these areas, they cannot avoid distance education and they must master the technical, organisational and pedagogical requirements which this implies.

Higher education's contribution to Europe's economic and social cohesion and to regional development is not only one of the key objectives of the *Single European Act*, it is also, for many institutions, a pre-condition of further development. This applies, in particular, to provincial and less well-known universities to which reference was already made in connection with the issue of collaboration between SMEs and higher education. The regional nature of these institutions had, in the past, an almost pejorative connotation, implying an absence or weakness of international connections (and of international recognition). Potentially, and increasingly so in actual fact, this is no longer the case since the launching and implementation of the COMETT and ERASMUS programmes. Transnational links of provincial higher education establishments are becoming the rule, and the former latent incompatibility between their regional and European dimensions has been replaced by a complementarity of these two characteristics.

Again, Europe after 1992 or the *Single European Act* will not, and cannot, force universities to be more interested and active in matters of regional development, but they represent a unique opportunity to do so, and, at the same time, provide a means towards facilitating the achievement of some of the more general goals of any university—and even of other non-university higher education institutions—namely, raising their international (and thereby also national) status and recognition.

It is often said that the *foreign language problem* is one of the main bottlenecks in the development of European co-operation. This applies to higher education as much as to other sectors, and this awareness is also at the root of the new Community *lingua* programme, an important part of which concerns the development of foreign language teaching in higher education. At least three points should be stressed in this connection.

First, a better knowledge of foreign languages (and of "foreign" cultures) is not just a matter of the 10% or less of students who are expected to spend part of their studies abroad; it concerns equally, if not more, the remaining 90% who will not have an opportunity to improve their foreign language skills almost automatically by an extended stay in another country.

Secondly, learning foreign languages is essential, not merely for a few special fields such as business administration but for virtually all disciplines and, indeed, for general higher education. Almost everywhere this goal is very far from being achieved and a massive effort is required. It can, of course, be argued that in this respect, secondary, and even primary, education must provide the necessary basis. However, to be effective, foreign language learning must be a continuing process spreading across all educational levels. Moreover, there is no time to wait until all or the majority of entrants to higher education will have received a sufficient basis in secondary school: 1992 is less than three years away. The massive effort advocated here has far-reaching implications: in curriculum development of almost any field of study, in assessment criteria, in the definition of degree requirements, in the use of new technologies, etc.

Thirdly, the question of which foreign languages should be given priority is far from settled. For obvious reasons, the *lingua* programme concerns those of the Community and, clearly, the massive effort mentioned above applies primarily to them. But for the competitiveness of Europe, as well as from a strictly cultural and scientific point of view, it is also essential to develop skills in other foreign languages, and especially (but not exclusively) of those with a wide diffusion such as Russian, Chinese, Japanese or Arabic. The role of higher education is of strategic importance in this respect.

The Strategic Marginality of European Resources

The financial resources made available to European higher education through the various major Community programmes are considerable, COMETT and ERASMUS will each provide close to 50 million ECU or more per year, LINGUA is of the same order of magnitude, and much larger amounts are coming from the multi-annual R&D scientific and technological Framework Programme (ESPRIT, RACE, etc.), with funds totalling well over 1 billion ECU per year. Last but not least, the three Structural Funds intended to develop the social and economic cohesion of the Community, and, in particular, to help the underprivileged regions, have at their disposal a total close to 15 billion ECU for the period 1987 – 1992. With the exception of COMETT and ERASMUS, other sectors besides higher education will, and already do, take advantage of these programmes: industry and SMEs in particular, vocational training, research centres outside higher education, local and regional authorities, various public and private associations, etc. Overall, however, the share of higher education in the new Community funds is quite important, although difficult to assess at this point.

Any observer familiar with budgets and programmes of international organisations, including those of the United Nations family (with the possible exception of the World Bank), cannot be but deeply impressed by the magnitude of the figures involved.

Certainly, never in history and nowhere in the world have higher education institutions of a mere 12 countries benefited from such large sums from a single non-national public source. Nevertheless, the available amounts must be considered as marginal.

They are marginal compared with the needs and budgets of the national higher education systems concerned. France alone spends about 5 billion ECU annually on higher education, twelve times as much as the combined total of ERASMUS and COMETT for the next five years.

They are marginal compared with R&D budgets of single large companies such as IBM, which devotes about 5 to 6 billion dollars per year to this purpose, almost the same figure as the total of the Community R&D Framework Programme for five years.

They are marginal compared even with the budgets of many of the larger higher educational institutions both in Europe and, *a fortiori* in the United States.

In brief, Community funds are not, and never will be, a manna available to European higher education to solve its financial problems; they will never cover more than a very small proportion of needs. Misunderstandings and over-expectations in this respect have been, and probably remain, common among European universities, their staff and their students. They can have very negative consequences with regard to both academia's commitment to European integration and its efforts at renewal in general. Fortunately, an awareness of the real significance and value of new European resources is growing, and this awareness has certainly to be strengthened further. In spite of the limited amounts made available to individual institutions and projects, at least three major and often decisive advantages arise from Community grants to higher education and other beneficiaries:

First, and as already mentioned, they provide a label and recognition. This is true even if very large companies with budgets many times larger than the support solicited or awarded, and which could undertake the proposed activity without any difficulty on their own.

Secondly, these grants often represent extremely effective "seed money": They have a powerful mobilising and multiplier effect. Because a Community contribution is available, others (local authorities, chambers of commerce, firms or other higher education institutions) will join in the financing of the project more easily—and sometimes on that condition alone.

Thirdly, they constitute, to some extent at least, "free money", which is often essential in view of the rigidity of many university budgets. Even very small sums amounting to a few thousand ECU might make it possible to cover expenses such as staff travel abroad or the cost of a meeting for which a strictly itemised budget does not allow but which might be essential for the implementation and success of the project.

There are, of course, exceptions where the financing of almost the whole or a large proportion of the project might depend on Community funds. They mainly concern some of the smaller institutions in disadvantaged regions of southern European countries but, overall, it must be clear to everybody that by far the most important financial contribution to modernising and adapting higher education to post-1992 Europe must come from sources other than the Community. This even applies to increasing student mobility, including the achievement of the originally proposed target of 10%.

Conclusions: Probability of Change and Cost of Non-change

The probability of change in response to post-1992 Europe is linked to a point raised earlier in this paper: Certain developments and reforms of higher education might take place in any case, with or without 1992. It will always be difficult to identify clearly which of the changes actually occurring are due, solely or principally, to the catalysing effect of the Single Internal Market, and which are the result of a more general, almost worldwide trend of "convergence in the structures and policies of systems of higher education". In fact, many of the goals and requirements discussed in this paper have been familiar to, and pursued by, many institutions since well before the adoption of the *Single European Act*: collaboration with industry, continuing education activities, regional involvement, etc. This in no way diminishes the importance of the Single Internal Market for higher education. It simply means that its objectives are quite compatible with, and reinforce, a more general existing trend. Sometimes such reinforcement may even be indispensable to achieve the expected result on an adequate scale.

The same is true of the development of a European dimension in higher education. In this respect, it can be argued that "universities are, by nature of their commitment to advancing universal knowledge, essentially international institutions" and that, in a sense, "Europeanisation" is but a particular form of internationalisation. Again, therefore, the International Market merely complements or strengthens not only a wider trend in progress for centuries but also an essential attribute historically rooted in the nature of higher education. The reality, however, is slightly different. Since at least the beginning of the nineteenth century, universities have also been rooted in national states and follow their respective policies and purposes. In practical terms, this has set severe limits on internationalisation of higher education. The chances are good that, thanks to post-1992 Europe, these limits will be extended far beyond where they presently lie, and that internationalisation mainly, but not exclusively, in the form of Europeanisation of higher education will spread rapidly so as to cover not only the Oxfords, Heidelbergs or Sorbonnes of this world, but almost the whole spectrum of advanced learning.

However, it is well known that higher education institutions in general, and universities in particular, resist change. The hypothesis of no change should therefore at least be explored and its costs assessed. We believe that it is a highly improbable contingency because of the combined effect of the general trend towards convergence together with the catalysing potential of the Single Internal Market, but two possibilities may be envisaged:

—the changes will be superficial or very partial (limited, for example, mainly to an increasing student mobility and to various university-industry projects without any more fundamental transformations);

—real changes and adaptations will occur much later, maybe 10 to 20 years after 1992.

What then will be the costs of such small, partial or much delayed changes? There is no easy answer to this question. The cost of non-Europe in general was the subject of a major study directed by Paolo Cecchini on behalf of the European Commission between 1986 and

1988. The results of this study suggest an overall amount of 200 billion ECU as a potential benefit of the completed Single Internal Market. This, then, with some simplifications, can be considered as the cost of not implementing and not achieving this objective. Unfortunately, it is impossible to undertake similar evaluation for higher education, mainly because the equation involves too many qualitative aspects and one can only speculate about several others. Certainly, this is not simply a matter of losing the potentially available Community funds which, we have seen, are strategic but quantitatively marginal. The other, and real, losses can be defined by rather general and almost trivial statements, for example:

—higher education will miss the opportunity of implementing more rapidly many of the reforms that are often overdue, even without the perspective of 1992;

—higher education will have much greater difficulty in improving quality and relevance to its students, the labour market, technological progress and society at large;

—internationalisation of higher education will be delayed and almost completely blocked in some of its sectors.

All these are costs of non-change and many others exist. In fact, they concern only one part of the issue: namely, the consequences for higher education of its hypothetical refusal to adapt to the conditions, requirements and possibilities of the Single Internal Market. Another part of the issue is the question "What will Europe of 1993 lose if higher education does not adapt and makes no contribution to it?" Here the answer might be more straightforward. We assume that this contribution is essential and greatly needed. But the Europe of the Single Internal Market and of the *Single European Act* will become a reality (albeit with some delays and some additional difficulties) even without the expected contribution of higher education. However, this would have two important consequences:

—higher education will be left behind (perhaps irremediably), and, in a sense, bypassed and marginalised, while others will, at least partly, take its place, e. g., research and training centres within industry and elsewhere in both the private and public sectors;

—the nature of European integration and the nature of Europe after 1992 will be in danger of remaining limited to their mainly economic, technological and purely political dimensions for a long time. The chances of Europe acquiring what Jacques Delors, President of the European Commission, called "*le supplement de l'ame*" will significantly diminish.

It may be that this is the principal and true cost of non-change of higher education in the perspective of Europe after 1992, and also the most important rationale for higher education to make a contribution to it.

1992年后的高等教育与欧洲[①]

塞里希[②]

宫　齐译

多元化与一元化：潜在趋势

欧共体所有与高等教育发展相关的材料都表明，1992年后不再是，也不应是一元化的发展局面。在欧共体国家中，高等教育体系的多元发展已硕果累累，因此必须在各高校和机构中给予全力保护。以下两大趋势比任何强大的一元潜在因素更加强大：①高等教育多元化自20世纪60年代起已先后出现于大多数欧洲国家，而且在一些传统的中央集权国家中，人们目睹了走向权力分散和更大范围机构自主的局面；②随着教师、学生的相互交流，合作学习方案的实施，合作研究项目的开发，各国间的接触日益频繁，结果导致了大量引借和不断增多的工作新方法的出现，从而使每一系统内部都有越来越多的选择范围。

因此，即使政治制度迫使各国高等教育趋于一致，结果也注定要以失败告终，因为这是高等教育发展中强大的历史、社会对抗力的结果。

预期变化的性质

纵观1993年国际市场，欧洲高等教育将要经历的变化可以从以下不同角度加以思考：①或多或少带有强制性的变化；②受到推动、促进而发生的变化；③1992年到来体现出的特别契机所带来的变化。

强制性的变化相对来讲比重不大，比如由于欧共体采取的一系列指令所带来的变革。目前已有许多约束力的决定，将来其他决定也会实施。因为这些决定主要关系到各成员国学生的平等待遇问题，关系到高等教育体系及机构的两个极为重要的方面：入学条件和学费。人们期待将来平等待遇问题在各成员国的教师队伍也能兑现，因为这在一些国家中已是久而未决的问题了。

受到推动、促进而发生的变化数量比上一种变化要多。其中绝大多数除了将与发展合作研究项目、学者交流、互派师生、校办工厂相关以外，还与组织基金和外语教学计划等欧共体主要计划相关。无疑这些计划所带来的欧共体的财力及资助将成为高等院校从事各类创新活动的有力刺激。要参与并得益于上述各项计划须采纳适当的办

① 为使译文逻辑清晰、重点突出，仅摘译原文重点和关键内容。

② 作者系欧洲教育、社会政策研究院（地处法国巴黎）创始人和现任院长。

事方针，鼓励开展具体活动，采取有组织的、科学的课程及教育步骤。这便是1992年以及未来欧洲对高等教育最大的（潜在和实际的）影响。

变化之三与前者密切相关。“如果我们不改革我们的机构和体制，我们势必要落在后面”，这一立论言简意赅。其实几乎任何改革皆如此。这不但适用于某些国家和体制，尤其是那些极端阻挠改革的国家和体制，同时这也适用于迄今为止变化不大的高等教育的某些领域，尽管每一体制在整体上已进行了若干实质性的调整，如教师任用制度、高校自主性、权力下放程度等。

基本要求

展望1992年后的欧洲，高等教育会出现哪些重大变化和改革呢？

至少就某种程度而言，对这一问题的答案不可避免是任意的，且能列出长长一串必须转变的和理想的发展结果。这里我们将侧重于与1992年提出的条件及变化全部过程密切相关的十个方面：

（1）课程设置的变化。展望1992年的未来及更为广泛地作为当代社会技术、社会和文化发展的组成部分，这些变化十分必要。所有相关学科都与“普遍教育”相联系；即每个学生都须习得作为其高等教育经验的那部分知识。

（2）后中等教育普遍区别体制的发展。这是必须达到的又一主要条件。在大多数国家，高校只是整个高教体制的组成部分。这一体制是叫“高等教育”，还是叫“后中等教育”，或者“第三级教育”只是个名称问题，其概念是明确的：这一体制预期所起的多重作用加快了机制类别多样化的步伐。显然，这又提出了中、高等教育之间，高等教育各主要部门之间的诸关系问题，而且也提出了普遍体制中高等学校的具体任务问题。

（3）深化机构自主，提高责任感、迅速反应。显而易见，这是欧洲高等教育目前及未来发展的中心议题，这里基础的实际核心是这一具体要求三个组成部分的相互联系。

（4）促进高等教育机构间的竞争。这点与前面的要求联系密切，因此几乎是1992年后欧洲高等教育总框架的自然结果和实质。这一框架意味着越来越激烈的竞争环境。它也适用于高等机构，尽管传统上在许多国家，竞争欲望和能量不是其真实面目。基本问题是建立能促使这一能量得以发挥的条件，同时又不妨害学术生命认可的规则和价值。

（5）确保高等教育机会平等。这至少是从20世纪60年代开始就一直普遍追求的长期目标。在过去的10年至12年的时间里，对实现这一目标或许缺少深入细致的工作，此间与大学生就业、财政、顺应经济劳务市场需求，以及质量相关问题成了优先考虑的对象。然而，社会种族群体、民族、地区之间，教育背景不同的学生之间，青年人与成年人之间，男女之间的问题却在议事日程上搁了起来。实现上面所提的更为广泛的机会平等观念决非轻而易举，它必须连同其他重要目标共同去探求。在这一方面，高等教育多元体制显然是任何理想解决方法的先决条件。

（6）连续性教育。这里无须重复强调连续性教育对整个欧洲未来，特别是对《单一欧洲法令》各目标实现的重要意义。这一问题不仅在理论上而且在实际上已为大多数高等教育机构所承认，尽管对许多机构来说连续性教育活动仍主要表现为收入来源的增加。

（7）高等教育与工业的合作。目前这种迫切需求好比连续性教育中不可缺少高校这一环节一样受到广泛承认。其基本原理此处无须详述。欧共体诸多主要计划，从ESPRIT计划到可米特项目，以及呈指数增长的高校与工业合作项目，使这成为一种不可逆转的趋势。

当然，还有许多问题没有解决。目前存在以下两个重要问题，它们的解决是1993年到来的关键。

问题之一：迫切需要更多中、小企业参与高校和工业的合作。虽然上述许多合作途径已经对实现这一目标提供了最有效的武器，但仍需要不懈的努力去挖掘新的、富于想象力的解决办法。

问题之二：高校与工业结合的本质是，它侧重于（甚至特别关系到）如工程学、企业管理及纯科学等领域。这又与另一趋势相汇合——即对人文科学、社会科学等某些传统学科的使用程度有时会呈戏剧性下跌，就此而言，高校已经出现了可怕的不平衡现象。高校与工业必须积极去寻找措施，以便使他们的合作也让“薄弱领域”有利可图。高校与工业合作的观念完全应当在生产和社会服务领域扩大为更广泛的高等教育与企业密切联系的协作形式。

（8）现代信息与通信技术。欧洲高等教育对此类技术的使用尚不充分。从某种意义上讲，许多国家的中、小学生在这一方面已经取得了既快又好的协调发展局面。虽说微机、数据库、信息网迅速在高校及其他机构普及，却只限于研究、管理领域，作为教学或教育手段尚不常见。尤其要指出它们对教育方式影响甚微，对人文科学、社会科学尤其如此。然而，它们在这一方面却有着巨大的潜力，迫切需要进一步挖掘，在面临高等教育新潮（成人、在职学员、贫困地区和下层社会学生）到来的今天更是势在必行。

在教学、科研中，更有效且大量地使用信息技术是高等教育面临的又一挑战。这一目标是1992年欧洲能够且应当鼓励达到的目标。

（9）高等教育对欧洲经济、社会融合及地区发展的贡献。这不仅仅是《单一欧洲法令》的主要目标之一，而且也是许多高校发展的条件之一。它尤其适用于地方性或知名度很低的高等学府。这些高校的“地区性”在以往带有近乎贬义的内涵，因为它缺乏或没有国际联系。可能（实际中也如此）在可米特项目和欧共体大学生交流行动计划出台及实施后，上述情况已不复存在。地区高等教育机构国家间的交往已成定局，以往在这些地区和欧洲范围内潜在的互不相容已经被这两个特征的互补所取代。

（10）外语问题。外语问题一向是欧洲合作发展的主要障碍之一，高等教育如此，其他部门也不例外。意识到这一点也是与高等教育外语教学发展重要部分相关的欧共体发展外语教学新方案的根基。

结论：变化的可能结局与不变的后果

无论如何，高等教育的发展和变化终将出现。然而，实际发生的哪些变化完全或基本上归因于单一国际市场催化作用，哪些属于更为普遍的、世界范围的“高等教育体制结构和政策方面聚合”趋势的影响，要澄清这些问题十分困难。

其实，讨论中的多数目标及要求已为诸多机构所熟悉和探求，如与工业合作、连续性教育活动、地方性参与等。这并没有抹杀国际市场对高等教育的重要作用，它只意味着其目标与更普遍的现存趋向十分一致并且强化了后者。有时要想在适当范围内取得预期效果，这种强化则是必不可少的。

欧洲高等教育领域的发展亦是如此。在这一方面，“从其承担着传授普遍知识义务的本质来看，高校实际上就是国际性机体”，在某种意义上的“欧洲化”不过是国际化的一种具体体现。至少从 19 世纪初开始，高校一直根植于本国的土壤，遵循各自的政策和目标。这实际上给高等教育国际化套上了种种桎梏。现在有利的局面已经出现，桎梏将被打破，主要（但决非唯一）以高等教育欧洲化形式出现的国际化将迅速席卷几乎整个高等学术领域。

众所周知，高等教育机构（尤其是高校）普遍抗拒变革。因而研究一下不变革的假说，并对其后果加以评估是十分必要的。我们相信，由于普遍聚合趋向的共同作用和国际市场催化的潜在推动，不变是根本不可能的，但也有必要正视以下两种可能：①表面变化或局部变化；②真正的变化和适应性的变化将很晚出现，也许要在 1992 年的二三十年以后。

那么，小的、局部的、推迟的变化会带来什么后果呢？

回答这一问题并非轻而易举。下面这些普普通通、平平常常的说法足以说明其真正损失：

①高等教育将丧失许多早应实施变革的契机；②高等教育将会在提高学生质量、促进技术进步、解决劳动力市场及社会普遍问题等方面遇到重重困难；③高等教育国际化将被推迟，甚至在某些部门几乎完全受阻。

这便是不变的代价，而且损失还不止如此。其实，这只是问题的一方面：即高等教育假定拒绝顺应国际市场的条件、要求及可能产生的后果。问题的另一方面表现为：如果高等教育倒行逆施、拒不贡献的话，1993 年的欧洲将有何损失？答案是直截了当的。我们认为，高等教育的贡献是基础的、必不可少的。尽管没有高等教育的预期贡献，国际市场和单一体的欧洲仍不失为一种现实存在，但这将导致以下两大结局：

①高等教育被抛在后面（也许无法挽回），而其他教育形式至少要部分取代前者的地位，如工业体内部的科研培训中心等。②欧洲一体化及 1992 年后欧洲的本质将出现长期局限于其主要经济、技术和纯政治范围的危险局面。因此也会丧失建立并全面实施第五次解放，实现欧共体内思想自由交流的机会。

展望 1992 年以后欧洲的前景，我们将看到高等教育不变革的真正的重大损失，它同时也提出了高等教育要为 1992 年以后的欧洲做出贡献的重要理论基础。

Selected Reading 3

Toward a History of Modern Sociolinguistics

Konrad Koerner

It appears to be a regular part of North American culture that when something is declared to be new, few people care to ask a question about what in effect distinguishes the allegedly novel idea or approach from the old. The past is soon forgotten, and people are happy to be part of a trendy present which holds out the promise of becoming the future. There are, of course, reasons for this phenomenon—historical, socio-political, and economic; however, an analysis of these reasons is not my concern here. I am simply trying to explain why linguists on this continent usually lack a historical consciousness regarding their own field of study and, as a result, can be easily led into believing claims of novelty, discontinuity, breakthrough, and revolution made by someone in favour of a new product or, for that matter, a theoretical stance. I still recall my own astonishment about the enthusiasm of my teachers for "sociolinguistics" during the late 1960s, which then was, as it is still today, largely associated with the name of William Labov (cf. Macauley 1988, 154 – 157). In this paper I refer mainly to this brand of sociolinguistics rather than the line of research pursued by scholars coming from sociology (e. g., Bernstein 1960, 1971; Fishman 1972), which is better defined by the phrase sociology of language; or research programs laid out by scholars with anthropological backgrounds, such as Hymes' ethnography of speaking (e. g., Hymes 1974), and by scholars who favor an interactionist, discourse analysis approach (e. g., Gumperz 1971).

Given what I noted in my opening sentence, I probably should not have been surprised to find next to nothing on the history of "sociolinguistics" when I first ventured to investigate the subject several years ago. But I expected a scholar like Dell Hymes, who has written on other aspects of the history of linguistics during the past twenty-five and more years (see Hymes 1983 for a collection of his papers in this area), and who published, among other things, a book called Foundations in Sociolinguistics (1974), to have enlightened us on the origins, sources, and development of the field. However, one searches in vain for any such account in the bibliography of this prolific writer. The closest thing that I could find to date on the history of sociolinguistics was Yakov Malkiel's (1976) paper, which traces its development from Romance scholarship via dialectological work. There are a few brief textbook accounts of the history of sociolinguistics (e. g., Wolfram and Fasold 1972, 26 – 32; Bell 1976, 28 – 29; Milroy 1987, 5 – 11), but these go little beyond acknowledging the existence of a link between work in dialectology and sociolinguistics. Some textbooks (e. g., Fasold 1984, Wardhaugh 1986) treat the subject without any historical perspective at all. This unsatisfactory situation has been somewhat remedied by the publication of the first tome of the recent sociolinguistics handbook (Ammon et al. 1988), which contains a large section on "history of sociolinguistics as a discipline", though only Hagen's contribution comes in any way close to what I am trying to do in this paper (Hagen 1988b).

William Labov, the leader of this field of research, should not be expected to have engaged himself in writing the history of sociolinguistics, of course, although his work shows much of the sources of his own background and approach (e. g., 1966a, 9 – 12), as we shall see in what follows. The pioneering organizer of the modern field of sociolinguistics does not need to involve himself in history-writing; he is far too busy with regular research work, and he knows that his place in the annals of the discipline is assured. We may also recall the disastrous results of Noam Chomsky's forays into the supposed ancestry of his own work, at least as far as serious historiographic research in linguistics is concerned (cf. Koerner 1983). Apart from presenting us with a distorted picture of the development of Western linguistic thought— not to mention the history of North American linguistics from Whitney to the 1950s— Chomsky's example encouraged others to produce similar Whig histories and, even worse, propaganda pieces for a particular faith.

It remains true, however, that a scientific field reaches its maturity only by becoming aware of its history and by becoming interested in having it documented (see, most recently, Shuy 1990 for a laudable effort in this direction). The present paper is a modest attempt to come to grips with the task of presenting the sources and early development of sociolinguistics, an area of research generally and erroneously thought to have arisen in the mid-1960s, perhaps as a result of the publication of the papers of the November 1963 San Francisco Conference on the Ethnography of Communication (Gumperz and Hymes 1964) and of the proceedings of the 1964 UCLA—Lake Arrowhead—conference devoted to the subject (Bright 1966), which no doubt served as a rallying point for this line of research and at which William Labov had ample opportunity to present his findings and have his views discussed (Labov 1964, 1966b).

The sources of modern sociolinguistics. My own research revealed that we could envisage the broad Labovian type of sociolinguistics to be the confluence, the synthesis, of various lines of research that go back to at least several generations of linguistic workers. The link between dialect geography and sociolinguistics has been made by various scholars (e. g., Trudgill 1983); it is too obvious to be overlooked, but this may explain in part why it has not been as frequently acknowledged as one might expect. Another line of linguistic thought goes back to the later nineteenth century, when scholars such as William Dwight Whitney (1827 –

1894), Heymann Steinthal (1823 - 1899), Michel Breal (1832 - 1915), Hermann Paul (1846 - 1921), Jan Baudouin de Courtenay (1846 - 1929), and others reacted against the view, usually associated with ideas propounded by August Schleicher (1821 - 1868) according to which linguistics should be thought of as a natural science and that language ought to be treated like a living organism. This change in philosophical outlook among linguists became fairly general in the wake of the publication of Wilhelm Dilthey's (1833 - 1911) *Einleitung in die Geisteswissenschaften* (1883) and the ensuing debate over the essential differences between *Naturwissenschaft* and *Geisteswissenschaft* in Germany and elsewhere (Koerner 1982, 187 - 188). This reference to the change in the intellectual climate is important, as it provides the background for a better understanding of the establishment of a specific line of research. So, in addition to dialectology, we may also have to recognize a particular line of approach to language and to questions of language change that has been sociological in orientation. As well, we may become aware of the more recent influx of work on bi- and multi-lingualism into sociolinguistic research.

The influence of Whitney, Paul, Baudouin de Courtenay, and others on Saussure is well established (see Koerner 1973 for details); it suggests at the same time that Saussure did not need Durkheim to be able to characterize language as a *fait social* (Bierbach 1978). To cite just one passage from Whitney's *Language and the Study of Language*, to which Saussure frequently referred in his lectures on general linguistics at the beginning of this century:

> *Speech is not a personal possession, but a social; it belongs, not to the individual, but to the member of society. No item of existing language is the work of an individual; for what we may severally choose to say is not language until it be accepted and employed by our fellows. The whole development of speech, though initiated by the acts of individuals, is wrought out by the community.* (*Whitney* 1867, 404)

I shall return to the importance of Whitney below. The role he played in European linguistics during the last quarter of the nineteenth century has been discussed elsewhere already (see Koerner 1980).

From dialect geography to sociolinguistics. As mentioned, Malkiel (1976) established a connection between dialectological work in Romance languages and sociolinguistics. In other words, we must go back to the beginnings of fieldwork in dialect geography during the last decades of the nineteenth century to see the sociological component slowly infiltrating linguistic geography. I am thinking in particular of the *Marburger Schule* established by Georg Wenker (1852 - 1911), which is still active today (Knoop et al. 1982) and the school created somewhat later by the Swiss Jules Gillieron (1854 - 1926) in Paris (Jaberg 1908), whose students Jacob Jud (1882 - 1952) and Karl Jaberg (1877 - 1958), together with the assistance of Paul Scheuermeier (1888 – 1973), Gerhard Rohlfs (1892 – 1984), and Max Leopold Wagner (1880 – 1962), compiled the voluminous *Atlas Linguistique et Ethnographique de l'Italie et de la Suisse Méridionale* (Jaberg and Jud 1928 – 1940). Both the German and the Swiss enterprises are of particular interest in the present context, as I shall indicate below.

To begin with, Max Weinreich (1894 – 1969), the father of the much better known Uriel Weinreich (1926 – 1967), did his doctoral dissertation on Yiddish with Ferdinand Wrede (1863 – 1934), Wenker's successor at the University of Marburg (Weinreich 1923). (From 1926 onwards, Wrede brought out the massive Deutscher Sprachatlas, initiated many years earlier by Wenker.) More interestingly perhaps, Wrede—whom Meillet cites in his famous 1905 paper (see Meillet 1921, 255) —much earlier drew parallels between ethnography and dialectology, distinguishing between individual linguistiche and social-linguistiche instances of borrowing among languages (Wrede 1902).

Perhaps more important in the present context is the fact that, in 1931, the Swiss Jud and Scheuermeier were brought over to this continent for the summer to train American students to undertake dialectological field work. The Austrian-born Hans Kurath (b. 1891) had secured a grant from the American Council of Learned Societies for this purpose. We know that Raven I. McDavid, Jr. (1911 – 1984), for instance, was one of those who participated in the research that led to the *Linguistic Atlas of New England* edited by Kurath and others (1939 – 1943). It seems significant, therefore, that McDavid published an article entitled "Dialect Geography and Social Science Problems" as early as 1946 [see also McDavid's autobiographical sketch (1980a)]. His 1948 "social analysis on Post-Vocalic /-r/ in South Carolina", however, has recently been hailed as a pioneering instance of variation study (Shuy 1990, 193). By the time of McDavid and O'Cain (1973) the connection between dialectology and sociolinguistics had been recognized, though perhaps more implicitly than publicly acknowledged.

Even outside established schools important dialectological work was done in the later nineteenth century; mention can be made of Schleicher's little-known study of his native dialect (Schleicher 1858) and of Jost Winteler's (1846 – 1929) celebrated Kerenzer Mundart (1875) as just two such examples. That the social component in language variation was recognized before the turn of the century may be gathered from Richard Lowe's (1863 – c. 1940) paper of 1882, which Hagen (1988b, 408) has referred to as the "only known early study on social dialect variation in cities", and the dialect work of yet another scholar of the time, Philipp Wegener (1848 – 1916), dealing with the same geographic area as Lowe, who noted the following in his 1891 contribution to Hermann Paul's Grundriss:

In the Magdeburg region, the rural workers go into the cities in large numbers to work there as masons, handy-men, or in the factories. The joint work brings them into regular contact with the urban workers; the low German rural worker usually does not mind being influenced by the common speech of the city dwellers, and this the more so, the larger the distance from his rural dialect and the higher his esteem for the advantages of urban life. (Wegener 1891, 937; my translation: KK)

I resist the temptation to give this statement a modern interpretation. I believe, however, that in observations like these we may discern an awareness of the "sociology of language" *avant la lettre*, and I am sure that many other such statements could be found in the early work of dialectologists. (See also Olmsted and Timm 1983 on Baudouin de Courtenay, a former student of Schleicher's, who conducted considerable field work from the 1870s onward) No doubt the actual contact in these linguistic investigations with speakers of different varieties of language in differing socioeconomic settings fostered such awareness, to the extent that it becomes at times difficult to distinguish sharply between dialectology and sociolinguistics in the work of these scholars, especially in areas of research that are now called URBAN DIALECTOLOGY.

In order to establish a more obvious connection between the different lines of development in the history of sociolinguistics, let me draw something like a genealogy. Before we are able to do so, however, a few additional links will have to be established. We mentioned Saussure's high esteem for Whitney, which probably goes back to his years at the Universities of Leipzig and Berlin (1876 – 1880). During his years in Paris, Saussure's most distinguished student was Antoine Meillet (1866 – 1936), who in turn had Andre Martinet (b. 1908) as his student. I mention this fact because Martinet wrote a monograph-length study of his native dialect in 1939, which was published after World War II (1946), and also because Labov, like Meillet and Martinet, has always been particularly interested in questions of language change. More important still, while a professor at Columbia University in New York City, Martinet had Uriel Weinreich as his student, both for the M. A. and the Ph. D. degrees. It was Weinreich's doctoral thesis of 1951 which led to the book he became famous for, namely, *Languages in Contact* (Weinreich 1953), a sociogeographical study of bilingualism whose title he had taken from a series of lectures given by Martinet (as Weinreich indicates in his acknowledgements, x). It should be added that Weinreich also studied under Jakob Jud in Zurich during the academic year 1948 – 1949 (Malkiel 1969), doing fieldwork in Switzerland, thus establishing another Swiss connection in sociolinguistics *avant la lettre*. Finally, we need only recall the fact that Labov (b. 1927) took his advanced degrees with Weinreich (see Labov 1963, 1966a) in order to establish a kind of genealogical line leading from Whitney to Labov and to contemporary sociolinguistics (see Fig. 1).

No doubt this is an overly simplistic lineage, and much more evidence, textual as well as biographical, must be supplied in order to offer a more adequate picture. My next section will add to this composite picture. But those familiar with Labov's work know of his frequent acknowledgement of debt to his teacher Weinreich and of his references to the work of Meillet, Saussure, Hermann Paul, and others, making this genealogy somewhat more credible.

The transition from dialectological work to sociolinguistic research is something like a natural development, as can be shown by reference to work done on Dutch during the first decades of this century. Although noting that "the sociological approach had scarcely found its way into linguistics", Jacobus Van Ginneken (1877 – 1945) attempted to bring about just this sort of approach in his two-volume *Handboek der Nederlandse taal* (Van Ginneken 1913 – 1914) as he indicated in the subtitle *De sociologische structuur van het Nederlands* (see Hagen 1988a, 271 – 272, for details). The next decade saw the publication of a work which Hagen (273) rightly characterizes as "a very advanced socio-linguistic study", namely, Gesinus Gerardus Kloeke's (1877 – 1963) *De Hollandsche expansie* (1927), which Bloomfield treated as paradigmatic for the discussion of isoglosses in his chapter on dialectology (Bloomfield 1933, 328 – 331). As the full title of his book indicates (see Kloeke 1927), the author is combining in his research language geography, sociology, and history; sound change is regarded as taking place by a process of social adaptation or borrowing from the speech of the upper classes by speakers from the socioeconomically lower classes.

Whitney
↓
Saussure
↓
Meillet
↓
Martinet
↓
Weinreich
↓
Labov

Fig. 1 From Whitney to Labov

Historical linguistics, language change, and sociolinguistics. While the dialectology-sociolinguistics connection is rather obvious, the link that exists between certain traditions in historical linguistic work and sociolinguistics is not. Interestingly enough, very early in his career, Labov made it clear that the focus of his research "has always been on the understanding of linguistic change" (1966b, 102). It is therefore not surprising that, realizing where he had come from, we can find the connection between sociolinguistics and early work on language change acknowledged in the work of Labov. For instance he states (1972, 267):

In 1905, *Meillet predicted that this century would be devoted to isolating the causes of language change within a social matrix in which language is embedded. But that did not happen. In fact, there were almost no empirical studies of language change in its social context in the* 50 *years following Meillet's pronouncement.*

Labov appears to be referring to Meillet's celebrated paper, "*Comment les mots changent desens*," which Meillet published in Emile Durkheim's (1858 – 1917) periodical *Annee sociologique*, and which still today is regarded as exemplary in the semantic change debate (see Arlotto 1972, 163 – 183, Lehmann 1973, 212 – 213). One may assume that Labov would have taken the by-now classical studies by Louis Gauchat (1866 – 1942) and by Eduard Hermann (1869 – 1950) as exceptions to his pronouncement (see Lehmann 1973, 163 – 164); however, one misses a reference to the work of Kloeke (Labov 1972, 23 and passim; 1966a, 11). Curiously enough, Kloeke is not mentioned in Weinreich's huge bibliography (1953, 123 – 146) either. Earlier in his book Labov quotes, with approval, the following (1972, 263):

Language is ... the social fact par excellence, the result of social contact. It has become one of the strongest bonds uniting societies, and it owes its development to the existence of the social group. [*Vendryes* 1925 (1921), 11]

Joseph Vendryes (1875 – 1960), first a pupil and later a long-time collaborator of Meillet's, fully shared his teacher's views on the social nature of language and on the desirability of establishing a sociological linguistics. His goal, like Meillet's and his school (cf. Bolelli 1979), was to pinpoint the causes of linguistic change and not simply describe the mechanism of linguistic evolution as was common practice among historical linguists, Neogrammarian or not, of the nineteenth and early twentieth centuries. While Meillet ventured little beyond the area of lexical change (which in many instances offers itself best to sociological interpretation as regards the reasons for meaning change, loss of words, and the like), Vendryes, as the title of his book suggests—although he, too, devotes two chapters to meaning change alone (192 – 211 and 212 – 230)—tried to argue that linguistic evolution is but a reflection of social evolution (352ff.).

Yet while other students of Meillet, such as Alf Sommerfelt (1892 – 1965) from the 1930s onwards (e.g., Sommerfelt 1932) and Marcel Cohen (1884 – 1974) in his later years, belabored the subject of a sociology of language, it is fair to say that little concrete advance was made in the explanation of language change on the basis of social factors (cf. Labov's remarks 1972, 267). However, Meillet's student Martinet did instill in his student Weinreich a strong interest in historical linguistics and the explanation of the causes of linguistic change, an interest he passed on to his student Labov (cf. Weinreich et al. 1968), as may be gathered from most of his research from the mid-1960s onwards (e. g., Labov 1982, a recent monograph-length account). In fact, Labov's work constitutes a synthesis of earlier attempts at a sociological approach to questions of language change, beginning with Meillet's paper of 1905 (if not much earlier) and dialectological research done in the United States since the 1930s, which in turn goes back to European traditions established during the last quarter of the nineteenth century. Even Whitney, who made such seemingly modern-sounding observations as the following, was European-trained: We regard every language ... as an institution, one of those which, in each community, make up its culture. Like all the constituent elements of culture, it is various in every community, even in the different individuals composing each (1875, 280).

Bilingualism, multilingualism, and languages in contact. There is yet a third line traceable in more recent work (ignoring the late-nineteenth-century debate on *Mischsprachen* and the like) that filtered, I believe, into much of modern-day work in sociolinguistics. I am not so much referring to straightforward research on bilingualism such as Werner Leopold (1896 – 1984) conducted in the 1930s and 1940s, which is more directly associated with "psycholinguistics", as to bilingualism research that is conscious of the socio-political environment in which it occurs. I am thinking in particular of the work of Einar Haugen (b. 1906) from the early 1950s onwards, especially his ground-breaking study of the Norwegian language in the United States (1953). In this context, it is interesting to note that Weinreich *père*, like his son a native speaker of Yiddish, published papers on bilingualism as early as 1931. It is easy to imagine that following the arrival of the Weinreichs on the North American continent, and given the multilingual situations that they must have encountered in New York City, their interest in plurilingualism and language contact would have increased. (In this last regard, Martinet's influence on Uriel Weinreich must have been of singular importance.)

In other words, the sources of modern-day sociolinguistics are diverse and complex, and they all had a bearing on the development of the various research programs from the 1960s onwards. In the North American context, where over ten percent of the population is of African ancestry, we should not forget the importance that was attached by the administrations of presidents Kennedy and Johnson to the study of Black English (see Drake 1977, 78 – 106, for details), research in which Labov was very prominent.

Concluding observations. Writing at the beginning of the century under the influence of Durkheimian sociology, Meillet did not have a name for the new approach to language and language change in particular. But just a few years later, in 1909, his compatriot Raoul de la Grasserie (1839 – 1914) spoke of *sociologie linguistique* in a programmatic article. The term sociolinguistics, however, did not make its appearance before 1952, somewhat too late to be employed in Haugen's and Weinreich's studies of 1953. Created by Haver C. Currie (b. 1908) and used in a programmatic paper dealing with what we would refer to as "(social) register" of speech (1952), the term "sociolinguistics" was picked up by Wallis (1956), the same year that Pickford offered a "sociological appraisal" of American dialectology. It appears, however, that it took almost ten more years before "sociolinguistics" became the generally accepted name for an important subfield of linguistic research (e. g., Bright 1966).

Considering the different sources of modern sociolinguistics traced in this paper, we might depict the evolution of the field with the help of the diagram (which is obviously incomplete) shown in Fig. 2. (The diagram excludes extralinguistic, in particular sociological and psychological, work that has exercised an influence on sociolinguistic theory and practice)

It is true that the appearance of a cover term for a particular field of research does not necessarily signal the beginning of a discipline, but it marks the point at which professional identification of a particular enterprise is regarded as desirable by at least some of its practitioners. If the awakening of interest in the history of sociolinguistics is any indication, it appears that the field is truly reaching its maturity.

Fig. 2 The Sources of Sociolinguistics

现代社会语言学史①

[加] K. 凯尔纳
官　齐译

本文主要指20世纪60年代末期以拉波夫为代表的社会语言学派，而不是指从社会学出发所进行的研究（如伯恩斯坦、费希曼——即语言的社会学学派），或人类学出身的学者所从事的研究（如海姆斯的《话语的人种史》），或倾向于话语分析方法的学者所做的研究（如甘伯兹）。

笔者一直期待能有像海姆斯这样一位在过去的25年或更长的时间里论述语言学史的若干问题，并撰写了一部题为“社会语言学基础”（1974）专著的学者也能在社会语言学的起因、来源及发展方面开拓我们的视野，可遗憾的是我们在这位著述颇丰的学者名下却无法找到这一方面的论著。我们所能见到的最为接近论及社会语言学史的文章为马尔基尔于1976年所写，其借助于方言研究的成果从罗曼语的学术成就出发追溯了社会语言学的发展。而教科书对社会语言学史的阐述往往只是轻描淡写一带而过，充其量也不过是承认方言研究和社会语言学的成就之间存在着联系；至于历史展望，一些课本中则全然不见。然而，后来《社会语言学》手册第一卷（安蒙等编，1988）用很大的篇幅对“作为独立学科的社会语言学史”进行了阐述，这多少使这不尽人意的局面有所缓和。

事实上，任何科学领域只有当其历史得到重视，并用大量的纪实材料对它进行记述时，它才走向了成熟。为此，本文立足于阐释社会语言学的来源及其早期发展。

现代社会语言学的来源

笔者的研究表明，我们可以设想广义拉波夫派社会语言学是几代语言学家不同的研究方法的集成。许多学者都在方言地理学与社会语言学之间建立了联系，这十分明显。语言思维的另一方法可追溯到19世纪后期（惠特尼、斯坦索尔、布雷尔、保罗、德科特尼等对此持反对意见），通常与施莱歇尔所提出的观点相关，按照他的观点，语言学应被看作自然科学，同时语言也应被看作活的机体。语言学家中出现的这种哲学观的改变，随着狄尔泰《人文科学绪论》一书的问世已十分普遍，于是在德国等地便相继出现了对自然科学和人文科学之间基本差别的讨论。由于这种学术气氛的变化对更好地了解特定研究方法的确立提供了背景知识，所以很有参考的必要。因而除了方言学以外，我们还要承认研究语言、研究那些以社会学为宗旨的语言变化问题的具体

① 为使译文逻辑清晰、重点突出，仅摘译原文重点和关键内容。

研究方法。此外，我们还需注意迄今汇入社会语言学研究主流的诸多论及双语或多语现象的学术成就。

惠特尼、保罗、德科特尼等人对索绪尔的影响无疑是存在的，这影响表明，索氏无须迪尔凯姆即可把语言描写成社会存在。20 世纪初，索氏在其普通语言学讲座里经常提到惠特尼的《语言与语言研究》，下面仅引其中一段："言语不是个人的财产，而是社会的财富；它不属于任何个人，而为社会全体所有。现存语言的所有组成部分绝非个人的成就，因为我们每个人所选择使用的语音只有在为我们人类所接受、所使用时才成为语言。言语发展的全部过程，虽然始于个人活动，却为人类社会所完成。"

从方言地理学到社会语言学

如上所述，马尔基尔（1976）在罗曼语的方言论著和社会语言学之间建立了联系。换言之，我们必须重新回顾方言地理学实地调查的初始阶段，以便弄清社会学部分逐渐渗入语言地理学的过程。笔者特别要提的是温克所奠立的马尔伯格学派，该学派迄今仍很活跃；此外还有瑞士学者日叶龙后来在巴黎创立的学派，其弟子贾德和朔伊尔迈耶等人编撰了多卷本的《意大利与南部瑞士语言学和人种志地图集》。

此后，温莱西在温克的承继人弗雷德的指导下完成了其关于依地语的博士论文。1931 年瑞士学者贾德和朔伊尔迈耶来到美国教授美国学生进行方言实地调查。麦克戴维便是调查研究的参与者之一，该研究使《新英格兰语图集》得以问世。而且更令人瞩目的是，早在 1946 年麦克戴维便发表了题为"方言地理学与社会科学问题"的论文。而他 1948 年发表的"对南卡罗来纳元音后的 / – r/的社会分析"目前被誉为变体研究方面的开拓之著。在麦克戴维和奥凯恩时代，方言学与社会语言学之间的联系已经得到承认（尽管还不是公开的）。

然而，语言变体中的社会部分在进入 20 世纪前早已得到承认，这一点可在吕 1882 年撰写的论文中找到证据，哈根曾把它称为"唯一的……关于城市社会方言变体的早期著名论述"，而同时期的另一位学者韦格纳与吕进行了同样的地理方面的研究，他曾这样写道："在马格德堡地区，农民大量涌进城市，在城里做瓦工、打小工或当工人。共同的工作使他们和市区的工人建立了经常的联系，讲低地德语的农民对于城市居民普通话的影响并不在意，而且越是这样，他们与其原有乡村方言的距离就越大，也就越崇尚城市生活的优越。"

在诸如此类的观察中，我们清楚地看到了对语言社会学的关注。而且这种关注在语言调查中，在与不同社会经济背景的不同语言变体的使用者的实际接触中得到了强化。在一定程度上讲，有时很难在这些学者的著述中严格划出方言学与社会语言学的界线，对于城市方言学尤其如此。

为了在社会语言学发展的不同研究方法之间建立起较为明显的联系，笔者将借助于系谱图示法。图示前，我们有必要澄清以下的一些联系。前面提到了索绪尔对惠特尼的推崇，这可能要追溯到他的莱比锡大学和柏林大学时期。索氏后来到了巴黎，在其任教期间梅耶成了他最得意的门生，而后来的马丁内便是梅耶的高足。1939 年马丁内完成了对其母语的专题研究，并发表于“二战”后的 1946 年。同梅耶与马丁内一样，拉波夫也一向对语言变化有着特殊的兴趣。需要指出的是，马丁内后来去美国任教，温莱西便是其麾下弟子。温莱西于 1951 年完成了题为“交际中的语言”的博士论文（该书于 1953 年正式发表），它是关于双语现象社会地理学研究的论著，也是其成名之作，书名来源于他的导师马丁内的系列讲座。

最后需要指出的一点是，著名社会语言学家拉波夫便出于温莱西的门下。这样从惠特尼到拉波夫和现代社会语言学的系谱便一目了然了。

图 1　从惠特尼到拉波夫

从方言研究到社会语言学研究的过渡正是发展的自然结果。这一点在 20 世纪初的十余年间的著作中已得到了证实。

历史语言学、语言变化及社会语言学

虽然方言学与社会语言学的联系已经有目共睹，但是历史语言学研究与社会语言学的某些传统之间的联系却非如此。有趣的是，拉波夫在其研究的初期曾清楚地表明，他的研究中心“永远在于探讨语言的变化”。例如，他写道：“1950 年，梅耶曾经预言，本世纪将主要致力于对语言所寓于的社会基体内的语言变化起因的分离工作，然而，事实并非如此。事实上，在梅耶该预言后的 50 年里几乎没有出现在其社会背景中对语言变化的经验式研究。”

这里，拉波夫似乎指的是梅耶的著名论文——“词义变化的方式”，该文迄今仍为讨论语义变化的典范。有人可能认为，拉波夫会把高查特和赫尔曼的“古典研究”作为梅耶预言的例外。拉波夫在其早期的著作中曾赞同地摘录了这样一段话：“语言是……最优秀的社会事实，是社会交际的产物。它已成为联结社会的强大纽带，它的发展归功于社会群体的存在。”（房德里耶斯）

房德里耶斯既是梅耶的学生，又是合作者；在语言的社会性质和建立一门社会的语言学方面与其导师可谓是志同道合。他的目标也和梅耶学派一样，强调语言变化的起因，而不是仅仅停留于19世纪或20世纪初历史语言学家那种惯用的对语言进化机制的描写。虽然，梅耶从词汇变化的圈子走出了大胆的一步，但他的弟子房德里耶斯（虽然仅在语义变化一题用去了两章的篇幅）却力图论证：语言演变不过是社会进化的反映。(p352)①

但梅耶的另一位弟子马丁内并没有给他的学生温莱西强烈灌输历史语言学的兴趣及对语言变化起因的解释，尽管如此，后者却把这种兴趣带给了他的学生拉波夫，这从拉波夫20世纪60年代中期直至后来的大多数研究里明显地体现出来。其实，拉波夫的著述便是用社会学方法探讨语言变化问题早期尝试的综合体现。甚至惠特尼这位似乎做出如下正确观察的学者也出身于欧式教育："我们把每一种语言……都看成一种惯例，它是每个社会中构成文化的成分之一，像文化的所有组成部分一样，不同社会语言也大相径庭，甚至不同的人也不尽相同。"

双语、多语现象及交际中的语言

现代研究的第三种方法渗透着社会语言学大部分当代著述，这里特别要提到的是豪根20世纪50年代后发表的论著，特别是他对美国挪威语的具有突破性的研究(1953)。此外，有趣的是温莱西的父亲早在1931年便发表了关于双语现象的论著。因此，不难想象，随着温莱西学派踏上北美大陆，纽约的多语现象环境必定是他们所面对的情景，对此他们研究多语现象及语言交际的兴致势必大增。

虽然，今天社会语言学的来源多种多样，十分繁杂，却都与20世纪60年代以后的各种研究计划的发展有所关联。在北美，有10%以上的非洲后裔，我们切不可无视肯尼迪、约翰逊执政期间在黑人英语研究方面的重要成就，其中首推拉波夫。

结 语

20世纪初，由于迪尔凯姆社会学对研究的影响，梅耶并没有命名所使用的研究语言，特别是语言变化的新方法。然而，在几年以后的1909年，他的本族学者格拉塞利在一篇重要文章中谈到了语言社会学。而社会语言学这一术语直到1952年后才得以问世，为柯里所创，首先被使用于一篇被称为言语的"（社会）语域"（1952）的重要论文中。随后，沃利斯（1956）也使用了这一术语，同年皮克福德提出了美国方言学的"社会评价"。但是"社会语言学"一语被普遍接受几乎是近十年之后，那时它才成为语言研究的一个重要分支。

谈到本文中所涉及的现代社会语言学的不同来源，我们不妨用下面的图表来描写这一领域的进展。

---

① 指房德里耶斯1925年发表的《语言：历史的语言学通论》一书。

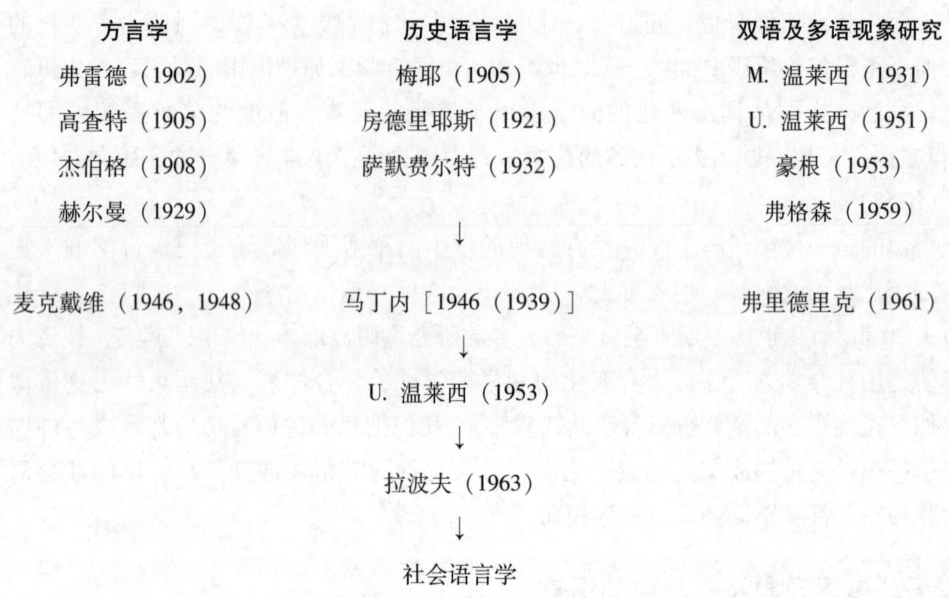

图2　社会语言学的不同来源

事实上，某一具体研究领域的表面称俏并不就意味着一个学科的开始，它只表明对具体领域的专业确定至少为它的研究者所公认是合乎需要的。如果说社会语言学史志趣的兴起展示了某种迹象的话，那么说它表明这一学科正在真正地走向成熟。

Selected Reading 4

On the Developing History of Psycholinguistics

J. F. Kess

Abstract

This paper describes the developing history of the discipline of psycholinguistics. It contrasts Wundtian psycholinguistics with modern psycholinguistics of the past 50 years, and outlines our progression through the Formative, Linguistic, Cognitive, and Cognitive Science periods in current psycholinguistic research. Particular attention is paid to models and metaphors based on a computational view of natural language and the mind as an information-processing device.

Introduction

Disciplines recite their own history once they have become established as separate and unique fields of intellectual endeavour. In so doing, they break the flow of events into periods or stages during which time theoretical or methodological concerns turned the discipline in some crucially different direction. When the field is an interdisciplinary one, there is usually some division of intellectual labour, and its practitioners usually erect signposts for their convenience as well as for their guidance. In this keynote address, I intend to survey the major developments in the interdisciplinary field of psycholinguistics to show how psycholinguistic studies have evolved since the turn of the century. But I should note that the history of psycholinguistics is a developing history, one in which the division of intellectual labour is constantly changing, but one in which collaborative research across the disciplines is still the norm. The success of the discipline of psycholinguistics has always depended upon what linguists and psychologists were willing to learn from one another, and it would appear that success will continue to depend upon that premise, despite its seeming absorption into the larger interdisciplinary field of Cognitive Science.

Early Divisions: Morris, Syntactics, Semantics, and Pragmatics

One of the earliest divisions was not even intended for psycholinguistics as a field, but its influence was unmistakable. This early set of signposts encompassed the total study of signs and symbols, and by inference the relationship between language and thought, and was established by Morris (1938), contribution to the *International Encyclopaedia of Unified Science*, Morris' approach to the study of signs and symbols was based on logical positivism, and his division of effort listed the three fields of syntactics, semantics, and pragmatics. For Morris, the field of syntactics dealt with the relationship of signs to signs. The field of semantics concerned itself with the relationship of signs to their meanings, and pragmatics with the relationship of signs to those who use them.

Some 30 years later, Miller (1964b) also used this logico-philosophical frame of reference in trying to explain a linguistically based approach to psycholinguistics to his fellow psychologists. He noted that the effect of such a scheme is to divide the field into problems of structure, of comprehension, and of belief, and that such a division of efforts provides its own hierarchy of activities for the relevant disciplines of linguistics, psychology, and philosophy.

Thus, syntactics focused on problems of structure, for at the lowest level it is necessary to understand the syntactic structure of a language. Syntactics has, in Morris' terms, traditionally been the interest of linguistics, even before generative transformational grammar made syntax, in the narrower sense of sentence structure, the departure point for modern analyses of language. Morris' sense of the term evokes the analysis of the formal relationship of signs to one another, in abstraction from the relationship of signs to objects or to their users. On the other hand, semantics has been more traditionally the interest of philosophy and later of anthropology. Semantics for Morris suggested problems of comprehension, in that comprehension meant perceiving the semantic content of a language. Lastly, psychology's interests were seen to be traditionally in pragmatics, with the psychologist trying to understand the ways in which humans acquire, understand, and exploit the linguistic system. Pragmatics for Morris implied problems of belief, in that once both structural analysis and semantic comprehension are achieved, then an understanding of pragmatic acceptance or rejection, and belief or disbelief, is possible.

Miller's (1964b) observation that this division corresponds roughly to the order in which the study of language had progressed was accurate enough for its time. It was also a predictor for the future, but only in its roughest form and not quite in the way that Miller had envisioned. It is still true, as Miller had suggested in the mid-1960s, that syntactics is the best-known area and semantics the next best. Pragmatics was, and still is, the least known field, though it too is receiving increasing attention. We can note, for example, the recent appearance of several journals in pragmatics, an international organization, and the first international congresses in pragmatics (Antwerp in 1987 and Barcelona in 1990).

But when Miller in the 1960s recalled Morris' tripartite classification from the 1930s, it was still true that the three fields could be apportioned between the disciplines in that way. And more to the point, when Miller reiterated these distinctions as having guided research up until the 1960s, he was attempting to demonstrate the importance of theoretical insights derived from linguistics to psycholinguistics. In the 1980s and 1990s, however, we no longer make such severe distinctions between theories of language and theories of language users. Nor do we now see the fields of endeavour as neatly broken into linguists just doing syntactic analysis and psychologists describing how humans acquire and use the system known as language. Changes have also occurred in the definitions of what semantics and pragmatics mean, and, perhaps most importantly, changes have also occurred in zones of interest. Psychologists are more aware of problems of structure and meaning in their research plans, and we linguists are now attuned to also constructing theories of language users and language acquirers.

Miller's (1964a, b) comments are best understood in the context of a Linguistic Period in psycholinguistics. Such comments act as an effective prompt to psychology in noting that in order to construct a theory of the language user, one first had to understand how that language user deals with syntactic and semantic aspects of language, with the realities of structure and meaning derived from language. Many now take such assumptions for granted, and new divisions have erected new interdisciplinary signposts to give directions as to where we should go and why.

Allow me to now sketch these more recent interpretations, in a way that will illustrate how the divisions of intellectual labour have been translated into a developing history of psycholinguistics which periodically redefines what psycholinguistics should be concerned with. It is, of course, worth reviewing the recent history of psycholinguistics just for the theoretical ideas which defined the field of interests from the 1950s to the 1980s. The perspective of theoretical commitment and methodological realization often provides the necessary insight into research beliefs which motivate research, but more importantly, this perspective also provides the relevant background for understanding the new ideas which proponents of a new paradigm rebel against which to create the developing history of the discipline.

A Historical Overview of Modern Psycholinguistics

The historical background

The term psycholinguistics suggests that this is a field which depends in some crucial way on the theories and intellectual interchange of both psychology and linguistics. There have been in fact two major eras in which psycholinguistic interests have flourished, one historical and one modern. The first took place around the turn of the century, primarily in Europe; the second took place in the 1950s and 1960s, primarily in America (Blumenthal 1987; Reber 1987). Blumenthal (1970, 1974) has painted Leipzig's Wilhelm Wundt as the influential master psycholinguist during that first era, for Wundt was prepared to demonstrate that language could be explained on the basis of psychological principles (see Wundt 1900, 1910 – 1920). This was also a period in the developing history of the social sciences when linguistics was prepared to exchange its older, romanticist evaluation of language on cultural and aesthetic principles, for a more modern, scientific approach to language. Wilhelm Wundt, and the new psychology, offered this possibility with the rigour and the enthusiasm that only a new scientific discipline can offer. Many younger linguists were keen to import this new rigour and scientific vision to linguistic theory and research, and for a time psychological concerns were directly reflected in the emerging field of linguistics. For example, we linguists all know Leonard Bloomfield as the prototypical structuralist, and often quote his famous 1933 book as the classic text of the structuralist period in linguistics. But few know his little known first book of 1914, even fewer have read it, and fewer still realize that it pays careful homage to the Wundtian psychology alluded to above.

After the devastating first war, there was a decline in the power and consequent influence of German intellectual life, and Wundtian cognitive psychology was correspondingly weakened in the attention it commanded. Thus, Bloomfield's later 1933 book parallels the newer aspirations of the powerfully emerging behaviourism. This is what accounts for the sharp split between mentalism and mechanism in Bloomfield's work, and the injunction against the former in all structuralist explanations of language description. Moreover, though Bloomfield himself was obviously sympathetic to behaviourist tenets, psychological theory no longer guides linguistic theory (see Kess 1983), and this is an intellectual posture which continues to characterize linguistics throughout this century.

Curiously, there was to be another era of intellectual unity, equally fertile, equally enthusiastic, and equally brief (see Reber 1987; McCauley 1987). This was the era after the late 1950s, and on into the 1960s, a time when linguistic theory fuelled the engines of psycholinguistic enterprise. Specifically, the form of linguistic theory was the type of linguistics founded on the theoretical pattern of generative transformational grammar, as first proposed by Noam Chomsky in 1957, elaborated in 1965, and universalized in 1968.

But this unity of purpose also faded after several decades of experimentation based on Chomskyan theory, leaving us now with a more balanced, and certainly a more eclectic view of what psycholinguistic theory should pursue in attempting to offer explanations for natural language. This paper pays particular attention to the history of psycholinguistics since that second ferment in the 1950s. The major reason for doing this is because this recent history reflects the changing roles of linguistics and psychology vis-a-vis one another in the developing discipline of psycholinguistics. It also represents a time when these two mature disciplines collaborated in meaningful and productive, but alternatively different, ways to approach the problems of the psychology of language.

The four major periods

Updating Maclay's useful (1973) classification of developmental steps in modern psycholinguistics, we can trace the field's progression through four major periods in that time span. The stages can be labelled as follows: ① formative; ② linguistic; ③ cognitive; ④cognitivescience.

Formative period

The first formal contacts between disciplines were established at a Social Science Research Council Summer Meeting at Cornell in 1951, and a Committee on Linguistics and Psychology was formed with Charles Osgood, a neo-behaviourist psychologist, as chairman. A second summer seminar was held at Indiana University in conjunction with the Linguistic Institute of 1953. The intellectual directions and content of such exchanges are chronicled in Osgood and Sebeok's (1954) *Psycholinguistics*, and the title of this text represents one of the first uses of the new hyphenated discipline of psycholinguistics. Though we have referred to research in the psychology of language around the turn of the century, the term psycholinguistics was simply unknown in Wundt's time.

This Committee on Linguistics and Psychology sponsored a number of smaller meetings on a variety of topics like language universals (see Greenberg 1966) and encouraged research into the possible relationships between language and thought. The most important of these was probably Carroll's *Southwest Project in Comparative Psycholinguistics*, which focused on investigating the linguistic relativity hypothesis. Relativism was not a novel concept, but had attracted renewed attention through the catalytic writings of Benjamin Lee Whorf (see, for example, Carroll and Casagrande 1958; Maclay 1958).

This first period in modern psycholinguistics boasted a symmetrical relationship between linguistics and psychology, because both were committed to an operationalist philosophy. Structuralism was the prevailing paradigm in linguistics and behaviourism was predominant in psychology. As a philosophy of science, an operationalist approach derives theoretical constructs from observable data by using a set of verifiable operations which are highly explicit and reliably replicated. Thus, structuralism in linguistics defined units like the phoneme and the morpheme in terms of operational procedures. For example, one used operationalized concepts like minimal contrast or complementary distribution to discover and then define a given phoneme or morpheme. These operational procedures were called discovery procedures and were used in interview situations like field work to discover the structure of unknown languages as well as the structure of familiar languages.

Similarly, the movement known as behaviourism in psychology gave primacy to observable data, and devoted its theoretical efforts to the elaboration of operational methods which guaranteed that any explanatory device (like drive or habit strength) was anchored in the real, physical world. For the strongest statement of such views, it is worth re-reading John B. Watson (1924) for an idea of the commitment to observability and the anathema status of mental constructs. Behaviourist methodology thus came to focus upon rigorous experimental design and the statistical analysis of data.

It is worth noting that, despite the introduction of mental constructs like the framework of explanation in both linguistics and psychology, the fields have retained a differing methodological orientation. Psychology has been and continues to be the study of individual differences, often based on studies of large subject populations. In contrast, theoretical linguistics has typically sought after the specific principles of a grammar, or even the generalized principles of universal grammar, by relying on individual data sets. Recent principles like grammaticality experienced problems with reliability across individual intuitions, and were simply modified by adding considerations like acceptability, dialect variation, and so forth.

The psychology that made common cause with linguistics in the Formative Period was not of this extreme behaviouristic bent. It was true that Skinner's contemporaneous work (1957) extended behaviouristic philosophy into the extreme position that has been termed Radical Behaviourism. But it was Hullean psychology that made common cause with linguistics in the Formative Period. Psychologists like C. E. Osgood postulated models of stimulus—response relationships that posited internal, and thus unobservable, mediational variables that earned such psychology the designation of Neo-behaviourism [see, for example, Osgood (1953)]. It was this group that was more active in psycholinguistics research.

It is worth mentioning a third partner in this Formative Period. Psycholinguistics, in the earliest stages of its modern development, had some fascination with mechanistic models of language processes and possible applications. Then it was information theory, and now it happens to be the computational model which encourages model testing in a direct success-or-fail mechanical sense. Information Theory, derived from the concerns of communications engineers, served largely as a source of ideas and models. For example, Shannon and Weaver (1949), communications engineers with Bell Telephone, defined a communication unit as a encoding/decoding unit, that is, much like a telephone set. And one had to then be concerned with how messages went from their sources to their destinations in the following fashion.

Source→transmitter/encoder →channel→ receiver/decoder →destination

Such communication channels might be subject to interference, or noise, a prime concern for communications engineering at the time. Not surprisingly, there was much emphasis on decoding and encoding processes on opposite ends of the channel, plus attention to the possible interference properties a channel might be subject to. Information Theory, and by extension, psycholinguistics, made use of this mechanical metaphor of language for a period in the 1950s. Psycholinguists, for a time at least, spoke in terms of investigating communicating units who produce/encode and receive/decode messages; a ready example can be seen in Osgood and Sebeok's (1954) statement that "psycholinguistics deals directly with the processes of encoding and decoding as they relate states of messages to states of communicators" . Now, armed with a different set of metaphors from computer modelling, we talk of central processing units, on-line processing, and modularity.

Though there was room for disagreement as to who did what in this Formative Period, none arose because of the obvious split in the division of labour. Linguists took the states of messages as their area of research inquiry, while psychologists took the states of communicators. By default, psychologists also took the encoding and decoding processes, perhaps because of the natural affinity between behaviourism and information theory. The striking characteristic of this period in psycholinguistics is its diversity, and when one asked what psycholinguistics did, the answer seemed to be "Everything!" Saporta (1961), a popular book of readings in the new paradigm, was essentially a juxtaposition of readings collected from the two disciplines, with little effort at integrating linguistics and psychology.

The first modern overview of psycholinguistics that appears in the *Annual Review of Psychology* (Rubenstein and Aborn 1960) thus notes "little helmsmanship", in the field, and is largely an account of traditional psychological endeavours. There is little mention of linguistics, except for a paragraph just noting linguists Noam Chomsky and his mentor Zellig Harris. The time seems ripe for the introduction of a new and unifying paradigm in the Kuhnian sense (see Kuhn 1970) . And this is just what happened! For a time, psycholinguistics found in generative transformational grammar a unifying paradigm, only to fragment and dissolve until the final unifying paradigm currently offered by Cognitive Science.

This paradigmatic uniformity can be easily found if we trace the evolution of the field as characterized by later reviews in the *Annual Review of Psychology*. Ervin-Tripp and Slobin (1966) and Fillenbaum (1971) very much reflect the centering focus of linguistic theory in Chomskyan terms. But time takes its toll, and it is equally worthy of noting that later reviews by Johnson-Laird (1974) and Danks and Glucksberg (1980) do not cite a single paper by Chomsky, though much of the experimental work reflects his ideas. And those ideas still have a certain influence; the hegemony of syntactic theory may be long past in both linguistics and psycholinguistics, but both fields continue to be profoundly affected by Chomskyan claims.

Linguistic period

It was during the Linguistic Period that psycholinguistics experienced its second historical period of total theoretical unity, and so it is worth pondering over this period somewhat longer. It is also necessary to understand its aims, as well as to gauge the reasons for the reactions which followed, to understand the following stages in the history of the discipline.

The rise of transformational generative grammar in linguistics was followed by its theoretical domination of psycholinguistics research for a time. It practically controlled important research in the decade from 1960 to 1970, and continued to inspire interesting questions right into the next decade and beyond. Chomsky (1957) had redirected linguistic concerns, and Chomsky (1959) had convincingly demonstrated that behaviourism could explain neither the acquisition nor the dynamic creativity of language behaviour. This destroyed the two cornerstones of psycholinguistic research which had served the formative period, for Chomsky argued that an operationalist philosophy cannot provide adequate grammars of natural languages. He further argued that a deductive approach is required, and that linguistic theory has as its proper domain the competence of speakers, and not their performance (Chomsky 1965). Thus, the previous division of labour was called into question, as well as the theoretical cornerstones upon which research activity had been based.

Chomskyan criticisms of behaviourism simply left psychologists of language without a champion, and the basic tenets of generative grammar itself come to dictate the shape of psycholinguistic research. In linguistics, this was a shift in paradigm, but in psycholinguistics this was really the introduction of one where there was none. Psycholinguistics was now to be based on what generative grammarians thought to be crucial to an understanding of language. The starting point was the study of competence, with the study of performance a secondary activity, if indeed even that important. It was generally agreed, at least by generative grammarians, that an understanding of competence would be crucial to understanding the nature of actual performance. Thus, the centrality of grammar was taken as a basic assumption, and the sentence emerged as the prime unit in this quest to understand grammar. Not surprisingly, most psycholinguistic experiments during this period dealt with the understanding and use of sentences, because the sentence played such an important role in defining the data and dimensions of transformational generative grammar.

Much of this orientation came through the psychologist George A. Miller, whose writings and experiments served as bridge between linguistic theory and psychological experimentation in the earliest years (for example, Miller 1964a, b). And some of the early titles of papers are suggestive of the centrality of grammar commitment; for example, consider titles like some psychological studies of grammar (Miller 1962) and some perceptual consequences of linguistic rules (Miller and Isard 1963). Some of these early experiments even hinted that production or perception of sentences could be isomorphic with the derivation of that sentence by the grammar. This notion, known as the Derivational Theory of Complexity, never received sufficient support to warrant its continuing presence as even a working hypothesis. Still, much of the information which experiments uncovered along the way was even more informative, and the experimental results showed that there was much more to be learned from linguistically inspired research than just this weak hypothesis.

The originator of transformational generative grammar, Noam Chomsky, had rejected this idea early on, and linguistics waxed hot and cold on how the grammar might be related to the actual derivation of sentences by the speaker and their subsequent interpretation by the listener. As a matter of fact, this ambivalence has been true until the present. It is only this last period that we are now in, the period that I label the Cognitive Science Period, that the notion of psychological reality has found acceptance. Although psychological reality is rarely called that anymore, and few debates rage as to whether it should be pursued, the concept seems to have won easy acceptance in linguistic theory, and even easier acceptance in cognitive science.

Because of generative grammar's pursuit of linguistic universals, and its demand for explanations instead of taxonomies of data, there was soon considerable interest in language acquisition as well (see Smith and Miller, 1966). Some early writings (like McNeill, 1964/1970) in developmental psycholinguistics wholly accepted the transformational approach, suggesting that the child enters the process of language learning with an innate predisposition for the general form of linguistic rules, and possibly even certain linguistic categories. Lenneberg's (1967) work on the biological foundations of language most fully developed the argument for innateness, chronicling the argument with evidence from other sciences, but relying for its original impetus from theoretical notions of nativism derived from linguistic theory. The basic argument is that the capacity for language acquisition is species-specific and is a genetically determined attribute of humans and humans alone. Consequently, where there had been scattered research, the field of developmental psycholinguistics and child language studies now bloomed with a richness and vigour which is still with us. In fact, there are now countless researchers among us attempting to discover what it is that children are expected to master in natural language and how they go about achieving this as they pass from stage to stage into linguistic maturity.

Cognitive period

The Linguistic Period eventually gives way to a richer, more interdisciplinary commitment in psycholinguistics. For one thing, the rapid pace with which formalizations changed in linguistic theory placed a heavy burden on even committed linguists, let alone psychologists, trying to keep track. There was ensuing fragmentation in the aims of transformational grammar, and in the formalisms, that it employed to achieve this, leading to a decline in the uniformity and optimism which marked earlier work (see Reber 1987). Other problems confronted linguistic theory in the form of the role of performance facts, data from language acquisition studies, and where to place semantics vis-a-vis syntax in a comprehensive grammatical theory. Having placed semantics, the next question would be what to include in semantics, for it directly interfaced with the range of world knowledge in a way that syntax never did. Not surprisingly, a third period arises, largely prompted by psychologists and philosophers of language. I do not mean to suggest that the Linguistic Period ends abruptly, nor that linguistic theory ceases to have an influence. But the shift in priorities by psycholinguists does imply a rejection of the direction of traffic from about 1970 on, and Unguistics no longer supplies psycholinguistic units, models, and methodologies in the exclusive way that it did for a decade (see Kess 1976a).

First of all, allow me to note that the cognitive in this Cognitive Period does not carry quite the same meaning that it did in earlier models of cognitive psychology. I might also note that there was also some similarity between Gestalt cognitive psychology and transformational grammar in their mutual rejection of behaviourism and the power of its explanatory principles (Neisser 1967). The crucial difference in the use of the term cognitive in the Cognitive Period rests more in the area of language acquisition and what was considered the separate and intrinsic capacity it took to learn language. The basic question is really "what does it mean to learn a language, and what does it take to do this?" The philosopher Fodor (1966) had already noted that what must be brought to bear is a set of general learning principles, and Lenneberg (1967) had also seen language in the broader sense of general biological and cognitive foundations.

The major premise that underlies a cognitive approach is the dependence of language upon human cognition in general. Many psycholinguists come to agree that language is but one of several outcomes of more fundamental cognitive processes. Perhaps Chomsky had himself pave the way with his offhand (1968) comment that linguistics is after all really a field concerned with human cognition, and that linguists are in that sense really cognitive psychologists. The best early representatives of this cognitive reorientation are Bever (1970) and Slobin (1973), with their suggestion of the cognitive basis for linguistic structures. A cognitive orientation seemed to reject the centrality and independence of grammar, and argued that the cognitive capacity described in grammatical accounts of competence is only one manifestation of human language and is neither prior to nor independent of other cognitive and behavioural systems involved in the acquisition and use of language. It was suggested that linguistic structures are not learned independently of semantic concepts and discourse functions, and more importantly, that cognitive principles must be assumed to govern the acquisition of linguistic structures. The acquisition of language was to be explained as a result of the interaction between the linguistic and other behavioural systems, such that the nature of linguistic systems is ultimately a product of more basic cognitive structures. Some even went so far as to suggest that transformational grammar itself was just a theory about having linguistic intuitions, with the implication that this type of language analysis is just a form of language behaviour and is thus no more closely related to the ultimate nature of language than any other linguistic aspect of learning, perceiving, and speaking.

Thus, although linguistic theory continued to play a role in psycholinguistic theory and practice, the role is not quite the same as before. Fodor et al. 's (1974) summation of psycholinguistic achievements based on linguistic theory (see also Kess 1976a) is easily that period's best state-of-the-art assessment of what was learned from linguistic input. Very simply, they review experiments which set out to investigate the psychological reality of grammatical structure and operations postulated by linguists and present a simple conclusion. Their review of this line of experimentation reconfirms the reality of the taxonomy of sentences, the notion of the sentence family and inter-sentential distances implied in transformational syntax. But their review does not reconfirm the psychological reality of transformations. In fact, their observation is that the sum total of experimental findings on generative grammar suggest that "experiments which undertake to demonstrate the psychological reality of the structural descriptions characteristically have better luck than those which undertake to demonstrate the psychological reality of the operations involved in grammatical derivations" (Fodor et al. 1974, 241). Thus, structural descriptions and units, like the sentence constituent specified therein, do appear to have some psychological status in organizational and memory tasks, but evidence for the claim that transformational processes, as set out by linguists' descriptions of the language, might play a role in the comprehension, storage, or recall was far weaker in comparison. Interestingly, Fodor et al. concluded that work on the psychological reality of syntactic structures may be "concerned less and less with the vindication of independently motivated linguistic analyses where the linguistic arguments are equivocal" (Fodor et al. 1974, 512) and that "it may well be that only direct experimentation on psychological reality will ultimately choose between competing syntactic theories" (Fodor et al. 1974, 512).

Cognitive science

The fourth and current period is more difficult to characterize, for it is one which we are presently in the middle of, and its final conclusions and contributions we have yet to see realized. One fact we are certain of, however psycholinguistics is in a state of transition, and there is no longer any one single prevailing school of thought in the discipline (see Rieber and Voyat 1981). Nor is there one in psychology or linguistics. Instead, one sees a tremendous amount of interdisciplinary activity, with researchers very much aware of developments in adjacent fields, often even contributing to those developments. More important, however, is the fact that scholars can no longer afford to ignore scientific answers in other fields, if those answers impinge on research problems in one's own field. This means that the explanations that we offer for problems in psycholinguistics must be compatible with solid explanations in psychology and linguistics. The disciplines can no longer afford to work separately to prepare idiosyncratic ad hoc solutions tenable only in that discipline.

The rubic under which this intellectual commitment appears is the superordinate discipline of cognitive science. And if cognitive science is truly the scientific understanding of how the human mind works (Johnson-Laird, 1983), then the demand for psychological reality in psycholinguistic theory is no longer novel or trivial.

In linguistics, the acceptance of this criterion as one which is necessary for a realistic and well-formulated theory of language is more a feature of the last decade than of the previous three periods. I see this, for example, in Halle et al.'s (1978) *Linguistic Theory and Psychological Reality*, knowing that this was not the kind of volume that would have appeared in such a matter-of-fact fashion earlier. In more general terms, the acceptance of this criterion is implicit in the collaborative participation of linguistics, psychology, and psycholinguistics in the development of cognitive science, one of the more noteworthy events of the last decade. Basically, the linguistic approach pressed into service here is now one which takes information processing constraints into account. Internal consistency and formal logic as correctness in a grammatical theory is accepted as a sine qua non and is no longer being argued here, for many grammatical theories can be internally correct according to such measures. We instead now argue the question of usefulness or compatibility of a system of grammatical description that is attuned to the problems, as well as the results, of psycholinguistic research. As an example, the treatment of such grammatical phenomena as the derivation of truncated passives or the ordering of centre-, left-, and right-embeddings can still be independently treated in a grammatical description, that is, independent from the way they operate for language users in terms of processual strategies. And many linguists have insisted that this is rightly so, and that this is all that linguistic theories should account for. On the other hand, many would now suggest that grammatical descriptions should be responsive to psycholinguistic findings and even incorporate them into useful grammars. Such grammars could be said to exhibit psychological reality, a term we might now reserve only for grammars which have relevance to language processing, and which are in turn constrained by language processing factors.

The problem of psychological validity is thus only a problem for those linguists who wish to make psychological claims about their theories and resultant grammars. Many of course do not wish to, many do so explicitly, and some do implicitly (see, for example, Bresnan 1982). But certainly, psychological reality is a desideratum for any linguistic theory which truly wishes explanatory power about the nature of language beyond the linguistic system itself. And it is certainly a requisite for any psycholinguistic theory that is worthy of the name. Such realistic theories of language would thus be expected to describe our language knowledge and linguistic abilities in a way that incorporates performance abilities that are crucial to information processing tasks.

One example of such an attempt to integrate linguistic and psycholinguistic information into a single theory of language is found in the lexical—functional theory of grammar (Bresnan 1981; Bresnan and Kaplan 1982; Kaplan and Bresnan 1982), also known by LFG as the acronym for lexical-functional grammar. Unlike many theories of grammatical description, it does concern itself very directly with the relationship between an adequate grammatical theory and language processing considerations. And in the innovative paper in the Halle et al's volume mentioned above, Bresnan (1978) makes claims that her grammatical postulates not only should be, but are, psychologically real. As a representative model of linguistic knowledge compatible with real language processing this theory actually does make a claim that a competence grammar of this sort is directly incorporated into a language processing model. Lexical-functional grammars do this by simply storing grammatical information directly in the lexical entry, assuming that it is easier to retrieve lexical information from memory rather than grammatical permutations like transformational rules which change the syntactic format of sentences. It is also sensitive to the well-established fact that we remember the semantic gist of sentences and discourse rather than their actual syntactic format.

This approach also avoids the problems that transformational grammar suffered when it was applied as a model of sentence processing and storage under the experimental paradigm known as the derivational theory of complexity. In a lexical-functional theory of grammar, it is assumed that grammatical information needed to relate or differentiate sentence types is stored in the lexical entry itself. Take, as an illustrative example, the relationship between the active and die passive sentence types. We now no longer need a hierarchy of sentences with the active sentence serving as a starting point in processual terms. Nor do we need to rank other sentences like passives or truncated passives as being more difficult, and in an order of difficulty which runs from active to passive to truncated passive sentences. A truncated passive sentence, like the dog was bitten, is not more complex than a full passive, like the dog was bitten by the cat, in this model, though this was the order of derivation in some previous generative frameworks. And, in fact, it is not more difficult in processing terms, as demonstrated by experimental results. Such a theoretical approach clearly acknowledges the fact that some linguists are responding to the need to present our linguistic knowledge of structure in a way that also reflects the way in which speaker-hearers of a language process those structures in real-time performance tasks like understanding, storing, and recalling those structures. The evaluative metric for an adequate description of a linguistic fact is no longer driven exclusively by purely internal criteria like simplicity, elegance of description, or even formal logic.

The other salient characteristic of the current cognitive science period is that the metaphors and models once again come from a third and external source, again one with engineering applications. That source is the burgeoning field of activity concerned with expert systems, artificial intelligence, and model-building and model-testing in computer science. Psycholinguistics, as well as its cooperating founding disciplines, now seems less eager to build a "science of the mind", on rationalistic deductive foundations alone. It declares aspirations of being a true "science of the mind", a "cognitive science", if you will. But our aspirations are not simply to model computational systems employing formal programs; our goal is to model and understand mental systems employing cognitive programs like knowledge, experience, inference, and decision-making, but which interface with natural language. Here the analogy ends, for computers are not humans, but only are allowed to make use of some of the information that humans employ. Unlike computer scientists, it is not sufficient to write a formal program of some cognitive ability, like sentence parsing, and accept the validity of that program on the simple basis of simply "it works, so it must be correct!" The validity of the program, or description of mental abilities in this example, is based on what humans do, how they perform cognitive tasks, and this is the difference between computer science and cognitive science. Still, the emergence of this new area has sharpened our perceptions of what we must attend to, and we now have an entirely new set of metaphors to guide us and a wide range of potential applications for our findings in both competence and performance tasks.

Winograd (1983) has recently offered a clever portrayal of paradigm shifts in linguistics as a series of shifts in the metaphors borrowed from the successful paradigms in the hard sciences. It is easy to see how any given shift in a historical period in psycholinguistics can be seen as coinciding with research directions in sister disciplines. It is also easier to see why we are presently involved in a transition period of intellectual growth and reorientation toward issues in cognitive science.

Allow me to start with the first of these four powerful metaphors. In the previous century, Darwinian evolutionary theory was reflected in linguistics as biology. Much attention was paid to language change, language variation, and language families. Language change was seen as operating in an evolutionary fashion of ongoing differentiation, with the outcome the delineation of different families of languages. Trees showing how a family of languages like Romance had developed from Latin within the Italic family had a striking similarity to how, say, Darwin's finches on the Galapagos Islands had differentiated.

In this century, the taxonomic orientation we saw in structuralism was a reflection of language as chemistry. Linguists set out to discover the units of language structure, such as the phonemic units that constitute the phonology of a language. The basic units in language could be combined and recombined like the basic valences in chemistry, but always had a fundamental integrity of their own as the building blocks of the specific language level being investigated.

In the 1950s, Chomsky's generative grammar, as first laid out in *Syntactic Structures* (Chomsky 1957), was a shift to viewing language as mathematics. The mode of enquiry was deductive, as is the case with mathematical inquiry, although the goal was an understanding of competence, the abstract characterization of the knowledge that native speakers have that makes them native speakers of a language. This knowledge, albeit a knowledge of language structures and language operations, was viewed as a mathematical object which could be described by a set of rules. A set of re-write rules was the formal mechanism which provided for explicitness in stating the sets affected by each distinct rule, and explicitness was a requirement that generative grammar prided itself on.

But now the models and metaphors come from elsewhere (Fodor 1983; Jackendoff 1987; Johnson-Laird 1988). A new focus of interest has emerged, one which has now put linguistics and psycholinguistics in league with the powerful influence of those mechanical devices that are having their effect on all fields of knowledge. The 1980s and 1990s now enjoy a fourth metaphor, a computational metaphor, obviously catalysed by the use of computers as models of language processing functions. Language is now seen as a symbolic process, often leading to decisions, typically based on knowledge and inference. Language is no longer the ultimate and only interesting knowledge set. It is true that human minds use natural language, and that computers use programmatic languages. But it is also true that both types of language manipulate symbols and make decisions on the basis of stored and inferred knowledge. It is inevitable that psycholinguistics, and linguistic theory, would have to become involved in a larger field of inquiry, that is, the nature of knowledge, the structure of mental representations, and how these are used in mental processes like reasoning and decision-making.

Chomskyan notions had in a way already set the stage for this new focus of interest, not so much by the observation that linguists were really cognitive psychologists (Chomsky 1968), but by the very nature of what the description of competence entailed. Generative grammar had attempted to characterize speakers' knowledge of their language, and this by its very nature entails understanding the cognitive processes underlying the language facility. The transfer is a natural one, and indeed, it is typical of the current period that names previously associated with formal syntax or semantics now are committed to problems of conceptual representation and the structure of human cognitive systems. For example, in discussing semantics and cognition, Jackendoff (1983) admits that the formal description of semantics in linguistics is really a problem of conceptual representation, common to all forms of cognition. Similarly, in formulating the cognitive grammar approach to analysing syntactic and semantic structure, Langacker (1987) espouses the basic premise that language is not a self-contained system separate from general cognitive systems. Langacker simply accepts that the findings of linguistics and cognitive psychology should be integrated.

An information-processing view of language requires that we understand how these mental representations operate, in tasks like acquisition of knowledge from discourse by direct extraction or by inference. This information-processing metaphor also leads us into examining the storage, recall, or cross-classification of knowledge, that is, whatever human language users do in the processes of reasoning and decision-making. In fact, the generative, cognitive, and computational paradigms are very similar in one respect. All three can be considered cognitive paradigms in their commitment to studying the structure of the knowledge possessed by humans who use language. The major difference among them is how knowledge about mental processes and representation involved in language use shall be accessed and represented, and the degree of commitment to incorporating the research findings from other disciplines into psycholinguistics.

This means that psycholinguistics no longer just takes into account findings from psychology and linguistics in its role as the final umbrella, or superordinate interdisciplinary category, for theory, research, and the findings of such research. Instead, one now sees psycholinguistics itself as also being subsumed under the larger scheme of research, in that broader interdisciplinary activity that has come to be labelled as cognitive science. The contributory disciplines in this new discipline are variously agreed upon as being psychology, linguistics, artificial intelligence, neuroscience, and philosophy (see Stillings et al. 1987), but with obvious inclusion for overlap areas of inquiry like psycholinguistics and cognitive anthropology. In many ways, the multidisciplinary commitment to the goals of cognitive science has effectively meant that the psychological reality of theories about natural language must be matched with information about natural language processing, and that this is now an actively desired goal. This is indeed an exciting time for research, with the ultimate promise an exacting and realistic science of the human mind and all that the mind is capable of, including, and particularly, language.

心理语言学的发展史①

［英］J. F. 凯斯
官　齐译

一、引言

本文旨在综览心理语言学这一交叉学科的主要发展过程。笔者认为，心理语言学的历史是一部知识劳动分野不断变动的发展史，尽管如此，跨学科的合作研究仍旧是其基本规范。心理语言学所取得的成就一直是语言学家和心理学家相互学习的结果，而且未来的成功也将取决于这种相互学习。

二、早期的划分：英里斯的句法、语义和语用

最早的一种知识劳动划分法虽然没有打算把心理语言学作为独立的领域，却产生了显而易见的影响。早期一系列研究记载了对符号和标记的全部研究成果，推断了语言和思维之间的关系，这要归功于莫里斯（Morris，1938）对《国际统一科学百科全书》的贡献。莫氏研究符号与标记的方法是以逻辑实证论为基础的，他的划分表现在句法学、语义学和语用学这三个领域。在他看来，句法学所研究的是符号之间的相互关系；语义学的研究对象是符号与意义的关系；而语用学则研究符号及其使用者之间的关系。

三十年后，米勒（Miller，1964b）也使用了这种逻辑哲学相关联的框架，力图为他那些从事心理学研究的同仁阐明基于语言学的心理学研究方式。他指出，这种方案的效力在于把这领域划分为结构问题、理解问题以及信念问题；这种研究划分法为语言学、心理学和哲学等相关学科提供了研究范畴。

于是，结构问题便成为句法学的研究中心，因为在最基础的层次上了解语言的句法结构十分必要。用莫里斯的话来说，句法一直是语言学家的传统兴趣所在，甚至在转换生成语法使句子成为现代语言分析的转折点之前也是如此。莫氏赋予这一术语的内涵，引起了对符号之间形式上的相关关系的分析。至于语义学，它始终是哲学及后来的人类学的研究热点。它提出了理解的问题，其中的理解是指对语言语义内容的理解。而心理学的传统研究中心在于语用研究，心理语言学家试图了解人类习得、理解乃至探讨语言体系的各种方式。在莫氏看来，语用学指信念问题，当结构分析和语义理解实现后，对语用的接受与拒绝（信念与怀疑）的理解便可能随之产生。

---

① 为使译文逻辑清晰、重点突出，仅摘译原文重点和关键内容。

米勒（1964b）发现，这种划分大体上符合语言研究的发展顺序。当时，这一发现无疑是正确的。该发现也是对未来的一种预测，但只是其最初形式。米勒在20世纪60年代中期指出，句法学是最知名的，语义学次之。这一点迄今仍然如此。尽管语用学目前已引起了越来越多的关注，但它无论是过去还是现在都是人们知之甚少的学科。

20世纪60年代，当米勒重温莫里斯20世纪30年代的三重分类形式时，这三个领域依然可按上述方式划分。米勒在重申这些直至20世纪60年代一直是研究方针的区分法时，力图表明来自语言学理论的洞悉力对心理语言学的重要意义。然而到了20世纪八九十年代，我们已不再对语言理论及语言使用者理论进行如此严格的区分；我们现在也不再将这些研究领域截然划分为仅从事句法分析的语言学和描写人类如何习得和使用称为语言系统的东西的心理学。与此同时，语义学和语用学的定义也发生了变化，而更重要的是研究的重点也改变了。心理学家在研究的规划中更加注重结构和意义的问题，而我们语言学家今天也力求与语言使用者和语言习得者的理论构建协调一致。

米勒（1964a，b）的评论对于心理学来说起到了有效的促进作用，他指出要构建语言使用者的理论，必须要理解语言使用者是如何处理语言的句法和语义，以及从语言延伸出的结构与意义的实际情况的。对于这一观点，许多人都坚信不疑，同时新的划分法为新的交叉学科指明了航向，明确了我们应探索的道路和缘由。

三、现代心理语言学历史纵览

1. 历史背景

心理语言学这一术语表明，该学科的研究从根本上说依附于心理学和语言学两个领域的理论和知识。心理语言学研究的兴盛主要表现为历史和现代两个时期。历史时期始于20世纪初，重点在欧洲；现代时期始于20世纪五六十年代，中心是美国。布鲁门塔尔（Blumenthal）曾把莱比锡的威廉·冯特（Wilhelm Wundt）誉为该时期颇有影响的心理语言学大师，因为冯氏对表明语言可以根据心理学原则进行阐释已有充分准备。这也是社会科学发展史的一个阶段，在这期间，语言学正准备用更加现代、科学的语言研究方法取代基于文化和美学原则的陈旧的浪漫主义语言进化论。冯氏和新兴的心理学以严密性与热心提供了只有新科学才能提供的可能性。许多年轻的语言学家渴望把这种崭新的既严密又科学的视野带进语言的理论与研究，同时，心理学的研究也直接反映到不断发展的语言学领域。例如，我们常常引用结构主义语言学的代表布龙菲尔德（Bloomfield）1933年的名著①，并把它作为结构主义时期语言学的经典；但他1914年发表的第一部专著却很少有人知晓，而了解他在该书中曾高度评价冯氏心理学这一点的人也就更寥寥无几了。

第一次世界大战后，冯氏认知心理学的影响也随之低落。而布龙菲尔德的著作

---

① 指《语言论》（*Language*），该书是作者在1914年发表的《语言学研究入门》（*Introduction to the Study of Language*）一书的基础上修订、增补后写成的。——译者注。

(1933) 正迎合了日益兴起的强有力的行为主义新倾向。这也被看作布龙菲尔德著作中心灵主义与机械主义的决裂，以及在所有语言描写的结构主义解释中对前者的排斥。尽管布氏本人明显地流露出对行为主义的同情，然而心理学理论已丧失了对语言学的指导作用，这一局面始终是20世纪语言学的特征。

现代时期始于20世纪50年代末，并且一直发展到20世纪60年代。这一时期，语言学理论，特别是基于乔姆斯基提出的转换生成语法理论模式的语言学理论，① 对于心理语言学的研究起到了触发作用。然而，经过以乔氏理论为基础的几十年实验，这种目标统一的局面已不复存在，横在我们面前的是一条更加平衡、折中的道路——为了解释自然语言心理语言学理论应探讨什么，本文将着重概述自20世纪50年代第二个高潮以来心理语言学的进展情况。

2. 四个主要阶段

(1) 形成阶段。

这一阶段的特点是语言学和心理学并驾齐驱，共同诉诸操作主义哲学。在语言学领域，结构主义占有统治地位，而心理学则以行为主义称雄。作为科学的哲学，操作主义的方法是通过使用极为明确、重复可靠的一系列可证操作活动从观察到的数据中获得理论构想。这样，语言学的结构主义便以操作程序来定义类似音位和语素这样的单位。例如使用最小对立体或互补分布去找出和定义具体的音位或语素。

尽管语言学和心理学都引进了类似解释框架这样的心理构建，但是它们仍保留着各自不同的方法取向。心理学一直以对庞大的实验对象的研究为基础，对个别差异进行探究；语言学却不同，它以个别数据的集合为依据，探求语法的具体原则，乃至探讨普遍语法的一般原则。

在形成阶段，与语言学志同道合的心理学并没有极端行为主义的倾向。尽管斯金纳 (Skinner) 同一时期的著作 (1957) 已把行为主义哲学扩展为激进行为主义的极端立场，但赫利恩 (Hullean) 心理学却与语言学保持着共同的目标。奥斯古德 (C. E. Osgood) 等心理学家则提出了刺激—反应关系的模式，讨论了为心理学赢得新行为主义雅称的内在的、无法观察的调解性变量。这一派当时在心理语言学的研究中十分活跃。

现代心理语言学发展的最初阶段对使语言过程和应用成为可能的机械模式有着浓厚的兴致。后来，产生了信息理论。信息理论来源于通信工程界的研究，主要作为思维和模式的来源。例如香农 (Shannon) 和韦弗 (Weaver) 等人把通信交际单位看作像电话一样的译码/解码过程。如：

来源→话筒/译码系统→线路→听筒/解码系统→终点

信息理论后来扩展到心理语言学。心理语言学家至少在一段时间里使用了调查交际单位——谁发出 (译码) 和接收 (解码)。奥斯古德和西贝欧克 (Sebeok) 下面的话

---

① 乔姆斯基在1957年发表了《句法结构》(*Syntactic Structures*) 一书，从此创立了转换生成语法学派，并被誉为“乔姆斯基革命”。——译者注。

便是最好的例证："心理语言学直接研究译码和解码过程，因为二者是连接信息和交际人状况的纽带。"

语言学家把信息状况作为自己的研究领域，而心理学家则把交际人状况作为研究对象。也许是由于行为主义与信息理论之间有自然姻亲的关系，心理学家同时也采用了译码和解码程序。在这一阶段中，心理语言学的显著特点表现为研究的多样化。

（2）语言学阶段。

这一阶段，心理语言学又一次进入了一个理论完全统一的历史时期。语言学中转换生成语法的诞生，一度在理论心理语言学研究领域占据了统治地位，而且实际上主宰了 1960—1970 年间的主要研究，乔姆斯基的著作（1957）一举扭转了语言学的研究方向并令人信服地表明：行为主义既不能解释语言习得，也不能说明语言行为的动态创造性。于是，前一阶段心理语言学研究的基石便被彻底粉碎了。乔姆斯基指出，机械主义哲学无法提出确切的自然语言语法，因此演绎法是必要的，语言理论包括把说话人的语言能力而不是语言行为作为适当范畴（1965）。

乔姆斯基对行为主义的批判使研究语言的心理学家无言以对，于是生成语法的基本原则便开始支配心理语言学研究。心理语言学也开始以生成语法学家认为的理解语言的关键东西为基础，把语言能力放在首位，而把语言行为放在其后进行研究：同时普遍接受了（至少生成语法学家是这样）语言能力的理解决定着对实际语言行为本质的理解的观点。这样，语法中心性便被视为基本设想，句子在理解语法的探索中亦成了首要单位，由于句子在定义数据和转换生成语法范畴方面起着重要的作用，这一时期大多数心理语言学的实验都与句子的理解和使用相关。

由于生成语法旨在探索语言的普遍特征和各种解释，而不是数据分类，所以很快便对语言习得产生了巨大的兴趣。心理语言学发展中的一些早期论著完全接受了转换的方法，并提出儿童是带着生来就有的语言规则普遍形式（甚至可能是某些语言范畴）的机制走入语言学习过程的。莱尼伯格（Lenneberg，1967）关于语言生物基础的著述最完善地发展了这种先天论的观点，并记述了来自其他科学证据的论点，而其依据则源于语言理论关于先天论概念的原始动力。其基本观点是：语言习得能力是物种的特殊能力，是人类（只有人类）遗传所决定的属性。事实上，迄今已有无数的研究者正在探寻，在自然语言里儿童所期待掌握的是什么？当他们一步步走向语言成熟又是如何达到该目的的？

（3）认知阶段。

后来，心理语言学更加丰富的多方面研究终于取代了语言学阶段。转换语法的目的及其为实现这一目的的形式主义方法出现了一连串的漏洞，从而打破了上述的统一局面。语言学理论所面临的其他问题表现为语言运用事实的作用、语言习得研究的数据，以及把综合语法理论中与句法相应的语义部分放在什么位置上合适等。这样，第三阶段便出现了，它主要是心理学家和语言哲学家共同努力的结果。然而，心理学家重点的转移意味着对过去研究方向的否定，语言学从此便失去了过去十几年里享有的提供心理语言学研究单位、模式和方法论的特权。

需要指出的是，在认知阶段中，认知与早期认知心理学模式中的概念已不完全一致。就反对行为主义及其解释性原则的能力而言，格式塔认知心理学与转换语法之间仍存在着某些共同点。认知阶段中认知这一术语的使用主要表现为更加强调语言习得和什么是语言所需要的独立且内在的能力。因此，“学习语言意味着什么，学习语言需要什么”，便成了最基本的问题。

构成认知方法基础的大前提是语言对人类普遍认知的依赖。许多心理语言学家都同意，语言是诸多比较基础性的认知过程的结果之一。也许乔姆斯基本人已经表明了这一点：语言学就是与人类认知相关的学科，从这种意义上讲，语言学家就是认知心理学家。贝弗（Bever，1970）和斯洛宾（Slobin，1973）提出了语言结构的认知基础。认知的定向似乎否定了语法中心及独立的观点，因为语法对语言的解释中所包含的认知能力仅仅是人类语言的表现形式之一，在语言习得和使用中它既不优先，也不独立于语言习得和其他认知和行为系统。而且语言结构的获得不是独立于语义概念与话语功能的，更重要的是，必须看到认知原则支配着语言结构的习得。语言习得一般被解释为语言与其他行为系统之间相互作用的结果，语音系统的本质最终也是更加基本的认知结构的产物。

虽然在心理语言学理论和实践中，语言学理论仍继续发挥作用，但与从前相比却大不一样。福多（Fodor）等人基于语言理论所做的心理语言学成果总结大体反映了这一阶段对从语言输入所汲取的知识的最出色的评价。显然，他们对旨在调查语法结构心理现实的实验和语言学家所提出的操作方式进行了评价，并得出了简单的结论。他们对实验的评论又一次证实了句子分类的现实、句子类别的概念和转换句法所指的句子距离。可是他们的评论没有重新证实转换的心理现实。其实，他们的观察表现为：生成语法实验的总发现表明，“与旨在揭示语法派生所包含的操作方式的心理现实实验相比，用于揭示结构描写的心理现实特点的实验更为幸运”。有趣的是，福多等人得出了这样的结论：句法结构心理现实方面的研究可能“与语言论点歧义的、独立激发的语言分析的证明关系越来越少”，同时“很可能只有对心理现实的直接实验才能最终在各种势不两立的句法理论中进行抉择”。

（4）认知科学。

对第四阶段（即现阶段）进行阐述是十分困难的，因为我们正置身于这个阶段，对于最终的结论和成就尚有待于进一步观察。目前心理语言学尚处于过渡状态，其中一派之说的一统天下已不复存在。心理学和语言学的情况都是如此。学者们已不再无视其他相邻领域的科学成果，这就意味着，我们对心理语言学问题所提出的解释必须同心理学和语言学中完整的解释并行不悖。

如果说认知科学就是科学地理解人类心理活动，那么心理语言学理论寻求心理现实无疑也是十分重要的。语言学中把接受这一标准视为现实与合格的语言理论的必要条件，这是第四阶段的最大特点。从更普遍的意义上讲，认知科学发展中语言学、心理学和心理语言学的合作参与已蕴涵了对这一标准的接受，这也是现阶段一件最令人瞩目的事情。从根本上说，这里暂用的语言学方法现在已经把信息过程的强制因素考虑了进来。语法理论中的内部一致与形式逻辑被看作正确准则，并被认为是绝对的必要条件，对此人们已没有任何异议。我们现在要辩论的是与心理语言学研究的问题以及结果相协调的语法描写系统的有效性和一致性问题。例如，对截短被动式的派生，以及对左、中、右内嵌式的序列等语法现象的处理，仍然可以在语法描写中独立完成。许多语言学家坚持认为这是正确的，而且是语言学理论应予解释的全部内容。

把语言学与心理语言学的信息汇入单独语言理论的尝试，见于词汇—功能语法理论。该理论与其他语法描写理论不同，直接关系到充分语法理论和语言过程思考之间的关系。作为语言知识与真实语言过程相一致的代表模式，该理论主张此类语言能力语法直接与语言过程模式相结合；对这种词汇—功能语法，只需把语法信息直接存入词汇条目便可完成，直接从存储中重新获得词汇信息，比改变句子句法形式的转换语法置换显然要容易得多。

这一方法避开了转换语法的许多棘手问题。词汇—功能语法主张，关联或区分不同类型句子所需要的语法信息存储于词汇条目中。例如，主动和被动句类之间的关系就是如此。我们现在已不再需要以主动句开始的句子作等级排列，同时也不再需要把被动句或截短被动句一类句子按难易程度归入较难的序列中。这一理论方法明确承认了这样的事实：一些语言学家对表现我们语言结构知识的需要做出了反应，其反应方式也反映出一种语言的听话人、说话人处理（理解、存储、重新获得）这些结构的方式。

目前，认知科学所处阶段的其他显著特点是，隐喻和模式再次来源于外在第三者，也即与工程应用相关。这一来源是与专家系统、人工智能，以及计算机科学的模式建立和模式检验相关的雏形领域。心理语言学及其协同的基础学科，现在似乎不那么热衷于仅仅以理性主义的演绎基础为依据建立“心理科学”了。它希望成为真正的“心理科学”——“认知科学”。然而，我们并不仅仅希望使用形式程序来建立计算机系统模式，我们的宗旨在于模拟和理解心智系统如何使用认知程序（如知识、经验、推论和决策），这显然与自然语言相关。计算机不同于人类，它只能利用人类所使用的部分信息。它不足以写出某些认知能力（如句子分析）的形式程序，这便是计算机科学与认知科学之间的差别所在。

在过去的几百年中，达尔文的进化论曾反映于作为生物学的语言之中。当时学者们把大部分精力集中于语言变化、语言变体、语族等方面的研究。语言变化以不断发展演变分化的进化形式运行，同时产生了不同的语族。

20世纪里，结构主义所表现出的分类定向便是作为化学的语言的产物。语言学家开始去发掘语言结构的不同单位，如构成语言音系的单位。语言的基本单位可以像化学基本化合价那样化合、再化合，但始终保留着其自身的基本完整形式，作为被调查特定语言层次的建筑材料。

进入20世纪50年代后，乔姆斯基的生成语法（《句法结构》1957）开始把语言当作数学来研究。调查方式采用演绎法，它像数学的调查方法一样，目的在于理解语言能力，即本族语的使用者具有的使其成为讲该语言的人的抽象知识。虽然这种知识是一种语言结构和语言运用的知识，它却被看作可以用一套规则来描述的数学客体。

今天，新的研究兴趣已经出现，它把语言学和心理学同那些对所有知识领域产生效力的机械机制的联系起来。20 世纪八九十年代所拥有的是第四代暗喻——计算机暗喻。语言被看作符号过程，人们主要以知识和推论为基础进行决策。语言不再是最终及唯一有趣的知识集合。事实是，人类使用自然语言进行思维，而计算机所使用的是程序语言。但这两种语言都使用符号，并且以储存、推论的知识为基础进行决策，这也是事实。因此，心理语言学、语言学理论将会进入更广阔的空间，研究知识的本质、心理表现的结构，乃至它们是如何被用于类似推理和决策这样的心理过程——也就不可避免了。

乔姆斯基的思想在某种程度上已为这一新的研究兴趣打开了大门。生成语法力图描写说话人的语言知识，这从本质上来说是提出了对于潜在语言能力的认知过程的理解问题。其实，转变既是自然结果，也是这一阶段的典型特征：以往与形式句法或语义学相关的名称现在已移向概念表达以及人类认知系统结构的问题。如在讨论语义学和认知时，杰肯道夫（Jackendoff，1983）承认，语言学的语义学形式描写不过是概念表达的问题，是认知形式的共性。同样，在系统阐述分析句法和语义结构的认知语法方式时，兰加科（Langacker，1987）采纳了这样一个基本前提：语言不是与普遍认知系统相割裂的自制体系。

语言的信息过程理论要求我们理解心理表现的运行情况，如通过直接提取或推论的方式从话语中获得知识。这种信息过程暗喻导致对储存、重新获得或知识的交叉分类方面（即人类语言使用者在推理和决策过程中的所作所为）的检查。实际上，从这方面看，生成、认知及计算机范例十分相似。就其参与对使用语言的人类所具有的知识结构的研究上看，上述三者均可看作认知范例，它们的主要区别表现在如何对语言使用中所包括的有关心理过程和心理表现的知识进行评估和表示，以及在多大程度上把其他学科的研究发现结合到心理语言学中去。

总之，心理语言学已不再仅仅局限于探讨心理学和语言学的发现，相反，我们现在已把这一学科纳入“认知科学”这一广阔的交叉领域。多学科参与认知科学研究有力地表明，关于自然语言理论的心理现实必须同自然语言过程的信息相一致，这是目前的理想目标。

Selected Reading 5

Ecolinguistics: State of the Art 1998

Alwin Fill

Ecolinguistics is an interdisciplinary and interactive field of study in which the natural sciences (most specifically biological ecology) and the humanities (philology and philosophy) interrelate. Generally, ecolinguistics starts from a holistic view of the world based on the ideas of such thinkers as Gregory Bateson, David Bohm, Fritjof Capra, Ilya Prigogine, Rupert Sheldrake and Frederic Vester. Since interrelation, networking, dialectics and diversity are key concepts of the discipline, uniformness is not regarded as a desirable aim in ecolinguistic theory and methodology. The paper discusses the different approaches, summarizes results and shows perspectives for future research in the field.

1. Introduction

Ecolinguistics began with a metaphor. Einar Haugen, in a talk given in August, 1970, spoke of the interactions between any given language and its environment (1972: 325), which he compared to the ecological relations between certain species of animals and plants in and with their environment. A different type of link between language and ecology was established in 1990, when Michael Halliday, speaking at the AILA Conference in Thessaloniki, stressed the connection between language on the one hand and growthism, classism and speciesism on the other, admonishing applied linguists not to ignore the role of their object of study in the growth of environmental problems. These two talks were "seminal" in the sense that they triggered two approaches to ecolinguistics which can be associated with the two authors mentioned:

(1) *Ecology is understood metaphorically and transferred to "language (s) in an environment"* (Haugen 1972).

(2) *Ecology is understood in its biological sense; the role of language in the development and aggravation of environmental (and other societal) problems is investigated; linguistic research is advocated as a factor in their possible solution* (Halliday 1992).

The two approaches are complementary rather than mutually exclusive. However, since the starting point of work in ecolinguistics is clearly either (1) or (2), it is advisable, for the purposes of this presentation, to separate the two strands of research. It will become clear in the discussion where the interface of the two theories is situated.

2. Ecology as Metaphor

2.1 The Ecology of Language (s)

Haugen's ecological metaphor enjoyed a remarkable popularity in the 1980s. Evidence for this is the following (incomplete) list of book titles, book chapters and articles in which the word ecology or a derivative of it is used in connection with language:

Mackey 1980: The Ecology of Language Shift
Bolinger 1980: ch. 15— An Ecology of Language
Haarmann 1980: subtitle: Elemente einer Sprachökologie
Denison 1982: A Linguistic Ecology for Europe
Finke 1983: part Ⅱ Ökologische konstruktive Linguistik
Enninger & Haynes eds. 1984: Studies in Language Ecology
Hagege 1985: Écolinguistique
Haarmann 1986: Language in Ethnicity: A View of Basic Ecological Relations
Fill 1987: subtitle: Versuch einer Ökologie der Sprache

In all these publications, biological ecology is transferred in some way or other to language (s); ecological concepts such as "environment" "conservation" "interaction" and "language world system" (transferred from "ecosystem"), are used for psycho- and sociolinguistic phenomena with the intention of helping to see these in new perspectives.

In the 1990's, the impetus of Haugen's metaphor seems to have weakened a little. There are as yet no books entitled Ecology of the South African Languages or A Linguistic Ecology of Great Britain. However, the metaphor continues to be used, particularly in the study of minority languages and of language imperialism in the Pacific Region. One author who has used it recently concerning this topic is Peter Mühlhäusler (e. g., 1992, 1996a), whose research on the relation between linguistic and biological diversity will be discussed in section 3. Another is Fernande Krier (*Université de Rennes II*), who in her *Esquisse Écolinguistique du Galicien* (1996: 55), defines ecolinguistics as follows: " (*L'écolinguistique*) *cherche à expliquer à l'aide de facteurs spécifiques pourquoi certaines langues sont menacées et d'autres ont des chances de survie.* " In her investigation of the environmental factors which may (or may not) contribute to the survival of Galician, a minority language in Portugal, she uses the ecolinguistic variables established by Harald Haarmann (1980, 1986); among these are ethnodemographic, ethnosociological, ethnocultural and other factors which constitute the environment of a language.

The "Ecology of Language (s)" in the Haugenian sense is a study urgently needed at a time when languages are disappearing faster and faster from decade to decade, and one would wish that more linguists were to take it up and embrace the cause of linguistic diversity. The task of investigating, documenting and perhaps saving the many endangered languages on this planet would be worth the while of more aspiring newcomers to ecolinguistics.

2.2 Ecological linguistics

The idea of transferring concepts, principles and methods from biological ecology to the study of language was soon extended by a group of German researchers (most of them from the University of Bielefeld) in an approach called ecological linguistics (*ökologische Sprachwissenschaft*). Perhaps inspired by Niklas Luhmann's ideas on "ecological communication", Peter Finke (1983, 1993, 1996) transferred the concept of the ecosystem (first introduced by Tansley in 1935) to language world systems and to cultural systems like science and language itself. Other scholars such as Wilhelm Trampe and Hans Strohner have followed suit and have used the ecosystem metaphor to show language and language use in their interaction with an "environment", i. e., the world, and to elucidate the interactive process of (inter) change which is going on all the time between language and the world (Trampe 1990: 155).

Ecological linguistics stands in contrast to structural models with which only a language itself, not its environment, can be investigated (Finke 1983: 54). Ecosystems are life systems, and language world systems are systems of experience (ibid.). In this approach, the comparison between biological ecology and language leads to the following critical hypothesis: in the same way as the creativity of life is threatened by our current treatment of nature, the creativity of language is endangered by our present use of it (Finke 1983: 61). Ecological linguistics thus includes a critical study of language and language practice, as carried out for instance by Trampe (1990, 1991), who criticizes the language of industrial agriculture with its techno-economic ideology: the word "production", for instance, replaces "growing" and "giving", and euphemizes the "taking away" and "killing" which actually happens.

Trampe's ecological criticism of language is, however, drawn into question by other ecolinguists, who see in it only a form of linguistic conservatism and old-fashioned purism. In particular, the use of environmental terms like pollution and degradation for processes of language change is criticized as merely a new form of the centuries old complaint about language decay (Jung 1996: 153). The idea of an ecological correctness is rejected by all authors, but the question as to whether ecolinguistics should contain a critique of language and language use or should only lead to greater language awareness remains one of the controversial topics in this field.

More recently, the ecosystem metaphor has been extended from language world systems to cultural systems in general (Finke 1996). The ecology of language has thus been supplemented by a cultural ecology which concerns itself with the evolution of cultural ecosystems from natural ecosystems with language as a kind of "missing link" in between. For a discussion of this theory the reader is referred to Finke (1996: 27 – 39), who also raises the intriguing question (p. 40) to what extent the "rules of language" are the descendants of the "rules of nature".

2.3 Other metaphoric approaches

The ecosystem metaphor has also been used (instead of the outdated machine metaphor or the computer metaphor) for cognitive processes going on in the human mind and quite generally for interpersonal communication, whose interactional processes are not satisfactorily explained with the traditional sender-receiver model (Strohner 1991/1996).

The ecological concepts of interaction, interplay and networking are also in evidence in research on such topics as "language and conflict" (Fill 1993: 57 – 80) and "language, women and men" (Fill 1993: 86 – 102). They could also be used for research on the origin of language, since they explain the dynamics of many phenomena much better than previous approaches. If ecolinguistic concepts like "interaction" (*Wechselwirkung*) and "dialectics", (Bang, Døør 1996) replace the old concepts of cause and effect the artificiality of time-honoured controversies like the following becomes apparent: was the development of language the cause of the lateralization of the brain or its consequence? Was language the cause of certain improvements in the living conditions of human beings (more proteins in foodstuffs etc.), or was it the other way around: improved living conditions caused a more rapid development of the brain and thus made the rise of language possible? A dialectical approach to these topics recognizes the interplay of all factors concerned without asking for an initial cause and thus makes these controversies superfluous.

Finally, "ecological" has also been transferred to linguistics in the sense of "transdisciplinary" and "non-exclusive" (Makkai 1993) or of "transcending traditional considerations of economy" —with a critique of (Gricean) principles of relevance and economy (Weinrich 1990).

3. Language and Environmental Problems

Ever since the AILA Conference of 1990 and the publication of Halliday's *New Ways of Meaning*, there has been a growing interest, within ecolinguistics, in the role played by language in ecological issues and the environmental problems which affect more and more groupings and individuals. Indeed, the name environmental linguistics has been suggested for such a study. However, the terms language ecology or linguistic ecology are to be preferred since they indicate that this research is being carried out within the general framework of ecolinguistic principles, as listed in the introduction to this paper.

3.1 Criticism of discourse

The topic "language and ecological problems" is approached by the different scholars on different levels and with different methodologies. The German linguist Matthias Jung (1989, 1994a, 1994b, 1996) uses text corpora from newspapers and investigates changes over time in environmental vocabulary. Jung draws into question the frequently heard assumption that lexical choices are made for manipulatory purposes. The following part of a diagram [adapted from Jung (1994a: 65) and originally published in *Allensbach Jahrbuch der Demoskopie* 1978 – 1983, p. 525] shows the different associations of two German words for nuclear energy (Atomkraft and Kernenergie):

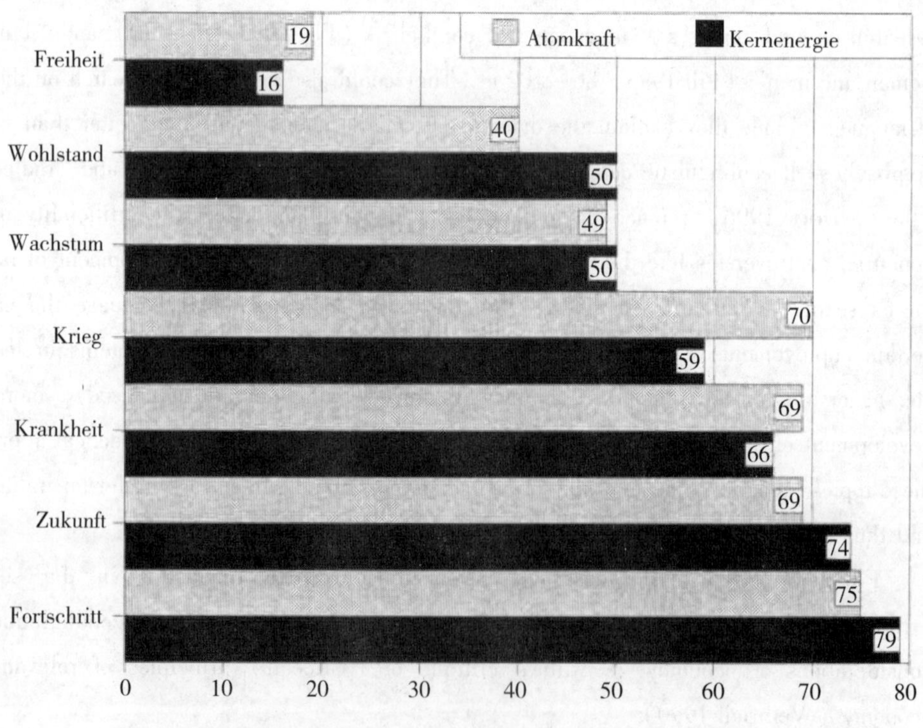

Atomkraft and Kernenergie—percentages of strong association

The only concept where the associations differ markedly is "Krieg" ("war"), which is much more strongly linked with Atomkraft than with Kernenergie. The argument brought forward by environmentalists that the word Kernenergie with its positive associations of healthy natural energy was used euphemistically and in a manipulatory way by the nuclear lobby is shown to be doubtful by Jung, who argues that "manipulation through language" is only another cliche nourished by such books as George Orwell's 1984 and Mackensen's *Verführung durch Sprache.*

Other authors use the framework of critical discourse analysis (as developed by Fairclough 1989, Kress 1989 and others) for a critical analysis of texts about environmental topics. Andrea Gerbig (1993, 1996) analyses collocational patterns in environmental texts concerning the ozone layer debate and shows that texts produced by opposing interest groups differ markedly in collocational frequencies (for instance, concerning the lexemes cause and responsible). Another linguistic parameter used by this author is the emphasis on or suppression of agency through the choice of active, passive and ergative constructions (cf. also Fairclough 1989: 123 – 125). The following is an example from Gerbig (1993: 63):

(1) ...cases of non-malignant skin cancer have been increasing over many years...

In this real example from an industry group text "the ergative choice expresses a self-caused process for which no—not even an implicit—agent is retrievable." This means a shift from the actor, i. e., the person or thing responsible for the action, to the action itself (Gerbig 1993: 63). That the industries which destroy the ozone layer are at least in part responsible for this process is suppressed.

Agency in environmental texts also plays a role in some of the work of Richard Alexander. The following are examples from a NIREX advertisement in which agency is expressed in different ways (Alexander 1996: 137f., his emphasis):

(2) *Britain* produces radioactive waste every day ...

(3) the safe disposal of *our* radioactive waste...

(4) some of the most stringent *safety requirements* in the world *will have to be met*...

Agent shift in (2) (*Britain* produces) and (3) (*our* radioactive waste) here implicates everyone in the production of nuclear waste; in (4) agent deletion through passivization (safety requirements will have to be met) is used as a "device for distracting attention away from the human actors who have to carry out the disposal process" (p. 138).

Agent (and patient!) deletion may also occur through the device of nominalization, as discussed by Goatly (1996: 555, cf_ also Fairclough 1989: 124). Following J. R. Martin, Goatly shows that in environmental texts nominalization may put less emphasis on the affected beings: for example, in describing the killing of seals, the use of nominal groups such as in (5) makes it unnecessary to mention the affected (i. e., the seals) at all.

(5) *a slaughtering operation*, *killing methods*, *killing techniques*, *a humane death*

Compound nouns may "reduce and downgrade the affected to modifier status: the seal hunt, the whitecoat harvest" (Goatly 1996: 555). (The latter example also shows a characteristically euphemistic metaphor in the word harvest or organized killing and thus explains the subtitle of Goatly's paper, "metaphors we die by")

The Danish scholars J. Døør and J. Chr. Bang use the categories of "Agency" and "Deixis" for their analysis of two Danish law texts on "organic production of agricultural products". This analysis reveals certain logical contradictions which result in making the ministry the agent in organic food production (!) and reducing the farmers to "recipients" and "applicants for grants", as in example (6) quoted in Bang & Døør (1993: 47):

(6) *Applicants for grants*...shall upon request produce evidence that the conditions for the grant have been fulfilled.

Bang and Døør's attempt at establishing an ecological theory of language is intended to lead to a fresh approach to the ethical dimension of the ecological crisis and to show that traditional linguistics, which ignores the ideological implications of deixis, is part of this crisis (Bang and Døør 1996a: 91).

3.2 Criticism of the language system

Besides critically analyzing discourse, ecolinguists have also scrutinized the language system for ecological and unecological features. One author who has criticized language on this level is of course Michael Halliday. The influence of language on the world is described by Halliday (1992: 73) as a "dialectic between the system and the instance", in which grammar provides the systemic options which, however, "resonate with the prevailing patterns of the culture" and are reinforced by being taken up in everyday discourse. Halliday's "linguistic constructivism" is a severe critique of the language system (or "grammar", as Halliday calls it). Halliday argues (1992: 84 - 87) that the ideologies of growthism, sexism and classism are contained in the grammar of our languages and that the unlimitedness of our resources and the special position of humans are also structurally inherent in the language system. In more detail, he argues that

(1) In our s. a. e. languages natural resources are shown to be unlimited with the use of uncountable nouns or "mass nouns" suggesting inexhaustibility (oil, energy, water, air, etc.).

(2) In pairs of contrasts like big and small the "growth word" is always the neutral term. It is always: how fast is the car (not how slow), how high is the building (not how low), how big is her income (not how small) etc.

(3) Our languages are reluctant to admit non-human agents: "what's that forest doing?" would be judged unacceptable by most speakers.

(4) The special position of the human species is expressed through the pronominal system (he/she as special pronouns for humans, it for all non-human beings) and through the exclusion of many collocations (think, know, believe, amiable, sympathetic, etc.) for animals and plants.

While ecolinguists like Gerbig, Bang, Døør and Alexander, in their analysis of environmental texts, have criticized the suppression of agents and experiencers, on this higher systemic level the very fact that language expresses such categories as "agent" "experiencer" and "recipient" has become the focus of critical attention. The point in question is that the grammar of s. a. e. languages, while in keeping with traditional Newtonian science, is out of step with modern ecological views of the world which question the traditional division into agent, experience, action and (temporal and local) positioning. This fragmentation of the universe is contained for instance in the familiar grammatical structure subject, predicate, object which separates agent, process and experiencer from one another. The role of language in this separation was recognized earlier by such non-linguist authors as Frederic Vester (1978), David Bohm (1980) and James Lovelock (1988), but has received little attention from thinkers in linguistics. However, among the more recent topics of ecolinguists, the connection between language and the unecological fragmentation of the world figures prominently.

Goatly (1996: 547f.), who adopts Lovelock's Gaia theory, mentions, among others, the following "ways in which congruent language use for describing material processes often represents the world in ways which are inconsonant with modern scientific theory, and Gaia theory in particular":

—A division into agentive participants, affected participants and circumstances... Such structures are an obstacle in conceiving the notion of undivided wholeness.

—The categorization of phenomena into processes and things, which is doubtful given the insights of modern physics.

In this context, ecolinguists also focus on the "anthropocentrism" of language, which perpetuates the separation of humans from the rest of creation. Frans Verhagen (1993: 117) puts the question: "How can language be used to shape a biocentric worldview away from an excessively anthropocentric and mechanistic worldview?", and Goatly (1996: 556) suggests that "an alternative Critical Discourse Analysis could target Anthropocentrism, including Marxist Humanism. Though we have reluctantly recognized that the world is not the centre of the universe, we have been slow to accept that humans may not be central either".

Linguistic anthropocentrism comes to the surface in the way languages name all natural phenomena from the point of view of their usefulness for humans (examples in Fill 1993: 104 – 130), but also in implicit references to humans, for instance in existential constructions and other verb phrases; for example, all verb forms in the following description of land (from a geography text book quoted by Kress 1989: 68f.) contain the implication "for humans":

...the soils are poor...the land is used for little else except extensive beef grazing...another land use, mining, is now of greater value...

"Land uses" by beings other than human are simply not provided for in the "grammar" of

English.

3.3 The ecologization of language

A question frequently raised in connection with ecolinguistic criticism of language is whether one should aim at changing language or whether language users should only be made aware of the linguistic facts criticized. Most ecolinguists turn against the idea of an ecological correctness and stress that their criticism of language is "non-conservative" (in the sense of "non-normative"), "gentle" and not intended to change the language system (Finke 1983: 66ff., Trampe 1990, Fill 1993: 115f.). This criticism is meant to be placed within the Critical Language Awareness Movement rather than in the neighbourhood of creating another newspeak. One author who does suggest a change of language so that it can take care of new ecological views of the world is the physicist David Bohm (1980: ch_2), who advocates the introduction of a new verbal modality called the Rheomode (Greek rhein— "to flow") which might serve to express "process" without expressing agent and experiencer.

An interesting hypothesis is put forward by Goatly (1996: 552), who suggests that our languages will, in the course of time, by themselves (i.e., by their users) adapt to the new ecological insights and change accordingly. Incipient signs of this change can be observed in the increasing use of ergative constructions (e.g., "The earth warms" —note, however Gerbig's criticism of these as discussed in 2.1) instead of transitive ones, and in the increase in reciprocal verbs (like meet, touch, interact, talk, converse, etc.), which express mutuality instead of dominance. This "deep ecologization" of language could be seen as a long evolutionary process of language change interactive with environmental processes—a process to be regarded in the framework of developments which might eventually slow down environmental degradation. Deep ecologization can be considered a counter-development to the "surface ecologization", of discourse, which is apparent in the prolific use of environmental vocabulary in the language of advertising (the so-called "green ads") and much of current political discourse.

4. Linguistic and Biological Diversity

The naming of natural phenomena is a topic which also figures prominently in the research of Muhlhausler (e.g., 1995, 1996a, 1996b), although Muhlhausler is more concerned with the ethnocentrism of this process. In his work, the ecolinguistic plea for the maintenance of linguistic diversity is linked with concern about biological diversity. Linguistic diversity, according to Muhlhausler, "reflects thousands of years of human accommodation to complex environmental conditions" (1996a: 270); biological diversity is taken account of in differing degrees by the different languages. He shows that discourse about new environments can actually have an influence on these, particularly in the form that lack of linguistic resources may contribute to environmental degradation (1996a, b). "The decline and loss of small languages, illustrated with examples from Australia and the Pacific Region, is not a self-contained phenomenon, but embedded in and related to a much larger range of ecological factors." (1996a: 275f.) Muhlhausler brings to light the relation between linguistic and biological factors by drawing from a great number of language world systems situated in Australia, Aotearoa (New Zealand) and the Pacific Region. The following example, which illustrates this relation, is taken from Muhlhausler (1996b: 107):

A particularly clear example of the consequences of...naming is that of the numerous small "marsupials" which once inhabited the Australian Continent in prolific numbers. Most of them ended up being called bush rat or native rat, and having got that name were regarded very much like a rat in Britain: at best useless, at worst dangerous pests that needed to be eradicated.

Muhlhausler then discusses recent attempts to rescue the dwindling population of small marsupials by renaming them or by reintroducing the old indigenous names. He shows that "the effects of names for individual animal species are paralleled by similar ones in the domain of plant names" (1996b: 108).

In Muhlhausler's research, concern for the environment (or convironment—a term which puts more emphasis on the togetherness of all beings) is combined with concern about the loss of linguistic diversity and the diminishing role of small languages. Muhlhausler's linguistic ecology makes use of both the metaphorical and the literal meaning of ecology and environment and is thus perhaps the most comprehensive approach within ecolinguistics to date.

5. Conclusion

Ecolinguistics is a study which goes far beyond syntax, semantics and pragmatics and which therefore requires some new theorizing as well as innovative ideas concerning empirical investigation. After the first 25 years of its existence, ecolinguistics has still a long way to go before all possible topics within it have been addressed, let alone investigated in suitable depth. The range of ecolinguistics is very wide, since it imposes the following tasks on the discipline of language study:

the finding of appropriate theories of language

the study of language systems as well as of texts

the study of universal features of language relevant to the ecological issue

the study of individual languages with regard to such features (with the possibility of contrastive approaches).

Studying the role of language in achieving "ecoliteracy" (Capra 1997: 289 – 295), i. e., in teaching ecological thinking to children and adults.

Ecolinguistics thus involves theoretical, methodological and empirical studies of language and offers new perspectives on all these levels for linguists interested in ecology. It can truly be claimed that here is a field of study worth being considered by linguistic talent in search of a challenging task.

当代生态语言学的研究现状[①]

[奥地利] 艾尔文·菲尔

范俊军　官　齐译

生态语言学是由自然科学（具体地说是“生物生态学”）和相关人文科学（即语文学和哲学）相结合而形成的交叉学科领域。总的来说，生态语言学产生于以巴特森、玻姆、卡普拉、普利高津、施尔德拉克和弗斯特等思想家的学说为基础的整体论世界观。由于关联关系、网络化、辩证法关系和多样性等术语已成为生态语言学的重要概念，因此生态语言学的理论学说和方法论不再将同一性（uniformness）作为其必要的研究目标。本文将讨论生态语言学的各种研究方法，总结梳理该领域的研究成果，并对学科的未来发展做出展望。

一、导言

生态语言学始于隐喻。1970 年 8 月，豪根（Einar Haugen）在一次报告中谈到“任何特定语言与它所处环境的相互作用关系”时，曾将这种关系比作特定动植物物种与其生存环境之间的生态关系。1990 年，韩礼德（Michael Halliday）在于希腊塞萨罗尼基举行的国际应用语言学大会上的发言中，强调了语言与生长状况（growthism）、种类特性以及物种形成之间的关系，告诫应用语言学家切不可忽视研究对象在不断增多的环境问题中所起的作用，从而奠定了语言与生态学之间的一种全然不同的研究范式。豪根和韩礼德的报告就促动使用两种方法研究生态语言学而言起到了“至关重要”的作用。以下两个方面与他们的思想相关联：①从隐喻角度理解的“生态学”概念转到“环境中的语言”；②从生物学意义上理解“生态学”概念，调查研究在环境（及其他社会问题）问题改善和加剧情况下语言所起的作用并倡导把语言研究作为可能的解决方案中的一个因素。

这两种观点并不相互排斥，而是相互补充。鉴于生态语言学研究的出发点无外乎这两种方法，因此为叙述方便，将二者分而述之则更为妥当，这样在讨论中，两种学说的“接合点”便会一目了然。

① 为使译文逻辑清晰、重点突出，仅摘译原文重点和关键内容。

二、作为隐喻的生态学

1. 语言生态学

豪根的生态学隐喻用法在20世纪80年代曾被广为使用。以下（不完全统计）专著、书的章节和论文都把“生态学”或其他派生词语与语言联系在一起，便是最好的证据：

麦基（Mackey，1980）的《语言转用的生态学》；博林格（Bolinger，1980，第15章）的《语言的生态学》；哈尔曼（Haarmann，1980），小标题为“语言生态学基础”；狄尼森（Denison，1982）的《面向欧洲的语言生态学》；芬克（Finke，1983）第二部分的“生态建构语言学”；昂尼吉、海尼斯合编（Enninger & Haynes eds，1984）的《语言生态学研究》；哈热日（Hagege，1985）的《生态语言学》；哈尔曼（1986）的《族群中的语言：基本生态关系概观》；菲尔（Fill，1987），小标题为“语言的生态学探讨”。

在所有这些著述中，生物生态学以不同的方式被用于语言研究领域。同时，一些诸如“环境”（environment）、“恒定性”（conservation）、“相互作用”（interaction）、“语言世界系统”（language world system）（源于“生态系统”）等生态学概念被用来研究心理语言学和社会语言学现象，以期帮助人们从新的视角审视这些现象。

进入20世纪90年代，豪根的隐喻说的影响似乎有所减弱。尽管迄今还没有出现诸如标题为“南非语言生态学”或“大不列颠语言生态学”之类的著作，但是生态学隐喻，特别是在有关太平洋地区少数民族语言以及语言帝国主义问题的研究中，仍然被研究者继续使用。米尔豪斯勒（Peter Mühlhäusler）是近来仍将生态学隐喻用于此类课题研究的学者之一，本文第三节将讨论他对语言与生物多样性关系的研究。另外一位学者是雷恩第二大学的科里叶（Fernande Krier），她在《加利西亚语生态语言学纲要》（*Esquisse Écolinguistique du Galicien*，第55页）一书中给生态语言学下了如下定义：“生态语言学力求借助一些特殊的要素，阐述为何有些语言的生存受到威胁，而另一些语言却得以幸存。”科里叶调查了葡萄牙的一种少数民族语言——加利西亚语，在研究所有可能或不可能影响该语言生存环境的因素时，她使用了哈尔曼建立的生态语言学变量，其中包括种族人口统计、种族社会、种族文化以及其他方面的各种因子，这些因子构成了一种语言的“环境”。

豪根学派的语言生态学是一项迫切需要进行的研究。在当代，随着年代的更替，语言消亡的速度越来越快。人们希望有更多的语言学家涉足这一领域探究语言多样性的根源。对于那些更热心于生态语言学的新研究者而言，调查、记录和抢救这个星球上众多的濒危语言是一项很有意义的工作。

2. 生态语言学

将生物生态学的概念、原理和方法用于语言研究的理念不久便被一些德国学者（多数来自比勒费尔德大学）进一步拓展，形成了“生态语言学”（ökologische

Sprachwissenschaft）学说和理论。可能受吕曼（Niklas Luhmann）有关“生态交际”（ecological communication）思想的启发，芬克（Peter Finke ）运用生态系统概念［由坦斯利（Tansley）1935 年首创］转指语言世界系统和文化系统，正如科学和语言本身一样。其他学者如特兰普（Wilhelm Trampe）和斯特罗纳（Hans Strohner）继承了这种观点，他们用生态系统做比喻，旨在说明语言以及与环境（如现实世界）相互作用中的语言使用行为，从而揭示了语言与现实世界之间一直在进行着的互变互动过程。

生态语言学观点与结构模型显然有明显差别，后者只用来研究语言本身，而不是外部环境。生态系统是一种生命系统，而语言世界系统则是经验系统。这一理论将生物生态与语言进行比较，结果引出了这样一个重要的理论假设：正如当今人类对待大自然的态度给生命创造力造成了威胁一样，人类时下对语言的使用也使语言的创造力出现了危机。因此，生态语言学包含了对语言和语言实践的批判性研究，正如特兰普所做的那样。特兰普批判了农业产业化中的语言现象及其“技术—经济”的意识形态，例如，“生产”（production）这个词取代了传统农业中的“生长”（growing）、“付出”（giving ）的意义，并且淡化了农业产业化过程中实际发生的“掠夺”（taking away）和“灭杀”（killing）行为。

不过，特兰普从生态学角度对语言的批评招致了其他生态语言学家的质疑，他们将其视为语言保守主义和已经过时的语言纯粹主义的一种表现。尤其是特兰普将诸如“污染”“退化”一类环境学术语用于描述语言变化的过程遭到了学者们的责难，认为这不过是一种抱怨语言退化的新的陈词滥调。尽管所有研究者都反对“生态正确论”的观点，但是生态语言学是否应该包含语言和语言使用的批评，还是应该旨在建立一种更广泛的语言意识，仍然是这一领域颇有争议的一个问题。

最近，生态系统隐喻已经由语言世界系统扩展到普遍的文化系统。文化生态学关注文化生态系统由自然生态系统的进化并把语言作为两者之间的“缺失链接”，从而弥补了语言生态学的不足。关于这一理论的探讨，读者可参阅芬克的有关论述，其中作者还提出了一个颇具吸引力的问题，即语言规则在多大程度上源于自然规则。

3. 其他 “隐喻” 的研究方法

生态系统隐喻（不是那种过时的机器隐喻或电脑隐喻）现在也用来说明发生在人类大脑里的认知活动过程，而在解释人际系统方面，其使用更是十分普遍，因为用传统的“传递—接受”隐喻模式，并不能令人满意地解释交际的互动过程。

相互作用、互动、网络系统等生态学概念，在诸如“语言与冲突”“语言、女人与男人”这类问题的研究中也常常使用。这些概念也可用于语言起源问题的研究，因为在解释许多现象的动力机制方面，它们大大优于以前的各种方法。如果用诸如“相互作用”“辩证”等生态语言学概念代替原因和结果这类旧概念，那么，下面这些久而未决的争论的人为因素就会变得清晰明朗：语言发展究竟是引起大脑功能单侧化的原因还是结果？语言是人类生活条件得以某种改善的因素，还是相反，即不断改善的生活条件促使大脑快速进化，结果使语言产生成为可能？用辩证的观点看待这些问题，就是承认所有相关因素的相互影响、相互作用而不是找出某种初始起因。这样一来，这种争论就纯属多余了。

最后，鉴于对相关性和经济性原则的批判，"生态的"这个概念用于语言学，也使其获得了"跨学科"和"非排他性"意义，或使之具有"超越传统经济观念"的意义。

三、语言与环境问题

自1990年国际应用语言学大会召开以及韩礼德《意义的新途径》一书出版以来，在生态语言学领域，研究者对下面的问题表现出越来越浓厚的兴趣：语言在各种生态问题中所起的作用以及对越来越多的族群和个人造成影响的环境问题。事实上，"环境语言学"这一名称就是针对此类研究提出的。不过，我则倾向于"语言生态学"（language ecology）或"语言学生态学"（linguistic ecology）这两个术语，这两个术语表明（正如我在导言中所言），此类研究是在生态语言学原理的总体理论框架内进行的。

1. 话语批评

关于"语言与生态问题"这个论题，不同的学者从不同方面、采用不同方法论进行了探究。德国语言学家马蒂亚斯·容（Matthias Jung）利用报纸文本语料，对环境词汇的时代变迁进行了研究。进而，他对我们常听到的"词汇选择是为了可操作的意图"这一假说提出了质疑。从下图（选自容，1994a：65。原文发表于《Allensbach民意调查年鉴1978—1983》，p. 525）可以看出，德语表示"核能"的两个词（Atomkraft和Kernenergie）的不同联想。

（图略）

只有"Krieg"（战争）一词的概念才能明显地区别联想差异，因为Krieg与Atomkraft（原子能）的联想关系远远高于与Kernenergie（核能）的联想。环境保护主义者提出，Kernenergie这个词带有健康自然能源的正面联想，核能游说者们采用委婉的、可操作的方式使用这个词。马蒂亚斯·容认为这种看法是值得怀疑的。他指出，"通过语言进行操作"只不过是某些书本杜撰出来的另一种老生常谈而已，比如奥韦尔（George Orwell）1984年的小说和麦肯森（Mackensen）的《语言的诱骗》。

另外一些学者运用批评话语分析（critical discourse analysis）的理论框架（费尔克拉夫、克雷斯等人创建），对有关环境话题的文本进行了批评性分析。安德烈亚·格比希（Andrea Gerbig）分析了有关臭氧层问题争论的环境文本中的搭配模式。结果表明，对立的利益群体所撰写出的文本在搭配频度上存在明显的差异（例如在论及原因和责任这两个词语时）。格比希使用的另一个语言参数是通过选用主动、被动和作格结构，对施受事关系（agency）加以强调或抑制。下面是格比希的例子：

（1）...cases of non-malignant skin cancer have been increasing over many years...（非恶性皮肤癌的病例在逐年增多）

这个真实的例子来自工业利益群体的语言文本。句中“选择作格意在表达这是一种自身造成的行为过程，对这一过程而言，没有任何，甚至一点暗示都没有——施事者可以幸免。这意味着把行为者（即应对行为负责的人和事）转换成行为本身”。对臭氧层造成破坏的产业群体至少应对这种过程（指皮肤癌病例不断上升——译者注）承担部分责任，而句中这种施事关系被抑制了。

理查德·亚历山大（Richard Alexander）所做的某些研究也表明，施受事关系在环境文本中起着一定的作用。下面的例子来自英国一个核废料处理组织（NIREX）的一份广告，其中施受事关系使用了不同的表达方式：

（2）*Britain* produces radioactive waste every day…（英国每天都生产大量的放射性废料）

（3）the safe disposal of *our* radioactive waste…（安全处理我们的放射性废料）

（4）some of the most stringent *safety requirements* in the world *will have to be met*…（世界上一些最为严格的安全要求将必须得到满足）

例（2）（*Britain* produces）和例（3）（*our* radioactive waste）变换了施事者，造成人人都制造核废料的含义指向；例（4）通过使用被动结构删除了施事（即 safety requirements will have to be met），使用这种手法，目的“在于转移人们对造成后果的肇事者的注意，而肇事者是必须采取这些安全处理措施的”。

删除施事者（或删除受事者）也可以通过名词化的方法来实现，如戈特利（Goatly）的有关讨论（还可参见费尔克拉夫）。在马丁（J. R. Martin）之后，戈特利的研究也表明，在环境文本中，将动词名词化可以弱化人们对受影响对象的关注。例如，在描述捕杀海豹事件时，如果使用诸如例（5）中的名词性词组，好像受害者（海豹）根本不值一提：

（5）*a slaughtering operation*，*killing methods*，*killing techniques*，*a humane death*

戈特利指出，复合名词可能“会把受害者弱化或降格至修饰语地位”，如：the seal hunt，the whitecoat harvest。（后例中用 harvest 一词指代有组织的猎杀行为，该词的使用有独特的委婉隐喻意味。这也恰恰说明了戈特利用“害死人的隐喻”做副标题之用心所在了）

丹麦学者杜尔（J. Døør）和邦（J. Chr. Bang）运用“施事”“直指”两个范畴，对两个丹麦语法律文本进行了分析，这两个文本都涉及“农产品的有机化生产”问题。分析揭示了文本中的逻辑矛盾，结果给人的印象是：政府部门成了有机食品生产中的施事者，而农民成了“接受者”和“授予物的申请者”。例（6）是杜尔和邦的论文引例：

（6）*Applicants for grants*…shall upon request produce evidence that the conditions for the grant have been fulfilled.

邦与杜尔为建立一种语言的生态理论做出了努力，其用意在于为生态危机伦理层面的探讨开辟一条新的研究途径，同时也想表明这样的观点：传统语言学理论忽视了语言指称范畴在思想意识上的含义，本身就是这种危机的组成部分。

2. 语言系统的批判

除了话语的批评性分析外，生态语言学家对语言系统的生态特征和非生态特征进行了缜密的探讨。从这方面对语言做批判分析的学者当推韩礼德。他将语言对世界的影响描述为“系统与事件之间的辩证法”。他认为，语法提供系统的所有选项，这些选项“与时下的文化形式相呼应”，并通过在日常话语中的使用而得到进一步强化。韩礼德的“语言建构论”对语言系统（或韩礼德所称的“语法”）提出了严厉的批评。他指出，生长特性、性别歧视、分类行为等思想意识，也体现在我们语言的语法中；同时自然资源的无限性、人类的特权地位这种思想意识已经成为语言系统中结构上的内在特性。韩礼德进而指出：

（1）欧洲各种通用的标准语中，不可数名词或“物质名词”（如 oil、energy、water、air 等）有“无限、无穷”之义，自然资源无限的观念从这类名词的使用中表现出来。

（2）像“大”与“小”这类成对的反义词、“成长词”（growth word）往往成了中性词。通常总是说“小车有多快？（不说小车有多慢）”“这楼有多高？（不说有多低）”“收入有多高（不说有多低）”等。

（3）我们的语言不愿意承认非人类的施事者。“那片森林在干什么？”这样的句子大多数人会认为不能接受。

（4）认为人类享有特殊地位的这种意识，通过语言的代词系统（如 he/she 用于指人，it 则指非人类的生物和事物）以及许多不能用于动植物的动词搭配（如 think、know、believe、amiable、sympathetic 等），表现得淋漓尽致。

如果说，格比希、邦、杜尔和亚历山大等生态语言学家在分析环境文本时，对施事和感受格（experiencers）的抑制现象提出了批评，那么从更高的系统层面看，正是因为语言表达了诸如“施动者”“感受者”“接受者”此类范畴这一事实，所以其成了批评关注的焦点。这里要谈到的一点就是，与传统的牛顿科学思想保持一致的欧洲通用标准语言的语法，与当代生态世界观已经不相适应；生态世界观正是对这种传统的范畴划分提出了质疑。这种对宇宙的“分解”（fragmentation）包含在诸如“主语”“述语”和“宾语”之类常见的语法结构中，这种语法结构把施事、过程、感受者相互区分开来。语言在这种划分中的作用早年曾为诸如韦斯特（Frederic Vester）、博姆（David Bohm）、拉夫洛克（James Lovelock）等非语言学界的学者所承认；而语言学界的思想家对此却很少注意。不过，在生态语言学家近期的研究中，将语言与世界的非生态性分解联系起来的做法明显地突显了出来。

戈特利运用拉夫洛克的盖亚理论（Gaia theory）对此进行了研究，其中他特别提到以下方法，“采用重合语言来描写物质过程的方式所表现出的世界往往与现代科学理论（尤其是盖亚理论）大相径庭”：

（1）划分施事参与者、受动参与者及环境等……这些结构有碍于构建不可切分的整体观。

（2）将所有现象分为过程与事物，这从现代物理学观点来看也是值得怀疑的。

在这一背景下，生态语言学家还着重探讨语言中的“人类中心主义”问题。人类中心说把人类同其他生物永久地割裂开来。费尔哈亨（Frans Verhagen）就提出了这样的问题：如何使用语言来确立一种生物中心主义世界观，而摆脱那种极端的人类中心的机械主义世界观？戈特利指出："批评性话语分析的一种选择，可以把包括马克思人道主义在内的人类中心说作为研究目标。尽管我们不大情愿承认这个世界不是宇宙的中心，但是对于接受人类也不可能是世界中心这个观点，我们则更加犹豫不定。"

语言学上的人类中心论不仅表现为语言从对人类的实用性角度来命名所有自然现象，而且也表现在隐含地指称人类方面，如某些存在结构和动词短语。例如，在下列描述土地状况的句子中，所有动词形式都隐含有"对人类而言"之意：

...the soils are poor...the land is used for little else except extensive beef grazing...another land use, mining, is now of greater value...

在这种英语"语法"里，除了人类之外，"land uses"（土地的使用）是不能用于其他生物的。

3. **语言的生态化**

一个经常提到的、同生态语言学的语言批评观相关的问题是，生态语言学家应该以改变语言状况为目标，还是仅仅让语言使用者对所批评的语言事实有所认识？多数生态语言学家都倾向于反对"生态正确性"的观点，并申明他们的语言批评观是"非保守主义的"（即非规范化意义上的）、"温和的"，而且也无意去改变语言系统。这种批评观的目的在于跻身于批评主义的语言觉醒运动，而不在于创造一种与之并驾齐驱的"新话"（newspeak）。不过，有一位学者确实提出了要改变语言，以使其包含新的生态世界观，他就是物理学家大卫·博姆。他建议采用一种称为"流"（Rheomode，希腊语意为"流"）的新的动词情态（verbal modality）——它可以无须区分施事者和感受者，而只用来表达"过程"（process）。

戈特利提出了一个很有意思的假说。随着时间的推移，我们的语言本身（或语言使用者）将自动地与这种新的生态意识相适应，并发生相应的变化。作格结构的使用频率正在上升，而及物动词结构渐渐被取代；相互动词（如 meet，touch，interact，talk，converse 等）的使用也在增多，这类动词表达的是共同性而不是支配性，这些都是我们能够观察到的语言自适应变化的早期征兆。语言的这种"深生态化"（deep ecologization）可以看作语言演变的一种长期进化过程。这个过程与环境过程交互作用，从发展的理论观点来看，这一过程可能逐渐减缓环境的退化。深生态化可以理解为对话语"浅生态化"（surface ecologization）的一种逆向发展。话语浅生态化在广告语言（即所谓"绿色广告"）以及许多现代政治话语中丰富的环境词汇的使用上已十分明显。

四、语言与生物的多样性

在米尔豪斯勒的研究中，自然现象的命名也是一个突出的课题，虽然他更多地侧重命名过程中的种族中心主义（ethnocentrism）。在他的研究中，生态语言学所追求的保持语言多样性问题与人们所关心的生物多样性问题联系在一起。在米尔豪斯勒看来，语言的多样性"反映了人类数千年来对复杂环境状况的适应性"，通过不同的语言可以不同程度地解释生物的多样性。他发现，有关新环境的话语实际上可以对该环境产生影响，尤其是在语言资源的缺乏可能引起环境退化的情况下。“小语种的衰落与消亡不是一种自足现象，它蕴涵在更为广泛的生态要素之中，并与之密切相关。这从澳大利亚和太平洋地区的语言实例中可以说明。”米尔豪斯勒对分布在澳大利亚、新西兰奥特亚罗（Aotearoa）以及太平洋地区众多的语言生态系统进行了调查研究，从中归纳抽取出若干语言和生物要素成分，阐明了其中的相互关系。下面引用米尔豪斯勒的有关例子来说明这一关系。

命名结果对自然生态造成影响的一个特别明显的例子就是，有许多种袋目小动物曾一度大量栖息在澳洲大陆上，但后来它们却被称为灌鼠或本地鼠；由于这些新名字，它们被人当作像英国老鼠一样的东西。这些动物至多成了无用的家伙，若从坏的方面看，则成了危险的有害动物，必须灭绝。

米尔豪斯勒接着讨论了最近所做的尝试，即通过重新取名或重新起用古老的土名字，来挽救这些数量日益减少的有袋小动物。他指出，单个动物物种的名称所产生的影响，也同样见于植物物种的命名方面。

在米尔豪斯勒的研究中，对环境［或共生境（convironment），这个术语更强调所有生物的共存］的关心同对语言多样性丧失和小语种作用日渐萎缩的关心结合在一起。他的语言生态学既涵盖了生态和环境的隐喻含义，也涵盖了它的字面意义，因而可能是生态语言学领域迄今最为全面的理论学说。

五、结论

生态语言学是一门超越句法学、语义学和语用学的学科。因此，这一学科就经验主义方面的研究而言，需要可理论化并具有创造性的新思想。尽管生态语言学迄今已经走过了20多年的历程，但要使这一研究领域所有可能的问题都得到涉及（且不谈研究的深度如何），生态语言学仍然有漫长的路要走。生态语言学的研究范围非常广泛，它给语言研究这门学科提出了以下任务：①探索各种适当的语言理论；②研究语言系统及语言文本；③研究与生态问题相关的语言普遍特征；④根据这些普遍特征，研究单个的具体语言（可采用对比的研究方式）；⑤研究语言在获得“生态读写能力”方面的作用，如教育儿童与成人进行生态思考。

生态语言学涉及语言理论探讨、方法论思考以及经验主义研究。在所有这些层面上，它为那些对生态学感兴趣的语言学家提供了新的视野。我们可以真正肯定地宣告，对于那些寻求挑战性问题研究的语言学家来说，这是一个值得探索的研究领域。

第三章

学术论文汉译英

Selected Reading 1

步态中的最小作用量原理

范毅方　Mushtaq Loan　樊瑜波　李知宇　罗冬林

摘要： 运用人类步态中的地面反弹力原理，我们发现人类步态中存在着最小作用量的现象。利用电子步态底垫系统，我们获得了步态中地面反弹力的变化情况，建立起地面反弹力合力的结构方程式。用一个作用函数来表示垂直力的离散程度，通过对步态的最优化分析，我们发现，最小作用量总是发生在一个跨步周期的1/2处。因此，在步态最小作用量原理的基础上，我们提出了一个关于机械能损耗的评估指标。我们认为这些观察结果可以使步态的评估更具可靠性。

步态分析利用生物力学的方法来探索人体运动的规律，因此，步态分析也可以服务于临床诊断和康复。步态参数指的是步行时的一些物理量，比如时空特点、人体运动学数量、动能量等。步态参数的相对对称是正常人自然步态的一个显著特征。相对对称性指数又被称为步态量化指数，是一种数学模型。该指数让对偏瘫病人行走功能的研究取得了可喜的成绩。随着步态测量仪器的研发，更多步态参数的步态评估指数得以确立。通过测力板或平面压力测量系统得出数据，在这些数据的基础上得出地面反弹力分布的步态评估指数以及峰值参数。最后再不断利用这些指数和参数来分析步态。这为医疗康复奠定了基础。步态指数评估的本质就是比较，也就是说，将正常人的步态作为康复评估的标准。但是，人的体形、坐标以及力量的不完全对称性成就了人类步态的独特性，同时也给建立步态参数、指数标准增加了难度。步态规律与一个人的年龄、性别以及体形并不相关，因此，在运用步态来科学地评估康复状况时，探索一个与年龄、性别及体形不相关的步态规律就显得尤为重要。

双足行走让人类步态不断进化，最终发展成为最佳步态，而人类的行为特征也得以形成。在发生物理过程时，大自然总是使某些重要的量取最小值。在人类行为特征不断演化的过程中，对一些问题的解释还存在争议，如：该演化过程是如何遵循最小作用量原理（以下简称 LAP）的？步态中的作用函数是什么？等等。本文旨在讨论步态中的最小作用量原理，提出更可靠、更标准的步态评估指数系统。

步态是在神经系统的控制下，通过肌骨系统产生合力并通过足作用于地面；地面的反弹力使人体产生运动。质心在垂直方向的变化可以通过人体环节在垂直方向上的时空关系来分析，也可以通过地面反弹力来分析。

根据人类步态的特点，某一特定时刻的地面反弹力合力的公式为：

$$F_{GRF}(T) = F_z^r(t) + F_z^l(t) \quad (1)$$ ①

其中，右脚和左脚的地面反弹力分别为 $F_z^r(t) = F_z(t)$ 和 $F_z^l(t) = F_z(t+t_0)$，T 为一足的一个跨步周期。它的区间为 $0 \leqslant t \leqslant T$。利用方程式（1），可以得出足的着地顺序以及地面反弹力的变化情况。将周期时间百分比化，用 $F_z(t)/mg$ 和 $F_z(t+t_0)/mg$ 使地面反弹力标准化，我们就能呈现地面反弹力的变化和足的着地顺序之间的关系了，如彩图 1 所示。

在确定了每一足的地面反弹力的变化情况之后，分析彩图 1 的光谱，我们发现，在每一个跨步周期中，$\frac{1}{Tmg}\int_0^T F_{GRF}(t)\mathrm{d}t - 1 = 0$。这样一来，$t_0$ 的变化会引起每一个跨步周期中 VGRF 分布情况的变化。而 F_{GRF} 的分布规律又决定了步行动作。例如，当 $t_0 = 0$ 时，就变成了双脚跳，而不是步行。为了分析足的着地顺序对地面反弹力合力分布情况的影响，我们引入了离散程度分布的概念。利用地面反弹力合力的离散程度

$$\sqrt{\frac{\Sigma(F_z(t)/mg + F_z(t+t_0)/mg)^2 - Tf}{Tf - 1}}$$

（f 表示测量系统的采集频率），我们得出了足的着地顺序与地面反弹力合力离散程度的关系。运用最优化的方法，我们发现了地面反弹力合力的作用函数 $\Psi(t_0)[= \sum_{t=1/f}^{T}(F_z(t) + F_z(t+t_0) - mg)^2]$ 在一个跨步周期的 1/2 处达到最佳值。如彩图 2 所示，这种变化是对称的，在跨步周期的 1/2 处，数值最小。因此，我们总结出，当步态中一个足的跨步周期的起始点正好在另一个足的跨步周期的中间位置时，双足地面反弹力的合力离散最小。

人体环节的运动需要主动肌、拮抗肌和协同肌共同完成；环节的伸展、屈曲动作都需要消耗机械能。由于在一个跨步周期中，$E_g = 0$，$E_k = \frac{1}{Tf}\sum \frac{1}{2}mv_t^2 > 0$，因此我们用 E_k 来描述步态当中垂直方向上机械能的消耗情况。彩图 3 说明，足的着地顺序影响了步态中垂直方向上的机械能变化。由此得出结论，步行时，足的着地时机选择在另一足跨步周期的中间位置时，连续步态在垂直方向上的机械能消耗最小。这就是步态的最小作用量原理。

利用地面反弹力变化来评估步态中垂直方向上的能量消耗，我们提出了以下能量耗损指数：

$$ID_E = \frac{\sum_{i=1}^{n} T_i \int_0^T |F_z(t) + F_z(t+t_0) - mg|\mathrm{d}t}{t\|_0^{T_1+\cdots+T_n}|F_{GRF}(t) - mg|\mathrm{d}t} \quad (2)$$

其中，n 表示跨步周期数。当 $n=3$ 时，以上的定义衍生出 Zebris FDM 步态分析系统。以上定义的优点在于测量者不需要计算质心的垂直加速度、速度以及位移。

用 Zebris FDM 测量系统进行步态分析，我们收集的数据都是最能代表正常步态，

① 我们假定左右脚的地面反弹力相同。

并能满足测试基本要求的。我们测试了一位左脚踝关节轻度扭伤的成年男性、一位正常男性和一位有轻度关节炎的老年人的步态。分析结果如彩图 4 所示。我们发现，一个健康的成年人在行走过程中，一个足的跨步周期的起始点会不由自主地落在另一足的跨步周期的 1/2 处。运用垂直方向上的机械能来评估受试者步行时的能量消耗，我们得出的估计值分别为：0. 931、0. 998 以及 0. 743。我们发现，与之前的结果进行对比，我们建立的评估指数能够更好地解释不同的步态。为了检验普遍性，我们扩大了样本量，测量了 173 人（95 名男学生，78 名女学生）。收集的数据如下表所示。利用 WinFDM，经统计分析得出左右脚的跨步周期分别为 1. 01(6)s、1. 00(6)s 。运用步态最小作用量原理计算得出左右跨步起始时刻与测试的左右脚跨步起始时刻之比分别为 0. 998(21) 和 0. 993(21)。这些估计值之间高度一致，表明步态最小作用量原理具有普遍性。

受试者的平均年龄、身高和体重

性别	人数	年龄（岁）	身高（m）	体重（kg）
男性	95	21. 1 ± 1. 31	1. 72 ± 0. 64	61. 8 ± 8. 3
女性	78	21. 8 ± 1. 3	1. 61 ± 0. 58	51. 3 ± 7. 6

将受试者的体重进行归一化，将跨步周期进行百分比化。彩图 5 显示的分别是男性受试者和女性受试者在一个跨步周期当中的地面反弹力、垂直机械能、质心速度以及位置。彩图 5 表明，当受试者的样本量足够大时（像我们的研究对象那样），一个跨步周期当中，男性和女性受试者的地面反弹力、垂直机械能、质心速度和位置都会极为相似。这表明本研究当中使用的评估指数对男女受试者都是有效的。

为检验足的着地顺序对地面反弹力合力的离散程度以及对垂直机械能消耗的影响，我们在彩图 6 中展示了受试者地面反弹力合力与垂直方向上机械能消耗的关系。相关性分析表明，这两者之间有着高度的关联性（$R = 0.976$，$p < 0.001$），地面反弹力离散程度越小，垂直方向上的机械能消耗就越小。

本研究在地面反弹力离散程度与垂直方向机械能消耗之间建立起了联系，得出了描述地面反弹力合力的方法。通过分析，我们总结出，地面反弹力离散程度最小时，垂直方向的机械能消耗也最小。我们还在最小作用量原理的基础上提出了关于机械能消耗的评估指数。我们得出的结果显示，步态中的最小作用量原理是普遍存在的。

正常人自然步态中有与生理因素（性别、年龄）、形态因素（身高、体重等）和步态因素（步频、步速）等无关的现象存在。一个足的跨步周期的起始点总是处于另一个足跨步周期的 1/2 处，这样的步态在垂直方向上的机械能消耗最小。建立跨步周期足的反弹力回归方程，用作用函数表示地面反弹力的离散程度，通过优化分析方法，我们发现了最小作用量原理。对 173 位测试者连续步态的分析证实了这一原理。结果显示，步态的演化是适应自然环境的结果，更是遵循最小作用量原理的结果。在现有的身体状态下，我们使用的步态是最节省能量的（甚至在踝关节受到一些轻微的损伤后也是如此）。这是人类的一种本能。因此，在运动康复中，应该着重身体功能的恢复。个人步态的唯一性应该是人体惯性参数、肌肉力量、运动协调性等方面存在差异的情况下遵循最小作用量原理形成的。对自然步态（赤足）中的剪应力的研究会丰富最小作用量原理的研究。该研究让我们相信，最小作用量原理极为深刻地影响了自然界的演化，乃至生命的进化过程。拉马克提出的生命进化中“用进，废退”的法则就是最小作用量原理的一种表现。对最小作用量原理的进一步研究对体育康复、生物识别技术以及双足机器人的步态控制等方面的研究都有重要的意义。

Least-Action Principle in Gait

Yifang Fan, Mushtaq Loan, Yubo Fan, Zhiyu Li and Donglin Luo

Translated by Zhiyu Li

Abstract: We apply the laws of human gait vertical ground reaction force and discover the existence of the phenomenon of least-action principle in gait. Using a capacitive mat transducer system, we obtain the variations of human gait vertical ground reaction force and establish a structure equation for the resultant of such a force. Defining the deviation of vertical force as an action function, we observe from our gait optimization analysis the least-action principle at half of the stride time. We develop an evaluation index of mechanical-energy consumption based upon the least-action principle in gait. We conclude that these observations can be employed to enhance the accountability of gait evaluation.

Gait analysis explores laws of body movement by biomechanical methods so that it can serve the clinical diagnosis and rehabilitation. Gait parameters refer to physical quantities while walking, for example, the space-time characteristics, kinesiological quantities and kinetic quantities. The relative symmetry of gait parameters is a notable feature of normal human natural gait. Phase symmetry index was proposed as gait quantization index and mathematical model and it has brought satisfactory result in the study of walking function of hemiplegic patients. With the development of gait measurement equipment, more gait evaluation indices of gait parameters have been defined. Gait evaluation index of vertical ground reaction force (VGRF) distribution and parameters of peak value based upon data collected from equipment such as force plate or planar pressure measurement system has been employed constantly to analyze gait, which provides foundation for medical rehabilitation. The essence of gait index evaluation is to compare, that is, to take the normal human gait as the standard of rehabilitation evaluation. However, the non-complete symmetry of human shape, coordinate and strength has formed the uniqueness of human gait, which has brought difficulty to the establishment of gait parameter index standard. Consequently, exploring a law that is irrelevant to one's age, gender or physical shape in gait has become very important when applying gait to scientifically evaluate the rehabilitation.

Bipedal walking has enabled the continuous evolution of human gait, which eventually brought about the optimized gait and formed a human behavioral trait. Nature always minimizes certain important quantities when a physical process takes place. In the continuous evolution of this human behavioral trait, explanations to issues such as how it observes the least-action principle (hereinafter referred to as LAP) and what the action function in gait is remain controversial. In this letter we address the issue of the principles of least-action in gait and propose a more reliable and standard gait evaluation index system.

Gait is under the control of the nervous system. Its musculoskeletal system generates resultant force, which acts on the ground by foot, and in turn, the consequent VGRF enables the human body to move. The vertical change of mass center can be analyzed either by the spacetime relation of human segments or by VGRF.

Following the human gait characteristics, the equation of certain moment's VGRF resultant force is

$$F_{GRF}(T) = F_z^r(t) + F_z^l(t) \text{①} \tag{1}$$

where $F_z^r(t) = F_z(t)$ and $F_z^l(t) = F_z(t+t_0)$, for $0 \leqslant t \leqslant T$, are the VGRFs of the right and left foot, respectively and T is one foot stride time. Using Eq. (1), one can obtain the landing sequences of the foot and its variations of VGRF. Rating the cycle time as a percentage and normalizing the reaction force by $F_z(t)/mg$ and $F_z(t+t_0)/mg$, we display the relationship between the variation of VGRF and the landing sequences of the foot in Fig. 1.

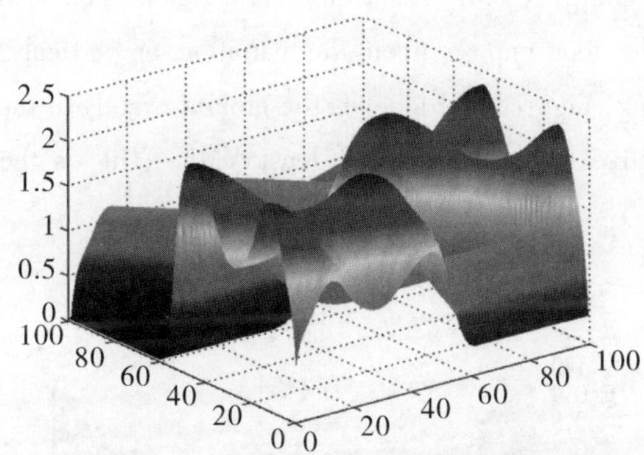

Fig. 1　(Colour on-line) Relationship between the landing sequences of the foot and its variations of VGRF

The variation range of both t and t_0 is defined over the range $[0, T]$.

Analyzing the spectrum in Fig. 1, we notice, after determining each foot's variation of vertical ground reaction force, that $\frac{1}{Tmg}\int_0^T F_{GRF}(t)\,dt - 1 = 0$ in each stride cycle. In this way, the change of t_0 leads to the change of the distribution of VGRF in a stride cycle. The distribution of F_{GRF} actually determines the walking movement. For example, when $t_0 = 0$, the walking will become jumping. In order to analyze the influence of foot land sequence to the distribution of VGRF resultant, we turn to the concept of deviation distribution. Using the

① We have assumed that the VGRF of both the left and right foot is the same.

deviation of VGRF resultant force,

$$\sqrt{\frac{\Sigma(F_z(t)/mg + F_z(t+t_0)/mg)^2 - Tf}{Tf-1}}$$

(f being the collection frequency of the measurement system), we develop the relationship between the landing sequence of one foot and its deviation of VGRF resultant force. Using the optimization method, we found that the action function $\Psi(t_0)[=\sum_{t=1/f}^{T}(F_z(t)+F_z(t+t_0)-mg)^2]$, of the resultant of VGRF in a gait cycle reaches an optimum value around $\frac{1}{2}T$. As can be seen in Fig. 2, this change is symmetric and has a minimal value about $\frac{1}{2}T$. Therefore, we conclude that in gait, when the starting time of one foot stride cycle time falls right at the half of the other foot stride time, the deviation of VGRF is the minimal.

The movement of human segment is done by a combination of prime movers, antagonist, and synergists. The extension and bending of a segment's movement consume mechanical energy. Since in a stride cycle, $E_g=0$, $E_k=\frac{1}{Tf}\sum\frac{1}{2}mv_t^2>0$, thus we use E_k to describe the vertical mechanical energy (VME) consumption in gait. Fig. 3 illustrates the effect the landing sequences of the foot impose upon the variation of vertical mechanical energy. It follows that while walking, one rearfoot touches the ground exactly at the half of the other foot's stride time and consecutive gaits consume the least VME. This is the so-called least-action principle in gait (LAPG).

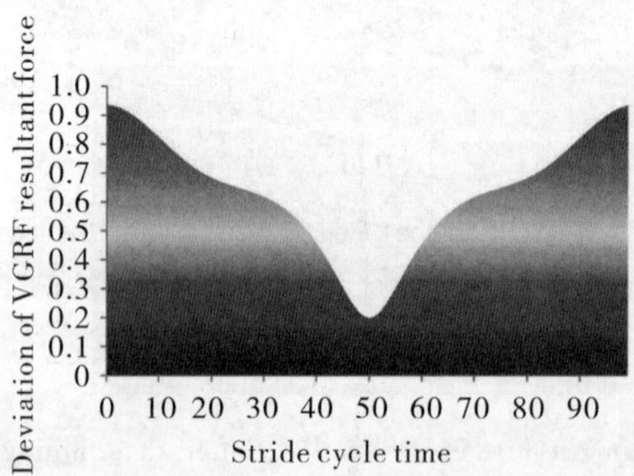

Fig. 2 (Colour on-line) The deviation of the resultant VGRF as a function of the stride cycle time

The stride time is rated as percentage by $(t/T)\times 100$.

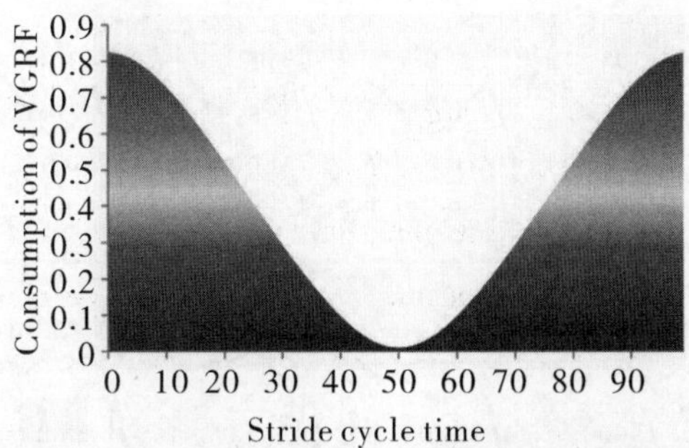

Fig. 3　(Colour on-line) Consumption of the vertical mechanical energy as a function of the stride cycle time

Using the variation of VGRF to evaluate the consumption of VME in gait, we propose an energy consumption index of the following form:

$$ID_E = \frac{\sum_{i=1}^{n} T_i \int_0^T |F_z(t) + F_z(t + t_0) - mg| \mathrm{d}t}{t \|_0^{T_1+\cdots+T_n} |F_{GRF}(t) - mg| \mathrm{d}t} \tag{2}$$

where n is the number of stride cycles. For $n = 3$, the above definition reproduces Zebris FDM Gait Analysis System. The advantage with the above definition is that one does not need to calculate vertical accelerated velocity, velocity and displacement of mass center.

Using the Zebris FDM Measurement System for gait analysis, we collect the data that best represent the usual normal gaits and meet the essential requirements of the test. We test the gait of one male adult with slight injury in his left ankle, a second male and one elderly male with rheumatic arthritis. The analysed results are displayed in Fig. 4. We notice that when a fit adult walks, the starting time of one foot in a stride cycle will spontaneously fall right at the half of the other foot's stride cycle time. Applying the VME to evaluate the energy consumption in gait for these subjects, we obtain the estimates of 0. 931, 0. 998 and 0. 743, respectively. A comparison with the earlier results shows that the established evaluation index can provide better accountability to different gaits. In order to examine its universality, we enlarged our sample size to 173 subjects (95 male and 78 female students). The collected data are tabulated in the following table. The statistical analysis to the results for gait, using WinFDM, yield the stride times of 1. 01(6)s and 1. 00(6)s for the left and right foot, respectively. The ratio between the starting time calculated by LAPG and that of the tested result for the left and right foot is estimated as 0. 998(21) and 0. 993(21), respectively. The excellent agreement between the estimates confirms the signature of the universality of LAPG.

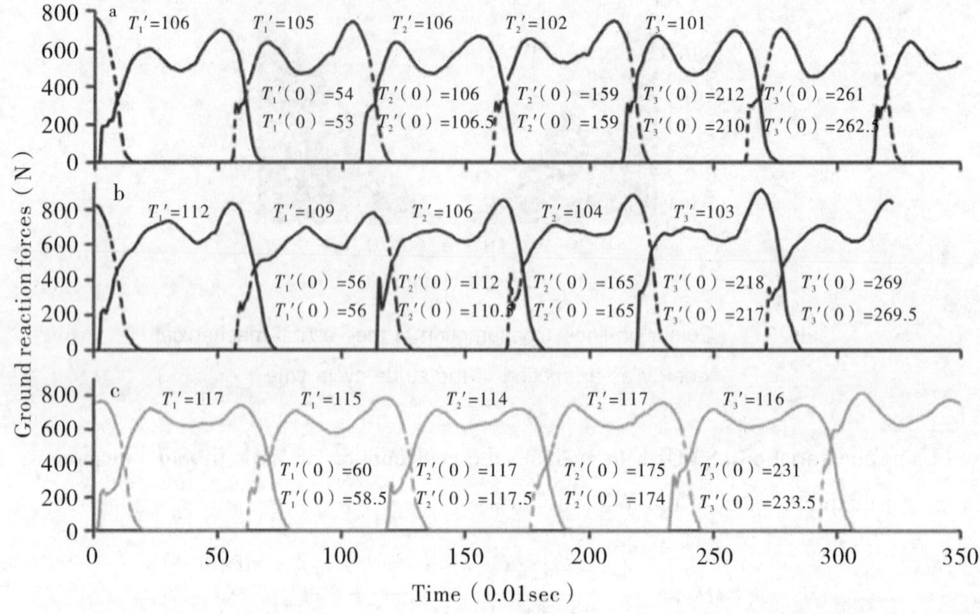

Fig. 4 Test result

Fig. 4a: feet pressure of a slightly injured adult, Fig. 4b: feet pressure of an adult, Fig. 4c: feet pressure of an elderly with rheumatoid arthritis.

Age, height and body mass of the subjects (Mean ± SD)

Gender	Sample size	Age (years)	Height (m)	Body mass (kg)
Male	95	21.1 ±1.31	1.72 ±0.64	61.8 ±8.3
Female	78	21.8 ±1.3	1.61 ±0.58	51.3 ±7.6

We normalized the subjects' weight and rated the stride time by percentage. Fig. 5 is the variations of male and female subjects' VGRF, VME, center of mass velocity and position in a stride cycle, respectively. Fig. 5 shows that when the sample size is big enough (like the one in our study), the variations of male and female's VGRF, VME, center of mass velocity and position in a stride cycle are quite similar. Thus, it confirms that the evaluation index in this study is valid to both male and female subjects.

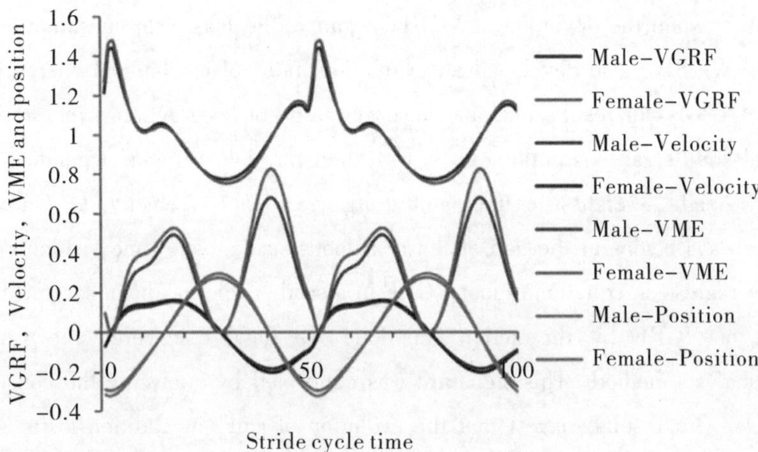

Fig. 5 (Colour on-line) Variations of VGRF, VME, center of mass velocity and position in a stride cycle

The unit of VGRF is a multiple of weight, that of velocity m/s. To make this figure more attractive, we multiplied VME values by 40, and center-of-mass position values by 20.

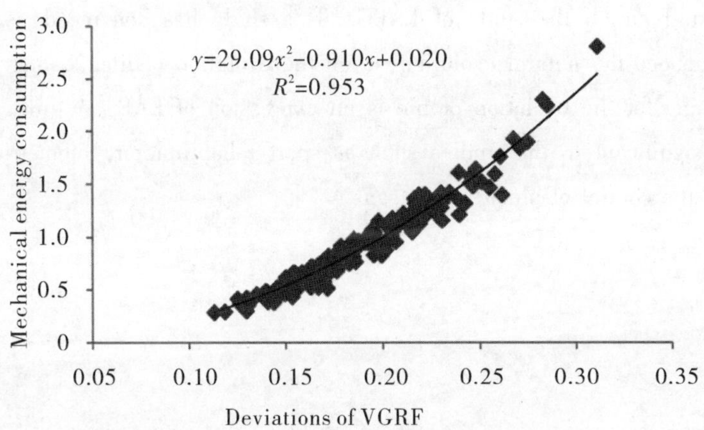

Fig. 6 (Colour on-line) Consumption of VME

The consumption of VME is represented by the function of the subject's deviation of VGRF. The solid curve is a quadratic fit to the data.

To examine the effect that the landing sequences of the foot exert upon both the deviation of VGRF resultant and the consumption of VME, we display our proposed relationship between the subject's deviation of VGRF and the consumption of VME in Fig. 6. An analysis of correlation reveals that the two quantities are highly correlated ($R = 0.976$, $p < 0.001$), a least deviation of VGRF results in least consumption of VME.

In this study, we have developed a relationship between the deviation of VGRF and its consumption of VME and established a description of VGRF resultant force. From our analysis we conclude that when the deviation of VGRF in gait is the least, its consumption of VME is also the least. We have also developed an evaluation index of mechanical-energy consumption based on the LAPG. Our results indicate the universality of least-action principle in gaits.

A normal adult's gait has nothing to do with their physiology (e. g. , gender, age), body shape (e. g. , height, weight) or their gait (e. g. , cadence, velocity) . One foot's stride starting time always begins at the half of the next foot's stride cycle time, which consumes the least VME. A regression equation of foot VGRF in a stride cycle has been set up. Representing the deviation of VGRF by the action function, we have discovered the LAPG by the optimization analysis method. This signature was confirmed by analyzing the consecutive gaits of 173 subjects. Our results suggest that the evolution of gait, in addition to its adaptation to the natural environment, is a consequence of following LAP. Human present physical condition uses the most energy-saving gait, even after a slight injury to the ankle. This could be considered as a human instinct. In sport rehabilitation, the therapy should be focused on the recovery of physical function. The uniqueness of each individual's gait is shaped when deviations of human-body inertial parameters, muscle strength, and motion coordination do exist, but they all follow LAPG. A research into the variations of natural gait (bare-footed) shear stress would enrich the study of LAPG. This study has convinced us that LAP has profoundly influenced the natural evolution, even the evolution of life. Lamarck's mechanism using and disusing for the evolution of life is an expression of LAP. A further research into LAPG will be significant to the studies such as sport rehabilitation, biometric identification techniques and the control of biped robots gaits.

Selected Reading 2

非病理性扁平足和高弓足的自然步态

范毅方　樊瑜波　李知宇　吕长生　罗冬林

摘要：关于非病理性扁平足和高弓足对人的步行活动是否有影响的问题，一直存在着争议。我们采用3D足部扫描系统，获得受试者在半承重站姿时的静态足印迹。根据这些足印迹，将受试者分为两组：扁平足和高弓足。通过地垫式足底压力系统来测试和记录受试者的连续自然步态。我们提出了两大指标：足底地面反弹力（VGRF）的分布和足印面积的变化率。用这些指标对这两组受试者的自然步态进行比较，我们发现：①支撑相时，足底的VGRF分布存在着显著的差异（$p<0.01$）；②跨步周期中，足印面积的变化率也存在着十分显著的差异（$p<0.01$）。经分析表明：行走时，足底的VGRF使扁平足承受了更大的肌肉张力；更小的足印面积变化率使得高弓足具有更好的稳定性。

前　言

足弓是人类进行行走等基本活动而不断进化的结果。人类是唯一有足弓的脊椎动物。一个横弓、一个内侧纵弓和一个外侧纵弓的解剖结构在人的活动中具有缓冲减震、保持稳定和产生推进力的功能。对于足弓的形态、结构和功能的研究从未停止过。

个体之间的足弓在形态和结构方面存在差异，这和年龄以及体重等因素有关。获得足弓形态的常用方法有：足印、X光、足底压力测量、激光扫描测量、MRI扫描等。用足印比值和足弓指数等指标可把足形分为正常足、高弓足和扁平足三类。形态上的扁平足和高弓足并不是扁平足症和高弓足症。研究结果表明，非病理性扁平足（柔性扁平足）不会影响人的生理生活质量，因此不需要治疗。其他研究表明，扁平足对速度、耐力和/或平衡等能力会有影响。因此高弓足者不适合当短跑运动员。非病理性扁平足和高弓足人群在步态上存在何种差异？这种差异会对步行产生影响吗？如果会，那么会产生怎样的影响呢？这些问题一直没有让人满意的答案。

形态是结构的表现。用3D足部扫描仪记录站立时的足印迹，根据足印迹比值选择扁平足和高弓足受试者。结构影响功能，足底压力分布能够定量地反映步态中足的结构、功能以及对整个身体的控制等信息。用步态分析系统来测试两组受试者的自然步态。通过分析足底VGRF的分布和足印面积的变化率，我们发现，两组受试者的步态确实存在差异。

材料和方法

本研究是在获得广州体育学院伦理委员会的批准后进行的。实验之前，受试者接受了关于实验的步骤和注意事项的集中指导，了解了实验的目标和要求。所有受试者都有签署书面同意书。

在选择过程中，我们得到了校医院骨伤科的协助，对受试者进行了检查，排除了有诸如仰趾外翻足、先天性马蹄内翻足或跖屈异常等病理性扁平足、高弓足症状的受试者。

受试者赤足站立下（双足用75%酒精进行消毒），用激光三维扫描获得在半体重下的足印迹。

用足印比值法分析足形。在足印内侧，自足跟内缘至趾关节内缘引一切线，测量足印迹空白区的最宽距离 *AB* 和这条线与足外侧边缘的距离 *ab*，实心区的宽度为 *bc*。计算 ab/bc 的值，$bc = 0$ 时，令 $ab/bc = 1$。当 $ab/bc \geqslant 0.786$ 时，为高弓足，当 $ab/bc \leqslant 0.258$ 时，为扁平足。由足印比例值的大小选择扁平足和高足弓各 12 人（6 男 6 女），足的形态结果见表 1。

表 1　受试者足部基本信息

项目（单位）	高弓足	扁平足
足长（mm）	241. 025 + 11. 664	243. 217 + 13. 486
足跟宽（mm）	±0. 358 + 4. 762	62. 950 + 2. 424
足宽（mm）	95. 783 + 5. 826	91. 283 + 6. 025
脚背高度（mm）	62. 075 + 3. 678	57. 450 + 3. 963 *
足弓指数	0. 257 ± 0. 007	0. 237 ± 0. 016 **
足印迹比值指数	0. 908 ± 0. 098	0. 246 ± 0. 092 **

$*p < \pm 0.05$，$**p < \pm 0.01$。

表 2　步态的基本运动学参数

项目（单位）	高弓足	扁平足
步长（cm）	68. 740 ± 5. 400	68. 158 ± 6. 547
步时（sec）	0. 507 ± 0. 026	0. 517 ± 0. 049
支撑相（%）	60. 784 ± 1. 419	61. 034 ± 2. 566
摆动相（%）	39. 21 ± 1. 419	38. 96 ± 2. 566
跨步长（cm）	137. 000 ± 10. 736	136. 783 ± 12. 989
跨步时间（sec）	1. 014 ± 0. 044	1. 034 ± 0. 095
步频（stride/min）	59. 313 ± 2. 496	57. 680 ± 5. 885
速度（m/sec）	4. 884 ± 0. 528	4. 751 ± 0. 761

测试开始时，受试者赤足站立。受试者走 2 ~ 3 步之后踏上平台。如果在平台上的第一步不完整，或受试者走出了平台或步态有明显的不连续，受试者就会被要求重新进行测试。采集符合测试要求的结果进行记录。结果如表 2 所示。对测试者的 VGRF

和跨步周期进行标准化（体重标准化为 1）。根据步态最小作用量原理（一个足的着地时机在另一个足跨步周期一半处），建立受试者左、右足的 VGRF 和 VGRF 合力与时间的关系，如彩图 7 所示。

结果与讨论

表 1 表明两类弓足在脚背高度方面存在着显著的差异（$p<0.05$），在足弓指数、足印迹比值指数方面也存在显著差异（$p<0.01$）。表 2 显示，足弓形态的显著差异在步频、步长和步速等步态参数方面没有表现出来。彩图 7 中两类足型的 VGRF 也有着相似的分布（当 VGRF 被体重归一化后，两类足型的 VGRF 分布有着惊人的相似）。由于足受到的 VGRF 影响着人体质心在垂直方向上的加速度变化、速度变化、位置变化和机械能变化，因此两类足弓者步行时的人体质心遵循着极为相似的动力学和运动学规律。

总之，我们不能依照步态参数来判断扁平足和高弓足。根据步长、步频和地面反弹力等步态参数，扁平足和高弓足并不会对人的生理和生活质量产生不良的影响的说法也是有道理的。

我们坚信结构影响功能这一原则是正确的。为了找出两类足弓之间的差异，我们对地面反弹力在足上的分布进行了分析。对受试者的体重、足长和站立时间进行标准化处理，得到了足上的 VGRF 分布情况，如彩图 8 所示。

彩图 8 表明非病理性扁平足和高弓足者，VGRF 在足跟部和中部的峰值均存在非常显著的差异（$p<0.01$），在第一跖骨头下方无差异，而在第一近节趾骨头下方的分布存在显著差异（$p<0.05$）。为了分析这些差异对步行的影响，根据两种足型的足弓指数建立了一个简化的足弓结构模型（三角构架），如彩图 9 所示。

彩图 9 表明，步行时，由于两类足弓的结构存在差异，足弓的肌肉所承受的拉力也有所不同。长时间行走时，扁平足更容易引起疲劳，而高弓足者更适合长时间行走，并且不会感到过于劳累。步行时，足底压力的分布和足弓下肌群承受的拉力均存在差异，这种差异符合了结构影响功能的原则。

稳定指数在步态分析中发挥了重要作用。步态的稳定常用两种足型的 VGRF、步长等步态参数的对称性来讨论。从彩图 8 可以看出，两类足型的步态参数的对称性是非常接近的。因此，采用步态参数的对称性来评价步行时的稳定性是有一定局限性的。

对人体运动中的稳定性分析，常用支撑面积指标来评定（如双足站立比单足站立的稳定性要好）。基于这样一种观点，我们来分析步行过程中足底支撑面积的变化。根据步态最小作用量原理，把一个跨步周期中足底的支撑面积标准化，得到两类足型在跨步周期中支撑面积的变化，如彩图 10 所示。

彩图 10 表明，在跨步周期中，两类足型的足底支撑面积的变化存在着差异，为了定量评价这种差异，用以下公式来定量评价步行中足底支撑面积的变化率。

$$\sigma=\frac{1}{fT}\sqrt{\sum_{t=1}^{T}(A(t)-\overline{A})^2} \tag{1}$$

式中，f 为设备的采集频率，T 为受试者的跨步周期时间，$A(t)$ 为跨步周期中某一时刻足底的支撑面积，$\overline{A}$ 为跨步周期中支撑面积的平均值。

由方程（1）的计算得到扁平足和高弓足者在步行中足底支撑面积的变化，分别为：0.147 ± 0.041，0.084 ± 0.034（$p < 0.01$）。人体站立时的稳定性要比行走时好的事实说明方程（1）计算的数值越小，稳定性就越好（最小值为零）。由此可见，方程（1）所表达的两类足型支撑面积的变化率定量描述了步行中的稳定性。

结　论

两类足弓的结构差异是造成步态中足底 VGRF 分布不同的原因。结构和 VGRF 分布的差异影响步行时足部肌肉的收缩力量，这是分析步行中足部肌肉疲劳的重要依据。足底上 VGRF 的分布能够很好地解释扁平足者长时间行走容易出现疼痛的现象。更小的足底支撑面积变化率，使得高弓足者在步行时具有更好的稳定性，而扁平足者由于缺乏稳定性，需要消耗更多的能量。这就很好地解释了扁平足者长时间行走容易疲劳的现象。

综上所述，神秘的人类步态远比我们想象的复杂得多。还有许多未知现象等着我们去发掘。新的步态评价指标的建立无疑是揭示未知现象的重要手段。足弓不仅能够减轻肌肉疲劳，而且能够减少能量的消耗。可以这么说，人类正是因为拥有了独一无二的足弓，才能走出非洲。

老年人的防摔问题一直是步态生物力学研究的重要问题。通过对两类足型的步态分析，扁平足老年人的步态问题应引起重视。另外，足型影响步行这个事实是否意味着我们可以通过鞋的设计来增强扁平足老人的稳定性呢？无论如何，足上的 VGRF 分布和足底支撑面积的变化都是重要的评价指标。

Natural Gaits of the Non-Pathological Flat Foot and High-Arched Foot

Yifang Fan, Yubo Fan, Zhiyu Li, Changsheng Lyu, Donglin Luo
Translated by Zhiyu Li

Abstract: There has been a controversy as to whether or not the non-pathological flat foot and high-arched foot have an effect on human walking activities. The 3D foot scanning system was employed to obtain static footprints from subjects adopting a half-weight-bearing stance. Based upon their footprints, the subjects were divided into two groups: the flat-footed and the high-arched. The plantar pressure measurement system was used to measure and record the subjects' successive natural gaits. Two indices were proposed: distribution of vertical ground reaction force (VGRF) of plantar and the rate of change of footprint areas. Using these two indices to compare the natural gaits of the two subject groups, we found that: ①in stance phase, there is a significant difference ($p < 0.01$) in the distributions of VGRF of plantar; ②in a stride cycle, there is also a significant difference ($p < 0.01$) in the rate of change of footprint area. Our analysis suggests that when walking, the VGRF of the plantar brings greater muscle tension to the flat-footed while a smaller rate of change of footprint area brings greater stability to the high-arched.

Introduction

Foot arches are the result of the successive evolution of basic human activities such as walking. Among the vertebrates, only humans have foot arches. The anatomic structure of one transverse, one medial longitudinal arch and one lateral longitudinal arch can perform the functions of buffering, amortizing, stabilizing and generating propulsion in human activities. Research into the shape, structure, and function of the foot arch has never ceased.

Differences exist in the shape and structure of each individual's foot arches, which is related to factors such as age and weight. The usual methods to collect the foot arch shape include footprinting, X-ray, plantar pressure measurement, laser scanning measurement and MRI scanning. Using indices such as the footprint ratio and foot arch index, we can divide the foot shape into three categories: normal, high-arched and flat. The morphological flat and high-arched foot are asymptomatic. Some research results demonstrate that the non-pathological flatfoot (flexible flat foot) does not affect one's physiology or quality of life and therefore does not require therapy. Others indicate that the flat foot exerts effects on velocity, stamina and/or balance while those possessing the high-arched foot are unsuitable sprint athletes. What difference exists in the gaits of people with the non-pathological flat foot and high-arched foot? Will this difference exert an effect upon walking? If so, how? As yet no satisfactory answers have been provided to these questions.

Shape is a representation of structure. A 3D foot scanner can be used to record the footprint of a person while standing. According to footprint ratio, flat-footed or high-arched subjects can be selected. Structure affects function. The distribution of plantar pressure can qualitatively reflect such information as the structure and function of the foot as well as the control of the whole body in gait. System Gait Analysis has been used to measure the natural gaits of both groups of subjects. Differences in gait between these two groups have been detected by analyzing both the distributions of VGRF of foot and the rate of change of footprint area.

Materials and Methods

This study was approved by the Ethics Committee of Guangzhou Institute of Physical Education. Before the experiments, the subjects were informed of the objectives, requirements and procedures of the experiments. All gave informed written consent to participate in the study.

During the selection process, we examined the prospective subjects with help from the Orthopedics Department of our clinic to screen and exclude subjects with pathological flat foot or high-arched foot symptoms such as talipes calcaneovalgus, congenital talipes equinovarus (CTEV) (club foot), or plantar flexion anomaly.

The subjects were asked to stand bare-footed after both feet had been sterilized with 75% ethyl alcohol, and their footprints of half weight were captured with a 3D laser scanner.

The footprint-ratio method was used to analyze the foot shape. For the inner side of the podogram, a tangent was drawn from the heel to the inner edge of the metatarsophalangeal joint to measure the widest distance AB of the hollow area of the footprint and the distance ab between this line and the edge of the outer side of the foot. The width of the solid area was bc. The value of ab/bc was calculated. When $bc = 0$, let $ab/bc = 1$. When $ab/bc \geqslant 0.786$, it was considered to be high-arched foot; when $ab/bc \leqslant 0.258$, a flat foot. Twelve subjects for each group (flat foot and high-arched foot) were chosen (6 males and 6 females for each group). Their foot shape results are shown in Table 1.

Table 1　Basic information of subjects' feet

Item (unit)	High-arched foot	Flat foot
Foot length (mm)	241. 025 + 11. 664	243. 217 + 13. 486
Heel breadth (mm)	± 0. 358 + 4. 762	62. 950 + 2. 424
Foot breadth (mm)	95. 783 + 5. 826	91. 283 + 6. 025
Hight of instep (mm)	62. 075 + 3. 678	57. 450 + 3. 963 *
Foot arch index	0. 257 ± 0. 007	0. 237 ± 0. 016 * *
Footprint ratio index	0. 908 ± 0. 098	0. 246 ± 0. 092 * *

* $p <$ ± 0. 05,　* * $p <$ ± 0. 01.

Table 2　Basic kinematic parameters of gait

Item (unit)	High-arched foot	Flat foot
Step length (cm)	68. 740 ± 5. 400	68. 158 ± 6. 547
Step time (sec)	0. 507 ± 0. 026	0. 517 ± 0. 049
Stance phase (%)	60. 784 ± 1. 419	61. 034 ± 2. 566
Swing phase (%)	39. 21 ± 1. 419	38. 96 ± 2. 566
Stride length (cm)	137. 000 ± 10. 736	136. 783 ± 12. 989
Stride time (sec)	1. 014 ± 0. 044	1. 034 ± 0. 095
Cadence (stride/min)	59. 313 ± 2. 496	57. 680 ± 5. 885
Velocity (m/sec)	4. 884 ± 0. 528	4. 751 ± 0. 761

The experiment started from the subject's standing position (bare-footed). After walking two or three steps, they stepped onto a platform. If the first step onto the platform was found to be incomplete or if the subject walked off the platform, or if the gait seemed apparently nonsuccessive, the subject was asked to try again. Data that met our requirements were collected. See Table 2. The VGRF and the stride cycle from the subject were standardized (their weight was normalized as 1). According to the least-action principle in gait (the time of initial foot contact falls right in the middle of the other foot's stride cycle), the relationships between the forces (VGRFs of left and right foot and their resultant force) and the time were established. See Fig. 1.

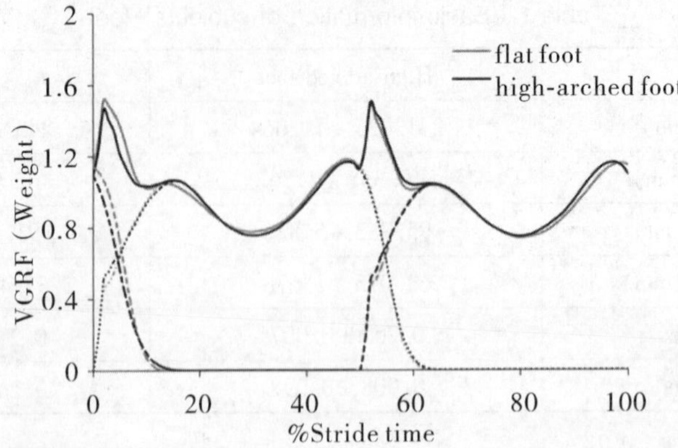

Fig. 1 Relationships between the stride time and VGRF

The blue (deep) dotted lines refer to the VGRFs of the high-arched left and right foot while the blue (deep) solid line refers to the resultant force of the high-arched foot. The red (light) dotted lines stand for the VGRFs of the flat left and right foot while the red (light) solid line for the resultant force of the flat foot. The VGRFs were obtained from the test report of Zebris FDM, the resultant force from $F_{sum}(t) = F_{left}(t) + F_{right}(t + t_0)$. According to the least-action principle in gait, $t_0 = \frac{1}{2}T$, where T is the stride cycle time.

Results and Discussion

Table 1 shows that there exists significant difference in the height of instep ($p < 0.05$), as well as a significant difference ($p < 0.01$) in the foot arch index and in the footprint-ratio index for both groups. Table 2 reveals there is no significant difference of foot arch shape in gait parameters such as stride frequency, length or velocity. Fig. 1 indicates a similar distribution of VGRF for both groups. (When VGRF is standardized according to weight, there is a substantial similarity of VGRF distribution between the two groups) Since the VGRF exerted on the foot affects variations of acceleration, velocity, position and mechanical energy of the body's center of mass vertically, while walking, the center of mass of the two groups shares almost the same kinetic and kinematic characteristics.

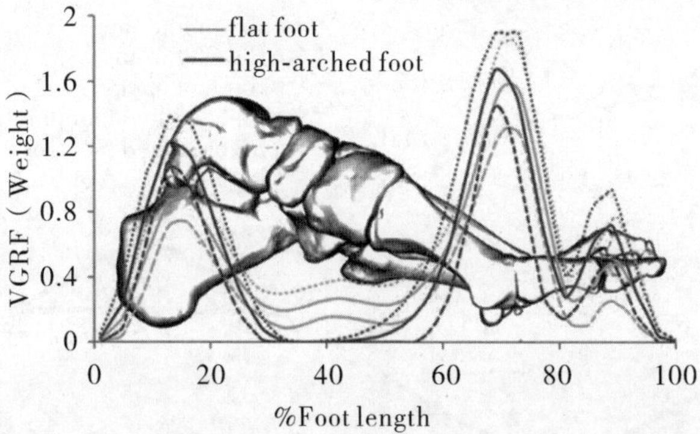

Fig. 2　Distributions of VGRF of foot in stance phase

The blue (deep) solid line refers to the plantar VGRF of the high-arched foot while the blue (deep) ribbon presents the standard error bars of the plantar VGRF of the high-arched foot. The red (light) solid line stands for the plantar VGRF of the flat foot while the red (light) ribbon for the standard error bars of the plantar VGRF of the flat foot. The VGRF has been standardized as 1 by weight, and the stride cycle time and foot length are rated by percentage.

Generally speaking, we cannot identify flat foot or high-arched foot from gait parameters. It is justifiable to say that based upon gait parameters such as stride length, frequency and GRF, neither the flat foot nor the high-arched foot lead to negative effects on physiology or living quality.

We are fully convinced that the principle that structure affects function is truthful. In order to discover the difference between the two foot arch types, we analyzed the distributions of VGRF of foot. The subject's weight, foot length and stance time were standardized. The distributions of VGRF of foot were obtained. See Fig. 2.

Fig. 2 exhibits that for both groups of subjects, significant difference ($p < 0.01$) exists in the peak value of VGRF in the heel and center. Virtually no significant difference can be identified under the first metatarsal bone, but significant difference ($p < 0.05$) can be noticed under the first proximal phalanx bone. In order to analyze how these differences affect walking, a simplified foot arch structure model (triangle truss) was created by a foot arch index from two types of foot arch. See Fig. 3.

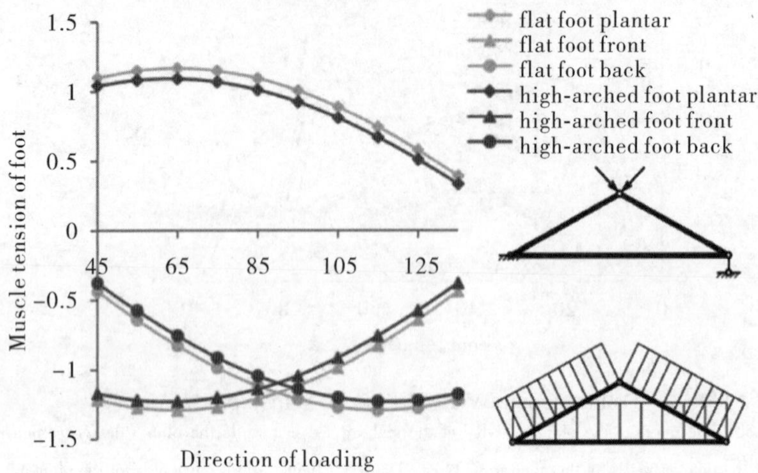

Fig. 3 Relationship between muscle tension and load

The foot arch is here simplified as a triangle truss, of which the truss width (foot length) is standardized as 1, the truss height (foot arch height) is the foot arch index 1/2, and the magnitude of the concentration force is 1. Its direction is changed from 45 degrees to 135 degrees, and its point application is at the top of the truss.

Fig. 3 indicates that when walking, the structural differences of both foot arch types produce differences in the muscle tension of the foot. When taking a long walk, the flat foot group will feel foot fatigue more easily while the high-arched foot group can walk longer and feel less foot fatigue. While walking, difference exists in the distributions of plantar pressure and the tension that the muscle group under the foot arch bears. This difference is again consistent with the principle that structure affects function.

Stability index plays an important role in gait analysis. Gait stability has been widely discussed by using the symmetry of gait parameters such as the VGRF or the stride length of both types of foot. Fig. 2 shows that the symmetry of gait parameters of both types is very close, indicating the limitation of using such a method to evaluate gait stability.

Stability analysis of human movement can often be evaluated by the stance area index (for example, the stability is greater when standing on both feet than on one foot) From this viewpoint, we analyzed the variations of plantar stance area while walking. According to the least-action principle in gait, when the plantar stance area of one stride cycle is standardized, the variation of the plantar stance area of both types of foot can be obtained. See Fig. 4.

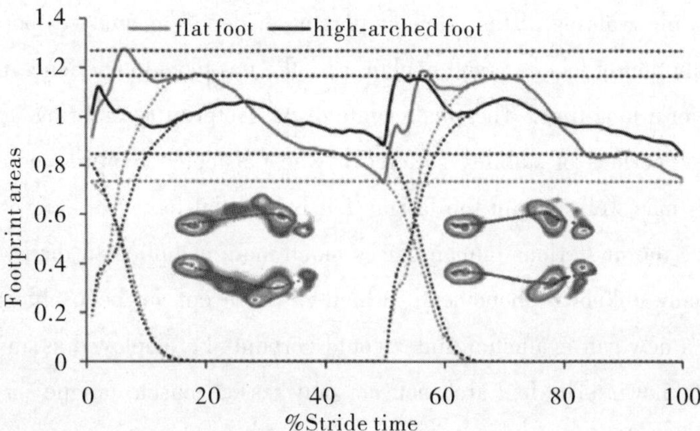

Fig. 4　Relationship between the footprint areas and stride time

The blue (deep) dotted lines stand for the plantar stance areas of the high-arched left and right foot while the blue (deep) solid line for the sum of plantar stance area of the high-arched foot. The blue (deep) horizontal dotted line presents the variation range of the sum of plantar stance area of the high-arched foot. The red (light) dotted lines stand for the plantar stance areas of the flat left and right foot while the red (light) solid line for the sum of plantar stance area of the flat foot. The red (light) horizontal dotted line presents the variation range of the sum of plantar stance area of the flat-footed. The footprint area is derived from the test report of Zebris FDM and the sum of plantar stance area is obtained from $F_{\text{sum}}(t) = F_{\text{left}}(t) + F_{\text{right}}(t + t_0)$. According to the least-action principle in gait, $t_0 = \frac{1}{2}T$, T stands for the stride cycle time.

Fig. 4 shows that in a stride cycle difference exists in the variations of plantar stance area from both types of subjects. In order to evaluate this difference quantitatively, the following equation is applied to assess the rate of plantar stance area while walking:

$$\sigma = \frac{1}{fT}\sqrt{\sum_{t=1}^{T}(A(t) - \overline{A})^2} \qquad (1)$$

where f stands for the collection frequency of the equipment, T, the stride cycle time of the subject, $A(t)$, the plantar stance area at a certain moment in a stride cycle and $\overline{A}$, the average value of footprint area in a stride cycle.

Calculation from Eq. (1) provides the variations of footprint areas for the flat-footed and the high-arched groups respectively while walking: 0.147 ± 0.041, 0.084 ± 0.034 ($p < 0.01$). The fact that the stability is greater when standing than when walking reveals that the smaller the value from the calculation of Eq. (1), the better the stability (the minimal value is zero). Accordingly, the rate of change of footprint area of both types resulting from Eq. (1) quantitatively describes stability while walking.

Conclusion

The structural difference in these types of foot arch causes significant difference of VGRF distribution of foot. The differences in structure and in VGRF distribution have an effect on foot muscle tension while walking. This offers important evidence to analyze foot muscle fatigue. The VGRF distribution of foot can well explain why the flat-footed experience pain more readily when they walk for a long time. The smaller rate of the footprint areas brings greater stability to the high-arched. The lack of stability suffered by the flat-footed requires more consumption of energy, and thus may well explain the fatigue felt by the flat-footed on long walks.

In summary, the mysterious human gait is much more complicated than we had expected. There exist so many unknown phenomena, which we have not yet been able to discover. The establishment of a new gait evaluation index could certainly be employed as an important means to disclose the unknown. The foot arch can not only lessen muscle fatigue, it can also reduce energy consumption. It was the unique foot arch that brought the human being walk out of Africa (so to speak).

How to prevent seniors from falling has always been a key issue in the biomechanical research of gait. The analysis of these two foot types may equally arouse attention to the gait of flat-footed seniors. In addition, does the fact that walking can be affected by foot type mean that we can enhance the gait stability for flat-footed seniors by the design of their shoes? In any case, the VGRF distribution of foot and the rate of change of footprint area can be employed as important evaluation indices.

Selected Reading 3

骨组织最优化原则

范毅方　樊瑜波　李知宇　Mushtaq Loan　吕长生　张　博

摘要：骨骼塑形及重建是一个优化过程，至今尚未有一个统一的理论或模式支撑。我们以 64 排 CT 扫描测量 384 块活体足骨，发现骨骼的质心大致与其形心相叠。这一现象表明，非均质材料（如骨骼）的优化过程，都遵循与均质材料一样的质心与形心重合定律。基于这一原则，我们建立了一个揭示密质骨质心和形心之间关系的指标，以及一个表明组织密度和分布半径之间关系的指标。通过这些指标来评估骨骼的强度，我们有了新的发现。

前　言

骨骼大小、形状和结构的优化是一种生理过程，而此过程是一个适应性反应。骨组织的适应性反应由各种内在活动产生，如骨骼构建与重塑，这些都最大化了骨骼的承载力。然而，对于骨骼的这些适应性变化遵循何种力学原理仍未有定论。

沃尔夫的骨骼适应性变化定律是骨骼塑形重建研究的理论基础，被弗罗斯特用于力学调控理论而得以改进，该理论表明了骨骼在组织水平上的转变。其机制的论述应该从细胞、分子或者基因层面来进行，虽然无论从哪个层面来说，都没有统一的理论和模式作为支撑。另外，研究骨骼承载力的复杂程度，在确定最少骨质是否能最大限度地承受外部荷载时，有相当的难度（比如目标优化分析中的目标功能或约束方程）。

我们假设非均质骨骼的优化过程遵循与均质材料一样的质心（COM）与形心（COS）重合定律。用亚毫米精度螺旋 CT 扫描了 32 个活体足，分析了 384 块足骨（每个足 12 块）的质心与形心的位置关系，结果验证了我们的假设是正确的。根据骨骼质心和形心叠加原理，我们利用一种评估方法测定了骨骼的强度。由评价指标得出的结果不同于根据其他评估方法得出的指标，如骨密度（BMD）。

材料和方法

【设备】

测试设备为荷兰飞利浦 Brilliance 64 排扫描仪，由珠江医院影像处理中心提供。扫描设定为：骨组织窗；电源功率：120kV；像素大小：0. 50mm；层距：0. 50mm。扫描过程：从脚部由上至下进行横切面扫描。

【软件】

测试所用的软件包括免费试用版的 SMSolver（Windows 系统的 2.5 版本结构力学求解器，http://www.civil.edu.cn/sms/），由交互式医学影像控制系统（Mimics，版本 10）完成三维建模，由 SPSS（版本 12）进行统计分析（上述软件由教育部生物力学与力生物学重点实验室提供）。

【受试者】

我们共收集了 384 块骨头的数据——均来自排球运动员（平均身高为 183.94 ± 3.90cm，平均体重为 69.80 ± 5.20kg，平均年龄为 21.88 ± 0.99 岁）和摔跤运动员（平均身高为 168.00 ± 5.68cm，平均体重为 65.52 ± 5.16kg，平均年龄为 21.00 ± 2.78 岁），例如，12 种足骨，每种各 32 块足骨，包括：跟骨、距骨、足舟骨、骰骨、外侧楔骨、中间楔骨、内侧楔骨、第一跖骨、第二跖骨，第三跖骨、第四跖骨、第五跖骨。

受试者为选自本学院的男排球运动员，以及选自省体校的男摔跤运动员。在测试前已确认各个对象已接受超过五年的专业训练。测试前已获取了各人的病史，并对他们进行了 X 光检查，排除了带有如足部病理变化、畸形或损伤的对象，以确保各人身体状况达到测试要求。

【概念界定】

设体微元（VE）位置坐标（x，y，z）对应于设备坐标系，g 代表体微元的灰度值，N 代表骨骼体微元数量，M 代表断层影像的体微元数量。在公式的辅助下，骨骼的物理量如质心和形心由下列公式定义：

$$\rho = \frac{\sum_{1}^{N} \rho_i}{N} \tag{1}$$

其中，$\rho_i = \dfrac{g_i}{g_w}$，$g_i$ 代表第 i 个体微元的灰度值，g_w 代表水的灰度值。设备经校准，空气灰度值调节至 0，因此水的灰度值为 1024。

骨骼形心定义为：

$$(x_s, y_s, z_s) = \left(\frac{\sum_{1}^{N} x_i}{N}, \frac{\sum_{1}^{N} y_i}{N}, \frac{\sum_{1}^{N} z_i}{N} \right) \tag{2}$$

骨骼质心定义为：

$$(x_c, y_c, z_c) = \left(\frac{\sum_{1}^{N} x_i \rho_i}{\sum_{1}^{N} \rho_i}, \frac{\sum_{1}^{N} y_i \rho_i}{\sum_{1}^{N} \rho_i}, \frac{\sum_{1}^{N} z_i \rho_i}{\sum_{1}^{N} \rho_i} \right) \tag{3}$$

形心与质心间的距离为

$$d_{cs} = \sqrt{(x_s - x_c)^2 + (y_s - y_c)^2 + (z_s - z_c)^2} \tag{4}$$

对于骨骼的 CT 数据，不妨设 $z_i = j$。当 j 为不变量，那么（$x_{(j)i}$，$y_{(j)i}$）代表第 j 个断层体微元集合，$\rho_{(j)i}$ 代表体微元密度，M_j 为断层体微元量。由公式 $\left(\dfrac{\sum_{1}^{M_j} x_{(j)i}}{M_j}, \dfrac{\sum_{1}^{M_j} y_{(j)i}}{M_j} \right)$ 算出横截面影像形心，由公式 $\left(\dfrac{\sum_{1}^{M_j} x_{(j)i} \rho_i}{\sum_{1}^{M_j} \rho_{(j)i}}, \dfrac{\sum_{1}^{M_j} y_{(j)i} \rho_i}{\sum_{1}^{M_j} \rho_{(j)i}} \right)$ 算出其质心，

由公式 $\sqrt{\left(\frac{\sum_1^{M_j} x_{(j)i}}{M_j} - \frac{\sum_1^{M_j} x_{(j)i}\rho_i}{\sum_1^{M_j} \rho_{(j)i}}\right)^2 + \left(\frac{\sum_1^{M_j} y_{(j)i}}{M_j} - \frac{\sum_1^{M_j} x_{(j)i}\rho_i}{\sum_1^{M_j} \rho_{(j)i}}\right)^2}$ 算出两点距离。

骨组织半径为

$$r = \frac{1}{N}\sum_1^N \sqrt{(x_i - x_s)^2 + (y_i - y_s)^2 + (z_i - z_s)^2} \tag{5}$$

相同密度的骨组织半径为

$$r_k = \frac{1}{Q}\sum_1^N \sqrt{(x_{(k)i} - x_s)^2 + (y_{(k)i} - y_s)^2 + (z_{(k)i} - z_s)^2} \tag{6}$$

其中 $k=\rho_i$。当 k 为常量，指代相同密度的骨组织。例如，当 $k=1.1$（g/cm^3），($x_{(1.1)i}$，$y_{(1.1)i}$，$z_{(1.1)i}$）表示一个 1.1 密度的体微元坐标。Q 为当密度为 1.1 时的体微元量。

【伦理声明】

本研究获得广州体育学院伦理委员会批准。受试者均完全知晓并自愿参与本项研究，签署书面知情同意书。

结果与讨论

下面我们把足骨分类，计算体积、表面积和骨密度。测量结果见表 1。

骨密度是分析骨骼强度的一个重要指标。表 1 说明在两组运动员的足骨对比中并不存在明显差异。这正确吗？

表 1　足骨体积、表面积和骨密度（均值 ± 标准差）

项目	摔跤运动员			排球运动员		
	体积（cm^3）	面积（cm^2）	密度（g/cm^3）	体积（cm^3）	面积（cm^2）	密度（g/cm^3）
跟骨	71.01 ±8.46	107.39 ±8.83	1.47 ±0.04	83.94 ±6.05	120.70 ±5.56	1.49 ±0.05
距骨	38.30 ±4.33	71.38 ±5.41	1.63 ±0.04	43.87 ±3.33	80.11 ±5.97	1.65 ±0.04
足舟骨	11.45 ±1.39	31.21 ±2.73	1.5 ±0.04	13.44 ±1.51	34.78 ±3.00	1.58 ±0.05
骰骨	13.87 ±1.61	33.14 ±2.77	1.4 ±0.04	15.09 ±2.69	35.24 ±4.78	1.47 ±0.05
外侧楔骨	5.91 ±0.69	19.09 ±1.56	1.51 ±0.04	6.79 ±0.61	20.99 ±1.28	1.53 ±0.06
中间楔骨	4.43 ±0.66	15.69 ±1.56	1.59 ±0.04	5.20 ±0.44	17.5 ±1.00	1.64 ±0.06
内侧楔骨	10.7 ±1.48	28.60 ±2.73	1.52 ±0.03	12.20 ±1.04	31.02 ±1.91	1.58 ±0.05
第一跖骨	16.94 ±2.23	44.90 ±3.89	1.62 ±0.05	20.93 ±2.25	51.94 ±3.47	1.65 ±0.05
第二跖骨	9.01 ±1.29	33.72 ±3.25	1.73 ±0.07	11.65 ±0.77	40.5 ±2.08	1.7 ±0.08
第三跖骨	7.72 ±0.58	30.23 ±1.60	1.70 ±0.05	8.99 ±1.07	34.50 ±2.61	1.68 ±0.07
第四跖骨	7.47 ±0.78	28.80 ±2.19	1.6 ±0.04	8.88 ±0.92	32.97 ±2.05	1.6 ±0.05
第五跖骨	8.83 ±1.09	30.92 ±2.64	1.72 ±0.05	9.65 ±1.07	33.73 ±2.49	1.71 ±0.05

均质材料的质心与形心完全重合，而非均质材料则不会如此精确。骨骼就是一种典型的非均质材料。CT 扫描把骨头划分为一个有限体微元集合。每个体微元和灰度值的坐标都可用。这使得计算骨质心与形心变得比较容易。设骨形心为坐标原点，建立骨骼质心与形心的位置关系。见彩图 11。

我们知道足舟骨与跟骨在体积、形态与密度等方面都存在明显的差异。而彩图 11 中，足舟骨和跟骨质心与形心之间的位置关系并无显著差异（$p > 0.05$）。在第一跖骨和第二跖骨间存在形态的相似性，而两者的质心与形心的位置关系则有明显的差异（$p < 0.01$）。因此，在测试精度范围内，非均质骨的质心与形心位置也的确具有高度重合现象。这种现象并不受骨的体积、密度或形态等因素影响。

当截面通过对称几何体的形心时，截面的形心和几何形心都在同一位置上。设骨的形心为坐标原点，即建立通过坐标原点的断层影像的质心和形心的关系。如彩图 12 所示。

彩图 12 中 a 图表明通过骨的形心的断层影像的质心与形心也高度重合，b 图表明断面和骨体形心存在差异。彩图 11 和彩图 12 表明质心和形心的高度重合不仅存在于骨体，也存在于横截面上。我们应该注意到，用截面的形心来决定骨的形心这一举措是很冒险的，因为骨的形态是不对称的。

骨骼被简化为桁梁结构，由内外两个正方形组成。外方形指代密质骨，内方形指代松质骨。在荷载和约束不变的情况下，结构强度随内部方形位置变化而变化。如彩图 13 所示。

彩图 13 表明，当受到相同的限制与负荷，内外方形形心高度重合的结构在剪力与力矩载荷量方面，优于缺乏如此高度重合的结构。因此，当平衡力的力作用线经过物体质心时，该结构的承载力达到了最大值。

虽然骨的形态和结构比彩图 13 的桁梁结构更加复杂，但是活体骨中的限制和负荷与彩图 13 中的结构相同——它们都由非平衡力起作用。因此可以假设，当形心（由骨表面形态决定）与质心（由骨密度分布决定）处于同一位置时，骨结构达到最佳强度。

总之，要达到骨功能要求，骨的体积、形态和密度都需要发生适应性变化。在此过程中，往往遵循质心高度重合形心的最优结构原则。相同地，功能决定结构也适用于最大限度的强度与最小量的材料之间的联系，或机械稳定性理论，或骨适应优化过程，以及沃尔夫定理（亦即骨转化定理），而质心和形心的高度重合则是一个定量的描述。

为什么质心与形心的高度重合是一个定量描述？以下所建立的关系可基于这样一个事实：密质骨的强度远大于松质骨；骨组织密度分布（与骨形心相关）与骨强度相关：①在密质骨形心与骨形心的关系当中，密质骨形心到骨形心的距离由骨组织半径进行标准化；②在骨组织密度与分布半径（与骨形心分布半径有关）当中，相同的密度组织半径由骨组织半径进行标准化。如彩图 14 所示。

彩图 14a 中，排球运动员的跟骨密质骨形心到骨形心之间的距离比摔跤运动员的要短，两者间距有显著的差异（$p < 0.05$），与表 1 的测量相反，表 1 中并未观测到任

何显著差异。我们观察到第五跖骨密质骨形心到骨形心的间距有类似走势。从表 1 第一至第五跖骨中，我们可以发现相似的走势，而最低密度出现在第一跖骨，这听上去并不合理。这体现了骨密度评价指标的局限性。例如，体积和关节部位的因素都有可能影响到骨密度。彩图 14a 中，两组运动员第一跖骨密质骨的形心和骨形心的间距最短。

排球运动员起跳后，制动姿态对跟骨会产生很大冲击。彩图 14b 中，从密质骨密度的角度来说，排球运动员跟骨的分布半径逐渐大于摔跤运动员，尤其与骨髓和松质骨组织的分布半径结果相比时（密度 $\rho<1.14$ 时，为骨髓，当 $1.14\leqslant\rho\leqslant1.65$ 时，松质骨保持原状，$\rho>1.65$ 时，为密质骨），这种差异十分显著。摔跤运动员激烈的身体角逐给其第五跖骨的前、后、左、右各个方向都造成了巨大的冲击。从密质骨密度的角度来说，摔跤运动员的第五跖骨的分布半径会逐渐大于排球运动员。

彩图 14 表明，骨质心与形心高度重合的定理、密质骨形心与骨形心的关系，以及组织密度与分布半径的关系的建立给骨强度的研究提供了一个崭新的方法。

质心与形心之间的高度重合现象会给生物力学研究带来怎样的启发呢？我们用骨骼 CT 数据分析另外的足部非骨组织的质心与形心。如彩图 15 所示。

彩图 15 表明，足部的踝部皮肤、踝关节的非骨组织，以及骨体形心周边的 ROI（Region of Interest）的质心与形心互相高度重合。细分下去，我们得知，如果细胞的质心与形心也遵循这个高度重合定律，那么便可建立一种力学的新方法用以研究像细胞生长与分裂这样的细胞活动。

一个连续闭合的几何体的形心与该几何体表面形态的形心高度重合。因此可通过细胞表面的数值模型获得细胞的形心数据。根据质心的力学原理（即内力并不能改变系统的质心运动），如果细胞受力，那么便可获得细胞的运动学特性。另外，我们可以根据细胞的运动学特性分析细胞外部力学信号的特征。当细胞形态不对称时，其几何的不变性及惯量主轴的唯一性可应用于研究细胞的转动力学问题。

结 论

骨骼的生理活动是一个优化过程。在这样一个适应性过程中，始终不变的是质心与形心高度重合的最优结构原则。其力学意义在于利用该优化结构去承载外部负荷。

我们提出骨组织形心与其骨形心间距这样一个概念，发现了间距（即密质骨形心与其骨形心之间的距离）与荷载类型的关系。这种关系与现象表明——冲击强度使密质骨形心向骨形心移动。这种位移标志着骨骼结构的功能性适应。中老年人的生理活动基本处于重构状态。当他们的骨质逐渐退化疏松，关注体育运动是否能减轻骨质流失，以此改变这种趋势尤为重要。这是一项意义重大、有价值的研究。

随着三维成像技术的进步，如果质心与形心高度重合的现象同样出现在细胞中，本文提出的原则将会在细胞动力学的研究中起到十分重要的作用。

Optimal Principle of Bone Structure

Yifang Fan, Yubo Fan, Zhiyu Li, Mushtaq Loan, Changsheng Lyu, Zhang Bo
Translated by Zhiyu Li

Abstract: Bone modeling and remodeling is an optimization process where no agreement has been reached regarding a unified theory or model. We measured 384 pieces of bone in vivo by 64-slice CT and discovered that the bone's center of mass approximately superposes its centroid of shape. This phenomenon indicates that the optimization process of nonhomogeneous materials such as bone follows the same law of superposition of center of mass and centroid of shape as that of homogeneous materials. Based upon this principle, an index revealing the relationship between the center of mass and centroid of shape of the compact bone is proposed. Another index revealing the relationship between tissue density and distribution radius is followed. Applying these indexes to evaluate the strength of bone, we have some new findings.

Introduction

The optimization of bone's size, shape and structure is a physical process and the process is an adaptive response. The adaptive responses of bone tissue generated by activities such as bone modeling and remodeling maximize its bearing load. However, it remains uncertain what principles of mechanics these adaptive changes of bone follow.

Wolff's law on bone's adaptive changes served as a prelude to the study of bone modeling and remodeling. Wolff's law was refined by Frost who promoted his mechanostat theory, describing the bone's transformation on the tissue level. An ideal description of its mechanism should be studied from the perspectives of cell, molecule or gene though no matter from which perspective, no agreement on a unified theory or model has been reached. What's more, the complexity of bone's loading has brought difficulties (such as the target function or constraint equation involved in the target optimization analysis) in defining whether the minimal material can sustain the maximal loading.

We assume that the optimization process of the nonhomogeneous bone follows the same law of superposition of its center of mass (COM) and centroid of shape (COS) of the homogeneous material. A spiral CT scanning with an accuracy of sub-millimeter is conducted to 32 feet in vivo. An analysis to the positional relationship between the COM and COS of 384 pieces of foot bone (12 pieces from each foot) verifies our assumption. According to the principle of superposition between the bone's COM and COS, an evaluation method is put forward to evaluate the bone strength. The result from our evaluation indexes is different from those derived from other evaluation methods such as the BMD (bone mineral density).

Materials and Methods

【Equipment】

The test equipment was Brilliance 64-slice Scanner by Philips, Netherlands, provided by Image Processing Center of Zhujiang Hospital. Scan settings were: frame bone tissue; power: 120kV; pixel size: 0.50mm; layer distance: 0.50mm. The scanning was conducted along both feet transect, from top to bottom.

【Software】

Software applied included a free trial of SMSolver (the structural mechanics solver for Windows, Version 2.5, http: // www. civil. edu. cn/sms/). The three-dimensional model was constructed by Mimics (Version 10) and the statistical analysis was performed by SPSS (Version 12) (provided by the Key Laboratory of Biomechanics and Mechanobiology of Ministry of Education).

【Subjects】

Altogether, we collected data of 384 pieces of bone—both from the volleyballers (with average height, weight and age of 183.94 ± 3.90cm, 69.80 ± 5.20kg and 21.88 ± 0.99year, respectively) and wrestlers (with average height, weight and age of 168.00 ± 5.68 cm, 65.52 ± 5.16kg and 21.00 ± 2.78year, respectively), i. e., 32 pieces of 12 types of bones: calcaneus, talus, navicular, cuboid, lateral cuneiform, intermediate cuneiform, medial cuneiform, first metatarsal, second metatarsal, third metatarsal, fourth metatarsal and the fifth metatarsal.

The subjects were male volleyballers from our institute and male wrestlers from Provincial Sports School. It was confirmed before the test that every subject had been trained as a professional athlete for more than five years. Before the test, each subject's medical history was inquired and all the subjects were x-rayed to exclude subjects with diseases such as foot pathological change, deformity or injury to make sure that their physical conditions meet the requirements of the test.

【Definition of the Concept】

Consider the volume element's (VE) position coordinates (x, y, z) with respect to equipment coordinate system. g stands for VE's gray value, N, the number of VE of the bone, M, the number of VE of the cross-sectional image. With the help of the following equation, bone's physical quantities such as the COM or COS are defined by the following equation.

The bone's density is defined as

$$\rho = \frac{\sum_{1}^{N} \rho_i}{N} \tag{1}$$

where $\rho_i = \frac{g_i}{g_w}$, g_i stands for the gray value of the i-th VE, g_w stands for the gray value of water. The equipment has been calibrated, the gray value of the air is set to 0 and that of the water is 1024.

The bone's COS is defined as

$$(x_s, y_s, z_s) = \left(\frac{\sum_1^N x_i}{N}, \frac{\sum_1^N y_i}{N}, \frac{\sum_1^N z_i}{N}\right) \tag{2}$$

The bone's COM is defined as

$$(x_c, y_c, z_c) = \left(\frac{\sum_1^N x_i\rho_i}{\sum_1^N \rho_i}, \frac{\sum_1^N y_i\rho_i}{\sum_1^N \rho_i}, \frac{\sum_1^N z_i\rho_i}{\sum_1^N \rho_i}\right) \tag{3}$$

The distance between the bone's COS and COM is

$$d_{cs} = \sqrt{(x_s - x_c)^2 + (y_s - y_c)^2 + (z_s - z_c)^2} \tag{4}$$

To the CT data of bone, let's set $z_i = j$. When j is set as a constant value, then $(x_{(j)i}, y_{(j)i})$ stands for the collection of the j-th cross-sectional VE, $\rho_{(j)i}$ stands for the density of VE, M_j stands for the number of cross-sectional VE. Calculate the cross-sectional image COS by $\left(\frac{\sum_1^{M_j} x_{(j)i}}{M_j}, \frac{\sum_1^{M_j} y_{(j)i}}{M_j}\right)$, its COM by $\left(\frac{\sum_1^{M_j} x_{(j)i}\rho_i}{\sum_1^{M_j} \rho_{(j)i}}, \frac{\sum_1^{M_j} y_{(j)i}\rho_i}{\sum_1^{M_j} \rho_{(j)i}}\right)$, and the distance between the two points by $\sqrt{\left(\frac{\sum_1^{M_j} x_{(j)i}}{M_j} - \frac{\sum_1^{M_j} x_{(j)i}\rho_i}{\sum_1^{M_j} \rho_{(j)i}}\right)^2 + \left(\frac{\sum_1^{M_j} y_{(j)i}}{M_j} - \frac{\sum_1^{M_j} x_{(j)i}\rho_i}{\sum_1^{M_j} \rho_{(j)i}}\right)^2}$

The bone tissue's radius is

$$r = \frac{1}{N}\sum_1^N \sqrt{(x_i - x_s)^2 + (y_i - y_s)^2 + (z_i - z_s)^2} \tag{5}$$

The same density tissue's radius is

$$r_k = \frac{1}{Q}\sum_1^N \sqrt{(x_{(k)i} - x_s)^2 + (y_{(k)i} - y_s)^2 + (z_{(k)i} - z_s)^2} \tag{6}$$

where $k = \rho_i$. When k is set as a constant value, it refers to the same density tissue of the bone. For example, when $k = 1.1$ (g/cm^3), $(x_{(1.1)i}, y_{(1.1)i}, z_{(1.1)i})$ indicates the VE's coordinates of a density of 1.1. Q is the number of VEs when the density is 1.1.

【Ethics Statement】

The study received approval from the Ethical Committee of Guangzhou Institute of Physical Education. The subjects provided fully informed consent to participate in this study by signing a written consent form.

Results and Discussion

Following, we separated foot bone to calculate the volume, surface area and BMD. The results for the extracted measurements are shown in Table 1.

BMD is an important index to analyze bone strength. Table 1 shows that no significant difference exists in the foot bone of both groups of athletics. Is that true?

Table 1　Foot bone volume, surface area and bone density (Mean ± SD)

Item	Wrestler			Volleyballer		
	Volume (cm^3)	Area (cm^2)	Density (g/cm^3)	Volume (cm^3)	Area (cm^2)	Density (g/cm^3)
Calcaneus	71. 01 ±8. 46	107. 39 ±8. 83	1. 47 ±0. 04	83. 94 ±6. 05	120. 70 ±5. 56	1. 49 ±0. 05
Talus	38. 30 ±4. 33	71. 38 ±5. 41	1. 63 ±0. 04	43. 87 ±3. 33	80. 11 ±5. 97	1. 65 ±0. 04
Navicular	11. 45 ±1. 39	31. 21 ±2. 73	1. 5 ±0. 04	13. 44 ±1. 51	34. 78 ±3. 00	1. 58 ±0. 05
Cuboid	13. 87 ±1. 61	33. 14 ±2. 77	1. 4 ±0. 04	15. 09 ±2. 69	35. 24 ±4. 78	1. 47 ±0. 05
Lateral cuneiform	5. 91 ±0. 69	19. 09 ±1. 56	1. 51 ±0. 04	6. 79 ±0. 61	20. 99 ±1. 28	1. 53 ±0. 06
Intermediate cuneiform	4. 43 ±0. 66	15. 69 ±1. 56	1. 59 ±0. 04	5. 20 ±0. 44	17. 5 ±1. 00	1. 64 ±0. 06
Medial cuneiform	10. 7 ±1. 48	28. 60 ±2. 73	1. 52 ±0. 03	12. 20 ±1. 04	31. 02 ±1. 91	1. 58 ±0. 05
First metatarsal	16. 94 ±2. 23	44. 90 ±3. 89	1. 62 ±0. 05	20. 93 ±2. 25	51. 94 ±3. 47	1. 65 ±0. 05
Second metatarsal	9. 01 ±1. 29	33. 72 ±3. 25	1. 73 ±0. 07	11. 65 ±0. 77	40. 5 ±2. 08	1. 7 ±0. 08
Third metatarsal	7. 72 ±0. 58	30. 23 ±1. 60	1. 70 ±0. 05	8. 99 ±1. 07	34. 50 ±2. 61	1. 68 ±0. 07
Fourth metatarsal	7. 47 ±0. 78	28. 80 ±2. 19	1. 6 ±0. 04	8. 88 ±0. 92	32. 97 ±2. 05	1. 6 ±0. 05
Fifth metatarsal	8. 83 ±1. 09	30. 92 ±2. 64	1. 72 ±0. 05	9. 65 ±1. 07	33. 73 ±2. 49	1. 71 ±0. 05

The COM and COS of homogeneous materials superpose exactly one another while those of non-homogeneous materials do not. Bone is a typical non-homogeneous material. Using CT scanning, bone will be separated into a collection of finite VE. The coordinates of each VE and gray value can be provided. This makes it easy to calculate the bone's COM and COS. Setting the bone's COS as the coordinate origin, the positional relationship between the bone's COM and COS can be established. See Fig. 1.

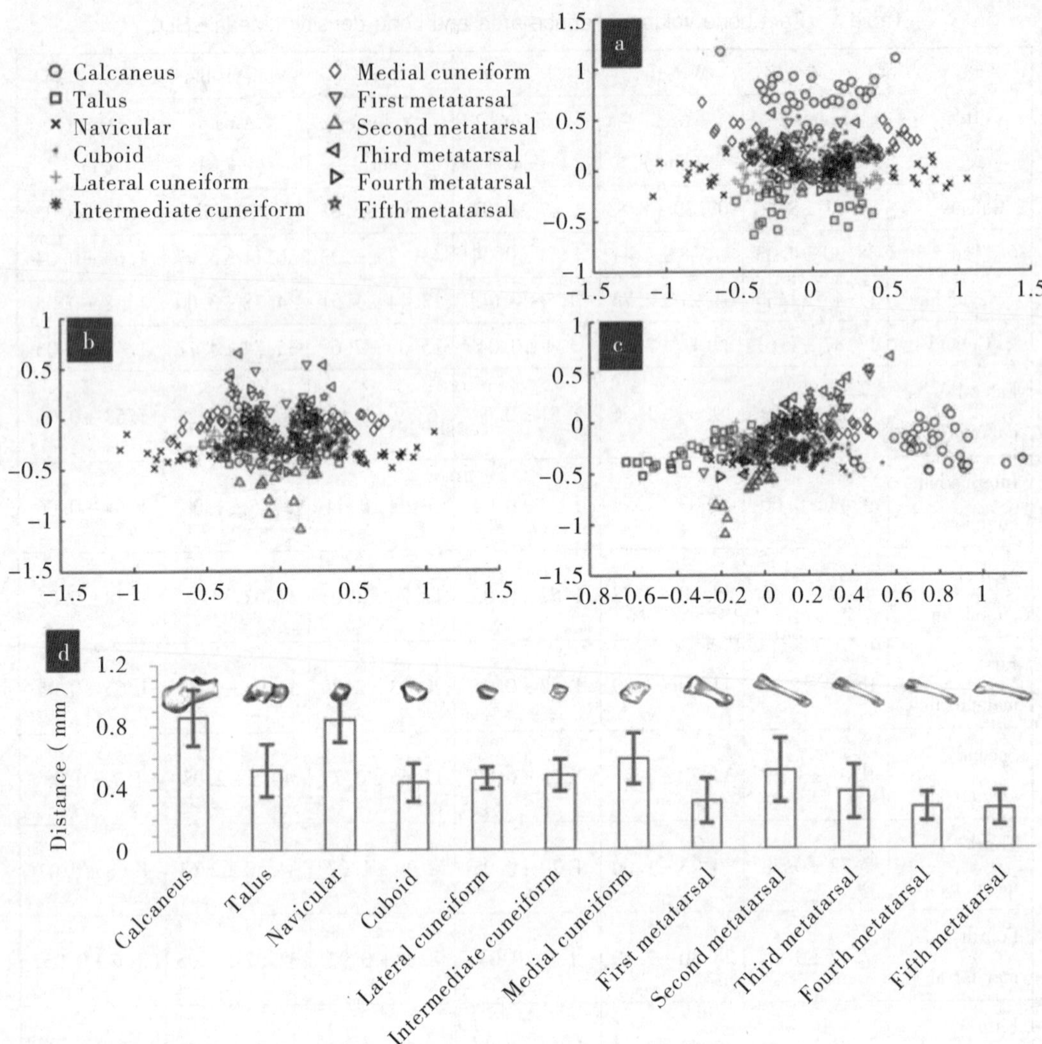

Fig. 1 Positional relationship between the bones' COM and COS

Fig. 1a reveals positional relationship between COM and COS on $x-y$ plane; Fig. 1b reveals positional relationship between COM and COS on $x-z$ plane; Fig. 1c reveals positional relationship between COM and COS on $y-z$ plane; Fig. 1d reveals distance between COM and COS. The bones' COS and COM are derived from the calculation of Eq. (2) and Eq. (3). When choosing coordinate system with origin at COM, the coordinates of COS relative to COM can be derived as $(x_s-x_c,\ y_s-y_c,\ z_s-z_c)$. By $(x_s-x_c,\ y_s-y_c)$, $(y_s-y_c,\ z_s-z_c)$ and $(x_s-x_c,\ z_s-z_c)$, 384 pieces' bone coordinates of COS with respect to COM can be located on $x-y$, $y-z$ and $x-z$ planes. See Fig. 1a, Fig. 1b and Fig. 1c (unit is mm). Through Eq. (4), the distance of these 384 pieces of bones' COS to the COM can be calculated, resulting in Fig. 1d.

It is known that significant difference exists in the size, density and shape of the navicular and calcaneus. However, Fig. 1 shows that there is no significant difference ($p>0.05$) in the positional superposition of the COM and COS of both. Shape similarity does exist between the first and second metatarsal, but there is significant difference ($p<0.01$) in the positional superposition of the COM and COS of both. Therefore, within the range of measurement accuracy, the phenomenon of superposition does exist in the positions of the COM and COS of non-homogeneous bone. It is furthermore unaffected by such different factors as bone size, density or shape.

When the cross-section passes through the COS of a symmetrical geometry, the COS of the cross-section and the COS of the geometry are in the same position. Setting the coordinate origin as the bone's COS, the relationship between the COM and COS of the cross-sectional image through the coordinate origin is set up. See Fig. 2.

Fig. 2a suggests that the COM and COS of the cross-sectional image through the COS of the bone also superpose. Fig. 2b shows difference in the COS position of the cross-section and that of the whole bone. Fig. 1 and Fig. 2 show that superposition of COM and COS does not only exist in the whole bone, but also in the cross-section. Attention should be paid to the fact that it is risky to determine the bone's COS by the cross-section's COS since the bone's shape is asymmetric.

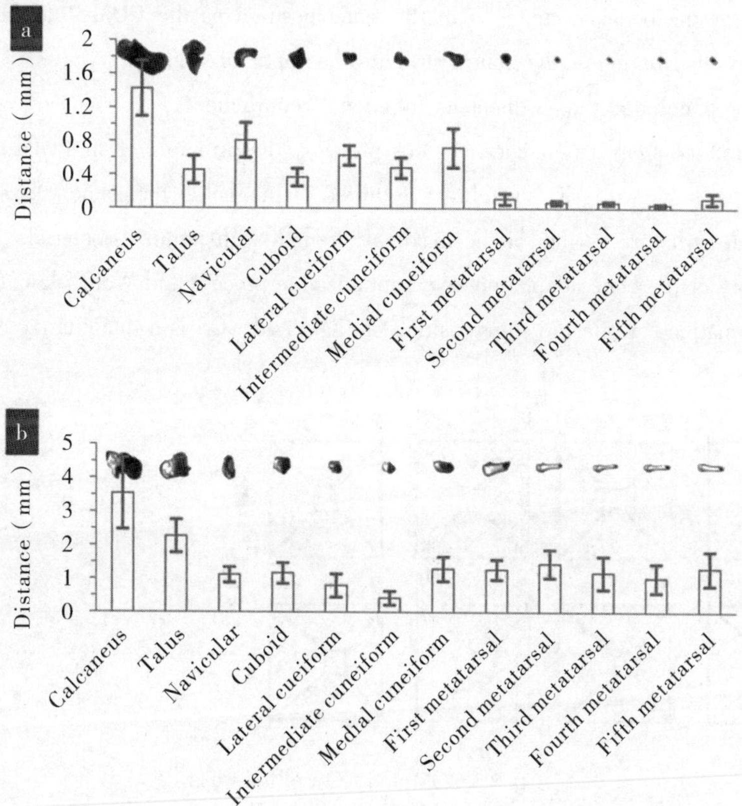

Fig. 2 Relationship between the COM and COS of the cross-sectional image

Fig. 2a reveals positional relationship between the COM and COS of the cross-sectional image through the coordinate origin; Fig. 2b reveals positional relationship between the COS of the cross-section and the COS of the bone. When the position value of the cross-sectional VE at z axis is approximately equal to the bone's COS, i. e., $z_i \approx z_s$, the cross-section is the tomography that goes through the bone's COS. Calculate the bone's cross-sectional COM and COS, and then calculate the distance between the two points by using the plane distance formula. Fig. 2a. and Fig. 2b show the distance between the cross-sectional COS and the COS of bone (x_s, y_s) on $x-y$ plane calculated by the plane distance formula.

The bone is then simplified to a truss structure, which is composed of an external square and an internal one. The external square refers to the cortical bone and the internal one to the cancellous bone. When the load and constraint remain the same, the structure strength changes when the position of the internal square changes. See Fig. 3.

Fig. 3 shows that bearing the same constraint and load, the structure where the COS of the internal square superposes with the COS of the external square is superior in the load-carrying capacity of shear and moment to the structure where there is not such a superposition. Therefore, when the force action line of the balance forces passes the COM of an object, the carrying capacity of the structure reaches its maximum.

Though the shape and structure of bone are more complicated than the truss in Fig. 3, the constraints and loads born by the bone in vivo are the same as the structure in Fig. 3—they are both acted upon by out-of-balance forces. It can thus be assumed that when the COS (determined by the bone's shape) is in the same position as the COM (determined by the bone's density distribution), the bone's structure has optimal strength.

It can be concluded that to meet its functional requirements, the bone's size, shape and density all produce adaptive changes. In this process, the principle of optimal structure where the COM superposes with COS is always followed. This holds the same idea that function determines the structure as that of the maximal strength with minimal materials, or mechanic stability theory or the bone adaptation as an optimization process and Wolff's law (i. e., law of bone transformation) while the superposition of COM and COS is a quantitative description.

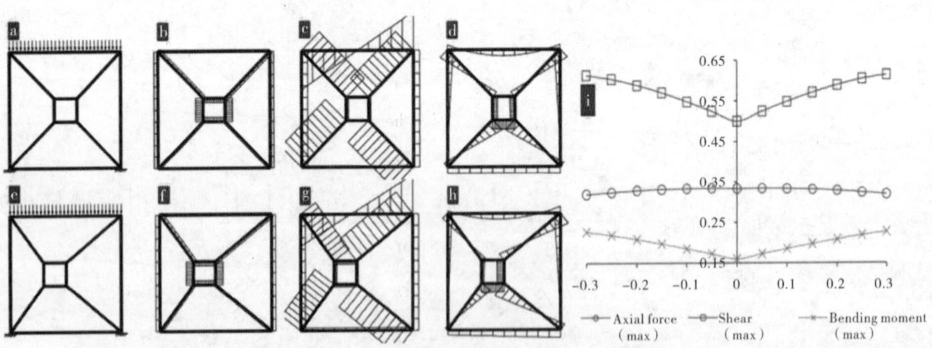

Fig. 3 COM and COS of the truss

Fig. 3a and Fig. 3e, structure by constraints and loads; Fig. 3b and Fig. 3f, axial force distribution in the structure; Fig. 3c and Fig. 3g, shear distribution in the structure; Fig. 3d and Fig. 3h, bending moment distribution in the structure. Fig. 3i, relationship between internal square position and strength. The rods in the structure are all rigid and the connections between the rods are rigid too. Two squares are drawn with a side length of 1 and 0. 2 respectively. Connect the vertices of the two squares and a simple structural mechanics model is forged. Set the two bottom vertices of the bigger square to connect with the hinge bearing on the ground. The top of the bigger square is subjected to distributed load (size is 1). The vertical coordinate of the smaller square COS superposes the bigger square. Change the horizontal coordinate to ±0. 3. By using the software of SMSolver, the calculation results are shown in Fig. 3a – Fig. 3i.

Why is the superposition of COM and COS a quantitative description? The following relationship can be established based upon the fact that the strength of compact bone is many times greater than that of the spongy bone, that the density distribution (relative to the bone's COS) of bone tissue is related to the bone's strength: ①the relationship between the COS of the compact bone and the COS of the bone where the distance from the compact bone's COS to the bone's COS is standardized by the bone tissue's radius; ②the relationship between the bone tissue's density and the distribution radius (relative to that of the bone's COS) where the same density tissue radius is standardized by the bone tissue's radius. See Fig. 4.

In Fig. 4a, the distance of the volleyballers' calcaneus compact bone's COS to the bone's COS is shorter than that of the wrestlers and it has a significant difference ($p < 0.05$), which is in contrast with estimates in Table 1 where no significant difference is observed. A similar trend is observed for the distance of fifth metatarsal compact bone's COS to the bones' COS. From Table 1, we can see that in the similar morphological first to fifth metatarsal, the lowest density goes to the first metatarsal, which does not sound very reasonable, suggesting the limitation of bone density assessment index, i. e., factors such as volume and joint segmental area might have affected bone density. In Fig. 4a, the distance of both athletic groups' first metatarsal compact bone's COS to the bone's COS is the shortest.

When a volleyballer takes off to spike, the braking movement has a great impact on the calcaneus. In Fig. 4b, the distribution radius of the volleyballers' calcaneus begins to become larger than that of the wrestlers from the density of compact bone on; especially when comparing this with the results from the marrow and spongy bone tissues (when density $\rho < 1.14$, it is the marrow; when $1.14 \leqslant \rho \leqslant 1.65$, the spongy bone and when $\rho > 1.65$, the compact bone), this difference is outstanding. The wrestlers' fierce body combats carry great strength to their fifth metatarsal from the front, rear, left and right. The distribution radius of the wrestlers' fifth metatarsal begins to become bigger from the density of compact bone than that of the volleyballers.

Fig. 4 shows that according to the superposition principle of the bone's COM and COS, the establishment of relationship between the compact bone's COS and the bone's COS and the relationship between the tissue's density and distribution radius has offered a new approach to study the bone's strength.

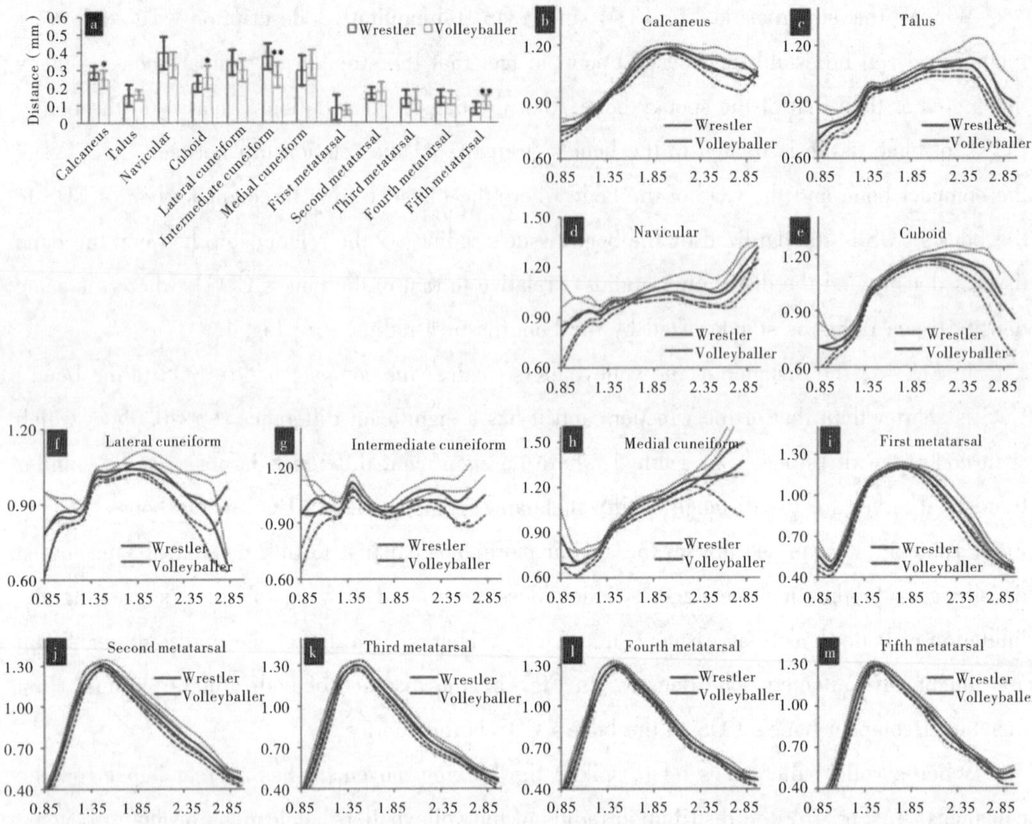

Fig. 4 Application of the superposition principle of the bone's COM and COS

Fig. 4a, positional relationship between the COS of the compact bone and the COS of the bone; Fig. 4b - Fig. 4m, relationship between the bone tissue's density and distribution radius, where axis x stands for the tissue's density and axis y for the standardized mean distribution radius of the tissue. The data were collected from 192 pieces of foot bones of the wrestlers and 192 ones of the volleyballers. $*p<0.05$, $**p>0.01$. When $\rho>1.65$, the bone tissue is defined as compact bone. Eq. (2) andEq. (3) are used to calculate the compact bone's COM and COS, while Eq. (4) is used to calculate the distance between the two points and Eq. (5) is used to calculatre the distribution radius of bone tissue. Fig. 4a is the result of the distance between the compact bone's COM and COS standardized by the bone tissue's radius. Eq. (6) is applied to calculate same density tissue radius. Then standardize it by the bone tissue's radius. See Fig. 4b - Fig. 4m.

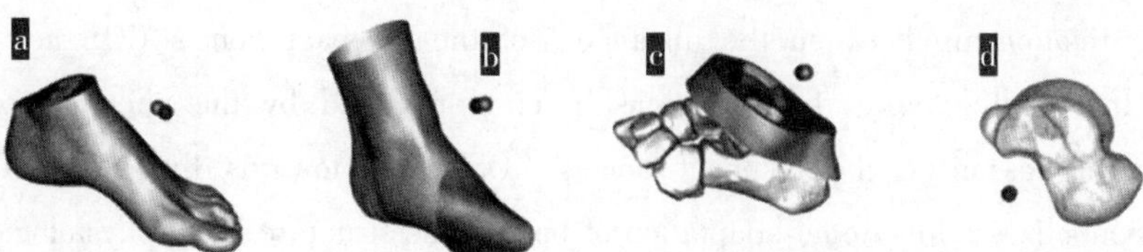

Fig. 5　COM and COS of non-bone tissues

Fig. 5a, positional relationship between the whole foot's COM and COS; Fig. 5b, positional relationship between the COM and COS of ankle skin; Fig. 5c, positional relationship between the COM and COS of non-bone tissues (a group of cross-sections selected around the ankle joint); Fig. 5d, positional relationship between the COM and COS when a ROI (region of interest) of 1 cm^3 is established around the COS of the talus. The grey ball stands for the COM position and the red ball for the COS position. The radius of the ball is 0. 5 mm. According to the definition of non-bone tissue density, Eq. (2) and Eq. (3) are used to calculate COM and COS of non-bone tissue. The three-dimensional model is constructed by the software of Mimics.

What insight will this phenomenon of superposition between the COM and COS bring to biomechanical research? Using the CT data of bone, we analyze the COM and COS of the other foot non-bone tissues. See Fig. 5.

Fig. 5 shows that the COM and COS of the whole foot, of its ankle skin, of the non-bone tissues around the ankle joint and of the ROI established around the whole bone's COS superpose highly. Further subdivisions tell us that if the COM and COS of the cell also follow this principle of high superposition, then a new method of dynamics can be set up to study activities such as cell growth and division.

The COS of a continuous closed geometry superposes with that of its surface (shape). The COS of the cell can thus be obtained through the numerical model of the cell surface. According to the dynamic principle of COM (i. e., the internal force cannot change the motion of the system's COM), if the forces acting on the cell are known, the cell's kinematic characteristics can be obtained. On the other hand, we can use the kinematic characteristics of the cell to analyze the characteristics of external mechanical signals. When the cell shape is asymmetrical, its geometric transformation invariance and the uniqueness of the principal moments of inertia axes can be applied to study issues such as the rotational dynamics of the cell.

Conclusion

The physiological activities of the bone are a process of optimization. In this adaptive changing process, what remains unchanged is the optimal structure principle of superposition of COM and COS. The mechanical significance of following the optimal structure principle is to use the optimal structure to bear the external load.

We propose the concept of distance between the tissue's COS and its bone's COS and discover the relationship between the distance (of the compact bone's COS and its bone's COS) and the loading type. This relationship is represented by the phenomenon that the impact strength has made the compact bone's COS move towards the bone's COS. This movement symbolizes a functional adaptation of bone in its structure. The physiological activity of the middle aged and seniors is mostly a reconstruction. When their bone masses are gradually decreasing, it is essential to look into the possibility of whether physical exercises can diminish the bone loss and change the movement's direction. This is a meaningful and worthwhile research.

With the advances of three-dimensional imaging technology, if this phenomenon of superposition of COM and COS also happens in cell, it will play a significant role in the study of cytokinetics.

Selected Reading 4

骨表面地图化技术

范毅方　樊瑜波　李知宇　吕长生　张　博

摘要： 骨形态是决定骨的结构功能的一个重要因素。对于非对称和非均质分布的活体骨，基于几何变换不变性和其惯量主轴的唯一性，我们提出骨表面地图化技术。利用螺旋 CT 扫描，我们可以对活体骨进行精确测量。基于建立在惯量主轴上的本体坐标，确定本初子午线和等高组等绘图基本要素。通过断层重建和断层边界展开等方法实现骨表面的地图化。经实验验证表明，表面地图化技术不但能反映活体骨的表面特征，同时也是研究骨形态变化的方法。无论是对器官、组织，还是对细胞的表面特征及变化规律，表面地图化技术都会有广泛的应用前景。

前　言

骨的外部形态是骨对力学环境和生理环境适应性的结果，相应地，骨形态会影响骨的结构功能。地图是根据数学规则把球面绘于平面上。这种绘制技术被称为展开。例如，圆的边界可展开成一条直线。当骨骼被简化为一系列有限的断层图像时，骨表面就是一系列的断层边界。当闭合的断层边界依据数学规律成像时，展开线就能形成骨表面地图。骨表面地图是显示骨形态的一种手段。因此，骨表面地图化是研究骨适应性和结构功能的方法。

地图化和平面化技术广泛应用于医学研究。这些技术都与展开技术密切相关（即基于数学规律的绘制技术）。平面化技术将三维物体转化为二维物体，而地图化技术在解析物体表面结构时发挥着重要作用。活体骨三维成像技术的进步使我们可以更好地对骨表面进行数字化，但地图化技术仍未有令人满意的系统化探索结果。尤其是在如何建立一个唯一的活体骨坐标系这方面，未有介绍，但要建立一个唯一的坐标系是绘制骨表面地图的先决条件。

在球形坐标系中，地球表面的点的位置由经纬线及等高线确定。子午线（0 度经线）和赤道线（0 度纬线）为矩形（或笛卡尔）坐标系的原点。除了体积差异之外，骨骼与地球皆为三维几何体。为了绘制骨骼表面地图，需要确定上述三个量。

海拔指代物体参照点之上的垂直距离，通常指海平面（即自海平面的平均距离）。对于骨骼的海拔，可定义为骨表面点相对于质心的均值距离。地球的子午线与赤道线是人为的定义，这给骨子午线及中纬线的定义带来了一定的难度。

一个物体的主轴转动惯量不仅与该物体的质量有关，也与其质量分布有关。转动惯量是一种张量，其形式类似于一个 3×3 矩阵。该张量的三个对角线元素分别为物体三个轴的转动惯量。这三个轴的转动惯量的和为该物体转动惯量的两倍。对于一个非对称物体，三个轴的转动惯量由其本体坐标所定，而它们的和保持不变。利用物体，比如骨骼的惯性轴矩的特性，当测量设备设置的直角坐标系原点位移到骨质心处，即形成骨骼本体坐标系。当在骨骼本体坐标系中进行坐标变换，即坐标系绕骨原点旋转时，可确定一个惯性积为零（即惯性张量的非对角元素）的坐标系。新的坐标系轴为骨骼的惯量主轴。

当用骨的惯量主轴确定三维模型的子午线与中纬线时，必须确保骨形不会受到坐标变换的影响。即使坐标变换，标量仍是不变量。骨表面可用有限个点云表示。点云的位置为一个标量，也就是说骨形不会受到坐标变换的影响。两两正交的惯量主轴可形成三个骨断面。两个断面的边界垂直于惯量主轴（惯量主轴或为最小值，或为最大值），分别代表子午线与中纬线。然后，骨子午线与中纬线可由骨惯量主轴确定。

本文测试并证明了形态非对称与结构各向异性活体骨惯量主轴的唯一性。实验结果表明，用惯量主轴设子午线，以及用断层边界（相对惯量主轴）的平均半径设轮廓线时，骨表面地图化方法是可行的。此骨表面地图化的技术提供了一种研究骨骼形态学的替代方法。它也可用于研究器官、组织或细胞的表面特性及变化。

材料和方法

【伦理声明】

本研究已获得广州体育学院伦理委员会批准。受试者均完全知晓并自愿参与本项研究，签署书面知情同意书。

【设备】

测试设备为荷兰飞利浦 Brilliance 64 排扫描仪，由珠江医院影像处理中心提供。扫描设定为：骨组织窗；电源功率：120kV；像素大小：0.50mm；层距：0.50mm。扫描过程：从脚部由上至下进行横切面扫描。

【软件】

三维建模由 Mimics（版本 10）和逆向工程进行，由 SPSS（版本 12）（由教育部生物力学与力生物学重点实验室提供）进行统计分析。

【受试者】

我们一共收集了源自 16 位运动员的足骨数据——8 位排球运动员（平均身高为 183.94±3.90cm，平均体重为 69.80±5.20kg，平均年龄为 21.88±0.99 岁）和 8 位摔跤运动员（平均身高为 168.00±5.68cm，平均体重为 65.52±5.16kg，平均年龄为 21.00±2.78 岁）。

受试者为选自本学院的男排球运动员，以及选自省体校的男摔跤运动员。在测试前已确认各受试者已接受超过五年的专业训练。测试前已获取各人的病史，并对他们进行了 X 光检查，排除了带有如足部病理变化、畸形或损伤的受试者，以确保各人身体状况达到测试要求。

【骨坐标系标准化】

各向同性扫描把足骨分成一系列体微元，扫描后能确定体微元的坐标，计算得出质心。把相对质心的体微元坐标设为（x_{oi}，y_{oi}，z_{oi}）（其中 o 在质心上），由下列方程确定主轴转动惯量：

$$\begin{cases} I_x = \sum (y_{oi}^2 + z_{oi}^2)\rho_i \Delta V \\ I_y = \sum (x_{oi}^2 + z_{oi}^2)\rho_i \Delta V \\ I_z = \sum (x_{oi}^2 + y_{oi}^2)\rho_i \Delta V \end{cases} \tag{1}$$

其中 ρ 为体微元密度，$\Delta V = \Delta x \Delta y \Delta z$、其中 Δx，Δy 与 Δz 分别为横向、纵向像素尺寸和 CT 图像层距。

设骨体依次绕 x，y，z 轴转动的角为 α，β，γ。确立下列关系：

$$\begin{cases} (I_y - I_z)_\alpha = \sum [(y_{oi}\cos\alpha - z_{oi}\sin\alpha)^2 - (y_{oi}\sin\alpha + z_{oi}\cos\alpha)^2]\rho_i \Delta V \\ (I_x - I_z)_\beta = \sum [(x_{\alpha i}\cos\beta - z_{\alpha i}\sin\beta)^2 - (z_{\alpha i}\cos\beta - x_{\alpha i}\sin\beta)^2]\rho_i \Delta V \\ (I_x - I_y)_\gamma = \sum [(x_{\beta i}\cos\gamma - y_{\beta i}\sin\gamma)^2 - (x_{\beta i}\sin\gamma + y_{\beta i}\cos\gamma)^2]\rho_i \Delta V \end{cases} \tag{2}$$

对方程（2）求导，令

$$\frac{\mathrm{d}(I_y - I_z)_\alpha}{\mathrm{d}\alpha} = 0, \frac{\mathrm{d}(I_x - I_z)_\beta}{\mathrm{d}\beta} = 0, \frac{\mathrm{d}(I_x - I_y)_\gamma}{\mathrm{d}\gamma} = 0$$

然后整理得

$$\begin{cases} \alpha = \frac{1}{2}\arctan\left(\frac{2\sum y_{oi}z_{oi}\rho_i \Delta V}{\sum y_{oi}^2\rho_i \Delta V - \sum z_{oi}^2\rho_i \Delta V}\right) \\ \beta = \frac{1}{2}\arctan\left(\frac{2\sum x_{\alpha i}z_{\alpha i}\rho_i \Delta V}{\sum y_{\alpha i}^2\rho_i \Delta V - \sum z_{\alpha i}^2\rho_i \Delta V}\right) \\ \gamma = \frac{1}{2}\arctan\left(\frac{2\sum x_{\beta i}y_{\beta i}\rho_i \Delta V}{\sum x_{\beta i}^2\rho_i \Delta V - \sum y_{\beta i}^2\rho_i \Delta V}\right) \end{cases} \tag{3}$$

方程（3）中，当且仅当 $I_x \neq I_y \neq I_z$，方程（3）有一系列的解。方程（3）中，$\sum y_{oi}z_{oi}\rho\Delta V$，$\sum x_{\alpha i}z_{\alpha i}\rho\Delta V$ 为惯性张量的惯性积。在［0，π］范围内，根据方程（3），有限转动可以使三个惯性积同时为零。

【重建】

将方程（3）的结果依次代入方程（2），把骨本体坐标轴定位在骨惯量主轴处。由于断层图像为数值化的，几何变换使得原本的断层图像如断层区域及其边界都发生了改变。那么，在几何变换后必须重建一个新的断层图像，可由下列方程完成：

$$\begin{cases} x_i = \text{trunc}\left(\dfrac{x_{oi} - \min(x_{oi})}{\Delta x}\right)\Delta x + \min(x_{oi}) \\ y_i = \text{trunc}\left(\dfrac{y_{oi} - \min(y_{oi})}{\Delta y}\right)\Delta y + \min(y_{oi}) \\ z_i = \text{trunc}\left(\dfrac{z_{oi} - \min(z_{oi})}{\Delta z}\right)\Delta z + \min(z_{oi}) \end{cases} \tag{4}$$

其中，(x_{oi}，y_{oi}，z_{oi}）指变换后的体微元位置，(x_i，y_i，z_i）指重建后的断层图像位置，trunc( ) 指取整函数。要保持 CT 图像的各向同性，仅由 $\Delta dx = \Delta dy = \Delta dz$ 满足方程（4)，像素大小和层距与原图像保持一致（或稍有出入)。

【边界检测】

CT 扫描把骨表面分成断层图像边界的集合。骨表面地图化成为展开断层边界的问题。进行 CT 扫描时，重置设备，即空气灰度值设为零。扫描过的骨断层图像由方程（4）重建，其断层边界由下列方程绘制：

$$\rho(x,y)_z \begin{cases} \rho(x,y)_z & \rho(x,y)_z > 0,\ \rho(x+1,y)_z = 0 \\ \rho(x,y)_z & \rho(x,y)_z > 0,\ \rho(x-1,y)_z = 0 \\ \rho(x,y)_z & \rho(x,y)_z > 0,\ \rho(x,y+1)_z = 0 \\ \rho(x,y)_z & \rho(x,y)_z > 0,\ \rho(x,y-1)_z = 0 \\ 0 & \text{other} \end{cases} \tag{5}$$

其中 z 为断层图像的序号，$(x, y)_z$ 为体微元的位置，$\rho(x, y)_z$ 为体微元密度。

【切线】

当骨表面地图化时，骨被切割，从圆状面可切下一个矩形，或一个菱形。无论怎么切割圆柱体表面，其面积都是一样的。但只有矩形是唯一的。

如何才能把骨切成唯一的形状呢？两惯量主轴处于一个平面上，该平面垂直于骨的最小或最大的惯量主轴。在此平面上，确定骨表面边界为子午线，作表面切割线来展开骨表面。也就是以下方程：

$$i = \begin{cases} 0 & x_z^i = x_z^c, y_z^i > y_z^c \\ 1 & x_z^i - x_z^c = -\Delta x, y_z^i > y_z^c \\ 2 & x_z^i - x_z^c = -2\Delta x, y_z^i > y_z^c \\ \vdots & \\ n-1 & x_z^i - x_z^c = 2\Delta x, y_z^i > y_z^c \\ n & x_z^i - x_z^c = \Delta x, y_z^i > y_z^c \end{cases} \tag{6}$$

其中（x_z^i, y_z^i）为体微元在断层边界上的位置，（x_z^c，y_z^c）为建立在惯性参考系中的质心，而 i 为切割后边界的体微元序号。

【等高线】

方程（6）将切割后断层边界上的体微元按序排列。将垂直于主转动惯量轴的断层图像平均半径定义为“海平面”，以之作为基准线，由此断层边界可用以下方程展开：

$$p(x,y)_z = p(i + x_z^c, h_z^i)_z \tag{7}$$

其中 z 与方程（5）的定义相同，$h_z^i = r_z^i - r_z^-$，$r_z^i = \sqrt{(x_z^i - x_z^c)^2 + (y_z^i - y_z^c)^2}$ 和 $r_z^- = \frac{\sum r_z^i}{n}$，$(x_z^i, y_z^i)$ 和 (x_z^c, y_z^c) 与方程（6）的坐标定义相同。

【摊平】

方程（4）至方程（7）把闭合表面展开成开放三维曲面。骨表面的三维曲面地图能进一步展开成二维平面。我们把骨表面用以下方程解析为一个平面：

$$p(x,y) = p\left(\int (l^2(i) + Z_i^2)\mathrm{d}i, \int (l^2(h) + Z_i^2)\mathrm{d}i\right) \tag{8}$$

其中 $p(x, y)$ 表示表面地图摊平后平面上体微元的位置，$l(i) = \sqrt{(z_i - z_{u-1})^2 + Z_i^2}$，$Z_i = \int |z_i - z_{i-1}| \mathrm{d}i$，$l(j) = \sqrt{(z_j - z_{j-1})^2 + Z_j^2}$ 和 $Z_j = \int |z_j - z_{j-1}| \mathrm{d}i$，其中 z 表示在骨表面地图化（i，j）坐标中的等高线值。

方程（4）至方程（8）表示骨表面地图化实际上是骨表面结构的模拟，是一种以图像为标志显示骨表面的立体模型，与真实人体的骨表面结构相一致。

结果与讨论

惯性张量表示我们能够发现惯性积同时为零的一系列本体坐标。三个主惯性矩的形成建立在惯量主轴的基础上。三个主惯性距得出的结果也只有三个：①三个量都相等；②其中两个相等；③三个各不相等。物体为同质时，第一种情况为球体；第二种情况为椭圆体，或是立方体、圆柱体或长方体。

第一种情况中，建立在惯量主轴上的坐标系有无数个，而第二种情况中，其中一条主轴的方向已确定，另外两条主轴尚未确定。因此，上述两种情况下，惯量主轴与切面形状之间不存在对应关系。而第三种情况中，相对惯量参考坐标系的骨惯量主轴方向余弦为唯一值，表明惯量主轴和切面形状之间是一一对应关系。

三个骨主惯性矩由其质量与质量分布确定。形态非对称与分布非均质的骨骼，是否会发生第三种情况？这要由实验来证明。用 Mimics 软件进行 CT 图像重建，建立运动员左足骨的三维模型。选取其第四跖骨。现在，查看骨标准化坐标系的结果：即本体坐标系转换为惯量主轴。如彩图 16 所示。

这表明，当 $I_x \neq I_y \neq I_z$ 时，建立一个坐标原点在质心上的本体坐标，通过有限转动，就可以确定惯量主轴。相对惯性参考系的惯量主轴方向余弦唯一（第三种情况），表明建立在惯量主轴上的本体坐标不仅说明了骨的位置方向，同时也证明了骨的表面形状，以及进行定量分析时形状的变化。

进行坐标系标准化后，骨表面位置发生了变化。骨表面地图化是展开断层边界的一种方法，也就是新的骨骼三维模型的断层重建。利用方程（4），我们重建受试者的第四跖骨。如彩图 17 所示。

彩图 17 表明，重建后的断层图像垂直于长惯量主轴。在断层图像边界上“海平面”的各个点连成了等高线。

以重合的足骨质心断层图像和足骨断层图像为例子，如彩图 18 所示。

彩图 18 表明方程（4）让体微元在平移后保持正方形，使新的断层图像维持闭合连续。断层边界形成了骨表面，也就是方程（5）中的描述。由两条惯量主轴构成的断层边界作子午线。方程（6）至方程（8）用作展开骨表面。

人体中，左右侧骨骼形态相互对称。这样的骨骼，无须用百分比大小描述其表面。一个物体左边或右边足部第一跖骨的地图化如彩图 19 所示。

彩图 14 ~ 彩图 16 表明，地图化技术具有实用性。该技术在生物动力学研究，以及在临床应用中是否具有价值，将决定我们的研究意义。为了检验地图化技术在未来研究中的应用，我们分别对 8 位摔跤运动员与 8 位排球运动员进行了第四跖骨的地图化分析。如彩图 20 所示。

彩图 20 说明，由第四跖骨定位展开地图的长宽标准，形成了大部分受试者第四跖骨的均值地图。源于两组运动员的该均值地图对比结果表明，排球运动员的第四跖骨表面凹凸度大于摔跤运动员，这与排球运动员在击球时足部承受较大压力的事实一致。

骨骼可保护身体，帮助身体做出动作。骨强度的分析一直是研究生物力学的重要一环，且我们已得出将骨地图化技术应用到骨强度分析的可能性。如彩图 20 所示。

彩图 21 表示由地图化技术得出的骨表面特征，这种方法也是研究骨形态学变化的定量方法，不仅两种指标——骨密度指标，骨组织密度和骨分布半径之间的关系指标——能用于分析骨强度，地图化技术也能实现这种分析。而这对临床骨强度分析也有帮助。

结　论

帕普里斯原理（Papoulis' theorem）的普及说明骨表面形状能保持其几何不变性，如平移、转化或维度变化。在保证骨表面各向同性的情况下，确保了活体骨的不同位置的 CT 扫描结果的一致性。骨表面地图化技术得益于余弦方向上的主惯量矩的惯性参考系相对稳定这个独特性质。形态几何不变性和主惯量矩坐标系唯一性这些特性，使骨表面地图化得以描述骨外部的形态学特性，这能够进一步推动对形态学机制的研究。活体骨的实验表明，骨表面地图化技术又开创了一个研究方法，并补充了三维骨成像技术的分析方法。

可以得出结论：形状非对称及分布非均质的活体骨存在一组唯一的惯量主轴。任意建立在质心上的本体坐标，经过坐标变换后，使本体坐标轴与惯量主轴相一致，表明本体坐标轴是惯量主轴上的唯一坐标轴。这可应用在均质非对称几何体以及非均质非对称几何体中。惯量主轴的唯一特征是确定活体骨能否地图化的关键。这种唯一性已经被证实，并使地图化技术得到运用。

我们通过人工定义本初子午线和赤道线绘制地球地图，但要对超过 200 块人骨进行地图化，如何用一个物理量去定义子午线与赤道线，是我们的研究团队尝试解决的问题——也就是用唯一的惯量主轴确定骨子午线和骨赤道线，随之用相对质心的骨表面各点均距设置“海平面”，最后依照数学规则对骨进行展开，如重建和边界测定，以实现骨表面的地图化。

骨形态学研究揭示了人类进化的重要意义。如在南方古猿阿法种的第四跖骨分析中发现阿法种的足部活动方式与现代人一样。罗斯和其团队开发的三维鉴定软件为科学家提供了方便，可利用古猿残骸定点形状（而非大小），更快更精确地鉴定其性别和血缘。上述一切都表明，在骨形态学探索方面仍旧有很大的潜力。因为人体器官、组织和细胞和骨骼一样，都是非对称的几何体，能依次进行地图化，我们相信这种骨表面地图化技术的应用前景十分广阔。

Bone Surface Mapping Method

Yifang Fan, Yubo Fan, Zhiyu Li, Changsheng Lyu, Bo Zhang
Translated by Zhiyu Li

Abstract: Bone shape is an important factor to determine the bone's structural function. For the asymmetrically shaped and anisotropically distributed bone in vivo, a surface mapping method is proposed on the bases of its geometric transformation invariance and its uniqueness of the principal axes of inertia. Using spiral CT scanning, we can make precise measurements to bone in vivo. The coordinate transformations lead to the principal axes of inertia, with which the prime meridian and the contour can be set. Methods such as tomographic reconstruction and boundary development are employed so that the surface of bone in vivo can be mapped. Experimental results show that the surface mapping method can reflect the shape features and help study the surface changes of bone in vivo. This method can be applied to research into the surface characteristics and changes of organ, tissue or cell whenever its digitalized surface is obtained.

Introduction

The shape of bone is the result of adaptation to mechanical environment and in return, the shape affects the structural function of bone. A map is a figure of a spherical surface drawn on a plane surface according to mathematical rules. The drawing method is called development. For example, the boundary of a circle can be developed as a straight line. When the bone is simplified as a set of finite tomographic images, the bone's surface is a set of tomographic boundaries. When the closed tomographic boundary is developed according to mathematical rules, the bone's surface map is thus formed by a set of developed lines. A bone's surface map is a way to reveal the bone's shape. The bone surface mapping, therefore, is used as an approach to study the adaptability of bone and its structural function.

Mapping and flattening methods have been widely used in medical research. They are both concerned with the development methods (i. e., drawing methods according to mathematical rules). The flattening method develops the 3-dimensional (3D) object to a 2-dimensional (2D) one while the mapping method plays an essential role in interpreting the surface structure of an object. The advancements and improvements of 3D imaging of bone in vivo have brought better methods to digitalize the surface of bone, but the mapping methods have not been systematically explored with satisfactory results. Specifically, how to establish a unique coordinate system of bone in vivo has not been introduced, but to set up a unique coordinate system is a prerequisite to draw the bone's surface map.

In the spherical coordinate system, the position of earth surface point is determined by the longitude, latitude and altitude. The prime meridian (0° longitude) and the equator line (0° latitude) are the origin of a rectangular (or Cartesian) coordinate system. Apart from the size difference, the bone and the earth are both a 3D geometry. In order to draw a bone's surface map, these three quantities need to be defined.

The altitude of the earth refers to the vertical distance of something above a reference point that usually refers to the sea level (i. e. the average distance from the sea surface). As to the bone's altitude, it can be defined as mean distance of the bone's surface points to the center of mass (COM). The prime meridian and equator line of the earth are artificial definitions, which bring difficulty to the definition of bone's prime meridian and equator line.

The magnitude of an object's moment of inertia is related not only to the object's mass but also to its mass distribution. It is a tensor whose form is similar to a 3 × 3 matrix. The three diagonal elements of the tensor are the three axis moments of inertia of an object, respectively. The sum of these three axis moments of inertia doubles the moment of inertia of that object. To an asymmetrical object, the magnitude of the three axis moments of inertia is determined by its body coordinate while their sum remains unvaried. Using the characteristics of an object's axis moment inertia, for an object like bone, when the origin of the rectangular coordinate system set by the measurement equipment is moved to the bone's COM, the bone's body coordinate system is formed. When the coordinate transformation, i. e., coordinate system rotates around bone's origin, is conducted to the bone's body coordinate system, a coordinate system with the products of inertia (i. e., the off-diagonal elements of a tensor) to be zero can be identified. The axis of the new coordinate system is the bone's principal axis of inertia (PAI).

When the bone's PAI is applied to determine the prime meridian and equator line of a 3D model, we must make sure that the bone's shape will not be affected by the coordinate transformation. The scalar remains invariant under coordinate transformation. The bone's surface can be presented by the finite point clouds. The point cloud position is a scalar, which means that the bone's shape will not be affected by the coordinate transformation. The pairwise orthogonal PAIs can form three bone cross-sections. The boundaries of the two sections vertical to PAI (the magnitude of principal moments of inertia is minimal or maximal) are to represent the prime meridian and equator line, respectively. Then, the bone's prime meridian and the equator line can be determined by the bone's PAIs.

This paper examines and verifies the uniqueness of PAIs of the asymmetrically shaped and anisotropically structured bone in vivo. The experimental results suggest that when PAI is used to set the prime meridian and when the average radius of the tomographic boundary (relative to PAI) is applied to set the contour, an approach to map the bone surface is practical. This bone surface mapping method provides an alternate method to study the bone's morphology. It can also be employed to study the surface characteristics and the changes of organ, tissue or cell.

Materials and Methods

【Ethics Statement】

The study received approval from the Ethical Committee of Guangzhou Institute of Physical Education. The subjects provided fully informed consent to participate in this study by signing a written consent form.

【Equipment】

The test equipment was Brilliance 64-slice Scanner by Philips, Netherlands, provided by Image Processing Center of Zhujiang Hospital. Scan settings were: frame bone tissue; power: 120kV; pixel size: 0.50mm; layer distance: 0.50mm. The scanning was conducted along both feet transect, from top to bottom.

【Software】

The 3D model was constructed by Mimics (Version 10) and Geomagic Studio, and the statistical analysis was performed by SPSS (Version 12) (provided by the Key Laboratory of Biomechanics and Mechanobiology of Ministry of Education).

【Subjects】

Altogether, we collected bone data of 16 athletes—8 volleyballers (with average height, weight and age of 183.94 ± 3.90cm, 69.80 ± 5.20kg and 21.88 ± 0.99year, respectively) and 8 wrestlers (with average height, weight and age of 168.00 ± 5.68 cm, 65.52 ± 5.16kg and 21.00 ± 2.78year, respectively).

The subjects were male volleyballers from our institute and male wrestlers from Provincial Sports School. It was confirmed before the test that every subject had been trained as a professional athlete for more than five years. Before the test, each subject's medical history was inquired and all the subjects were x-rayed to exclude subjects with diseases such as foot pathological change, deformity or injury to make sure that their physical conditions meet the requirements of the test.

【Standardized Coordinate System of Bone】

An isotropic scanning separates the bone into a collection of volume element. After the scanning, the coordinates of volume element become known. Then the COM can be obtained after calculation. Let the coordinates of volume element relative to COM be (x_{oi}, y_{oi}, z_{oi}) (where o is located in COM), and then the magnitude of the principal moments of inertia is represented by:

$$\begin{cases} I_x = \sum (y_{oi}^2 + z_{oi}^2)\rho_i \Delta V \\ I_y = \sum (x_{oi}^2 + z_{oi}^2)\rho_i \Delta V \\ I_z = \sum (x_{oi}^2 + y_{oi}^2)\rho_i \Delta V \end{cases} \quad (1)$$

where ρ is the density of volume element, $\Delta V = \Delta x \Delta y \Delta z$, where Δx, Δy and Δz are the horizontal, vertical pixel sizes and the layer distance of CT images, respectively.

Let the angles made with the x, y, z axes be α, β, γ. The following equations are set up:

$$\begin{cases} (I_y - I_z)_\alpha = \sum[(y_{oi}\cos\alpha - z_{oi}\sin\alpha)^2 - (y_{oi}\sin\alpha + z_{oi}\cos\alpha)^2]\rho_i\Delta V \\ (I_x - I_z)_\beta = \sum[(x_{\alpha i}\cos\beta + z_{\alpha i}\sin\beta)^2 - (z_{\alpha i}\cos\beta - x_{\alpha i}\sin\beta)^2]\rho_i\Delta V \\ (I_x - I_y)_\gamma = \sum[(x_{\beta i}\cos\gamma - y_{\beta i}\sin\gamma)^2 - (x_{\beta i}\sin\gamma + y_{\beta i}\cos\gamma)^2]\rho_i\Delta V \end{cases} \tag{2}$$

Differentiate Eq. (2), and let

$$\frac{\mathrm{d}(I_y - I_z)_\alpha}{\mathrm{d}\alpha} = 0,\ \frac{\mathrm{d}(I_x - I_z)_\beta}{\mathrm{d}\beta} = 0,\ \frac{\mathrm{d}(I_x - I_y)_\gamma}{\mathrm{d}\gamma} = 0$$

Then

$$\begin{cases} \alpha = \dfrac{1}{2}\arctan\left(\dfrac{2\sum y_{oi}z_{oi}\rho_i\Delta V}{\sum y_{oi}^2\rho_i\Delta V - \sum z_{oi}^2\rho_i\Delta V}\right) \\ \beta = \dfrac{1}{2}\arctan\left(\dfrac{2\sum x_{\alpha i}z_{\alpha i}\rho_i\Delta V}{\sum y_{\alpha i}^2\rho_i\Delta V - \sum z_{\alpha i}^2\rho_i\Delta V}\right) \\ \gamma = \dfrac{1}{2}\arctan\left(\dfrac{2\sum x_{\beta i}y_{\beta i}\rho_i\Delta V}{\sum x_{\beta i}^2\rho_i\Delta V - \sum y_{\beta i}^2\rho_i\Delta V}\right) \end{cases} \tag{3}$$

Eq. (3) shows that if and only if $I_x \neq I_y \neq I_z$ will Eq. (3) have a set of solutions. In Eq. (3), $\sum y_{oi}z_{oi}\rho\Delta V$, and $\sum x_{\alpha i}z_{\alpha i}\rho\Delta V$ are inertia products of inertia tensor. Within the range of $[0, \pi]$, according to Eq. (3), limited rotations find a set of body axes for which the products of inertia vanish.

【Reconstruction】

When the result of Eq. (3) is replaced for that in Eq. (2) accordingly, a set of bone body axes is positioned on bone's PAI. Since the tomographic images are numerical, the transformation leads to changes of the original tomographic images such as the tomographic area and boundary. It is necessary, then, to reconstruct a tomographic image after transformation, which can be performed by the following equation:

$$\begin{cases} x_i = \mathrm{trunc}\left(\dfrac{x_{oi} - \min(x_{oi})}{\Delta x}\right)\Delta x + \min(x_{oi}) \\ y_i = \mathrm{trunc}\left(\dfrac{y_{oi} - \min(y_{oi})}{\Delta y}\right)\Delta y + \min(y_{oi}) \\ z_i = \mathrm{trunc}\left(\dfrac{z_{oi} - \min(z_{oi})}{\Delta z}\right)\Delta z + \min(z_{oi}) \end{cases} \tag{4}$$

where (x_{oi}, y_{oi}, z_{oi}) stands for the position of volume element after transformation,

(x_i, y_i, z_i) for that of the reconstructed tomogram and trunc( ) for a function that truncates a number to an integer by removing the fractional part of the number. To keep the CT images isotropic, Eq. (4) is satisfied only by $\Delta dx = \Delta dy = \Delta dz$, and pixel size and layer distance are kept the same of (or a little more than) those of the original image.

【Boundary Detection】

CT scanning separates the bone surface into a collection of the tomographic image boundaries. The mapping of the bone surface has become an issue to develop the tomographic boundary. When performing a CT scanning, the equipment is reset, i. e., the gray value of the air is set as zero. The scanned tomographic images of bone are restructured by Eq. (4), and their tomographic boundaries are drawn by the following equation:

$$\rho(x,y)_z \begin{cases} \rho(x,y)_z & \rho(x,y)_z > 0,\ \rho(x+1,y)_z = 0 \\ \rho(x,y)_z & \rho(x,y)_z > 0,\ \rho(x-1,y)_z = 0 \\ \rho(x,y)_z & \rho(x,y)_z > 0,\ \rho(x,y+1)_z = 0 \\ \rho(x,y)_z & \rho(x,y)_z > 0,\ \rho(x,y-1)_z = 0 \\ 0 & \text{other} \end{cases} \tag{5}$$

where z is the sequence number of tomographic images, $(x, y)_z$ is the position of volume element and $\rho(x,y)_z$ is the density of volume element.

【Cutting Line】

When mapping the bone surface, the bone is cut from a cylindrical surface to a rectangle, or a rhombus. However the cylindrical surface is cut, its ultimate area would be the same. But there is only one in shape of rectangle.

How to cut the bone into only one form? Two PAIs are in a plane perpendicular to the minimal or maximal PAI of bone. On this plane, the bone surface boundary is defined as the prime meridian, which is used as the surface cutting line to develop the bone surface. The following equation makes it happen:

$$i = \begin{cases} 0 & x_z^i = x_z^c,\ y_z^i > y_z^c \\ 1 & x_z^i - x_z^c = -\Delta x,\ y_z^i > y_z^c \\ 2 & x_z^i - x_z^c = -2\Delta x,\ y_z^i > y_z^c \\ \vdots & \\ n-1 & x_z^i - x_z^c = 2\Delta x,\ y_z^i > y_z^c \\ n & x_z^i - x_z^c = \Delta x,\ y_z^i > y_z^c \end{cases} \tag{6}$$

where (x_z^i, y_z^i) is the position of the volume element at the tomographic boundary, (x_z^c, y_z^c) is the COM relative to the inertia reference frame and i is the sequence number of volume element at the boundary after being cut.

【Contour】

Eq. (6) sequences the volume elements at the tomographic boundary which has been cut. The average radius of the tomographic image perpendicular to PAI is defined as the sea level, which is used as a datum line so that the tomographic boundary can be developed by the following equation:

$$p(x,y)_z = p(i + x_z^c, h_z^i)_z \tag{7}$$

where z shares the same definition of that in Eq. (5), $h_z^i = r_z^i - r_z^-$, $r_z^i = \sqrt{(x_z^i - x_z^c)^2 + (y_z^i - y_z^c)^2}$ and $r_z^- = \frac{\sum r_z^i}{n}$, (x_z^i, y_z^i) and (x_z^c, y_z^c) have the same definitions with those in Eq. (6).

【Flattening】

Eq. (4) to Eq. (7) develop the closed surface into an open 3D curved one. The 3D curved map of the bone surface can be further developed into a 2D plane. We translate the bone surface into a plane by the following equation:

$$p(x,y) = p\left(\int (l^2(i) + Z_i^2) \mathrm{d}i, \int (l^2(h) + Z_i^2) \mathrm{d}i\right) \tag{8}$$

where $p(x, y)$ presents the position of volume element in a plane whose surface map has been flattened. $l(i) = \sqrt{(z_i - z_{u-1})^2 + Z_i^2}$, $Z_i = \int |z_i - z_{i-1}| \mathrm{d}i$, $l(j) = \sqrt{(z_j - z_{j-1})^2 + Z_j^2}$, and $Z_j = \int |z_j - z_{j-1}| \mathrm{d}i$ where z stands for the value of contour on (i, j) in bone surface mapping.

Eq. (4) to Eq. (8) suggest that the mapping of the bone surface actually serves as a simulation of the bone surface structure. It is a space model of an image symbol to represent the bone surface. It remains consistent with the real body of the bone surface structure.

Results and Discussion

The inertia tensor suggests that we can find a set of body axes where products of inertia will be zero at the same time. Three principal moments of inertia are formed relative to PAI. The magnitudes of these three principal moments of inertia come out with only three results: ①all are equal; ②two out of three are equal; ③all are different. When the object is homogeneous, in the first case, it is a sphere; in the second, an ellipsoid, a cube, a cylinder or a rectangular.

In the first case, there are numerous coordinate systems set upon PAIs, while in the second case, the orientation of one principal axis is determined, but not the other two. Therefore, in the first and second case, there is not a corresponding relation between PAIs and the shape. In the third case, however, the direction cosines of the bone's PAI relative to inertia reference frame are unique, suggesting a one-to-one corresponding relation between PAIs and shape.

The magnitude of the bone's three principal moments of inertia is determined by its mass and mass distribution. As to the bone, whose shape is asymmetrical and its distribution non-homogeneous, will the third case be applied? This needs experimental verification. Using Mimics software, a reconstruction to the CT image is conducted and a 3D model of the athlete's left foot bone is built. The fourth metatarsal of the athlete is picked. Now, look at the result from the standardized coordinate system (SCS) of bone, i. e. , body coordinate system is transformed into PAIs. See Fig. 1.

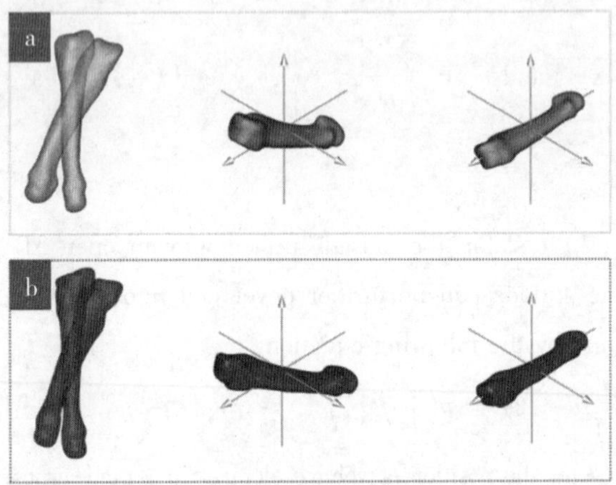

Fig. 1 SCS of the fourth metatarsal

Fig. 1a is the SCS of the fourth metatarsal of the wrestlers. Fig. 1b is the SCS of the fourth metatarsal of the volleyballers. The application of Mimics software leads to the 3D model of the fourth metatarsal. The 3D model is then reconstructed and saved as text file by "point cloud" process (the menu in the Mimics). Applying Eq. (3), SCS is conducted and then Geomagic Studio is used to wrap or smooth shade the processed point cloud data. Next, save the 3D model as a STL (standard template library) file. Last, input the standardized 3D model of the fourth metatarsal into Mimics. The left figure is a comparison of bone before and after using SCS, the middle figure is the posture of bone in body coordinate system before using SCS while the right one is the posture of bone in body coordinate system after using SCS. When the coordinate of the equipment is translated to the bone's COM, two different postures of the two subjects' fourth metatarsal can be spotted. But after using SCS, the bone's body coordinate axes are translated into the bone's PAIs, where the postures can be unified in the coordinate system.

This shows, when $I_x \neq I_y \neq I_z$, a set of body axes whose coordinate origins are located at the COM of bone are set up. After limited rotations, PAIs can be spotted. The direction cosines of bone's PAI relative to the inertia reference frame characterization are unique (i. e. the third case), which means that the body axes set upon PAIs not only depict the position and posture of bone, but also verify the bone surface shape and its changes when making a quantitative analysis.

After using SCS, the bone's surface position is changed. The proposed bone surface mapping is a method to develop the tomographic boundary, suggesting that the tomographic reconstruction of new bone's 3D model. Using Eq. (4), we rebuild the fourth metatarsal of a subject. See Fig. 2.

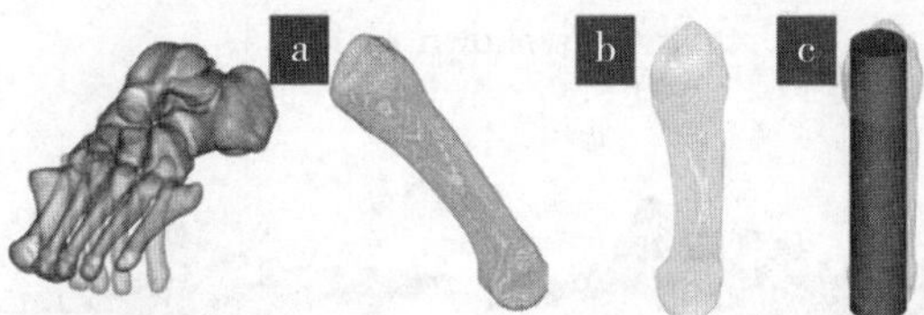

Fig. 2　Tomographic reconstruction of the fourth metatarsal after using SCS

Fig. 2a is the tomography of the fourth metatarsal before using SCS. Fig. 2b is the tomography of the fourth metatarsal after using SCS. Fig. 2c is the tomography and sea level of the fourth metatarsal after using SCS. According to the morphological features of the fourth metatarsal, set the average value of the distance between the fourth metatarsal's bone tissue to long PAI (the magnitude of principal moments of inertia is minimal) to be the radius. The central axis of the cylinder and the long PAI will superpose. The left figure shows the postures of 1st to 5th metatarsals before and after using SCS. If a cylinder is placed in Fig. 2a, the bone's tomography is not vertical to the central axis of the cylinder, but a reconstruction of tomography after using SCS is vertical to the central axis of the cylinder (i. e. the principal axis of minimal moment of inertia) . The tomography of the non-vertical central axis of the cylinder is determined by the posture of the subject when being measured. A different posture leads to a different tomography. Without using SCS, the development of the tomographic boundary of the bone's surface map is not unique whereas using SCS brings a unique map of the bone's surface.

Fig. 2 shows that, after being reconstructed, the tomographic image is vertical to the long PAI. The points relative to the sea level on the tomographic image boundary form the altitude.

Take one case of superposed tomographic image of the foot bone's COS of the tomography and that of the bone for example. See Fig. 3.

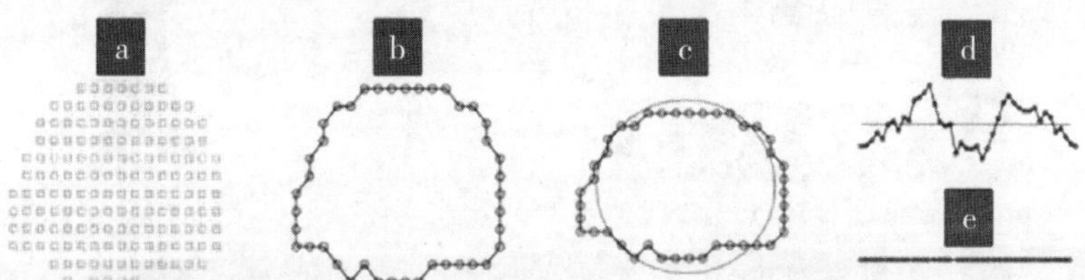

Fig. 3　Methods to develop the bone's tomographic image

Fig. 3a is the reconstructed tomogram by applying Eq. (4) after using SCS. Fig. 3b is the tomographic boundary extracted by Eq. (5) . Fig. 3c is the circle set up by the average radius of the tomographic image, where the center is on the COM of the tomographic image. Fig. 3d is the developed tomographic boundaries by Eq. (6) and Eq. (7) based upon the circumference taken as sea level. Fig. 3e is the flattened tomographic boundaries by Eq. (8) .

Fig. 3 shows that Eq. (4) keeps the volume elements to be a square and makes the new tomogram remain closed and continuous after the transformation. The tomographic boundaries constitute the bone's surface, which is drawn from Eq. (5) . The tomographic boundary formed by the two PAIs is taken for the prime meridian. Eq. (6) to Eq. (8) are used to develop the bone surface.

In human body, the left-side bones have symmetrical shapes with the right-side ones. To such bones, there is no need to express their surface as a percentage. The mapping of one subject's left or right foot first metatarsal is shown in Fig. 4.

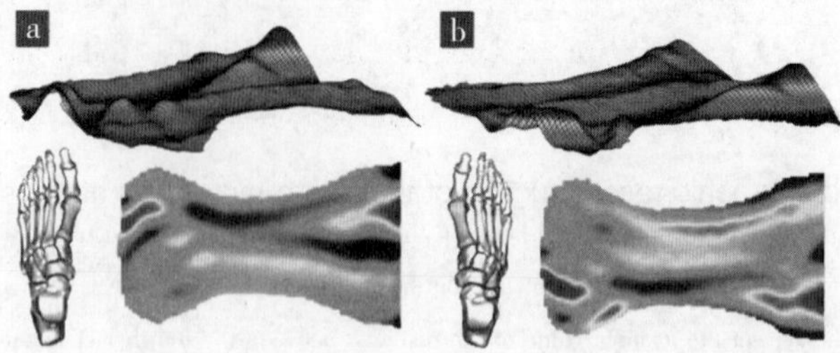

Fig. 4 Mapping of human symmetrical bone

Fig. 4a is one subject's left foot first metatarsal. Fig. 4b is one subject's right foot first metatarsal. The cutting line is the minimal PAI of the first metatarsal. (Some sections of the head and base of the first metatarsal are not on the cutting line. As a result, these sections are not included in the map)

Fig. 1 to Fig. 4 suggest that the mapping method is practical. Whether the method is valuable in bone's biomechanical study and in clinical application will determine the significance of our study. To examine the application of the mapping method in future research, we conduct a mapping analysis to the fourth metatarsal of the eight wrestlers and volleyballers, respectively. See Fig. 5.

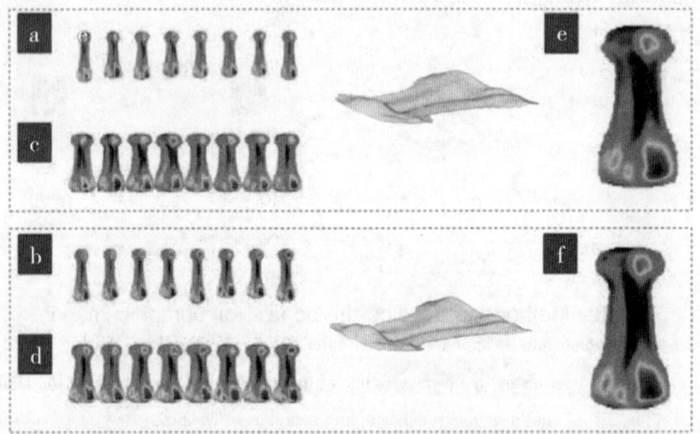

Fig. 5 Mapping analysis to the fourth metatarsal

Fig. 5a and Fig. 5b are the mapping of the fourth metatarsal (left foot) of eight wrestlers and volleyballers, respectively. Fig. 5c and Fig. 5d are the mapping of the fourth metatarsal (left foot) after standardization of length and width of eight wrestlers and volleyballers, respectively. Fig. 5e and Fig. 5f are the mapping of the fourth metatarsal (left foot) average value from eight wrestlers and volleyballers, respectively. Eq. (3) is applied to SCS of the athletes' fourth metatarsals (left foot) and then the tomography is reconstructed. Eq. (4) to Eq. (7) are employed to develop the reconstructed tomography. See Fig. 5a and Fig. 5b. To standardize the length and width of the metatarsal map brings the same length and width. See Fig. 5c and Fig. 5d. Statistical analysis is conducted on the standardized metatarsal map to calculate the average value of the eight metatarsal maps at the same position. See Fig. 5e and Fig. 5f.

Fig. 5 shows that the standardization of length and width of the map of the positioned development of the fourth metatarsal has brought about the average value map of the fourth metatarsal from many subjects. The result from the comparison of the average value map of the fourth metatarsal from two groups of athletes suggests that the degree of convex and concave surfaces of the fourth metatarsal from the volleyballers is greater than that of the wrestlers, which is consistent with the fact that volleyballers bear greater impact when spiking and blocking.

Bone can function as a body protection and as an aid to body movement. Analysis of bone strength has always been an important issue studied in biomechanics research. The possibility to apply the bone mapping method to analyze bone strength is explored. See Fig. 6.

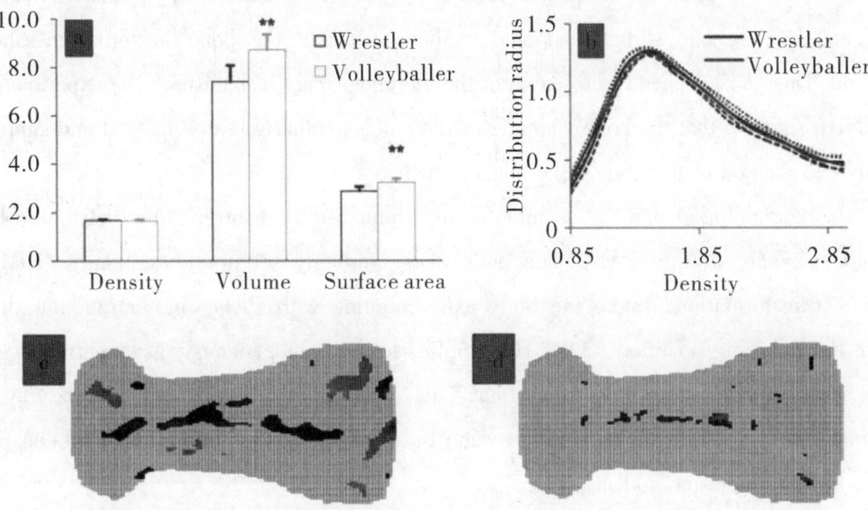

Fig. 6 Analysis of bone strength to the fourth metatarsal (left foot) of eight wrestlers and volleyballers

Fig. 6a is the comparison of bone density, volume and area of the fourth metatarsal (left foot) of eight wrestlers and volleyballers. Fig. 6b is the relationship between the fourth metatarsal (left foot) bone tissue density and the tissue distribution radius from eight wrestlers and volleyballers. Fig. 6c is the differences of the map of the fourth metatarsal (left foot) average value from eight wrestlers and volleyballers. Fig. 6d is the P-value distribution of the fourth metatarsal (left foot) map from eight wrestlers and volleyballers. In Fig. 6a, the bone's density is defined as $\rho = \frac{\sum_1^N \rho_i}{N}$, where $\rho_i = \frac{g_i}{g_w}$, g_i stands for the gray value of the i-th volume element, g_w stands for the gray value of water. Volume and area are results from Mimics software. In Fig. 6c, when $p_v(x, y) - p_w(x, y) > \lambda$, or $p_v(x, y) - p_w(x, y) < -\lambda$, $p_v(x, y) - p_w(x, y)$ is colored, where $p_v(x, y)$ and $p_w(x, y)$ stand for the altitude values for the positions of (x, y) of the fourth metatarsal from volleyballers and wrestlers, respectively, where blue shows $< -\lambda$ and red $> \lambda$ ($\lambda = 0.5$). In Fig. 6d, the calculation is done by SPSS, where blue shows $p < 0.05$ and red $p < 0.01$.

Fig. 6 shows the surface features of bone by the mapping method. It also serves as a quantitative method to study the morphological changes of bone, i. e., not only can the indexes of both bone density and the relation between bone tissue density and its distribution radius be used to analyze the bone strength, but also can the mapping method. This can contribute to the bone strength analysis clinically.

Conclusion

The generalization of Papoulis' theorem elucidates that bone surface shape keeps its geometric invariance, such as rotation, translation or dimension change. This ensures the consistency of the CT scanning results of different positions of bone in vivo when its isotropy is ascertained. The uniqueness of the relative consistency of the inertia reference system of principal moments of inertia on direction cosines contributes to the bone surface mapping method. The characters such as the geometric invariance and the uniqueness of the coordinate system of the principal moments of inertia, enable the bone surface mapping method to depict the bone's external morphological characters. This can advance the research of the morphological mechanisms. The experiment of the bone in vivo signifies that the bone mapping method adds another research method and supplements the analytical method of the bone's 3D imaging method.

It can be concluded that the asymmetrically shaped and anisotropically distributed bone in vivo holds a set of unique PAIs. The body axes randomly set upon the bone's COM, after coordinate transformation, make the body axes coincide with PAIs, indicating that the body axes are the only one set upon PAIs. This applies to the homogeneously asymmetrical geometry as well as the anisotropically asymmetrical one. The unique feature of PAIs is the key to determine whether or not the bone in vivo can be mapped. This uniqueness has been proved, and thus the mapping method is applicable.

We can draw a map of earth by an artificially defined prime meridian and equator line. But to map more than 200 pieces of human bone, how to employ a physical quantity to define the prime meridian and equator line is what our research team is trying to work out—to use the unique PAIs of the bone to determine the bone's prime meridian and equator line and then to use the mean distance of the bone surface points relative to the bone's COM to set the sea level and finally develop the bone according to the mathematical rules such as reconstruction and boundary detection so that the bone's surface can be mapped.

The morphological research of bone reveals the significance of human evolution. For example, the analysis of the fourth metatarsal of Australopithecus afarensis indicates that the afarensis foot functioned like that of modern humans. Ross and her colleagues' 3D – ID software can allow scientists to use the remains that there is still much potential to be explored in the morphology to focus on the shape (instead of size) to identify the sex and blood. Since human organ, tissue and cell are all asymmetrical ancestry with a better speed and accuracy, these all suggest geometries like bone which can be mapped accordingly, we believe that the application of this bone surface mapping method will be promising.

Selected Reading 5

基于步行足底冲量检测肌肉骨骼衰老及损伤的筛选方法

范毅方　樊瑜波　李知宇　Tony Newman　吕长生　周　毅

摘要：就如何通过步行足底冲量解释肌肉骨骼系统的损伤或老化目前尚未达成共识。我们通过定义足底冲量主轴这一概念实现足底冲量的标准化。基于标准化的足底冲量建立两个指标：足底压力记录时序和沿冲量主轴的足底冲量分布。使用这两个指标对足底压力板收集到的足底冲量进行分析，受试者分为三组：跟腱断裂组；老年组（62～71岁）；青年组（19～23岁）。研究发现，跟腱断裂者的足底冲量分布曲线随步行速度的变化是混乱的。通过对比青年人与老年人的足底冲量分布曲线，可知青年人与老年人的趾骨足底压力记录时序存在显著差异。于是我们的假设得到了验证：足底冲量检测能够成为反映评估肌肉骨骼系统损伤和老化程度的一种方法。

前　言

步行足底冲量是步行时足与支撑面相互作用的结果。利用 Titianova 等人发明的压力测量系统可以获取足底冲量信息。但步行足底冲量分析还没有在临床诊断、康复评估方面得到广泛应用。其主要原因是缺乏令人信服的有效表达运动器官损伤、衰老等状况的可靠证据。这已成为步行足印迹诊断被广泛使用的瓶颈。随着老龄化社会的到来和运动损伤病例的增加，如何更好地评估这两种人群的足部健康变得越来越重要。

步行时，足底压力测试设备由压力传感器把足与支撑面之间相互作用的力分割成单位（传感器面积）上的压力。压力传感器不仅能捕捉某一时刻的相互作用力，还能捕捉相互作用过程的开始时间和结束时间。足底触地（ICG）和离地（TCG）的时间被称为压力记录时序（PRTS），某一时刻传感器的压力值，称为瞬时压力。赤足行走时，在支撑阶段，瞬时压力的时间积分即为单位冲量。赤足步行，支撑阶段与足接触的传感器单位冲量的总和为足底冲量。

行走足印记的行进角度、足印迹大小、足底压力和足底冲量不仅受个体身体形态结构的影响，也与步速和步行足底冲量有关。平均数值的意义表明，平均足底冲量可以反映足底冲量的整体概况，而平均压力记录时序可以反映足底冲量形成过程的特征。健康人的很多指标（平均值）在临床和康复中被用作诊断标准。因此如何消除足底冲量之间的差异，使其一定程度上满足计算平均值数据的标准，是解决步行足印迹诊断的关键问题。

在本研究中，我们定义了一个物理量单位，意为冲量与其到总冲量中心距离平方乘积的总和的物理量。数学分析表明这个量有主轴存在，该主轴称为足底冲量主轴（PIPA）。与形态非对称、分布非均质物体惯量主轴具有唯一性一样，足底冲量主轴也是唯一的。这意味着，使用足底冲量主轴对足底冲量进行标准化，计算沿足底冲量主轴上足底触地、离地时序，对足底冲量分布长度进行百分化，并对支撑时间进行归一化，建立沿足底冲量主轴上压力记录时序指标。将定位后的足底冲量长度和宽度百分化后，再将每个单位冲量除以总冲量。这样我们就建立了沿足底冲量主轴的足底冲量分布指标。

我们假设个体的足底冲量包含其肌肉骨骼系统损伤和老化的信息：功能影响表现。如果假设成立，那么我们可以依据步行足底冲量建立一个反映肌肉骨骼系统损伤和老化的评估指标。将老年人的自然步态和青年人的自然步态、慢速步态、快速步态进行比较分析，结果显示沿足底冲量主轴的压力记录时序可以反映肌肉骨骼系统的老化情况。将跟腱断裂者与青年人不同步速状态下的 PRTS 指标比较分析，结果显示沿足底冲量主轴的足底冲量分布指标可以反映肌肉骨骼系统的损伤情况。由此我们的假设得到了验证。

材料和方法

【伦理声明】

本研究已获得广州体育学院伦理委员会批准。受试者均完全知晓并自愿参与本项研究，签署书面知情同意书。

【行走足底压力测试设备】

行走足底压力测量设备：地垫式足底压力系统：Zebris FDM System Gait Analysis（Long platform），平台：56（W）cm × 608（L）cm，平台每端延长 1. 2m；传感器分布：1sensor/cm^2；采样率：100Hz；软件：WinFDM。测试结果（每一时刻的单位足底压力数据）以文本格式输出供研究使用。足印迹图像生成用 MATLAB 软件绘制，背景图（background）（足的三维结构图）用 Mimics 软件绘制。

【测试对象及要求】

受试者分为三组。第一组：20 名健康青年人（10 名男性：21. 1 ± 1. 31 岁，1. 72 ± 0. 64m，61. 8 ± 8. 3kg；10 名女性：21. 7 ± 1. 3 岁，1. 61 ± 0. 57m，51. 2 ± 7. 6kg）；第二组：30 名健康老年人（14 名男性：68. 1 ± 3. 31year，1. 69 ± 0. 85m，63. 8 ± 8. 3kg；16 名女性：66. 5 ± 3. 1 岁，1. 59 ± 0. 67m，50. 2 ± 6. 6kg）第三组：7 名跟腱断裂男性，其基本信息见表 1。这三组受试者的基本步态信息见表 2。

表 1　跟腱断裂病人信息

病人	身高（cm）	体重（kg）	年龄（岁）	跟腱断裂原因
1	171	78	60	2000 年 1 月打篮球时右脚跟腱断裂
2	175	83	41	2002 年 7 月打篮球时左脚跟腱断裂
3	165	69	45	2003 年 7 月打篮球时右脚跟腱断裂
4	160	65	44	2005 年 5 月体操训练时左脚跟腱断裂
5	166	65	46	2007 年 4 月打篮球时左脚跟腱断裂
6	180	78	34	2011 年 4 月打篮球时左脚跟腱断裂
7	167	75	48	2011 年 6 月打篮球时右脚跟腱断裂

表 2　足底冲量主轴上足底触地时间的时间序列（足底冲量长度按百分比评价）

%	Normal（$n=20$）	Fast（$n=20$）	Slow（$n=20$）	Elderly（$n=30$）
1	0. 020 ±0. 018	0. 017 ±0. 011	0. 032 ±0. 021	0. 031 ±0. 029
2	0. 023 ±0. 013	0. 021 ±0. 009	0. 032 ±0. 016	0. 032 ±0. 026
3	0. 026 ±0. 010	0. 025 ±0. 010	0. 033 ±0. 013	0. 034 ±0. 024
4	0. 029 ±0. 010	0. 029 ±0. 013	0. 033 ±0. 013	0. 035 ±0. 022
5	0. 030 ±0. 012	0. 031 ±0. 015	0. 033 ±0. 014	0. 036 ±0. 022
6	0. 031 ±0. 009	0. 030 ±0. 012	0. 035 ±0. 012	0. 038 ±0. 020
7	0. 032 ±0. 009	0. 030 ±0. 011	0. 037 ±0. 013	0. 040 ±0. 019
8	0. 033 ±0. 012	0. 029 ±0. 011	0. 040 ±0. 016	0. 042 ±0. 020
9	0. 037 ±0. 015	0. 030 ±0. 011	0. 044 ±0. 020	0. 045 ±0. 022
10	0. 041 ±0. 015	0. 034 ±0. 013	0. 049 ±0. 019	0. 051 ±0. 022
11	0. 045 ±0. 016	0. 037 ±0. 016	0. 054 ±0. 018	0. 056 ±0. 020
12	0. 049 ±0. 017	0. 042 ±0. 018	0. 059 ±0. 018	0. 062 ±0. 019
13	0. 053 ±0. 015	0. 047 ±0. 019	0. 062 ±0. 018	0. 068 ±0. 019
14	0. 055 ±0. 013	0. 051 ±0. 017	0. 063 ±0. 016	0. 072 ±0. 020
15	0. 058 ±0. 013	0. 055 ±0. 016	0. 064 ±0. 016	0. 074 ±0. 020
16	0. 061 ±0. 015	0. 058 ±0. 015	0. 064 ±0. 018	0. 074 ±0. 020
17	0. 063 ±0. 017	0. 060 ±0. 014	0. 062 ±0. 021	0. 073 ±0. 021
18	0. 064 ±0. 018	0. 061 ±0. 014	0. 060 ±0. 022	0. 070 ±0. 020
19	0. 063 ±0. 020	0. 062 ±0. 017	0. 058 ±0. 024	0. 065 ±0. 021
20	0. 060 ±0. 021	0. 060 ±0. 020	0. 055 ±0. 025	0. 060 ±0. 022
21	0. 056 ±0. 022	0. 058 ±0. 020	0. 052 ±0. 026	0. 053 ±0. 021
22	0. 053 ±0. 021	0. 055 ±0. 019	0. 050 ±0. 025	0. 046 ±0. 021
23	0. 050 ±0. 019	0. 052 ±0. 017	0. 047 ±0. 024	0. 040 ±0. 019

（续上表）

%	Normal（$n=20$）	Fast（$n=20$）	Slow（$n=20$）	Elderly（$n=30$）
24	0.047±0.016	0.049±0.015	0.046±0.022	0.035±0.017
25	0.046±0.014	0.048±0.013	0.046±0.018	0.034±0.015
26	0.045±0.013	0.046±0.011	0.047±0.017	0.036±0.013◆
27	0.047±0.014	0.047±0.011	0.049±0.016	0.039±0.013
28	0.051±0.015	0.050±0.011	0.056±0.017	0.045±0.014
29	0.056±0.016	0.055±0.013	0.065±0.019	0.054±0.014
30	0.063±0.015	0.060±0.016	0.076±0.022▼	0.065±0.014
31	0.072±0.014	0.067±0.019	0.079±0.027▼	0.075±0.016
32	0.071±0.015	0.074±0.021	0.104±0.032▼	0.077±0.018
33	0.072±0.019	0.071±0.023	0.120±0.039▼	0.078±0.020
34	0.102±0.022	0.070±0.024	0.135±0.043▼	0.109±0.022
35	0.111±0.024	0.079±0.028	0.149±0.045▼	0.120±0.024
36	0.119±0.027	0.110±0.032	0.162±0.047▼	0.133±0.027
37	0.127±0.031	0.118±0.035	0.174±0.049▼	0.145±0.031
38	0.134±0.037	0.124±0.038	0.185±0.052▼	0.157±0.032
39	0.147±0.048	0.130±0.038	0.195±0.058▼	0.167±0.034
40	0.160±0.058	0.134±0.038	0.203±0.063▼	0.177±0.037
41	0.171±0.069	0.141±0.037	0.210±0.065	0.184±0.040
42	0.181±0.077	0.149±0.038	0.216±0.065	0.192±0.044
43	0.186±0.076	0.155±0.042	0.224±0.062	0.198±0.050
44	0.189±0.076	0.161±0.045	0.231±0.061	0.206±0.057
45	0.192±0.074	0.165±0.046	0.236±0.064	0.211±0.062
46	0.193±0.071	0.167±0.047	0.238±0.068	0.217±0.064
47	0.193±0.070	0.167±0.046	0.238±0.070	0.225±0.067
48	0.194±0.068	0.166±0.045	0.239±0.069	0.230±0.066
49	0.195±0.068	0.164±0.044	0.240±0.068	0.236±0.066
50	0.200±0.068	0.163±0.046	0.245±0.064	0.242±0.068
51	0.205±0.070	0.162±0.050★	0.249±0.062	0.248±0.072
52	0.213±0.072	0.168±0.052★	0.255±0.063	0.255±0.075
53	0.220±0.074	0.173±0.056★	0.261±0.066	0.261±0.081
54	0.225±0.071	0.181±0.059★	0.268±0.067	0.267±0.078
55	0.230±0.070	0.188±0.063	0.275±0.070	0.273±0.075
56	0.236±0.067	0.193±0.061★	0.283±0.069	0.280±0.068

（续上表）

%	Normal（$n=20$）	Fast（$n=20$）	Slow（$n=20$）	Elderly（$n=30$）
57	0. 245 ±0. 064	0. 203 ±0. 060★	0. 291 ±0. 067	0. 285 ±0. 058
58	0. 260 ±0. 058	0. 220 ±0. 059★	0. 299 ±0. 062	0. 291 ±0. 050
59	0. 274 ±0. 052	0. 241 ±0. 060	0. 306 ±0. 056	0. 296 ±0. 046
60	0. 287 ±0. 048	0. 264 ±0. 060	0. 310 ±0. 049	0. 298 ±0. 045
61	0. 296 ±0. 044	0. 283 ±0. 051	0. 312 ±0. 045	0. 301 ±0. 046
62	0. 296 ±0. 042	0. 292 ±0. 046	0. 310 ±0. 040	0. 298 ±0. 047
63	0. 294 ±0. 040	0. 296 ±0. 042	0. 304 ±0. 036	0. 291 ±0. 044
64	0. 287 ±0. 038	0. 293 ±0. 041	0. 296 ±0. 033	0. 281 ±0. 041
65	0. 277 ±0. 038	0. 286 ±0. 039	0. 284 ±0. 031	0. 269 ±0. 038
66	0. 268 ±0. 040	0. 275 ±0. 038	0. 270 ±0. 033	0. 256 ±0. 033
68	0. 249 ±0. 040	0. 252 ±0. 037	0. 247 ±0. 034	0. 239 ±0. 028
69	0. 242 ±0. 036	0. 243 ±0. 035	0. 241 ±0. 033	0. 232 ±0. 027
70	0. 238 ±0. 033	0. 237 ±0. 032	0. 239 ±0. 031	0. 228 ±0. 026
71	0. 235 ±0. 030	0. 236 ±0. 029	0. 238 ±0. 029	0. 223 ±0. 024
72	0. 232 ±0. 029	0. 235 ±0. 028	0. 237 ±0. 028	0. 219 ±0. 022
73	0. 230 ±0. 029	0. 237 ±0. 029	0. 237 ±0. 028	0. 215 ±0. 020
74	0. 229 ±0. 027	0. 239 ±0. 029	0. 235 ±0. 030	0. 212 ±0. 020
75	0. 230 ±0. 026	0. 244 ±0. 031	0. 233 ±0. 033	0. 213 ±0. 020
76	0. 234 ±0. 026	0. 249 ±0. 031	0. 229 ±0. 033	0. 215 ±0. 022
77	0. 238 ±0. 026	0. 256 ±0. 032	0. 226 ±0. 034	0. 219 ±0. 025
78	0. 245 ±0. 024	0. 267 ±0. 034★	0. 228 ±0. 036	0. 224 ±0. 029
79	0. 256 ±0. 025	0. 283 ±0. 041★	0. 236 ±0. 039	0. 232 ±0. 037
80	0. 271 ±0. 027	0. 304 ±0. 049★	0. 250 ±0. 040	0. 246 ±0. 045
81	0. 291 ±0. 031	0. 327 ±0. 056★	0. 270 ±0. 041	0. 263 ±0. 053
82	0. 316 ±0. 041	0. 354 ±0. 063★	0. 292 ±0. 046	0. 284 ±0. 058
83	0. 347 ±0. 050	0. 385 ±0. 067★	0. 320 ±0. 049	0. 308 ±0. 062
84	0. 383 ±0. 057	0. 423 ±0. 068	0. 353 ±0. 053	0. 336 ±0. 066
85	0. 421 ±0. 063	0. 461 ±0. 068	0. 387 ±0. 058	0. 365 ±0. 069
86	0. 454 ±0. 062	0. 495 ±0. 064★	0. 422 ±0. 059	0. 395 ±0. 068
87	0. 483 ±0. 057	0. 521 ±0. 057★	0. 457 ±0. 058	0. 421 ±0. 065
88	0. 509 ±0. 055	0. 543 ±0. 051	0. 491 ±0. 058	0. 448 ±0. 064?
89	0. 533 ±0. 055	0. 562 ±0. 049	0. 520 ±0. 058	0. 466 ±0. 065?
90	0. 546 ±0. 053	0. 574 ±0. 046	0. 537 ±0. 059	0. 476 ±0. 061?

（续上表）

%	Normal（$n=20$）	Fast（$n=20$）	Slow（$n=20$）	Elderly（$n=30$）
91	0. 546 ±0. 054	0. 570 ±0. 046	0. 544 ±0. 060	0. 484 ±0. 059?
92	0. 545 ±0. 055	0. 562 ±0. 048	0. 551 ±0. 062	0. 489 ±0. 062?
93	0. 542 ±0. 059	0. 554 ±0. 051	0. 556 ±0. 065	0. 486 ±0. 066?
94	0. 538 ±0. 063	0. 546 ±0. 059	0. 556 ±0. 068	0. 498 ±0. 065?
95	0. 548 ±0. 056	0. 552 ±0. 054	0. 565 ±0. 063	0. 515 ±0. 063?
96	0. 557 ±0. 050	0. 560 ±0. 050	0. 574 ±0. 058	0. 533 ±0. 063
97	0. 567 ±0. 047	0. 569 ±0. 047	0. 585 ±0. 054	0. 556 ±0. 066
98	0. 608 ±0. 035	0. 606 ±0. 048	0. 625 ±0. 043	0. 604 ±0. 065
99	0. 657 ±0. 030	0. 654 ±0. 053	0. 673 ±0. 036	0. 654 ±0. 067
100	0. 707 ±0. 040	0. 701 ±0. 066	0. 720 ±0. 038	0. 703 ±0. 071

◆$p<0.05$ 表明老年受试者常速步态与青年受试者常速步态、快速步态和慢速步态之间触地时序（ICG）的显著性差异。

▼$p<0.05$ 表明青年受试者的快速步态与年青受试者的常速步态、慢速步态和老年受试者常速步态下的足底触地时序之间存在显著差异。

★$p<0.05$ 表明青年受试者的慢速步态与青年受试者的常速步态、快速步态和老年受试者常速步态下的足底触地时序之间存在显著差异。t 检验采用双尾分布、两样本不等方差（异方差）。

对受试者进行问卷调查，选择无下肢韧带损伤病史者。根据受试者每年的体检报告，确保选择的受试者无神经系统与肌肉骨骼系统的疾病与损伤。根据医院提供的诊断报告确定第三组七名跟腱断裂者的病史情况。

对不同步速进行测试时，不用节拍器和运动参照物来干预受试者的步速，强调按照自己的习惯行走。为了使受试者有感性认识，给受试者以正常、快速和慢速步行的示范（示范者是受过多次训练的，其三种状态的速度值分别约为 1. 05m/s，1. 35m/s，1. 86m/s，且较为稳定）。

测试前，测试者双足用75%酒精进行消毒，赤足站立。然后受试者双足并拢（赤脚）站于 platform 前端。当受试者平稳站立后（约 3 秒钟），实验助理给出行走指示。设备操作员按键收集数据。受试者停止行走后，根据实验助理的指示返回。如果发现第一脚在 platform 上不完整、测试过程走出 platform 或步态有明显的不连贯时，重新测试，从第二脚在 platform 上开始，采集符合要求的结果记录。每位受试者取 6 个连续步行足印迹进行分析。

【步行足底冲量主轴】

定义一个物理量数值：所有单位冲量与其到总冲量中心距离平方乘积的总和。从 Zebris 步态测试分析系统得到的足底冲量，其分量形式为：

$$\begin{cases} I_x = \sum y^2 Ip_{ij} \\ I_y = \sum x^2 Ip_{ij} \end{cases} \tag{1}$$

式中，Ip_{ij}表示与足相互作用的传感器冲量，i、j 分别表示传感器的行列号。单位冲量用 $Ip_{ij}=\int_0^{T_s}P_{(i,j)}(t)\,\mathrm{d}t$ 计算，T_s表示支撑时间，$P_{(i,j)}(t)$ 表示位置为 (i,j) 的传感器在时刻 t 的瞬时压力值。(x,j) 表示 Ip_{ij} 相对足底冲量中心的位置，足底冲量中心用 $\left(\frac{\Sigma iIp_{ij}}{\Sigma iIp_{ij}},\frac{\Sigma jIp_{ij}}{\Sigma Ip_{ij}}\right)$ 计算。

设足底冲量绕通过足底冲量中心的垂直轴转动的角位移为 α。我们可以建立以下关系：

$$(I_x-I_y)_\alpha=\sum\left[(x^2\cos\alpha-y^2\sin\alpha)-(x^2\sin\alpha+y^2\cos\alpha)\right]Ip_{ij}\tag{2}$$

对方程（2）求导，并令

$$\frac{\mathrm{d}(I_x-I_y)_\alpha}{\mathrm{d}\alpha}=0$$

整理后得到

$$\alpha=\frac{1}{2}\arctan\left(\frac{2\sum xyIp_{ij}}{\sum x^2Ip_{ij}-\sum y^2Ip_{ij}}\right)\tag{3}$$

足底冲量分布形态是非对称的，这导致方程（1）中始终有 $I_x\neq I_y$ 存在。像形态非对称、分布非均质物体惯量主轴一样，在 $[0,\pi]$ 范围内，足底冲量通过有限转动（绕通过足印迹冲量中心的垂直轴转动）总可以使 $\Sigma xyIp_{ij}$ 为零。这时通过足底冲量中心的轴我们称为足底冲量主轴。

【沿足底冲量主轴的步行足底冲量分布】

沿足底冲量主轴的足底冲量位置（x_{cl}，y_{cl}）用下列公式计算：

$$x_{cl}=\frac{\sum_{l=1}^{n_l}\int_0^{T_s}P_{(i,j)}(t)x_l\mathrm{d}t}{\sum_{l=1}^{n_l}\int_0^{T_s}P_{(i,j)}(t)\mathrm{d}t},\quad y_{cl}=\frac{\sum_{l=1}^{n_l}\int_0^{T_s}P_{(i,j)}(t)y_l\mathrm{d}t}{\sum_{l=1}^{n_l}\int_0^{T_s}P_{(i,j)}(t)\mathrm{d}t}\tag{4}$$

式中 $P_{(i,j)}(t)$ 和 T_s 与其在方程（1）中的定义相同，n_l 表示在足长度位置 l 上与足相互作用的传感器数量（足底冲量分布宽度的单位数量）。

【沿足底冲量主轴上压力记录时序】

根据步态特征，步行中足触地与离地的过程是连续的（其表现为：足底的同一位置在一个步态周期中触地与离地各只有一次。也就是说在行走一步的过程中，足底面的每一个点都只接触地面一次）。设足底位置（x，y）的触地与离地时间分别为 $t^O_{(x,y)}$ 和 $t^T_{(x,y)}$，那么沿足底冲量主轴的足底触地（ICG）、离地（TCG）时序为：

$$\bar{t}^O_l=\frac{\sum_{l=1}^{n_l}t^O_{(x,y)}}{n_l},\quad \bar{t}^T_t=\frac{\sum_{l=1}^{n_l}t^T_{(x,y)}}{n_l}\tag{5}$$

式中 $\bar{t}^O_l$、$\bar{t}^T_l$ 分别表示足底冲量主轴上位置为 l 的触地、离地时间。n_l 与其在方程（4）中的定义相同。

[沿足长度上足底冲量]

在足长度上位置为 l 的足底冲量分布为：

$$Ip(l) = \frac{1}{n_l}\sum_{l=1}^{n_l}\int_0^{T_s} p(ij)\,\mathrm{d}t \tag{6}$$

式中 T_s 和 n_l 与方程（4）中的定义相同。

结果与讨论

用方程（1）计算足底冲量中心。由方程（3）计算各足底冲量旋转角，以这个角度将足底冲量绕通过足底冲量中心的垂直轴转动。如彩图 22 所示。

由彩图 22 可知，当足底冲量被确定后，足底冲量主轴是唯一的，这种唯一性保证了足底冲量标准化处理结果的可靠性。在步态分析中，步行足底冲量行进角被定义为一个与步行方向及步行足印迹的形态有关的量，它是一个测量值。这种基于足底冲量主轴的方法为实现步行足底冲量的标准化提供了另一种解析。

“定位”是指用足底冲量主轴的物理量代表足印迹的行进角。当足底冲量定位时，对每个足底冲量分布的长度和宽度进行百分化，用总冲量对单位冲量进行归一化。得到不同步速下的平均足底冲量，如彩图 23 所示。

彩图 23 中通过足底冲量主轴对足底冲量进行标准化。完成足底冲量分布的长度和宽度百分化及用总冲量对单位冲量的归一化，就消除了个体在步行足底冲量进程角、足型和体重方面差异的影响因素。然后我们就可以得到青年人不同步速下的平均足底冲量。而平均足底冲量可以反映出一个足底冲量的整体概况。

用方程（4）计算沿足底冲量主轴上的足底冲量分布曲线位置，绘制左右足的足底冲量分布曲线。如彩图 24 所示。

彩图 24 表明，基于平均足底冲量，可以建立沿足底冲量主轴的足底冲量分布曲线。用这个指标对青年人不同步速下足底冲量进行分析，结果表明：左右足足底冲量分布曲线在足跟部和足前掌形成两个交汇点。随着步速的变化，两条分布曲线第一个交汇点出现的顺序为慢速—正常—快速，第二个交汇点出现的顺序为快速—正常—慢速，这样的顺序使得两个交汇点之间的距离随步速增加而不断缩短。因此我们的假设得以证实——足底冲量包含了肌肉骨骼系统的损伤信息，那么健康人左右足足底冲量分布曲线的交汇点随步速的变化规律，将成为运动器官损伤者的诊断方法。

跟腱断裂者足底冲量分布曲线（左右两足）见彩图 25。

彩图 25 表明，跟腱断裂者在不同步速下，左右足足底冲量分布曲线的交汇点位置与彩图 3 中健康青年人的相比，有两个共同特征：①位置顺序混乱，这种混乱同时导致两个交汇点距离异常；②快速步行时，连接第 1（足跟部）和第 2（足前掌）两个交汇点，连线与足的矢状轴形成一个夹角，当角度大于零时，为右侧跟腱断裂者，当角度小于零时，为左侧跟腱断裂者。但即使是健康的受试者该角度也不为零，该现象需要进一步的研究讨论。

足底冲量定位后，用方程（5）计算沿足底冲量主轴的足底触地、离地时序。然后百分化足底冲量分布的长度并将支撑时间标准化为 1 秒，得到结果如彩图 26 所示。彩图 26 表明足底触地、离地时序与步速有关。对于青年人，步速对触地时序分布的影响相对较小，尤其在足跟、足前掌和足趾部位；步速主要影响离地时序分布，具体表现为：从足跟至足前掌，随步速的增加离地时间增加；随着步速的增加，足前掌相对支撑时间增大。这样的支撑时间分布符合了不同步速下地面反作用的分布。也就是说，这种沿足底冲量主轴的压力记录时序的计算方法是可靠的。

彩图 26 还表明老年人的触地时序与青年人的存在差异。为了说明该差异我们分析了老年人和青年人沿足底冲量主轴的触地时序，见表格 2。由表格 2 可知，建立沿足底冲量主轴上第一趾触地时序指数，老年人的该指标与青年人在各种步速下的该指标均存在显著差异，而青年人不同步速之间无统计学差异。为何会如此？通过公式（6）计算出沿足长度的足底冲量分布，我们可以得到每个受试者沿足长度的连续六个足底冲量的平均值。见彩图 27。

彩图 26 的 C 图显示跖骨与地面的相互作用发生于支撑相的结束阶段，且前后摩擦力向前，起到保持行走速度的作用。彩图 27 显示当青年人行走速度加快时，其第一趾的足底冲量增加。我们知道，肌肉系统的衰老会导致跖骨功能减弱。因冲量为一定时间内作用力造成的矢量，所以为了弥补这种肌力下降造成的损失，只有通过增加作用时间来增加作用效果。以彩图 26 中的中老年人跖骨与地面的作用时间为例，对支撑时间归一化后，通过提前触地时间来实现作用时间的增加。

肌肉骨骼系统的损伤与衰老会造成步行时步态参数的改变。但步态参数也许并不能用于预测损伤的信息何时衰弱、消失，衰老的信息何时出现。例如，跟腱重建 24 个月后步态参数恢复正常，但研究表明，无论时间长短，跟腱断裂残留信息始终存在。步速与老年人健康相关，但我们不能只用步速去判定老年人的健康状况，因为慢行也许是个人习惯。而我们建立的指标能够反映出老年人自然步态下足趾的压力记录时序与青年人自然、快速、慢速步态下的压力记录时序存在差异。这些证据表明，步行足底冲量能够反映评估人体肌肉骨骼的损伤、衰老状况。

本研究的局限性：①第一交汇点与第二交汇点连线形成的夹角是否与跟腱断裂有关，为什么健康受试者该夹角亦不为零？这是不是由个体左右脚的功能差异引起的？该现象需要设计新的步态实验来进一步研究。②老年人足趾触地时序与青年人存在差异的原因尚不明确。该现象是否由肌肉骨骼系统或神经系统的衰老引起需要进一步通过实验来解释说明。另外，虽然无法从 ROC 曲线（接受者操作特性曲线）中得知检测疾病的发生率，但其仍然是评估诊断试验灵敏度的有效方法。今后我们将会利用 ROC 曲线确定本次实验方法的临床意义和有效性。

结　论

健康人步态参数，如步长、步速等，作为临床诊断和康复评定的依据，已得到了广泛的应用。为了使这些指标更具有应用价值，用腿长或髋关节高度来消除个体之间的体型差异的标准化处理，已取得了非常有趣的（也是科学的）结果，如根据步长及髋关节高度对恐龙步速的推测。在应用前景上，步行足底冲量也不例外。

步行足底冲量的标准化，涉及足底冲量进程角、足印迹的大小、足底压力以及足底冲量等多个量。在这方面，Keijser 等人做了启发性的工作，本研究用一个解析确定足底冲量主轴，基于足底冲量主轴进行足底冲量标准化的方法保证了准确性。对于传感器而言，压力记录时序是一个逻辑量同时也是一个时间量（特别是当足底某一位置在某一段支撑时间接触地面而在另一段支撑时间与地面不接触时。“接触”与“没接触”是一个逻辑量，对于这样一个逻辑记录量我们不能认定该位置在连续的行走过程中没有接触地面，也不能直接计算其平均值），而对于经足底冲量主轴定位后的足底冲量，基于沿足底冲量主轴的压力记录时序计算方法解决了这个量的代数运算问题。

行走是一个足与支撑面相互作用的运动过程。在这个过程中，当身体环节的运动发生改变时，相互作用力也发生改变，因为力是物体间的相互作用。肌肉骨骼系统损伤、衰老改变了身体环节的运动，因此，步行足底冲量能够反映肌肉骨骼系统损伤、衰老的状况。采用沿足底冲量主轴的压力记录时序和足底冲量分布指标对跟腱断裂者、老年人与青年人的步行足底冲量进行分析，其结果也验证了这一点。

由此可见，采用足底冲量主轴对足底冲量进行定位、标准化，基于定位、标准化的足底冲量，我们可以建立沿足底冲量主轴的压力记录时序和足底冲量分布指标。如果通过大量的样本实验该评估指标的有效性得到验证，那么足底冲量分析法便可以在临床医学和康复医学等方面得到广泛应用。

Screening Method Based on Walking Plantar Impulse for Detecting Musculoskeletal Senescence and Injury

Yifang Fan, Yubo Fan, Zhiyu Li, Tony Newman, Changsheng Lyu, Yi Zhou
Translated by Zhiyu Li

Abstract: No consensus has been reached on how musculoskeletal system injuries or aging can be explained by a walking plantar impulse. We standardize the plantar impulse by defining a principal axis of plantar impulse. Based upon this standardized plantar impulse, two indexes are presented: plantar pressure record time series and plantar-impulse distribution along the principal axis of plantar impulse. These indexes are applied to analyze the plantar impulse collected by plantar pressure plates from three sources: Achilles tendon ruptures; elderly people (ages 62 – 71); and young people (ages 19 – 23). Our findings reveal that plantar-impulse distribution curves for Achilles tendon ruptures change irregularly with subjects' walking speed changes. When comparing distribution curves of the young, we see a significant difference in the elderly subjects' phalanges plantar pressure record time series. This verifies our hypothesis that a plantar impulse can function as a means to assess and evaluate musculoskeletal system injuries and aging.

Introduction

A walking plantar impulse expresses the action of the foot on a support surface. Titianova et al. developed the pressure sensor system to acquire plantar impulse information. But walking plantar impulse analysis is not widely used in clinical diagnosis or rehabilitation assessment. The lack of convincing and effective representation of conditions such as musculoskeletal system injuries or aging has bottlenecked the wide application of a plantar impulse. The arrival of an aging society and the increase of sports injuries call for more approaches to better assess and evaluate these two groups's foot health.

When walking, the interaction between a foot and its support surface—obtained from the plantar pressure measurement device can be differentiated by pressure sensors into the force of unit area. A pressure sensor will not only capture the interaction force at a specific instant, but it will also capture the initial and terminal time of the interaction process. The combination of plantar initial contact ground (ICG) and terminal contact ground (TCG) time is called the pressure record time series (PRTS) and the resulting pressure value reading from pressure sensors is called the instantaneous pressure. When walking bare-footedly, at stance phase, the temporal integration of the instantaneous pressure is called unit impulse, and the sum of each unit impulse that the foot makes contact with is a plantar impulse.

The walking-footprint progression angle, walking-footprint size, plantar pressure and plantar impulse are influenced not only by individual body shape and structure, but also by walking speed, and walking plantar impulse. The definition of an average value indicates that average plantar impulse can generalize the whole plantar impulse and the average PRTS can reflect the characteristics of how the plantar impulse is shaped. Healthy people's many indexes (mean) are used to identify abnormalities in clinical and rehabilitation medicine, which means that when differences between plantar impulses are eliminated, to such an extent that they can meet the requirements of average value, it solves the critical problem of plantar impulse analysis.

In this study, a distribution of plantar impulse is defined as a physical quantity, which is the sum of all the products formed by multiplying the magnitude of each unit impulse by the square of its distance to the plantar impulse center. Mathematical analysis indicates that this quantity has a principal axis, which is called the plantar-impulse principal axis (PIPA) . Just like the uniqueness of a principal axis of inertia of an asymmetrically shaped and anisotropically structured object, the PIPA is also unique. This means that we can use the PIPA to standardize the plantar impulse, to calculate the initial and terminal contact ground time series along the PIPA, to rate plantar-impulse distribution length by percentage, to normalize stance time and to establish a PRTS index along the PIPA. After rating the length and width of the processed plantar impulse by percentage, every unit impulse is divided by total impulse. Thus, we establish a plantar-impulse distribution index along the PIPA.

We assume that a plantar impulse contains information about musculoskeletal system injuries and aging: function affects behavior. If our hypothesis holds, then it is possible to build an evaluation index to reflect musculoskeletal system injuries and aging based on walking plantar impulse. Our comparative analysis of the elderly subjects' free gait with the young subjects' free, fast and slow gait shows that the PRTS index along PIPA can reflect the musculoskeletal system's senescence, while that of different speeds from the Achilles tendon ruptures (ATRs) and from the young shows that plantar-impulse distribution index along the PIPA can reflect the musculoskeletal system's injury, confirming our hypothesis.

Materials and Methods

【Ethics Statement】

The study received approval from the Ethical Committee of Guangzhou Institute of Physical Education. The subjects provided fully informed consent to participate in this study by signing a written consent form.

【Walking Plantar Pressure Test Equipment】

Walking plantar pressure measuring equipment: Zebris FDM System Gait Analysis (Long platform) . Platform: 56 (W) cm × 608 (L) cm, with an additional 1.2m at each end of the platform; sensor intensity: 1sensor/cm^2; sampling rate: 100Hz. software: WinFDM. Test results were output as text file (unit plantar pressure data at every instant of time) to be used in this study. Image processing was done by MATLAB and background (i. e. , foot's three-dimension image) was done by Mimics.

【Test Subjects and Requirements】

Our subjects were divided into three groups. The first group: twenty healthy subjects (10 male subjects: 21. 1 ±1. 31 year, 1. 72 ±0. 64m, 61. 8 ±8. 3kg; 10 female subjects: 21. 7 ± 1. 3 year, 1. 61 ± 0. 57m, 51. 2 ± 7. 6kg) The second group: thirty healthy elderly subjects (14 male subjects: 68. 1 ± 3. 31year, 1. 69 ± 0. 85m, 63. 8 ± 8. 3kg; 16 female subjects: 66. 5 ±3. 1 year, 1. 59 ± 0. 67m, 50. 2 ± 6. 6kg) The third group: seven male subjects with ATRs: see Table 1 for details. For these subjects' basic gait information, see Table 2.

Table 1 Detailed information of ATRs

Subject	Height (cm)	Weight (kg)	Age (year)	Cause of ATRs
1	171	78	60	with rightfoot ATR when playing basketball in January, 2000
2	175	83	41	with leftfoot ATR when playing basketball in July, 2002
3	165	69	45	with rightfoot ATR when playing basketball in July, 2003
4	160	65	44	with leftfoot ATR in gymnastics training in May, 2005
5	166	65	46	with leftfoot ATR when playing basketball in April, 2007
6	180	78	34	with leftfoot ATR when playing basketball in April, 2011
7	167	75	48	with rightfoot ATR when playing basketball in June, 2011

Table 2 ICG time series along PIPA (Plantar impulse length is rated by percentage)

%	Normal (n =20)	Fast (n =20)	Slow (n =20)	Elderly (n =30)
1	0. 020 ±0. 018	0. 017 ±0. 011	0. 032 ±0. 021	0. 031 ±0. 029
2	0. 023 ±0. 013	0. 021 ±0. 009	0. 032 ±0. 016	0. 032 ±0. 026
3	0. 026 ±0. 010	0. 025 ±0. 010	0. 033 ±0. 013	0. 034 ±0. 024
4	0. 029 ±0. 010	0. 029 ±0. 013	0. 033 ±0. 013	0. 035 ±0. 022
5	0. 030 ±0. 012	0. 031 ±0. 015	0. 033 ±0. 014	0. 036 ±0. 022
6	0. 031 ±0. 009	0. 030 ±0. 012	0. 035 ±0. 012	0. 038 ±0. 020
7	0. 032 ±0. 009	0. 030 ±0. 011	0. 037 ±0. 013	0. 040 ±0. 019
8	0. 033 ±0. 012	0. 029 ±0. 011	0. 040 ±0. 016	0. 042 ±0. 020
9	0. 037 ±0. 015	0. 030 ±0. 011	0. 044 ±0. 020	0. 045 ±0. 022

(to be continued)

%	Normal（$n=20$）	Fast（$n=20$）	Slow（$n=20$）	Elderly（$n=30$）
10	0.041 ±0.015	0.034 ±0.013	0.049 ±0.019	0.051 ±0.022
11	0.045 ±0.016	0.037 ±0.016	0.054 ±0.018	0.056 ±0.020
12	0.049 ±0.017	0.042 ±0.018	0.059 ±0.018	0.062 ±0.019
13	0.053 ±0.015	0.047 ±0.019	0.062 ±0.018	0.068 ±0.019
14	0.055 ±0.013	0.051 ±0.017	0.063 ±0.016	0.072 ±0.020
15	0.058 ±0.013	0.055 ±0.016	0.064 ±0.016	0.074 ±0.020
16	0.061 ±0.015	0.058 ±0.015	0.064 ±0.018	0.074 ±0.020
17	0.063 ±0.017	0.060 ±0.014	0.062 ±0.021	0.073 ±0.021
18	0.064 ±0.018	0.061 ±0.014	0.060 ±0.022	0.070 ±0.020
19	0.063 ±0.020	0.062 ±0.017	0.058 ±0.024	0.065 ±0.021
20	0.060 ±0.021	0.060 ±0.020	0.055 ±0.025	0.060 ±0.022
21	0.056 ±0.022	0.058 ±0.020	0.052 ±0.026	0.053 ±0.021
22	0.053 ±0.021	0.055 ±0.019	0.050 ±0.025	0.046 ±0.021
23	0.050 ±0.019	0.052 ±0.017	0.047 ±0.024	0.040 ±0.019
24	0.047 ±0.016	0.049 ±0.015	0.046 ±0.022	0.035 ±0.017
25	0.046 ±0.014	0.048 ±0.013	0.046 ±0.018	0.034 ±0.015
26	0.045 ±0.013	0.046 ±0.011	0.047 ±0.017	0.036 ±0.013◆
27	0.047 ±0.014	0.047 ±0.011	0.049 ±0.016	0.039 ±0.013
28	0.051 ±0.015	0.050 ±0.011	0.056 ±0.017	0.045 ±0.014
29	0.056 ±0.016	0.055 ±0.013	0.065 ±0.019	0.054 ±0.014
30	0.063 ±0.015	0.060 ±0.016	0.076 ±0.022▼	0.065 ±0.014
31	0.072 ±0.014	0.067 ±0.019	0.079 ±0.027▼	0.075 ±0.016
32	0.071 ±0.015	0.074 ±0.021	0.104 ±0.032▼	0.077 ±0.018
33	0.072 ±0.019	0.071 ±0.023	0.120 ±0.039▼	0.078 ±0.020
34	0.102 ±0.022	0.070 ±0.024	0.135 ±0.043▼	0.109 ±0.022
35	0.111 ±0.024	0.079 ±0.028	0.149 ±0.045▼	0.120 ±0.024
36	0.119 ±0.027	0.110 ±0.032	0.162 ±0.047▼	0.133 ±0.027
37	0.127 ±0.031	0.118 ±0.035	0.174 ±0.049▼	0.145 ±0.031
38	0.134 ±0.037	0.124 ±0.038	0.185 ±0.052▼	0.157 ±0.032
39	0.147 ±0.048	0.130 ±0.038	0.195 ±0.058▼	0.167 ±0.034
40	0.160 ±0.058	0.134 ±0.038	0.203 ±0.063▼	0.177 ±0.037
41	0.171 ±0.069	0.141 ±0.037	0.210 ±0.065	0.184 ±0.040
42	0.181 ±0.077	0.149 ±0.038	0.216 ±0.065	0.192 ±0.044

（to be continued）

%	Normal（$n=20$）	Fast（$n=20$）	Slow（$n=20$）	Elderly（$n=30$）
43	0.186 ±0.076	0.155 ±0.042	0.224 ±0.062	0.198 ±0.050
44	0.189 ±0.076	0.161 ±0.045	0.231 ±0.061	0.206 ±0.057
45	0.192 ±0.074	0.165 ±0.046	0.236 ±0.064	0.211 ±0.062
46	0.193 ±0.071	0.167 ±0.047	0.238 ±0.068	0.217 ±0.064
47	0.193 ±0.070	0.167 ±0.046	0.238 ±0.070	0.225 ±0.067
48	0.194 ±0.068	0.166 ±0.045	0.239 ±0.069	0.230 ±0.066
49	0.195 ±0.068	0.164 ±0.044	0.240 ±0.068	0.236 ±0.066
50	0.200 ±0.068	0.163 ±0.046	0.245 ±0.064	0.242 ±0.068
51	0.205 ±0.070	0.162 ±0.050★	0.249 ±0.062	0.248 ±0.072
52	0.213 ±0.072	0.168 ±0.052★	0.255 ±0.063	0.255 ±0.075
53	0.220 ±0.074	0.173 ±0.056★	0.261 ±0.066	0.261 ±0.081
54	0.225 ±0.071	0.181 ±0.059★	0.268 ±0.067	0.267 ±0.078
55	0.230 ±0.070	0.188 ±0.063	0.275 ±0.070	0.273 ±0.075
56	0.236 ±0.067	0.193 ±0.061★	0.283 ±0.069	0.280 ±0.068
57	0.245 ±0.064	0.203 ±0.060★	0.291 ±0.067	0.285 ±0.058
58	0.260 ±0.058	0.220 ±0.059★	0.299 ±0.062	0.291 ±0.050
59	0.274 ±0.052	0.241 ±0.060	0.306 ±0.056	0.296 ±0.046
60	0.287 ±0.048	0.264 ±0.060	0.310 ±0.049	0.298 ±0.045
61	0.296 ±0.044	0.283 ±0.051	0.312 ±0.045	0.301 ±0.046
62	0.296 ±0.042	0.292 ±0.046	0.310 ±0.040	0.298 ±0.047
63	0.294 ±0.040	0.296 ±0.042	0.304 ±0.036	0.291 ±0.044
64	0.287 ±0.038	0.293 ±0.041	0.296 ±0.033	0.281 ±0.041
65	0.277 ±0.038	0.286 ±0.039	0.284 ±0.031	0.269 ±0.038
66	0.268 ±0.040	0.275 ±0.038	0.270 ±0.033	0.256 ±0.033
68	0.249 ±0.040	0.252 ±0.037	0.247 ±0.034	0.239 ±0.028
69	0.242 ±0.036	0.243 ±0.035	0.241 ±0.033	0.232 ±0.027
70	0.238 ±0.033	0.237 ±0.032	0.239 ±0.031	0.228 ±0.026
71	0.235 ±0.030	0.236 ±0.029	0.238 ±0.029	0.223 ±0.024
72	0.232 ±0.029	0.235 ±0.028	0.237 ±0.028	0.219 ±0.022
73	0.230 ±0.029	0.237 ±0.029	0.237 ±0.028	0.215 ±0.020
74	0.229 ±0.027	0.239 ±0.029	0.235 ±0.030	0.212 ±0.020
75	0.230 ±0.026	0.244 ±0.031	0.233 ±0.033	0.213 ±0.020
76	0.234 ±0.026	0.249 ±0.031	0.229 ±0.033	0.215 ±0.022

(to be continued)

%	Normal ($n=20$)	Fast ($n=20$)	Slow ($n=20$)	Elderly ($n=30$)
77	0. 238 ±0. 026	0. 256 ±0. 032	0. 226 ±0. 034	0. 219 ±0. 025
78	0. 245 ±0. 024	0. 267 ±0. 034★	0. 228 ±0. 036	0. 224 ±0. 029
79	0. 256 ±0. 025	0. 283 ±0. 041★	0. 236 ±0. 039	0. 232 ±0. 037
80	0. 271 ±0. 027	0. 304 ±0. 049★	0. 250 ±0. 040	0. 246 ±0. 045
81	0. 291 ±0. 031	0. 327 ±0. 056★	0. 270 ±0. 041	0. 263 ±0. 053
82	0. 316 ±0. 041	0. 354 ±0. 063★	0. 292 ±0. 046	0. 284 ±0. 058
83	0. 347 ±0. 050	0. 385 ±0. 067★	0. 320 ±0. 049	0. 308 ±0. 062
84	0. 383 ±0. 057	0. 423 ±0. 068	0. 353 ±0. 053	0. 336 ±0. 066
85	0. 421 ±0. 063	0. 461 ±0. 068	0. 387 ±0. 058	0. 365 ±0. 069
86	0. 454 ±0. 062	0. 495 ±0. 064★	0. 422 ±0. 059	0. 395 ±0. 068
87	0. 483 ±0. 057	0. 521 ±0. 057★	0. 457 ±0. 058	0. 421 ±0. 065
88	0. 509 ±0. 055	0. 543 ±0. 051	0. 491 ±0. 058	0. 448 ±0. 064?
89	0. 533 ±0. 055	0. 562 ±0. 049	0. 520 ±0. 058	0. 466 ±0. 065?
90	0. 546 ±0. 053	0. 574 ±0. 046	0. 537 ±0. 059	0. 476 ±0. 061?
91	0. 546 ±0. 054	0. 570 ±0. 046	0. 544 ±0. 060	0. 484 ±0. 059?
92	0. 545 ±0. 055	0. 562 ±0. 048	0. 551 ±0. 062	0. 489 ±0. 062?
93	0. 542 ±0. 059	0. 554 ±0. 051	0. 556 ±0. 065	0. 486 ±0. 066?
94	0. 538 ±0. 063	0. 546 ±0. 059	0. 556 ±0. 068	0. 498 ±0. 065?
95	0. 548 ±0. 056	0. 552 ±0. 054	0. 565 ±0. 063	0. 515 ±0. 063?
96	0. 557 ±0. 050	0. 560 ±0. 050	0. 574 ±0. 058	0. 533 ±0. 063
97	0. 567 ±0. 047	0. 569 ±0. 047	0. 585 ±0. 054	0. 556 ±0. 066
98	0. 608 ±0. 035	0. 606 ±0. 048	0. 625 ±0. 043	0. 604 ±0. 065
99	0. 657 ±0. 030	0. 654 ±0. 053	0. 673 ±0. 036	0. 654 ±0. 067
100	0. 707 ±0. 040	0. 701 ±0. 066	0. 720 ±0. 038	0. 703 ±0. 071

◆$p<0.05$, showing the significant difference between the ICGs from the elderly subjects' free gait and those from the young subjects' free, fast and slow gait.

▼$p<0.05$, showing the significant difference between the ICGs from the young subjects' fast gait and those from the young subjects' free, slow gait and the elderly subjects' free gait.

★$p<0.05$, showing the significant difference between the ICGs from the young subjects' slow gait and those from the young subjects' free, fast and the elderly subjects' free gait. *t*-test uses the two-tailed distribution, two-sample unequal variance (heteroscedastic).

A questionnaire was given to the candidates to exclude those with lower extremity ligament injury history. Each subject's annual medical check-up report was screened to exclude those with disease or trauma in their nervous and/or musculoskeletal system. Medical reports provided by the hospital were used to choose seven subjects with ATRs.

When measuring at different speeds, no metronome or moving reference was used to intervene with the subjects' walking speed. The subjects were asked to walk in their usual habit. In order to impress perceptual awareness upon the subjects, models of walking at free, fast and slow speeds were given before the test. (The values of the three speeds modeled by our demonstrator were 1.05m/s, 1.35m/s, 1.86m/s, respectively, and they were relatively stable)

Before the test began, subjects were asked to stand bare-footed after both feet had been sterilized with 75% ethyl alcohol. Then subjects began from standing with feet together (barefooted) at the start of the platform. When the subjects stood steadily (for about 3 seconds), the laboratory assistant gave instructions to begin walking. The equipment operator pressed the key of the equipment to collect the data. When the subjects stopped, they returned after being instructed to do so by the laboratory assistant. If the first step onto the platform was found to be incomplete, or if the subject walked off the platform, or if the gait seemed apparently nonsuccessive, the subject was asked to try again. Data that met our requirements were collected from their second step on the platform. Six successive steps from each subject were collected and then analyzed.

【Walking Plantar-impulse Principal Axis】

We define a physical quantity which is the sum of all the products formed by multiplying the magnitude of each unit impulse by the square of its distance to the impulse center. The plantar impulse is provided by Zebris FDM System Gait Analysis, with a component as:

$$\begin{cases} I_x = \sum y^2 Ip_{ij} \\ I_y = \sum x^2 Ip_{ij} \end{cases} \tag{1}$$

where Ip_{ij} stands for the impulse of the interaction between foot and sensors, i and j stand for row and column number of sensor respectively. The unit impulse can be calculated by $Ip_{ij} = \int_0^{T_s} p_{(i,j)}(t)\,dt$, where T_s refers to stance time, $P_{(i,j)}(t)$ to instantaneous pressure value of sensor at instant t, and (x, j) for position of Ip_{ij} relative to plantar-impulse center, which is calculated by $\left(\frac{\sum iIp_{ij}}{\sum iIp_{ij}}, \frac{\sum jIp_{ij}}{\sum Ip_{ij}}\right)$.

Set the angle displacement to be α, where plantar impulse rotates around the vertical axis that goes through plantar-impulse center. We can set up the following relation:

$$(I_x - I_y)_\alpha = \sum [(x^2\cos\alpha - y^2\sin\alpha) - (x^2\sin\alpha + y^2\cos\alpha)] Ip_{ij} \tag{2}$$

Differentiate Eq. (2) and set

$$\frac{d(I_x - I_y)_\alpha}{d\alpha} = 0$$

Then, we will obtain

$$\alpha = \frac{1}{2}\arctan\left(\frac{2\sum xyIp_{ij}}{\sum x^2 Ip_{ij} - \sum y^2 Ip_{ij}}\right) \tag{3}$$

The shape of plantar-impulse distribution is asymmetrical, which leads to $I_x \neq I_y$ in Eq. (1). Just like the uniqueness of principal axis of inertia of the asymmetrically shaped and anisotropically structured object, within the range of [0, π] the limited rotation of the plantar-impulse can always bring the result of $\sum xyIp_{ij}$ to be zero. The axis that goes through plantar impulse center is called the PIPA.

【Walking Plantar-impulse Distribution Along PIPA】

Along PIPA, the plantar impulse position (x_{cl}, y_{cl}) is calculated by the following equation:

$$x_{cl} = \frac{\sum_{l=1}^{n_l}\int_0^{T_s} P_{(i,j)}(t)\,x_l\,\mathrm{d}t}{\sum_{l=1}^{n_l}\int_0^{T_s} P_{(i,j)}(t)\,\mathrm{d}t},\quad y_{cl} = \frac{\sum_{l=1}^{n_l}\int_0^{T_s} P_{(i,j)}(t)\,y_l\,\mathrm{d}t}{\sum_{l=1}^{n_l}\int_0^{T_s} P_{(i,j)}(t)\,\mathrm{d}t} \tag{4}$$

where $P_{(i,j)}(t)$ and T_s have the same definitions as those in Eq. (1), and n_l stands for the number of sensors (unit number of plantar-impulse distribution width) that interact with the foot at the foot length position l.

【PRTS Along PIPA】

According to gait characteristics, the progression of plantar contact (initial to terminal) with the ground is continuous, which can be represented by the fact that the same plantar position will initiate and terminate foot contact once, respectively, in one gait cycle. That is to say, each plantar surface point contacts the ground only once during a step. If the plantar position (x, y) is set as $t^O_{(x,y)}$ and $t^T_{(x,y)}$, respectively, then the plantar ICG and TCG time series along PIPA will be

$$\bar{t}^O_l = \frac{\sum_{l=1}^{n_l} t^O_{(x,y)}}{n_l},\quad \bar{t}^T_l = \frac{\sum_{l=1}^{n_l} t^T_{(x,y)}}{n_l} \tag{5}$$

where $\bar{t}^O_l$ and $\bar{t}^T_l$ stand for the ICG and TCG time series at the position l along PIPA. n_l shares the same definition as that in Eq. (4).

【Plantar Impulse Along Foot Length】

The plantar-impulse distribution along foot length position l will be:

$$Ip(l) = \frac{1}{n_l}\sum_{l=1}^{n_l}\int_0^{T_s} p(ij)\,\mathrm{d}t \tag{6}$$

where T_s and n_l have the same definitions as those in Eq. (4).

Results and Discussion

Eq. (1) is used to calculate the plantar-impulse center. Eq. (3) is used to calculate each plantar-impulse rotation angle, which is applied by the plantar impulse to rotate around the vertical axis that goes through the plantar-impulse center. See Fig. 1.

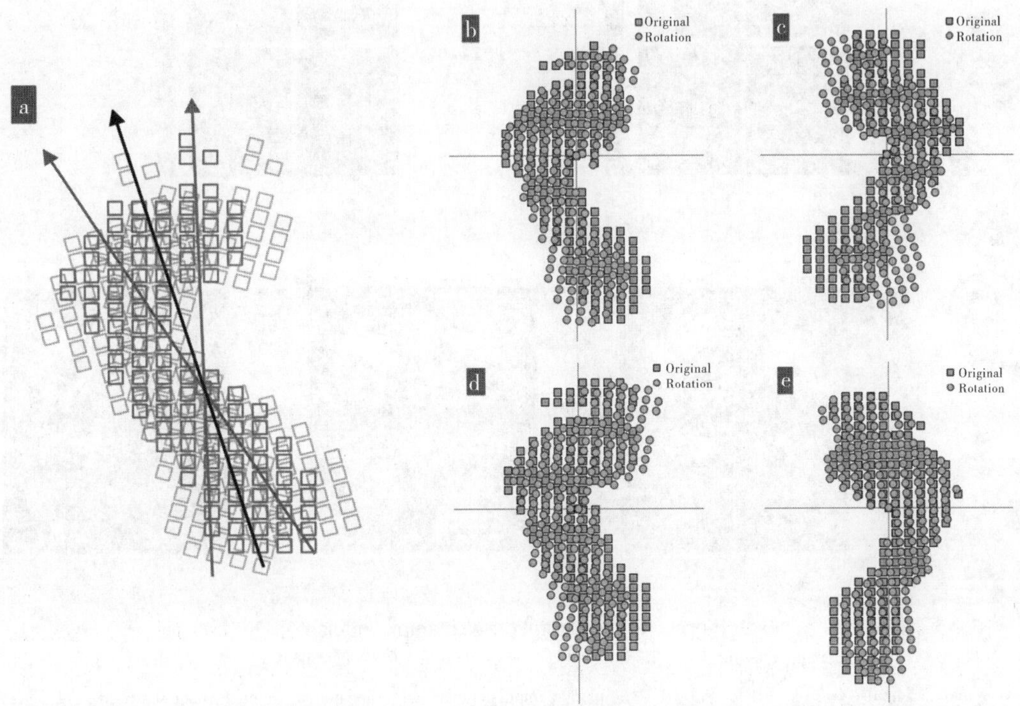

Fig. 1　Plantar impulse fixed along PIPA

Fig. 1a is the plantar-impulse rotation around the vertical axis that goes through plantar-impulse center. Fig. 1b is the first plantar impulse (left foot) before and after the plantar impulse is fixed. Fig. 1c is the second plantar impulse (right foot) before and after the plantar impulse is fixed. Fig. 1d is the third plantar impulse (left foot) before and after the plantar impulse is fixed. Fig. 1e is the fourth plantar impulse (right foot) before and after the plantar impulse is fixed. In these figures, black stands for the original plantar impulse before it is fixed, red for the plantar impulse position after it is fixed. A principal axis is identified after the first plantar impulse rotates 7.66 degrees, the second 214.37 degrees, the third 10.25 degrees and the fourth −5.00 degrees.

Fig. 1 shows that when the plantar impulse is identified, its principal axis is unique, which guarantees the reliability of the standardization of the plantar impulse. In gait analysis, the walking plantar-impulse progression angle is a quantity related to walking direction and walking-footprint shape, which is a measurement value. This method, based upon the PIPA, provides an alternative analytical solution to standardize walking plantar impulse.

"Fixing" refers to the use of the physical quantity of PIPA to represent footprint progression angle. When the plantar impulse is fixed, each walking plantar-impulse distribution length and width is rated by percentage, and the unit impulse is normalized by total impulse. The average plantar impulse at different speeds is shown in Fig. 2.

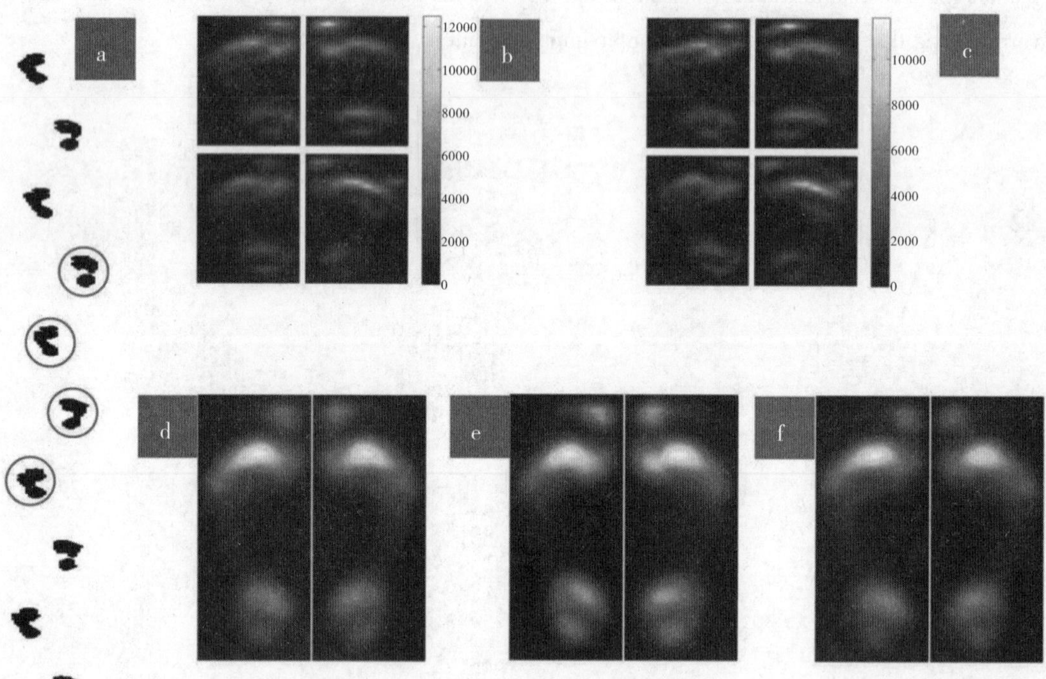

Fig. 2 Standardization of plantar impulse

Fig. 2a is the plantar impulse measured by Zebris FDM. Fig. 2b is the four continuous plantar impulses. Fig. 2c is the every plantar impulse fixed by PIPA. Fig. 2d is the plantar impulse of free gait after plantar impulse is standardized. Fig. 2e is the plantar impulse at fast speed gait after plantar impulse is standardized. Fig. 2f is the plantar impulse at slow speed gait after plantar impulse is standardized. Fig. 2b and Fig. 2c are from the same subject. Fig. 2d to Fig. 2f are the average plantar impulse from twenty healthy young subjects (each with six plantar impulses, three from left and right, respectively).

Fig. 2 shows the plantar impulse standardized by PIPA. Once the plantar-impulse distribution length and width are rated by percentage and the plantar unit impulse is normalized by total impulse, effects of individual difference in walking plantar-impulse progression angle, foot type and weight are eliminated. Then the average plantar impulse from healthy young subjects at different walking speeds is obtained. Thus, the average plantar impulse can reflect the overall shape of a plantar impulse.

Eq. (4) is applied to calculate the plantar-impulse distribution curve position. The distribution curve of left and right foot is drawn. See Fig. 3.

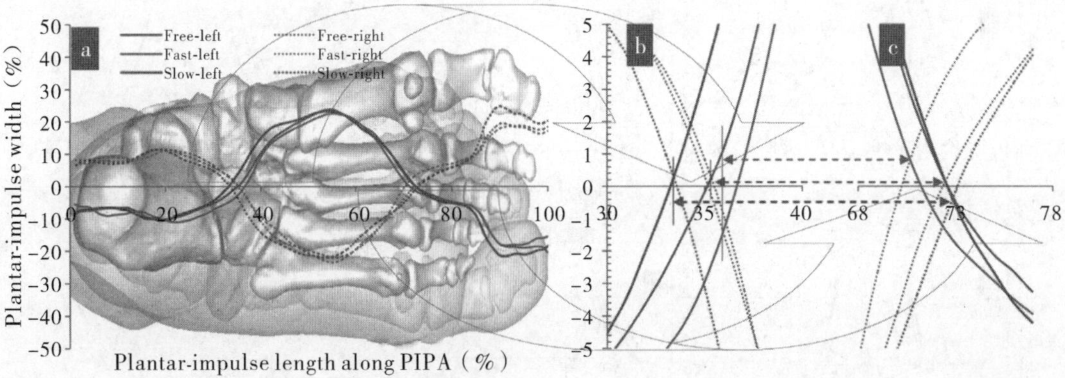

Fig. 3　Distribution curve of plantar impulse

Fig. 3a is the distribution curve of plantar impulse from the healthy young subjects at three walking speeds. Fig. 3b is the intersection point (first intersection point) at heel. Fig. 3c is the intersection point (second intersection point) at forefoot. The x-axis stands for the middle line in foot width.

Fig. 3 shows that based upon the average plantar impulse, the distribution curve of plantar impulse can be obtained along PIPA. The index can be used to analyze young subjects' different walking speeds, which brings the result that the distribution curves of plantar impulse form two intersection points—one at the heel and the other at the forefoot. When walking speed varies, the sequence of the first intersection point from the two distribution curves is slow-free-fast speed while that of the second intersection point is fast-free-slow. These sequences shorten the distance between two intersection points when walking speed increases. Our hypothesis that the plantar impulse reveals musculoskeletal system injuries is thus verified. The variation of intersection points changing with walking speed from the healthy subjects in this study can thus be used as an assessment method to identify musculoskeletal system injuries.

The plantar-impulse distribution curve (both left and right foot) from the ATRs is shown in Fig. 4.

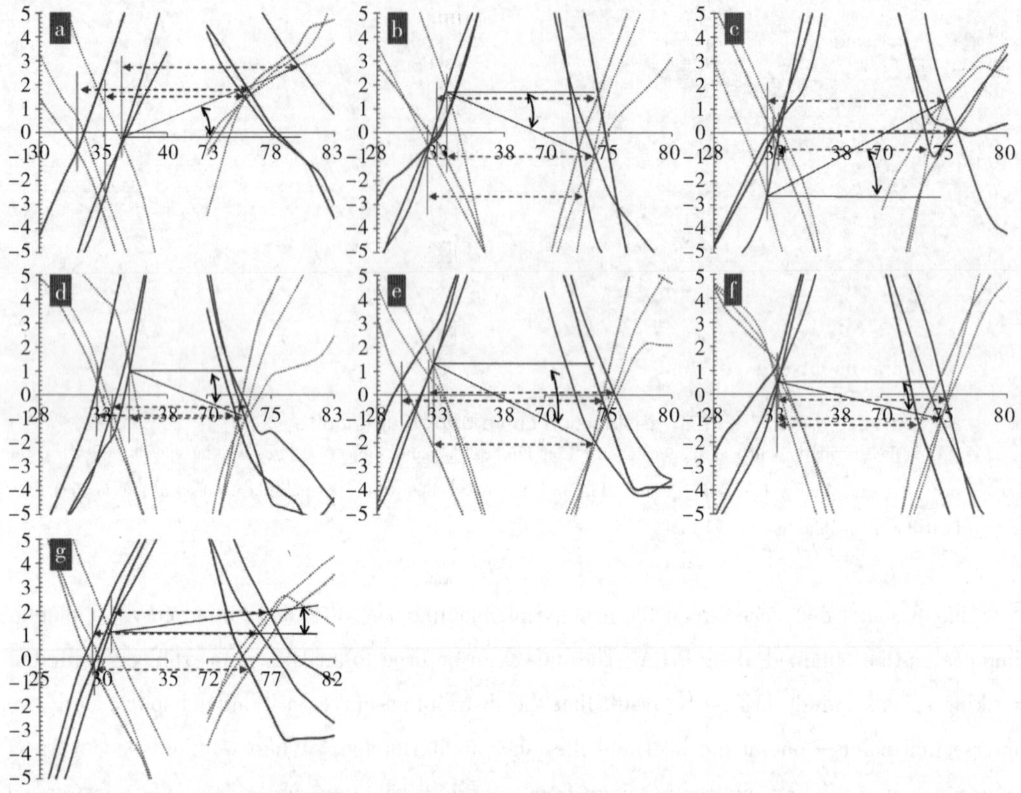

Fig. 4 Distribution curve of plantar impulse from the ATRs

Fig. 4 shows the intersection point (first intersection point) at heel and intersection point (second intersection point) at forefoot, where horizontal axis refers to the plantar-impulse length while the vertical one for plantar impulse.

Fig. 4 shows that at different speeds, the intersection point's position of left/right plantar-impulse distribution curve from the ATRs, in comparison with those from the young subjects, has two characteristics in common: ①the position sequence is irregular, which leads to the distance abnormality of two intersection points; ②when walking at fast speed, the connection line between two intersection points, i. e., one that connects the first (at heel) and the second intersection point (at forefoot) and the sagittal axis of foot forms an angle: when the angle is greater than zero, it indicates a right foot ATR; when it is less than zero, a left foot ATR. But even the angle of the healthy subjects is not zero. This needs further exploration and discussion.

After the plantar impulse is fixed, Eq. (5) is used to calculate the ICG and TCG time series along PIPA. Next, we rate the plantar-impulse distribution length by percentage and standardize the stance time as 1 second. The results are shown in Fig. 5. Fig. 5 shows that plantar ICG and TCG time series are related to walking speed. For the healthy young, the effect from walking speed upon the distribution of ICG time series distribution is relatively small, especially in the heel, forefoot or toe; the effect is mainly upon the distribution of TCG time series, i. e. , from heel to forefoot, the TCG time increases with an increase in walking speed; forefoot relative stance phase time increases with an increase in walking speed. This stance time distribution is consistent with the ground reaction force distribution at different walking speeds, indicating that this method to calculate PRTS along PIPA is reliable.

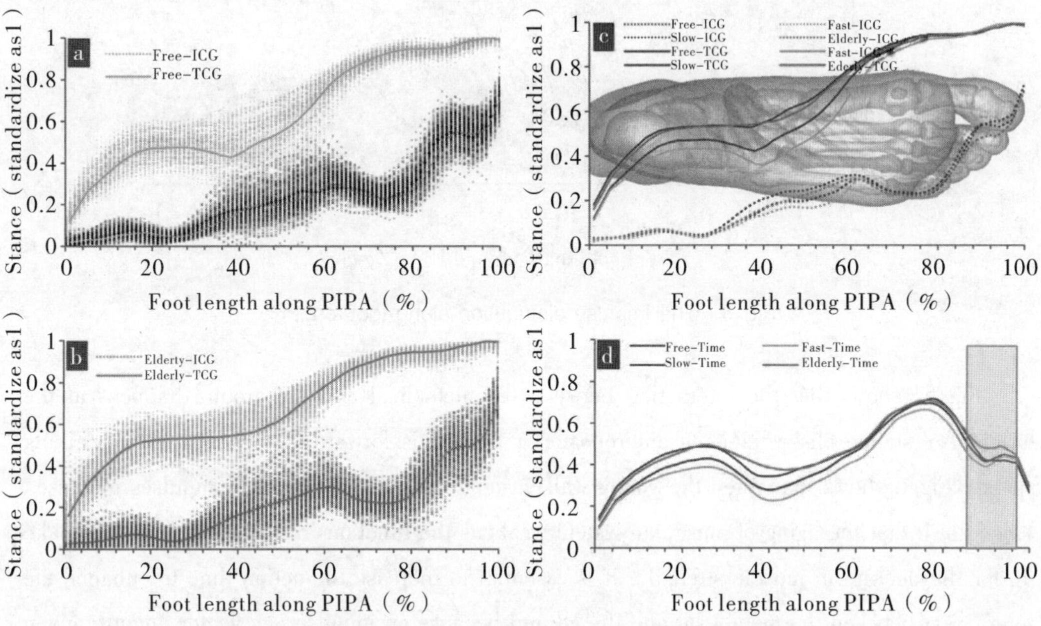

Fig. 5　Plantar ICG and TCG time series along PIPA

Fig. 5a is the plantar ICG and TCG time series along PIPA of healthy young subjects while walking at free gait. Fig. 5b is the plantar ICG and TCG time series along PIPA of the healthy elderly subjects while walking at free gait. Fig. 5c is the plantar ICG and TCG time series along PIPA of young subjects' free, fast and slow speed gait and the healthy elderly subjects' free gait. Fig. 5d is the plantar stance time distribution along PIPA. Six continuous plantar impulses of the subject were initially collected (three from each foot) . This average value can be employed as a toe ICG time series index along PIPA. We calculate the plantar stance time on PIPA by using $\bar{t}_l^T - \bar{t}_l^O$.

Fig. 5 also shows the difference between the healthy elderly subjects' ICG time series and that of the healthy young subjects. In order to demonstrate this difference, we analyze the ICG time series along PIPA from both the elderly and young. See Table 2. Table 2 shows that a toe's (1st toe) ICG time series index is created along PIPA, where the elderly subjects' index is significantly different from that of the young at different walking speeds while for the young subjects, no significant difference can be spotted at different walking speeds. Why did this happen? We use Eq. (6) to calculate plantar-impulse distribution along foot length. The mean value of impulse from each subject's six continuous plantar impulses along foot length is drawn. See Fig. 6.

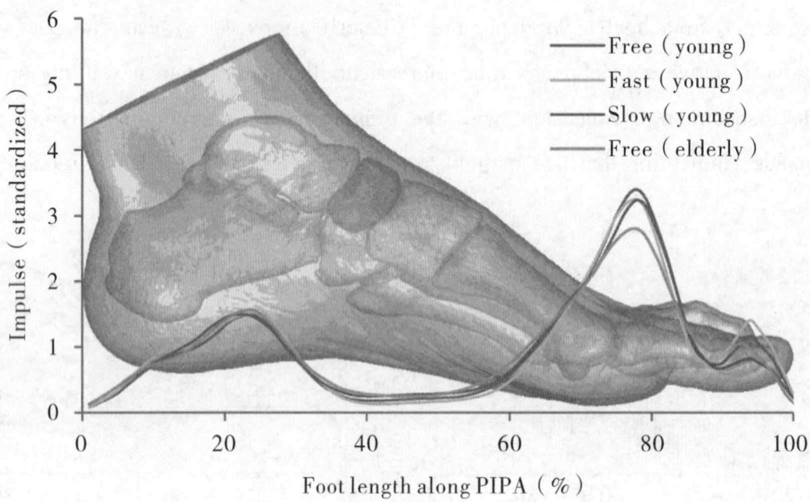

Fig. 6 The impulse distribution along foot length

Fig. 5c shows that the interaction between the metatarsal and the ground happens at the terminal of stance phase, and its anteroposterior friction is forward, which keeps the walking speed. Fig. 6 shows that when the young walk faster, their first toe plantar impulses increase. It is known that the aging of muscular system weakens the functions of the metatarsal. To make up for the decline in muscle strength, it is essential to increase the action time to enhance the interaction between the metatarsal and the ground because an impulse is a vector quantity given by the force over time. The reaction time between the elderly metatarsal and the ground in Fig. 5d serves as an example. When the stance time is normalized, the increase of this reaction time is achieved by an earlier ICG.

Injuries and aging of the human musculoskeletal systems can cause changes to the gait parameters at walking speed. But these gait parameters may not be used to predict when injury information will fade or disappear nor when aging information will emerge. For example, ATR reconstruction can return to normal after 24 months. But our research results can tell that ATR information always can be identified no matter how long ago an ATR happened. Walking speed is related to elderly subjects' health, but we cannot examine their health just by walking speed because some elderly subjects just walk slowly: this might be their habit. The index that we created can reflect the difference between the elderly subjects' toe PRTS at their free gait with that from the young subjects at their free, fast and slow gait, which suggests that the walking plantar impulse can serve as an index to analyze and evaluate musculoskeletal system injuries and aging.

Limitations of this research include: ①If the angle formed by the connection line between the first intersection point and the second intersection point has something to do with the ATR, why is the angle formed from the healthy subjects not zero? Is this caused by the difference in the function of an individual's left and right foot? A new gait experiment should be designed to explain this phenomenon. ②The reason why the elderly subjects' ICG time series of the toe is different from that of the young subjects is not clear. Further research is needed to explain whether this phenomenon is caused by the musculoskeletal or neural system. In addition, though the receiver operating characteristic (ROC) curve cannot tell the incidence of the disease being tested, it serves as an effective method to evaluate the diagnostic test sensitivity. In our future study, we will apply ROC curves to determine the clinical value and validity of our method.

Conclusion

Basic gait parameters such as stride length and speed have been widely applied to make clinical diagnoses and to evaluate rehabilitation. Interesting and scientific results have been reached to eliminate individuals' differences by applying these indexes such as stride length and hip height. For example, to estimate dinosaur's walking speed by its stride length and hip height. The walking plantar impulse may not be an exception.

The standardization of the plantar impulse involves many quantities—plantar-impulse progression angle, size, plantar pressure, and plantar impulse. Contributions from Keijser and other scientists have been enlightening. In our study, an analytical solution is applied to identify PIPA. The method to standardize the plantar impulse based upon the PIPA has guaranteed the accuracy. To the sensor, PRTS might serve as a logical data type as well as a time quantity. (Specifically, a certain position of foot contacts the ground in a stance phase while it does not contact the ground in another stance phase. "To have" or "not to have" is a logical quantity. To such a logical record quantity, we cannot say that in successive walking, this position does not contact the ground; neither can we calculate its mean value directly) On the plantar impulse that has been fixed by PIPA, a calculation method based upon PRTS along PIPA can solve the algebraic operation problem for this quantity.

Walking is a moving process when the foot interacts with its support surface. In this process, when the movement of body segments changes, so does its interaction because it is the result of the interaction between objects. Musculoskeletal system injuries and aging have changed the movement of body segment. In turn, the walking plantar impulse can reflect the status of musculoskeletal system injuries and aging. Indexes PRTS along PIPA and distribution of plantar impulse are applied to analyze ATRs, elderly and young subjects' plantar impulse. The results verify that this works.

In conclusion, we can use PIPA to locate and standardize plantar impulse, and we can use the located and standardized plantar impulse to create indexes of PRTS and plantar-impulse distribution along PIPA. If this assessment index is validated by large size samples, this plantar-impulse analysis method may be widely used in clinical and rehabilitation medicine.

Selected Reading 6

站立足印迹诊断方法

范毅方　樊瑜波　李知宇　Tony Newman　吕长生　范雨舟

摘要：压力中心是评估站立平衡的常见方法。虽然该方法仍不完善，但现在尚未有更好的评估方法。实验设计了三种站立姿势：双脚并拢站立，双脚分开与肩同宽站立，双脚分开比肩稍宽站立。实验用基于平台的压力测量系统收集（站立足印迹的）瞬时足底压力，我们定义了一个物理量——瞬时站立足印迹主轴，通过该物理量我们建立了一个评估站立平衡的指标。比较我们新建立的指标和压力中心指标对不同站立姿势稳定性的评估结果，我们可知站立足印迹主轴指标可以更好地反映站立姿势的改变。分析显示，站立足印迹主轴指标可以很好地弥补压力中心指标对两足间相对位置及站立姿势的改变缺乏灵敏度这一缺点。这一结论意味着站立足印迹主轴在评估站立平衡方面有广泛的应用价值。

前　言

平衡是人体的一种姿势。人体移动或受外力作用时能够自动调整并保持平衡姿势是人体的一种能力。平衡稳定性不仅与骨骼肌肉系统、耳前庭系统、本体感觉系统、视觉系统有关，还与身高、体重、年龄、性别等有关。保持站立平衡是一种简单有效的评估个体平衡能力的方法。平衡测试仪（平衡测量仪表系统）是评估站立平衡的可靠工具。

平衡测试仪主要由三部分组成——传感器、计算机和应用软件。安装了多个力传感器的平台可以在足与支撑面相互作用时确定垂直方向上合力作用点的位置。该点的位置即为压力中心（COP）。压力中心在横断面的改变与压力中心移动路径、速度以及其椭圆面积的改变，可以定量地反映了个体的站立平衡稳定性。垂直方向的合力位置可以基本描述站立平衡，使用足底压力测量仪器可以测量站立平衡能力。利用传感器矩阵结构我们可以建立支撑面指标和足底压力分布指标。尽管通过这些指标我们可以得到许多站立状态的信息，但当双脚间位置或足部姿势发生改变时，这些指标无法反映出变化。这些变化在站立平衡评估方面有着重要作用。在站立姿势时，足位置及姿势的变化会影响肌肉的工作，从而影响站立能力。

站立时，足底压力测量设备可以通过压力传感器测量足和支承面之间的相互作用力。交互式传感器的压力分布构成了一个几何图形。在某一特定时刻，交互式传感器瞬时压力值的分布被称为站立足印迹。站立足印迹被定义为一个单位压力与其到总压力中心距离平方乘积的物理量。数学分析可知该物理量有主轴，即为站立足印迹主轴（SFPA）。主轴这个概念在使用测力板的站立分析中已得到应用。因此，这两个概念是不同的。

我们假设足底压力可以反映在站立时由足位置和足部姿态的变化产生的影响。由此设计实验，受试者均为健康的青年人，实验设置了三种站立姿势：双脚并拢站立，双脚分开与肩同宽站立，双脚分开比肩稍宽站立。然后使用站立足印迹主轴和压力中心两种方法分别对三种站立姿势进行评估。结果显示，三种站立姿势的站立足印迹主轴和压力中心值从大到小排列顺序相同，皆为：双脚并拢站立＞双脚分开与肩同宽站立＞双脚分开比肩稍宽站立。由此可知，站立足印迹主轴可以作为评估站立平衡稳定性的方法。此外，当双脚并拢站立时几位受试者的压力中心值均正常，但站立足印迹主轴值显示异常。分析发现异常是由站立足印迹主轴对双脚距离、姿势以及压力分布的反应更灵敏造成的，这就意味着站立足印迹主轴有着压力中心所缺乏的优点——足够的灵敏度。

根据精度测量，一个健康人的身体形态结构是大致对称的。也就是说，从理论上讲，足部站立姿势和压力分布也应该是大约对称且稳定的。所以站立足印迹主轴指标更为重要，因为它可以反映足部站立姿势和压力分布的对称性，可以用这一指标来评估人体器官的生长、发育和衰老情况，而且在损伤评定和康复评估中该指标也可以发挥重要作用。

材料和方法

【伦理声明】

本研究已获得广州体育学院伦理委员会批准。受试者均完全知晓并自愿参与本项研究，签署书面知情同意书。

【实验设备】

Zebris FDM 步态分析系统（长平台）。平台：56（W）cm × 608（L）cm；传感器分布：1sensor/cm^2；采样率：100Hz；软件：WinFDM v1.2.2。

在本次实验中，WinFDM 如下设置：测量设备：Zebsdk Driver；属性：FDM WIDAB USB；测量方法：站立姿势分析；配置：FDM；设备收集数据频率：100Hz；每位受试者每种站立姿势的数据收集时间：11.5s（共三种站立姿势：双脚并拢站立，双脚分开与肩同宽站立，双脚分开比肩稍宽站立）；数据输出格式：ASCII 文件；得出数据用 EXCEL 软件分析，图像用 EXCEL 软件绘制，背景图用 MATLAB 软件绘制。

【测试对象及要求】

32 名青年男性（在校学生，年龄：21.31 ± 1.25 岁，身高：1.74 ± 0.04m，体重：63.82 ± 8.1kg），选择标准：首先采用问卷调查选择无肌肉骨骼、耳前庭、本体感觉及视觉疾病者，然后检查受试者每年的体检报告，确保选择的受试者无神经系统与肌肉骨骼系统的疾病与损伤。

然后告知所选受试者实验内容及要求（即演示三种站立姿势的宽度）：双脚并拢站

立（10.435±1.037cm），双脚分开与肩同宽站立（28.939±3.343cm），双脚分开比肩稍宽站立（51.066±7.043cm）。实验室助理向受试者说明解释三种站立姿势。

平衡测试前，受试者赤足（双脚用75%酒精进行消毒）做出三种站立姿势。收集数据前，实验室助理对不正确的姿势进行纠正。受试者站稳（保持约5~10秒）后，实验室助理给出开始指示。设备操作员按下收集数据按钮，记录结果并将实验中瞬时足底压力数据以ASCII格式输出。

【压力中心和站立足印迹主轴的计算】

通过以下公式计算压力中心在 t 时刻的位置 (x, y)：

$$\begin{cases} x = \dfrac{\sum\sum iP_{ij}(t)}{\sum\sum P_{ij}(t)} - x_0 \\ y = \dfrac{\sum\sum jP_{ij}(t)}{\sum\sum P_{ij}(t)} - y_0 \end{cases} \tag{1}$$

其中 $P_{ij}(t)$ 代表传感器位置在 t 时刻的瞬时压力值。站立阶段压力中心位置 (x_0, y_0) 的总和计算公式为：

$$\left(\frac{\sum\sum i\int P_{ij}(t)\,\mathrm{d}t}{\sum\sum\int P_{ij}(t)\,\mathrm{d}t}, \frac{\sum\sum j\int P_{ij}(t)\,\mathrm{d}t}{\sum\sum\int P_{ij}(t)\,\mathrm{d}t}\right)$$

定义一个单位压力与其到压力中心距离平方乘积的物理量。对于足底压力测量设备得到的站立足印迹，其分量形式为：

$$\begin{cases} SF_x = \sum (j-y)^2 P_{ij}(t) \\ SF_y = \sum (j-x)^2 P_{ij}(t) \end{cases} \tag{2}$$

其中 (x, y)、(i, j) 和 $P_{ij}(t)$ 同方程（1）中的定义。

设站立足印迹绕压力中心垂直轴的角位移为 α，通过方程（2）可以建立如下关系：

$$(SF_x - SF_y)_\alpha = \sum(((i-x)^2\cos\alpha - (j-y)^2\sin\alpha) - ((i-x)^2\sin\alpha + (j-y)^2\cos\alpha))P_{ij}(t) \tag{3}$$

然后对方程（3）求导，使：

$$\frac{\mathrm{d}(SF_x - SF_y)_\alpha}{\mathrm{d}\alpha} = 0$$

我们可得：

$$\alpha = \frac{1}{2}\arctan\left(\frac{2\sum(i-x)(j-y)P_{ij}(t)}{\sum(i-x)^2P_{ij}(t) - \sum(j-y)^2P_{ij}(t)}\right) - \alpha_0 \tag{4}$$

其中：

$$\alpha_0 = \frac{1}{2}\arctan\left(\frac{2\sum(i-x)(j-y)\int P_{ij}(t)\,\mathrm{d}t}{\sum(i-x)^2\int P_{ij}(t)\,\mathrm{d}t - \sum(j-y)^2\int P_{ij}(t)\,\mathrm{d}t}\right)$$

结果与讨论

通过方程（1）计算每位受试者的瞬时压力中心（相对于受试者站立时的总压力中心）。通过方程（4）计算受试者的瞬时站立足印迹主轴（相对于受试者站立时的总站立足印迹主轴）。设 (x_0, y_0) 为坐标原点并计算出每位受试者每种站立姿势的瞬时压力中心。设 α_0 为对称轴并画出每位受试者每种站立姿势的瞬时站立足印迹主轴（见彩图 28）。

在彩图 28a ~ 28c 中，双脚并拢站立与另外两种站立姿势的压力中心存在显著差异（$p < 0.01$），而双脚分开站立的两种姿势的压力中心无显著差异（$p < 0.748$）。在彩图 28d ~ 28f中，比较大于零的数值和小于零的数值，双脚并拢站立与另外两种站立姿势的站立足印迹主轴存在显著差异，而双脚分开与肩同宽站立和双脚分开比肩稍宽站立两种姿势的站立足印迹主轴亦存在显著差异（$p < 0.01$）。

为什么在分析三种站立姿势的稳定性时，站立足印迹主轴指标比压力中心指标更为准确呢？我们可以从测力平台得到 6 个数值：三个力和三个力矩。通过力矩可知在 t 时到压力中心的位置。压力中心位置的改变是评估个体平衡能力的重要工具。足底压力测量平台可以收集垂直方向上的作用力，并通过传感器和足相互作用的瞬时压力可得出压力中心的位置。站立时，虽然足与支撑面的相互作用处于同一平面，但测力板可能无法反映支撑区域的大小，也就是说，在测量重量相同的球体和平板体时，测力板得到的测量结果相同。但足底压力测量平台能够区分两种不同形状物体的支撑面积。

此外，我们可以看到两个常用指标是如何发挥作用的：前后压力中心（ACOP）位移和内外侧压力中心（MCOP）位移（见彩图 28）。

由彩图 28 可知：前后压力中心和内外侧压力中心两个指标可以反映三种站立姿势的稳定性变化。那么这是否意味着压力中心评估站立平衡的方法是有缺陷的呢？事实并非如此（见彩图 29）。

由彩图 28、彩图 29 可知：双脚并拢站立时前后压力中心和内外侧压力中心位移的对称性优于站立足印迹主轴方向的对称性。双脚分开与肩同宽站立时，站立足印迹主轴方向的对称性比前后压力中心位移的对称性要好。表 1 对这种差异进行了进一步解释。

表 1　前后压力中心位移、内外侧压力中心位移与站立足印迹主轴方向

姿势	前后压力中心位移	内外侧压力中心位移	站立足印迹主轴方向
姿势 I[a]	0. 00060. 480	0. 00060. 414	0. 000611. 760
姿势 II[b]	0. 00060. 182	0. 00060. 314	0. 00060. 639
姿势 III[c]	0. 00060. 174	0. 00060. 306	0. 00060. 296

a，双脚并拢站立，b，双脚分开与肩同宽站立，c，双脚分开比肩稍宽站立。

由彩图 28、彩图 29 及表 1 可知：站立时，将压力中心位移的平均值或站立足印迹主轴方向的平均值设为坐标原点，那么该位移和方向的相对平均值可形成对称的图形。

因为标准差反映离散度，由表1可知：站立足印迹主轴指标对三种站姿的反映比前后压力中心和内外侧压力中心更为精确。

力学上的结构重心、支撑面等指标对反映静态稳定有着重要意义。一般情况下，支撑面积越大，重心越低，稳定性越好。由人体的解剖学和力学结构的特点可知，比较双脚并拢站立与另外两种站立姿势时，压力中心和站立足印迹主轴的评估结果在力学上与结构稳定性方面应具有一致性。双脚分开比肩稍宽站立时，重心更低，支撑面积较双脚并拢时更大，因此具有更好的稳定性。从这个方面来看，站立足印迹主轴评估结果与力学分析的结果更为吻合。

另外一个引起我们注意的现象是：彩图28a中受试者压力中心反映数值显示正常（同相关文献中的结果相比较），而在彩图28d中一些数值则显示异常（同彩图28e、彩图28f中数值相比较）。我们通过比较足位置、姿势的改变与压力中心、站立足印迹主轴的关系来分析该异常现象。“克隆”一只脚的瞬时站立足印迹，即将一只脚的足底压力对称地复制到另一只脚上。然后我们对足位置、姿势，以及足底压力与压力中心和站立足印迹主轴的关系进行分析。见彩图31。

由彩图31可知：①将两只脚的压力中心设为坐标原点，每只脚向上或向下对称移动，总足底压力中心保持不变，但其站立足印迹主轴则发生明显变化。②左脚或右脚的压力分布百分比变化时（即左脚与右脚的压力分布比例发生变化），压力中心发生变化（坐标 y 值不变，x 值发生变化）且变化不如双脚靠近时站立足印迹主轴的变化显著。③单部（仅单脚）绕压力中心转动时，压力中心不发生变化，但站立足印迹主轴发生变化。以上说明，站立足印迹主轴可与压力中心一样成为站立平衡的评估方法。而且压力中心在反映双脚足底压力总量分布时缺乏灵敏度，对足位置前后变化及足旋转等变化无反应，站立足印迹主轴弥补了压力中心的这些缺点。

另一点值得注意的是：由资料文献可知，前后压力中心和内外侧压力中心的位置指数是由足与测力板的接触位置决定的。两脚的压力中心以同样的方式改变时，足与测力板之间位置的改变将会导致前后压力中心和内外侧压力中心位置指数的改变。我们如何确定受试者前后轴与内外侧轴的坐标与测力板的坐标系一致，而站立足印迹主轴与受试者在测力板上的站立位置无关呢?

压力中心的计算方法与绕压力中心轴旋转的扭矩（该物理量为单位压力与其到压力中心的距离的乘积）的计算方法相似。站立足印迹主轴的计算方法与惯性积的计算相似，惯性积为单位压力与其距压力中心距离平方的乘积，当其绕压力中心轴转动时（且当分布不对称时），就会产生惯性积的可变分量。从数学角度上讲，张量为几何实体，力矩（moment）为一阶张量，惯性积为二阶张量。这就解释了为什么站立足印迹主轴可以同压力中心一样进行站立平衡评估。而且站立足印迹主轴可以更好地反映双脚之间的距离与姿势改变。

最后分析一下彩图28d中的异常。已知对于一个均质对称（相对于质心对称）的物体（例如一个圆圈或球体），其有无数条惯量主轴（所有通过质心的轴都是主轴），因此其惯量主轴并不唯一。虽然足部形状并不是对称的，但通过调整足位置和姿势可以使站立足印迹主轴达到45°［公式（4）中45°正切无解］。由彩图28和彩图29可知，为了避免无解情况，应以双脚分开与肩同宽和双脚分开比肩稍宽两种站立姿势进行平衡评估。

由于我们的实验设备主要用于步态分析，无法满足最优实验条件即20～30s的实验时长。建议使用面积为40（W）cm×60（L）cm、传感器分布为4sensor/cm^{2}的足底压力测试平台进行实验。

应　用

从结构力学的角度分析，个体稳定性随着双脚间距的增加而增加。从骨骼肌肉系统衰老的角度分析，青年人的稳定性优于老年人。为了验证其正确性，以青年受试者前后压力中心位移，内外侧压力中心位移以及站立足印迹主轴顺时针和逆时针轴方向的平均值为对称指标，我们对30名老年人（14名男性：68.1±3.31岁，1.69±0.85cm，63.8±8.3kg；16名女性：66.6±3.1岁，1.59±0.67m，50.2±6.6kg）的站立姿势（双脚分开与肩同宽，25.925±3.328cm）进行了测试。测试时长为11.5秒，测试结果见表2。

表2　站立姿势的对称性（均值6倍标准偏差）

		姿势 I[a,*]	姿势 II[b,*]	姿势 III[c,*]	姿势 II[b,**]
前后压力中心位移	前	0.377±0.136	0.142±0.109	0.132±0.082	0.201±0.151
	后	0.371±0.125	0.116±0.047	0.128±0.047	0.186±0.106
	假定值	0.667	0.271	0.889	0.657
内外侧压力中心位移	左	0.319±0.122	0.257±0.136	0.244±0.098	0.442±0.206
	右	0.335±0.143	0.230±0.078	0.241±0.077	0.430±0.183
	假定值	0.518	0.404	0.826	0.821
站立足印迹主轴方向	顺时针	8.447±13.353	0.472±0.210	0.220±0.105	0.647±0.376
	逆时针	5.713±6.801	0.488±0.321	0.218±0.105	0.577±0.271
	假定值	0.323	0.76	0.993	0.413

a，双脚并拢站立，b，双脚分开与肩同宽站立，c，双脚分开比肩稍宽站立，*青年受试者，**老年受试者。位移单位为厘米，方向单位为度。

由表2可知：①对青年人来说，内外侧压力中心和前后压力中心的对称性并不随着双脚间距离的增加而增加，而站立足印迹主轴却随之增加。②内外侧压力中心和前后压力中心的结果显示老年人的数值对称性优于青年人，而站立足印迹主轴的结果则显示青年人的数值对称性优于老年人。

我们尚未找到这些现象背后的机制，过大的标准差意味着也许样本容量不足，又或者受试者有着未被发现的结构问题，但可以确定的是——站立足印迹主轴可用于站立平衡的评估。

结　论

物理量方面，压力中心通过一个类似于矩阵的物理量计算得出，矩阵为一个张量；而站立足印迹主轴则通过一个类似于惯性积的物理量计算得出，惯性积为二阶张量。这就解释了两种指标在反映足位置和姿势时的差异性，这也是本次研究的一个重要发现。此外，一个理想的站立姿势站立足印迹主轴值应该为零，压力中心应位于双脚中间，但因为足部的形状和其足底压力分布，确定压力中心确切位置并不容易。一个理论参照值（例如最好的投射角度为45°）对评估的进行十分重要。

由力传感器组成的平衡测试系统可以量化站立平衡的评估结果，但由压力传感器组成的平衡测试系统可以显示瞬时足底压力的分布情况。我们通过定义足底压力主轴这一概念，提供一个新的评估方法。站立足印迹主轴与足底压力分布和双脚间相对位置有关。这样即可弥补压力中心指数对双脚相对位置缺乏灵敏度的缺点。站立足印迹主轴可以独立地对站立平衡进行评估，也可与压力中心指数相结合共同进行评估。

站立是人的一项基本活动，其不仅关系到行走，也与跌倒密切相关。这就是站立稳定性评估在老年预防医学方面获得了更多的关注的原因。相信基于站立足印迹主轴的站立足印迹诊断方法将会在青少年医学、老年医学以及康复医学等领域得到广泛应用。

Standing Footprint Diagnostic Method

Yifang Fan, Yubo Fan, Zhiyu Li, Tony Newman, Changsheng Lyu, Yuzhou Fan
Translated by Zhiyu Li

Abstract: Center of pressure is commonly used to evaluate standing balance. Even though it is incomplete, no better evaluation method has been presented. We designed our experiment with three standing postures: standing with feet together, standing with feet shoulder width apart, and standing with feet slightly wider than shoulder width. Our platform-based pressure system collected the instantaneous plantar pressure (standing footprint). A physical quantity of instantaneous standing footprint principal axis was defined, and it was used to construct an index to evaluate standing balance. Comparison between results from our newly-established index and those from the center of pressure index to evaluate the stability of different standing postures revealed that the standing footprint principal axis index could better respond to the standing posture change than the existing one. Analysis indicated that the insensitive response to the relative position between feet and to the standing posture change from the center of pressure could be better detected by the standing footprint principal axis index. This predicts a wide application of standing footprint principal axis index when evaluating standing balance.

Introduction

Balance is a posture the body keeps and it is an ability to automatically adjust and maintain posture when moving or when acted on by external force. Balance stability is not only associated with the musculoskeletal, vestibular, proprioceptive, and visual system but also with height, weight, age, and gender. Standing balance is a simple and effective method to assess one's balance ability, and the Balance Tester (the instrument system for balance) is a reliable tool to assess standing balance.

The Balance Tester is mainly composed of three parts—sensors, computers, and application software. A platform installed with multiple force sensors can suggest the position of the vertical resultant force's point of application when the foot/feet and the supporting surface interact. This position is called the center of pressure (COP). The changes of the COP on the transverse plane, together with the changes from the COP path length and the COP velocity elliptical area, quantitatively reflect one's standing balance stability. Standing balance can mainly be described by the position of vertical resultant force, and a plantar pressure measurement device is used to measure standing balance ability. The application of a sensor matrix structure makes it possible to establish indices of support area and plantar pressure distribution. Although these indices can present much standing information, they do not respond to changes when the position between the feet changes or when the feet posture changes, which is a desirable feature of standing balance evaluation. The influence of foot position and posture variations in standing posture affects muscle work, and thus standing ability.

When standing, plantar pressure measurement equipment can collect the interaction force between the foot and the supporting surface by pressure sensors. The interactive sensor pressure distribution forms a geometric pattern. The distribution of instantaneous pressure values of the interactive sensors at a specific instant is called standing footprint. Standing footprint is defined as a physical quantity, which is produced by multiplying a unit pressure by the square of its distance to the total COP. Mathematical analysis reveals a principal axis of this quantity, which is called standing footprint principal axis (SFPA). The concept of principal axis has been applied in the standing analysis where the force plate is used. These two concepts, therefore, are different.

We hypothesized that plantar pressure could reflect the influence of foot position and posture variations in standing posture. Three standing postures were designed for healthy young adults in our research: standing with feet together, standing with feet shoulder width apart and standing with feet slightly wider than shoulder width. Then SFPA and COP were used to evaluate three different standing postures, respectively. The results showed that both SFPA and COP values were greater when standing with feet together than when standing with feet shoulder width apart, and that those values from the latter were greater than when standing with feet slightly wider than shoulder width. This suggested that SFPA could serve as a method to evaluate standing balance stability. In addition, when standing with feet together, COP values for several participants were normal, but abnormal SFPA values appeared. Our analysis found that the abnormality was caused by the sensitivity of SFPA to the feet distance, posture, and pressure distribution, which meant that SFPA could provide what COP lacks—sufficient sensitivity.

Under measurement accuracy, a healthy body's shape and structure are approximately symmetrical, which means, theoretically, standing feet posture and pressure distribution should be approximately symmetrical and stable as well. This adds importance to the SFPA index because the fact that it can reflect the standing foot posture and pressure distribution symmetry means it can be used to evaluate the growth, development and aging of the human organism, and it can also play an important role in injury assessment and rehabilitation evaluation.

Materials and Methods

【Ethics Statement】

The study received approval from the Ethical Committee of our institute. The participants provided fully informed consent to participate in this study by signing a written consent form.

【Test Equipment】

Zebris FDM System Gait Analysis (long platform). Platform: 56 (W) cm × 608 (L) cm; sensor intensity: 1sensor/cm^2; sampling rate: 100Hz; software: WinFDM v1.2.2.

In this study, WinFDM was set as follows: measurement device: Zebsdk Driver; properties: FDM WIDAB USB; measurement method: stance analysis. Its configurations: FDM; equipment collecting data frequency: 100Hz. Duration to collect data for each participant: 11.5s. (for each of three different stance conditions: standing with feet together, standing with feet shoulder width apart and standing with feet slightly wider than shoulder width) Data output: ASCII files. Data were then analyzed by EXCEL, figures drawn by EXCEL and background drawn by MATLAB.

【Test Subjects and Requirements】

The subjects were thirty-two young adult males (undergraduates, age: 21.31 ± 1.25 year, height: 1.74 ±0.04m, mass: 63.82 ±8.31kg). Selection procedure was as follows: first, a questionnaire was given to exclude those with a history of musculoskeletal, vestibular, proprioceptive and visual disease. Then the subjects' annual medical reports were reviewed to screen those with neural and musculoskeletal disease and trauma.

Next, the selected subjects were told the contents and requirements of the test, i.e., to perform three stance widths: standing with feet together (10.435 ± 1.037cm), standing with feet shoulder width apart (28.939 ± 3.343cm) and standing with feet slightly wider than shoulder width (51.066 ± 7.043cm). One laboratory assistant demonstrated all three postures to the participants.

Before the balance test, the bare-footed subjects (whose feet were sterilized with 75% alcohol) performed the three standing postures. Before the data were collected, the laboratory assistant had a chance to correct any improper postures. When the subjects stood still (for about 5 – 10s), the laboratory assistant gave instructions to begin. The equipment operator pressed the key of the equipment to collect the data, recorded the results and output the data of plantar pressure data as ASCII files for each instant of this study.

【COP and Calculation of SFPA】

The positions of COP (x, y) at instant t were calculated by the following equation:

$$\begin{cases} x = \dfrac{\sum\sum iP_{ij}(t)}{\sum\sum P_{ij}(t)} - x_0 \\ y = \dfrac{\sum\sum jP_{ij}(t)}{\sum\sum P_{ij}(t)} - y_0 \end{cases} \tag{1}$$

where $P_{ij}(t)$ referred to the pressure value of sensor positions at a specific instant t. The sum of COP positions of the standing phase (x_0, y_0) were calculated by

$$\left(\frac{\sum\sum i\int P_{ij}(t)\,\mathrm{d}t}{\sum\sum\int P_{ij}(t)\,\mathrm{d}t},\frac{\sum\sum j\int P_{ij}(t)\,\mathrm{d}t}{\sum\sum\int P_{ij}(t)\,\mathrm{d}t}\right)$$

We defined a physical quantity to be the product by multiplying a unit pressure by the square of its distance to the COP. The component of the standing footprint obtained from plantar pressure measurement equipment was

$$\begin{cases} SF_x = \sum (j-y)^2 P_{ij}(t) \\ SF_y = \sum (i-x)^2 P_{ij}(t) \end{cases} \tag{2}$$

where (x, y), (i, j) and $P_{ij}(t)$ shared the same definitions in Eq. (1).

Set the angular displacement of the standing footprint rotating the COP's vertical axis as α. By Eq. (2), the following relation was established:

$$(SF_x - SF_y)_\alpha = \sum(((i-x)^2\cos\alpha - (j-y)^2\sin\alpha) - ((i-x)^2\sin\alpha + (j-y)^2\cos\alpha))P_{ij}(t) \tag{3}$$

Next, we differentiated Eq. (3) and let

$$\frac{\mathrm{d}(SF_x - SF_y)\alpha}{\mathrm{d}\alpha} = 0$$

Then we got

$$\alpha = \frac{1}{2}\arctan\left(\frac{2\sum(i-x)(j-y)P_{ij}(t)}{\sum(i-x)^2P_{ij}(t) - \sum(j-y)^2P_{ij}(t)}\right) - \alpha_0 \tag{4}$$

where

$$\alpha_0 = \frac{1}{2}\arctan\left(\frac{2\sum(i-x)(j-y)\int P_{ij}(t)\,\mathrm{d}t}{\sum(i-x)^2\int P_{ij}(t)\,\mathrm{d}t - \sum(j-y)^2\int P_{ij}(t)\,\mathrm{d}t}\right)$$

Results and Discussion

Each participant's COP at each instant was given by Eq. (1) (relative to each participant's total COP when standing). Each participant's SFPA at each instant was given by Eq. (4) (relative to each participant's total SFPA when standing). Set (x_0, y_0) as coordinate origin and draw each participant's COP at each instant for each standing posture. Set α_0 as symmetry axis and draw each participant's SFPA at each instant for each standing posture (see Fig. 1).

In Figs. 1a – Fig. 1c, significant difference ($p < 0.01$) exists between when standing with feet together and the other two postures, while no significant difference ($p < 0.748$) exists between these two postures. In Fig. 1d – Fig. 1f, comparing values greater than zero and those less than zero, significant difference ($p < 0.01$) exists between when standing with feet together and the other two postures, and significant difference ($p < 0.01$) also exists between when standing with feet shoulder width apart and when standing with feet slightly wider than shoulder width.

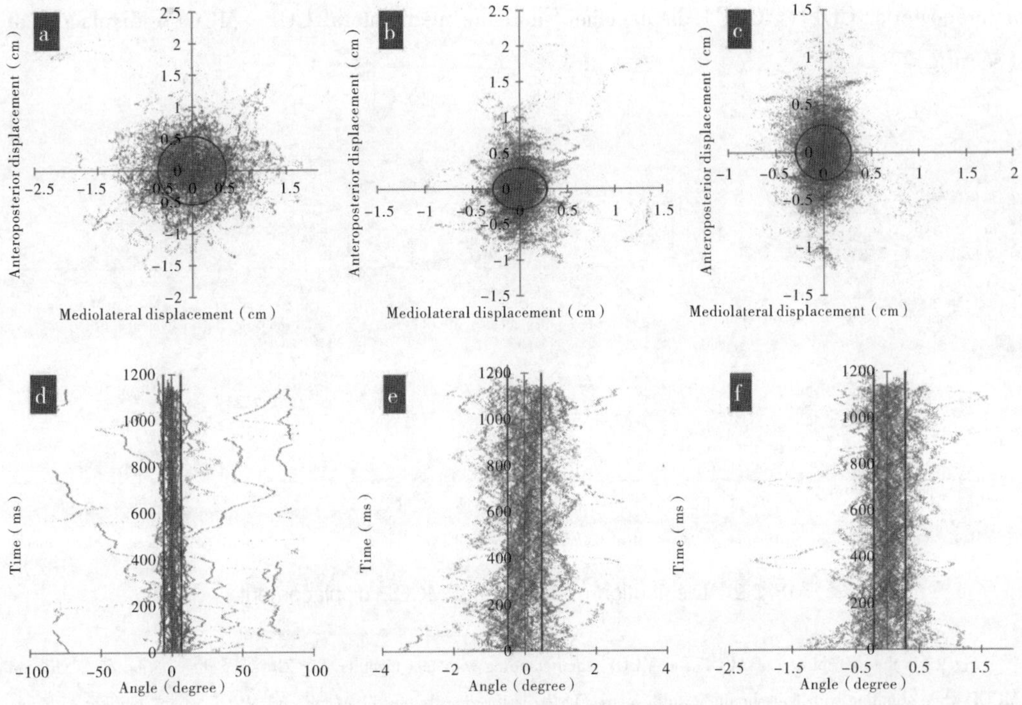

Fig. 1　Distribution of COP and SFPA

Fig. 1a is the COP distribution when standing with feet together. Fig. 1b is the COP distribution when standing with feet shoulder width apart. Fig. 1c is the COP distribution when standing with feet slightly wider than shoulder width. Fig. 1d is the SFPA distribution when standing with feet together. Fig. 1e is the SFPA distribution when standing with feet shoulder width apart. Fig. 1f is the SFPA distribution when standing with feet slightly wider than shoulder width. In Fig. 1a – Fig. 1c, the red circle stands for all participant's COP average radius at each instant. The values for three postures are 0.5391cm, 0.287cm, and 0.288cm, respectively. In Fig. 1d – Fig. 1f, the red line stands for each participant's SFPA value that is greater than zero at each instant, 8.455 degrees, 0.469 degrees, and 0.232 degrees, respectively. The green line stands for each participant's SFPA value that is less than zero at each instant, −5.701 degrees, −0.499 degrees, and −0.235 degrees, respectively.

Why can SFPA be used to provide the stability difference of these three postures more accurately than the index of COP? Six quantities can be gained from a force platform: three forces and three moments. The moment can reveal the position of COP at instant *t*. The change of COP position serves as an important tool to evaluate one's balance ability. The plantar pressure platform can collect the vertical reaction force and provide the position of COP according to the instantaneous pressure values from sensors interacted with foot. When standing, the interaction between a foot and its support surface is on the same plane, but the force plate cannot reflect the size of the support area, indicating that the force plate may provide the same result for a ball or plate of the same weight. But a plantar pressure platform can differentiate two different shapes' support areas.

In addition, we can observe how the two commonly-used indices are used: the anteroposterior COP (ACOP) displacement and the mediolateral COP (MCOP) displacement (see Fig. 2).

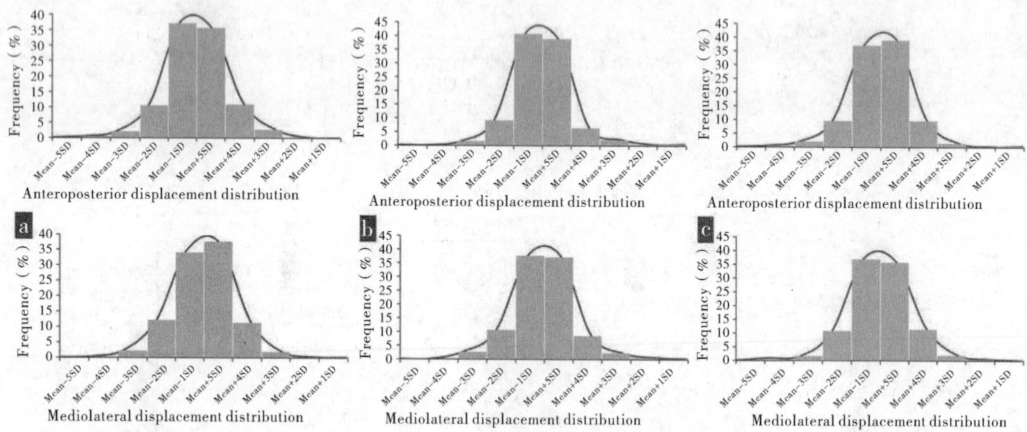

Fig. 2 Distribution of ACOP and MCOP displacement

Fig. 2a is the distribution of ACOP and MCOP when standing with feet together. Fig. 2b is the distribution of ACOP and MCOP when standing with feet shoulder width apart. Fig. 2c is the distribution of ACOP and MCOP when standing with feet slightly wider than shoulder. The calculation of the position value in the figures: first calculate the mean value of the position of ACOP and MCOP when standing, and then calculate the COP position of each instant relative to the mean value.

Fig. 2 shows that for these three postures, the ACOP and MCOP indices can tell the changes of stability. Does it mean that using COP to evaluate standing balance is defective? But this is not the case (see Fig. 3).

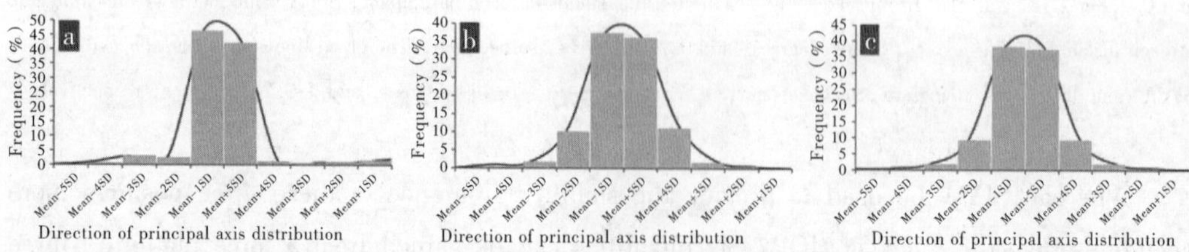

Fig. 3 Direction distribution of SFPA

Fig. 3a is the direction distribution of SFPA when standing with feet together. Fig. 3b is the direction distribution of SFPA when standing with feet shoulder width apart. Fig. 3c is the direction distribution of SFPA when standing with feet slightly wider than shoulder. The calculation of the direction value in the figures: first calculate the mean value of the direction of SFPA when standing, and then calculate the direction value of each instant relative to the mean value.

Fig. 2 and Fig. 3 show that when standing with feet together, the symmetry of ACOP and MCOP displacement is better than that of direction of SFPA, when standing with feet shoulder width apart the symmetry of the direction of SFPA is better than that of the ACOP displacement, and when standing with feet slightly wider than shoulder width, the symmetry of the width direction of SFPA is better than that of the ACOP and MCOP displacement. To further explain this difference, see Table 1.

Table 1　ACOP, MCOP displacement, and direction of SFPA (Mean 6 SD)

Posture	ACOP displacement	MCOP displacement	Direction of SFPA
Posture I[a]	0. 00060. 480	0. 00060. 414	0. 000611. 760
Posture II[b]	0. 00060. 182	0. 00060. 314	0. 00060. 639
Posture III[c]	0. 00060. 174	0. 00060. 306	0. 00060. 296

a, standing with feet together. b, standing with feet shoulder width apart. c, standing with feet slightly wider than shoulder width.

Fig. 2, Fig. 3, and Table 1 show that when standing, when the mean value of displacement of COP or that of the direction of SFPA is set as the coordinate origin, the relative mean value of displacement and direction forms a symmetric pattern. Since the standard deviation reflects the dispersion, Table 1 tells that the SFPA index expresses these three postures more accurately than the ACOP and MCOP indices.

Mechanically, indices such as the center of gravity of the structure and the support area are important to reflect static stability. Generally speaking, the larger the support area, the lower the center of gravity, thus better stability. The anatomical and mechanical structure features of the human body reveal that when comparing the posture while standing with feet together vs. the other two postures, the results from COP and SFPA evaluation should have consistent structure stability mechanically. When standing with feet slightly wider than shoulder width, the center of gravity should be lower and the support area larger than when standing with feet together, leading to better stability. In this aspect, the SFPA evaluation result is more consistent with that of the mechanical analysis.

Another phenomenon draws our attention: in Fig. 1a, values from the participants reflected by COP are normal (comparing with the results from relevant references) while in Fig. 1d, some values are abnormal (comparing values from Fig. 1e and Fig. 1f). We compare how the feet position and posture may affect COP and SFPA to analyze this abnormality. One foot's instantaneous standing footprint is cloned, i. e., to copy one foot's plantar pressure to the other foot symmetrically. Then we analyze the relation between the position, posture, plantar pressures and COP and SFPA (see Fig. 4).

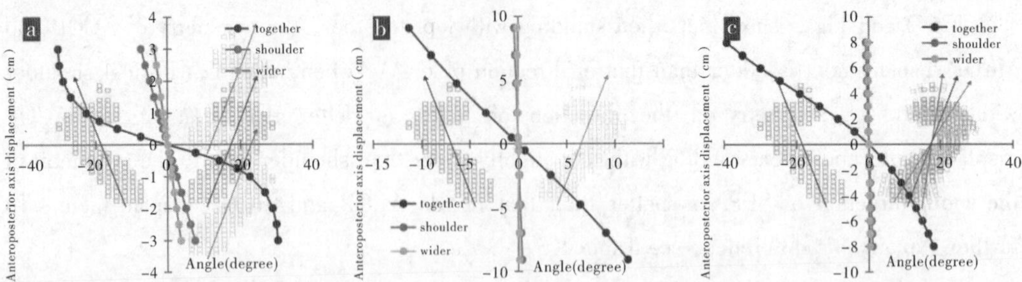

Fig. 4 Relation between position, posture, plantar pressures and COP and SFPA

Fig. 4a shows the relation between anteroposterior position change of both feet and SFPA. Fig4. b shows the relation between plantar pressure change of both feet and COP and SFPA. Fig4. c shows the relation between the rotation of foot and SFPA. In Fig. 4a, left and right foot move anteroposterior symmetrically, i. e. , when the left foot moves forward, the right foot moves backward. In Fig. 4b, when left foot plantar pressure remains unchanged, the right foot plantar pressure multiplies a coefficient (e. g. , 1. 1 or 0. 9) so that the plantar pressures from left and right foot are inconsistent. In Fig. 4c, when left foot remains unchanged, the right foot rotates around its COP. One foot's instantaneous pressure is 323. 26N and there are 115 sensors, indicating the standing footprint area is 115cm^2. The foot's SFPA is ± 16. 52° (right foot is positive and left negative). Let the COP distance between the foot and the cloned one be 11. 67cm when standing with feet together. When standing with feet shoulder width apart, the distance is 28. 67cm and when standing with feet slightly wider than shoulder width, the distance is 51. 67cm.

Fig. 4 shows that: ①When two feet's COP is set as coordinate origin, each foot moves symmetrically upward or downward. The total plantar pressure's COP remains the same, but that of the SFPA changes significantly. ② When the percentage of left/right foot's pressure distribution changes (the pressure distribution ratio of left foot to right foot changes), COP changes (coordinate value of y remains unchanged, but x is changed) and the change is not as significant as that from SFPA when the feet are nearer. ③ When one foot rotates its COP (foot's not feet's), COP does not change, but SFPA changes. This shows that SFPA can work as well as COP to evaluate standing balance. It can also make up for the sensitivity that COP lacks when reflecting the distribution of both feet's total plantar pressure and for the defect occurring when there is no response to the anteroposterior change of position and to the foot's rotation.

Then one fact captures our attention: in the literature, the position index of ACOP and MCOP is determined by the contact position between the foot and the force plate. When both feet's COP positions change the same way, the changed position between the foot and the force plate will bring different results from position index of ACOP and MCOP. How can we ensure that the participants' coordinate from anteroposterior axis and mediolateral axis is consistent with the body coordinate system of the force plate while SFPA has nothing to do with the position when the participant is standing on the plate?

The calculation of COP is similar to that of torque (a physical quantity, which is the product of a unit pressure multiplied by the COP of the distance), which rotates around the

COP's axis. The calculation of SFPA is similar to the product of inertia, which is the product by multiplying a unit pressure by the square of its distance to the COP, resulting in the changeable product of inertia components when it rotates around the COP's axis (and when the distribution is asymmetrical). Mathematically, tensors are geometric objects. Moment is a first-order tensor and product of inertia is a second-order tensor. That justifies why SFPA can function as well as COP to evaluate standing balance. The difference is that SFPA can better explain the distance and posture between feet.

Finally, we analyze the abnormality in Fig. 1d. It is known that for the homogeneous and symmetrical (relative to center of mass) object (such as a circle, a sphere), there are numerous principal axes of inertia (and all the axes that go through the center of mass are all principal axes), revealing that its principal axes of inertia are not unique. Even though the foot's shape is asymmetrical, the position and posture between the feet (and posture) can make SFPA reach 45° (the arctangent in Eq. (4) has no solution at 45°). Fig. 2 and Fig. 3 indicate that in order to avoid this, it is recommended to evaluate balance when standing with feet shoulder width apart and when standing with feet slightly wider than shoulder width.

Since our equipment is mainly used to analyze gait, it cannot meet the requirement to do optimum testing at 20 – 30s trial periods. It is recommended to use a plantar pressure platform of 40 (W) cm × 60 (L) cm (area) and 4 sensors/cm^2.

Application

From the perspective of structural mechanics, one's stability grows with the increasing distance between two feet. From the perspective of the aging musculoskeletal system, the young adults have better stability than the elderly. To verify its validity, using the mean value of young participants' ACOP displacement, MCOP displacement, clockwise and counterclockwise direction of SFPA as symmetrical indices, we tested the standing posture (standing with feet shoulder width apart, 25.925 ± 3.328cm) of 30 healthy elderly people (14 male participants: 68.1 ± 3.31 year, 1.69 ± 0.85m, 63.8 ± 8.3kg; 16 female participants: 66.6 ± 3.1 year, 1.59 ± 0.67m, 50.2 ± 6.6kg). The testing time is 11.5s. The results are shown in Table 2.

Table 2　Symmetry of standing posture (Mean 6 SD)

		Posture I[a, *]	Posture II[b, *]	Posture III[c, *]	Posture II[b, **]
ACOP displacement	Anterior	0.377 ± 0.136	0.142 ± 0.109	0.132 ± 0.082	0.201 ± 0.151
	Posterior	0.371 ± 0.125	0.116 ± 0.047	0.128 ± 0.047	0.186 ± 0.106
	P-value	0.667	0.271	0.889	0.657

(to be continued)

		Posture I[a, *]	Posture II[b, *]	Posture III[c, *]	Posture II[b, **]
MCOP displacement	Left	0. 319 ±0. 122	0. 257 ±0. 136	0. 244 ±0. 098	0. 442 ±0. 206
	Right	0. 335 ±0. 143	0. 230 ±0. 078	0. 241 ±0. 077	0. 430 ±0. 183
	P-value	0. 518	0. 404	0. 826	0. 821
Direction of SFPA	Clockwise	8. 447 ±13. 353	0. 472 ±0. 210	0. 220 ±0. 105	0. 647 ±0. 376
	Counter clockwise	5. 713 ±6. 801	0. 488 ±0. 321	0. 218 ±0. 105	0. 577 ±0. 271
	P-value	0. 323	0. 76	0. 993	0. 413

a, standing with feet together. b, standing with feet shoulder width apart. c, standing with feet slightly wider than shoulder width. * young participants. * * elderly participants. The displacement unit is cm and the direction unit is degree.

Table 2 shows that ① To the young adults, the symmetry of MCOP and ACOP does not grow with the increasing distance between two feet, but their SPAI does; ②The results from MCOP and ACOP reveal better symmetry from the elderly than that from the young while SPAI tells better symmetry from the young than that from the elderly.

We could not yet explain the mechanism behind these phenomena, and maybe the larger standard deviation implies that the sample size remains to be a problem, or maybe the participants have their unidentified structural issues, but one thing is certain—SPAI can be used to evaluate standing balance.

Conclusion

In terms of physical quantities, COP derives from a quantity similar to matrix, which is a tensor; while SFPA derives from a quantity similar to product of inertia, which is a second-order tensor. That explains the difference to reflect feet position and posture and that is an important discovery of this study. In addition, for an ideal standing position, SFPA should be zero. COP lies in the middle of two feet, but it is not easy to determine the exact position because of the foot's shape and its plantar pressure distribution. A theoretical reference value (for example, the best projectile angle of 45) can be of great importance to the evaluation.

The balance test system formed by force sensors can quantify the evaluation of standing balance, but the balance test system formed by pressure sensors can present the distribution of plantar pressure at each instant. When the concept of plantar pressure principal axis is introduced, a new evaluation method is presented. SFPA is related to foot pressure distribution, and to the relative position between feet. The defect that COP index is not sensitive to the changes of relative position of feet is avoided. SFPA can evaluate standing balance dependently (with COP) or independently.

Standing is a basic activity, which is related to walking as well as to falling. That is why standing stability evaluation has captured more attention in preventive medicine for the elderly. We predict that SFPA-based standing footprint diagnostic method will have a wide application in fields such as adolescent medicine, geriatrics and rehabilitation medicine.

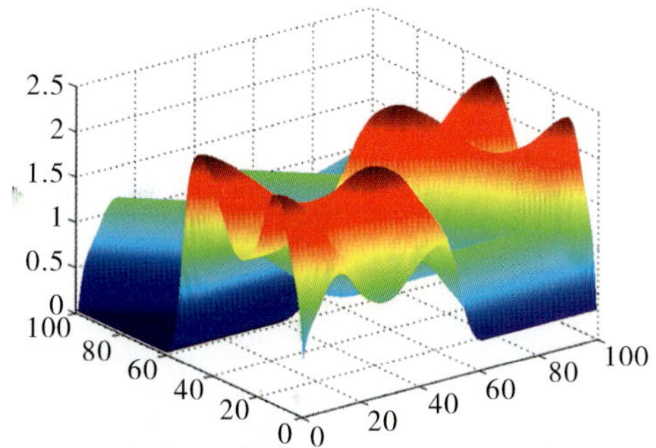

图1　足的着地顺序与 VGRF 变化之间的关系

t 和 t_0 的变化范围都定义在 [0, T] 区间上。

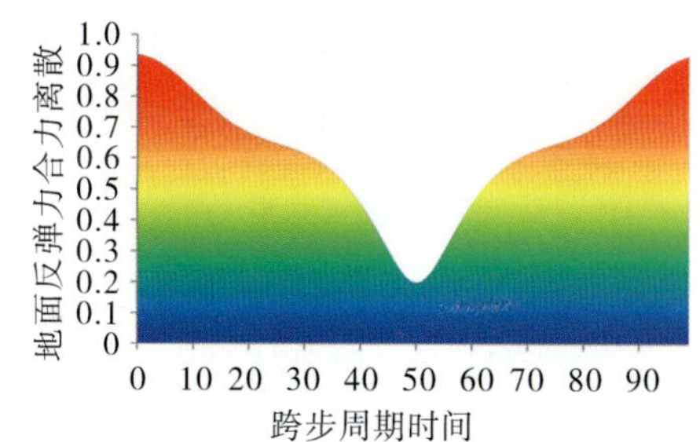

图2　跨步周期中地面反弹力合力离散

跨步时间被百分化，由（t/T）×100 确定。

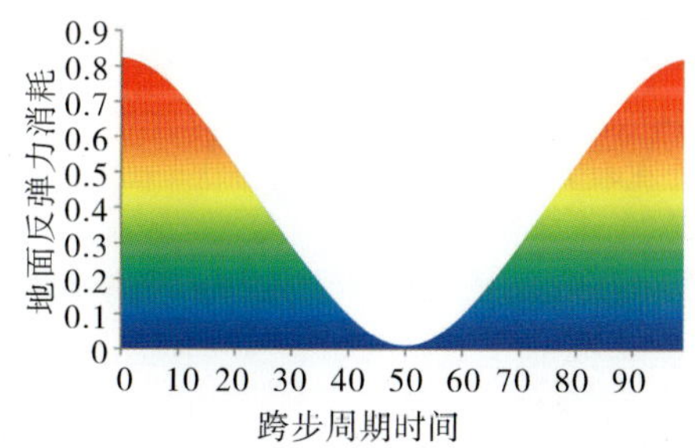

图3　跨步周期中地面反弹力消耗

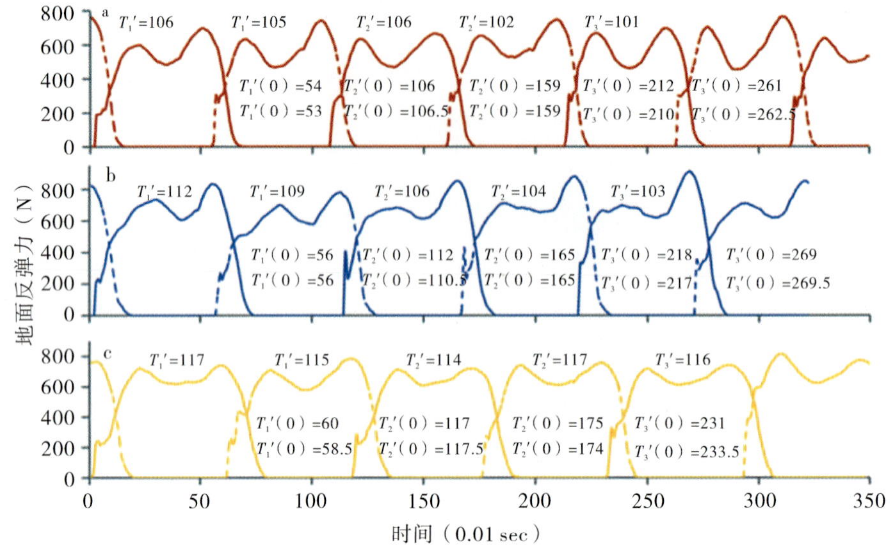

图4　分析结果

图a为一脚踝轻度扭伤的成年人的足底压力；图b为一正常成年人的足底压力；图c为一有轻度风湿性关节炎症的老年人的足底压力。

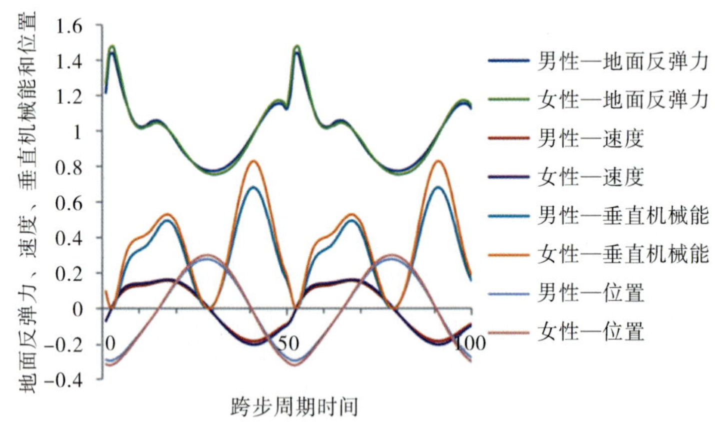

图5　一个跨步周期当中地面反弹力、垂直机械能、质心速度和位置的变化情况

地面反弹力是体重的倍数，也是速率的倍数。为了让这个数据更为显眼，我们将垂直机械能的数值扩大40倍，将质心位置的数值扩大20倍。

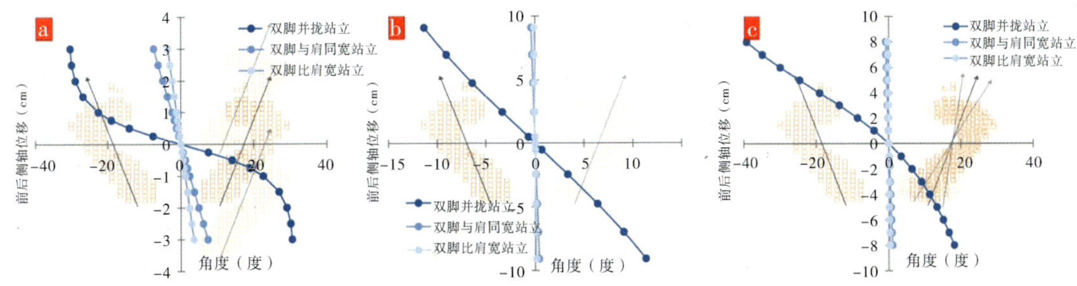

图 31　足位置、姿势、足底压力和压力中心、站立足印迹主轴的关系

图 a 所示为双脚前后位置的改变与站立足印迹主轴的关系；图 b 所示为双脚足底压力的改变与站立足印迹主轴、压力中心的关系；图 c 所示为足旋转与站立足印迹主轴的关系。图 a 左右脚前后对称移动（即左脚向前移动而右脚向后移动）；图 b 左脚足底压力不变，右脚足底压力乘以一个系数（如 1.1 或 0.9），使左右脚足底压力不相同。图 c 左脚保持不变，右脚绕其压力中心旋转。一只脚的瞬时压力为 323.26N，共有 115 个传感器即站立足印迹面积为 $115cm^2$。足站立足印迹主轴为 ±16.52°（右脚为正，左脚为负）。双脚并拢站立时足与复制足的压力中心间距为 11.67cm；双脚分开与肩同宽站立时压力中心间距为 28.67cm；双脚分开比肩稍宽站立时压力中心间距为 51.67cm。

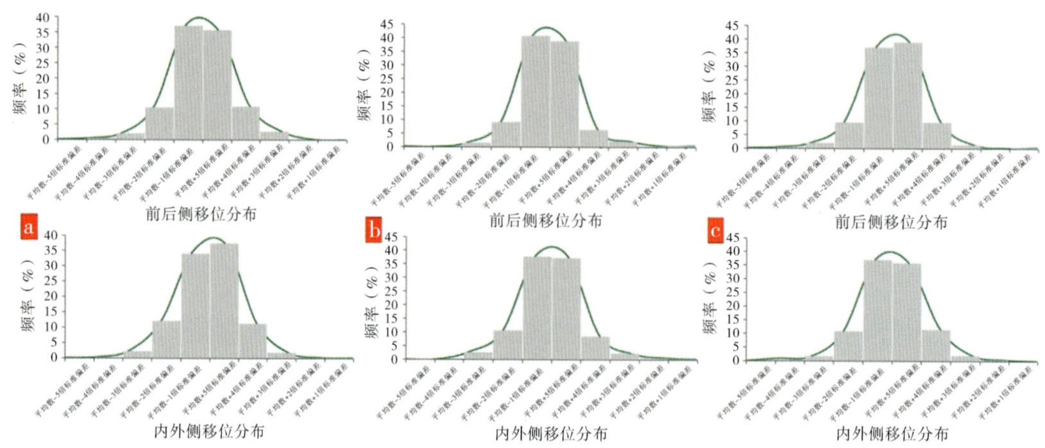

图 29　压力中心和内外侧压力中心位移分布

图 a 所示为双脚并拢站立时前后压力中心和内外侧压力中心分布；图 b 所示为双脚分开与肩同宽站立时前后压力中心和内外侧压力中心分布；图 c 所示为双脚分开比肩稍宽站立时前后压力中心和内外侧压力中心分布。图中位置数值计算方法：首先计算站立时前后压力中心与 M 压力中心位置的平均值，然后计算相对平均值的瞬时压力中心位置。

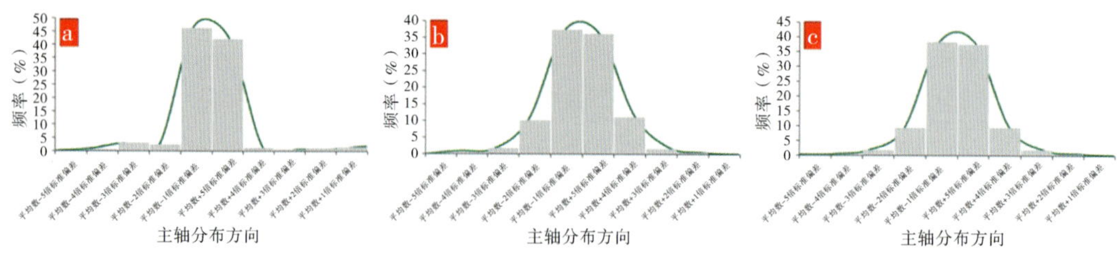

图 30　站立足印迹主轴方向分布

图 a 所示为双脚并拢站立时站立足印迹主轴方向分布；图 b 所示为双脚分开与肩同宽站立时站立足印迹主轴方向分布；图 c 所示为双脚分开比肩稍宽站立时站立足印迹主轴方向分布。图中方向数值计算方法：首先计算站立时站立足印迹主轴方向的平均值，然后计算相对平均值的瞬时方向值。

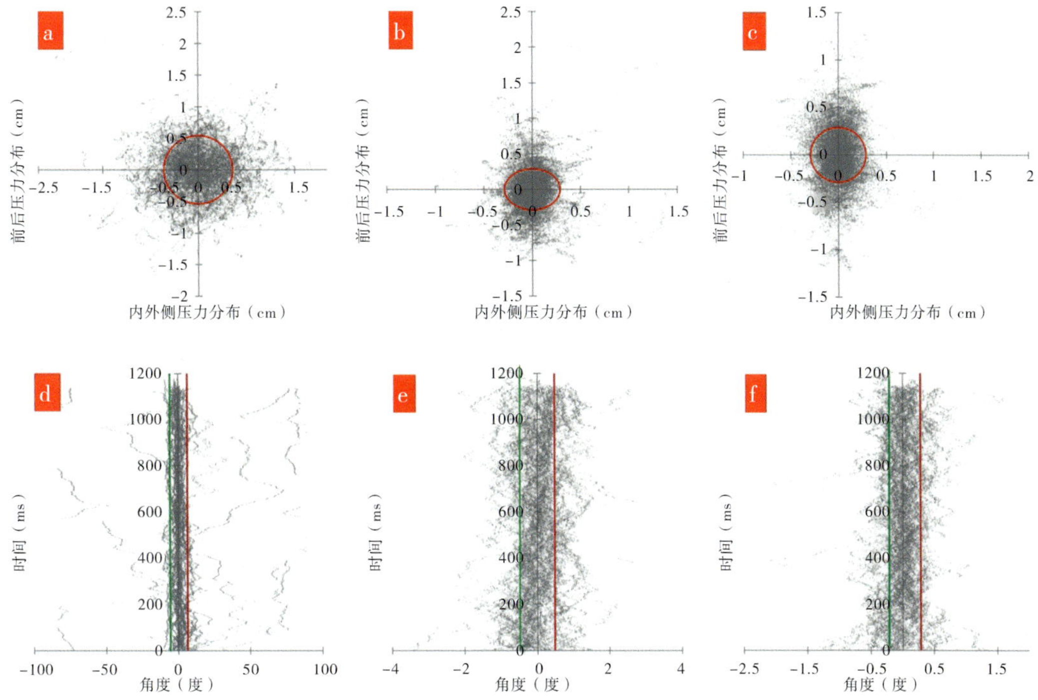

图 28　压力中心和站立足印迹主轴分布

图 a 所示为双脚并拢站立时压力中心分布；图 b 所示为双脚分开与肩同宽站立时压力中心分布；图 c 所示为双脚分开比肩稍宽站立时压力中心分布；图 d 所示为双脚并拢站立时站立足印迹主轴分布；图 e 所示为双脚分开与肩同宽站立时站立足印迹主轴分布；图 f 所示为双脚分开比肩稍宽站立时站立足印迹主轴分布。图 a 至图 c 的红色圆圈代表所有受试者瞬时压力中心的平均半径。三种姿势的该数值分别为：0.5391cm，0.287cm，0.288cm。图 d 至图 f 的红线代表每位受试者瞬时站立足印迹主轴数值大于零，且分别为：8.455°，0.469°，0.232°；绿线代表每位受试者瞬时站立足印迹主轴数值小于零，且分别为：-5.701°，-0.499°，-0.235°。

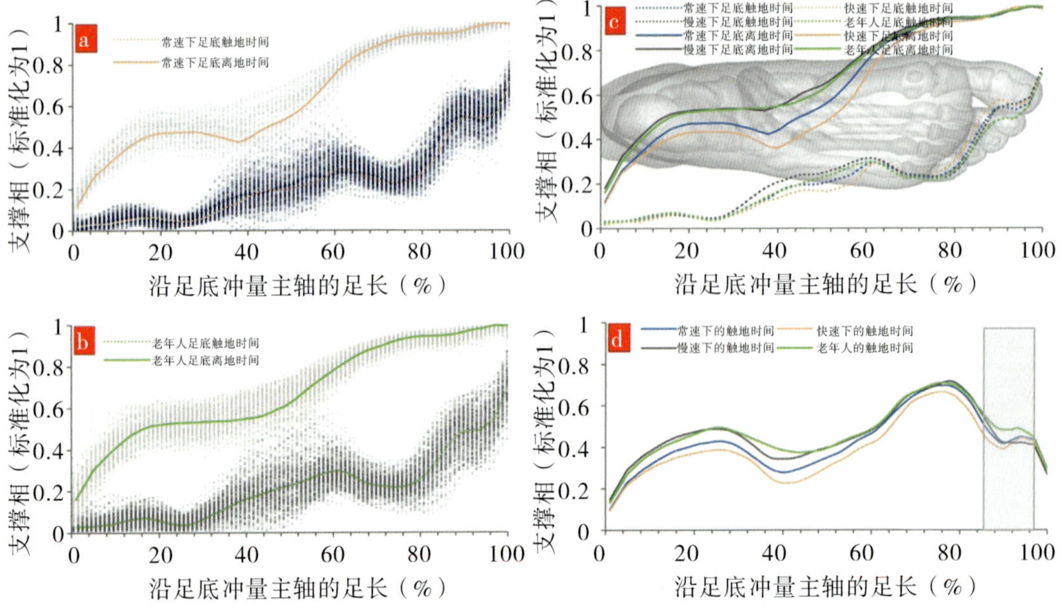

图 26　沿足底冲量主轴的足底着地、离地时序

图 a 所示为青年人自然步态下沿足底冲量主轴的足底着地、离地时序。图 b 所示为老年人自然步态下沿足底冲量主轴的足底着地、离地时序。图 c 所示为青年人自然、快速和慢速步速与老年人自然步态下沿足底冲量主轴的足底着地、离地时序。图 d 所示为沿足底冲量主轴的足底支撑相时间分布。取受试者 6 个连续的足印迹（左右各 3 个）。此平均值为沿足底冲量主轴足趾着地时序指标。用 $\bar{t}_l^T - \bar{t}_l^O$ 计算支撑相时间。

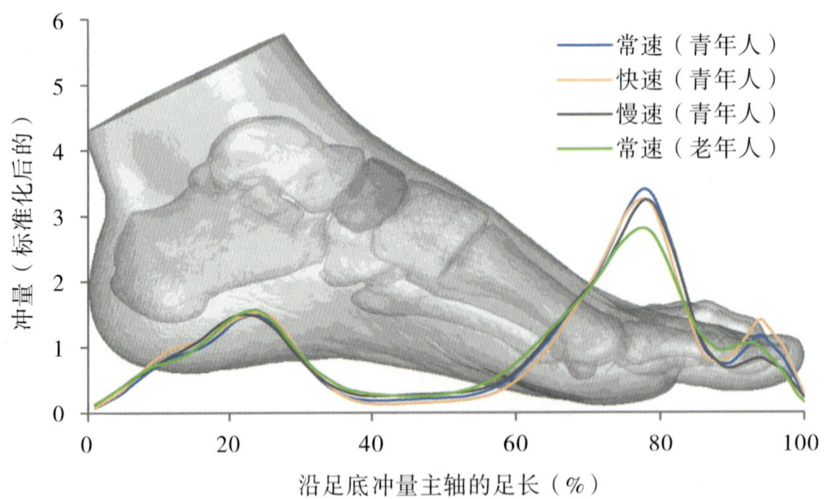

图 27　沿足长的冲量分布

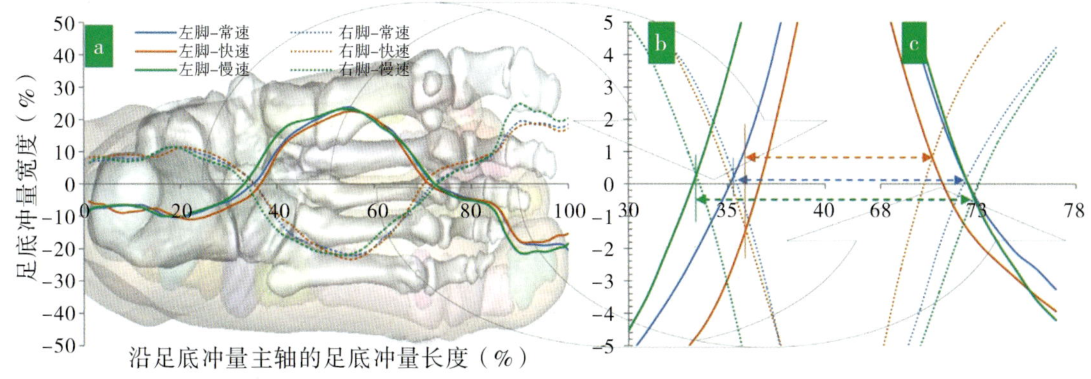

图 24 足底冲量的分布曲线

图 a 为健康年轻受试者的三个步速的足底冲量分布曲线。图 b 所示为脚跟交叉点（第一交叉点）。图 c 所示为前脚交叉点（第二交叉点）。x 轴代表足部宽度中线。

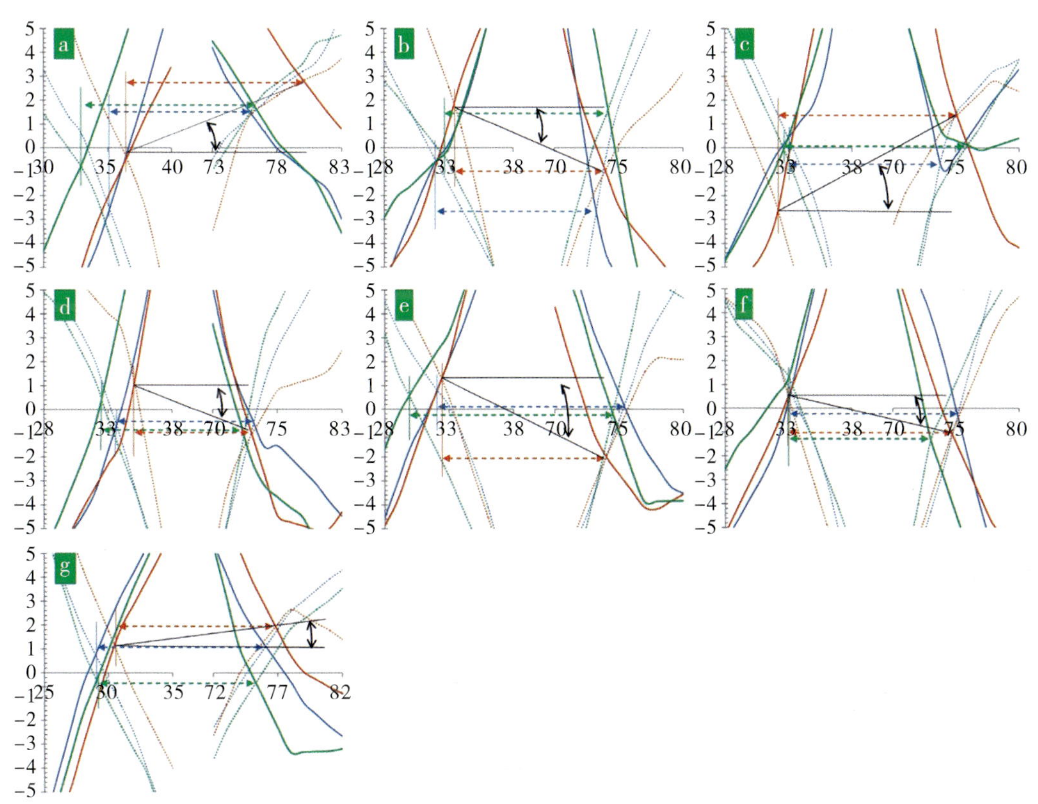

图 25 跟腱断裂病人足底冲量的分布曲线

图 a 至图 g 所示为脚跟交叉点（第一交叉点）和前脚交叉点（第二交叉点），其中水平轴指的是足底冲量长度，而垂直轴指的是足底冲量。

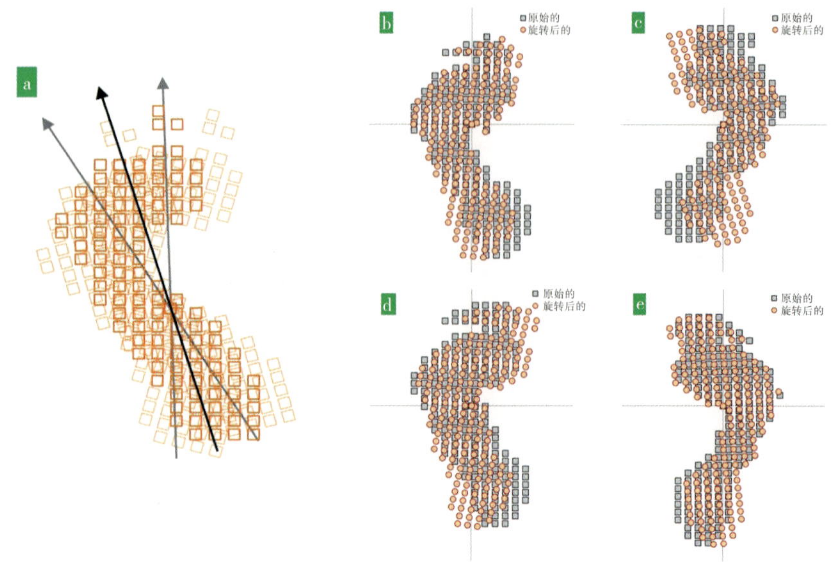

图 22　沿足底冲量主轴的足底冲量

图 a 为绕通过足底冲量中心垂直轴旋转的足底冲量。图 b 为足底冲量定位前后的第一次足底冲量（左脚）。图 c 为足底冲量定位前后的第二次足底冲量（右脚）。图 d 为足底冲量定位前后的第三次足底冲量（左脚）。图 e 为足底冲量定位前后的第四次足底冲量（右脚）。在这些图中，黑色表示定位前原始足底冲量，红色表示定位后足底冲量。在第一个足底冲量旋转 7.66°，第二个 214.37°，第三个 10.25°和第四个 -5.00°之后确定主轴。

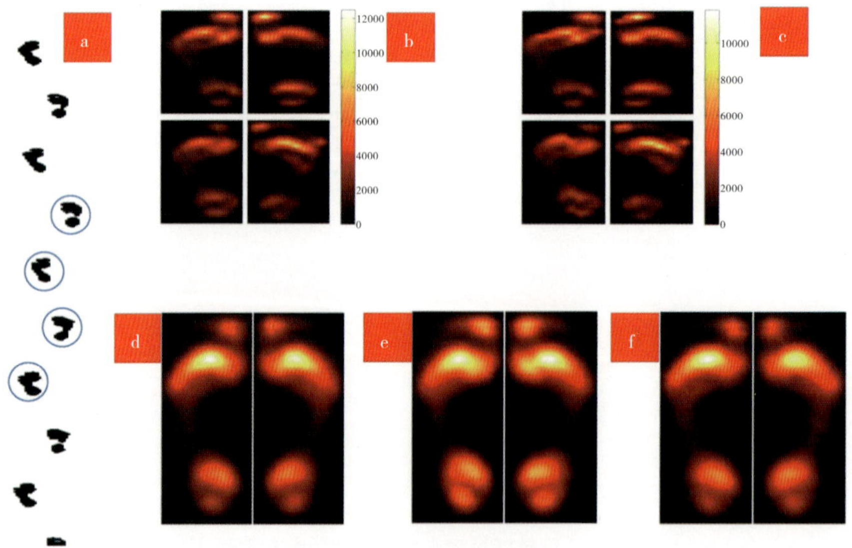

图 23　足底冲量标准化

图 a 为用 Zebris FDM 测试的足底冲量。图 b 为 4 个连续的足底冲量。图 c 为用足底冲量主轴定位的每一足底冲量。图 d 为足底冲量标准化后自然步态的足底冲量。图 e 为足底冲量标准化后快速步态的足底冲量。图 f 为足底冲量标准化后慢速步态的足底冲量。图 b、图 c 来自同一名受试者。图 d 至图 f 为 20 名健康青年受试者（每人 6 个足印迹，左右各 3 个）。

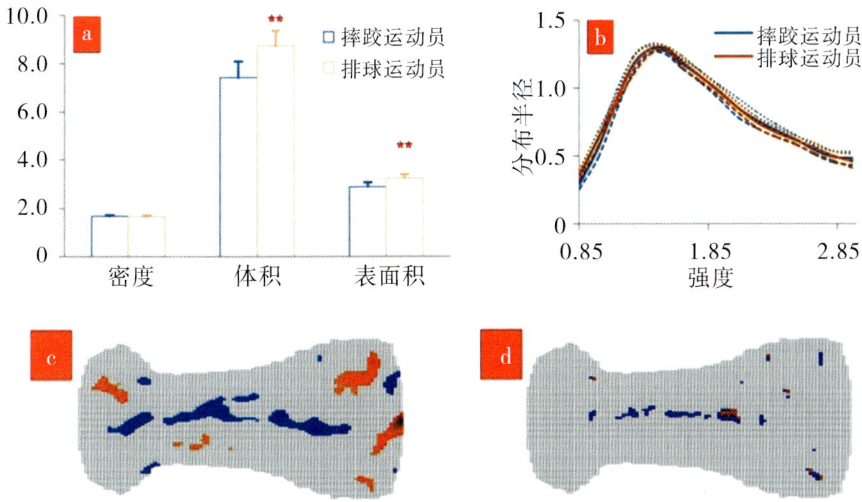

图 21　8 位摔跤运动员与排球运动员第四跖骨（左足）骨强度分析

图 a 为两组运动员第四跖骨（左足）骨密度、体积和面积对比。图 b 为两组运动员第四跖骨（左足）骨组织密度和组织分布半径之间的关系。图 c 为两组运动员第四跖骨（左足）均值地图差异。图 d 为两组运动员第四跖骨（左足）地图 P（压力）值分布。在图 a 中，骨密度定义为 $\rho = \frac{\sum_{1}^{N}\rho_i}{N}$，其中 $\rho_i = \frac{g_i}{g_w}$，g_i 代表第 i 个体微元灰度值，g_w 代表水的灰度值。由 Mimics 得出体积和面积。图 c 中，当 $p_v(x, y) - p_w(x, y) > \lambda$，或者 $p_v(x, y) - p_w(x, y) < -\lambda$，$p_v(x, y) - p_w(x, y)$ 被着色，其中 $p_v(x, y)$ 和 $p_w(x, y)$ 分别代表排球运动员和摔跤运动员第四跖骨的（x，y）坐标位置等高线值，蓝色表示 $< -\lambda$，红色表示 $> \lambda$（$\lambda = 0.5$）。图 d 中，由 SPSS 完成运算，其中蓝色代表示 $p < 0.05$，红色表示 $p < 0.01$。

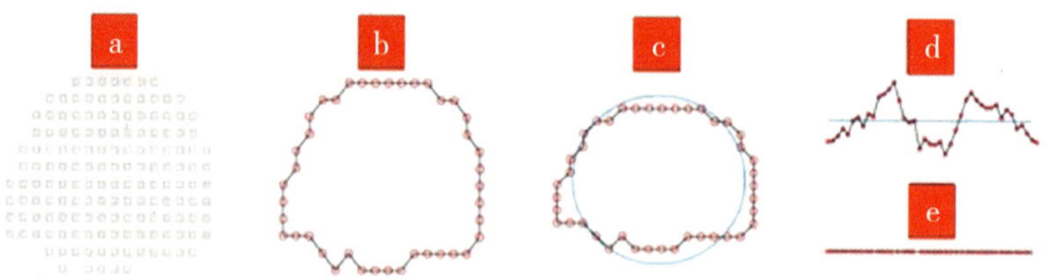

图 18　骨断层图像展开法

图 a 为进行 SCS 后应用方程（4）得出的重建断层图。图 b 为从方程（5）提取的断层边界。图 c 为断层图像平均半径得出的圆，其圆心位于断层图的质心上。图 d 为以圆周方程（6）和方程（7）所展开的断层边界，视圆周作“海平面”。图 e 为由方程（8）摊平的断层边界。

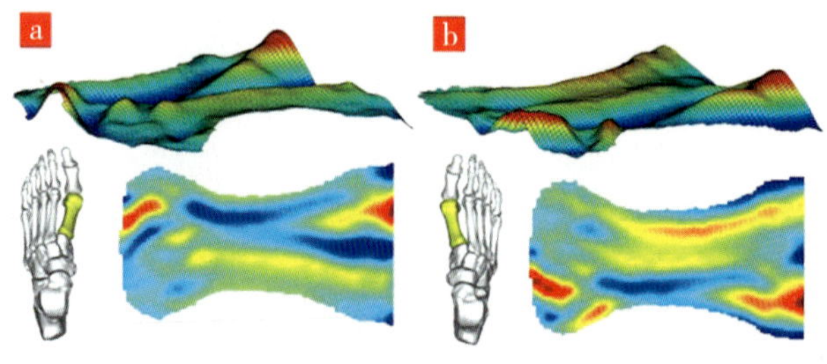

图 19　人对称足骨地图化

图 a 为一受试者左足第一跖骨。图 b 为一受试者右足第一跖骨。切线为第一跖骨最小惯量主轴（第一跖骨某部分始端和底端并不在切线上，因此这些部分并不包括在地图中）。

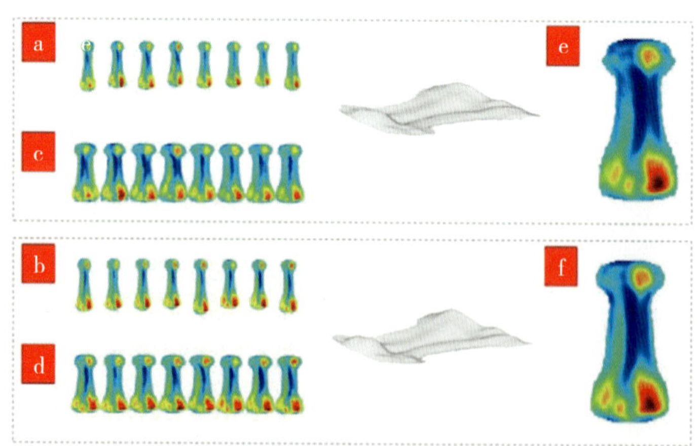

图 20　第四跖骨的地图化分析

图 a 和图 b 分别为 8 位摔跤运动员和排球运动员第四跖骨（左足）的地图化图。图 c 与图 d 分别为两组运动员（左足）第四跖骨长宽标准化后的地图化图。图 e 至图 f 分别为两组运动员（左足）第四跖骨均值地图化图。对两组运动员第四跖骨（左足）依照方程（3）进行 SCS，重建断层图像。运用方程（4）至方程（7）展开重建的图像，如图 a 与图 b 所示。为了标准化跖骨地图的长宽值，引入相同的长宽值，如图 c 与图 d 所示。在标准化跖骨地图上进行统计分析，从而计算同一位置上八幅跖骨地图的均值，如图 e 与图 f 所示。

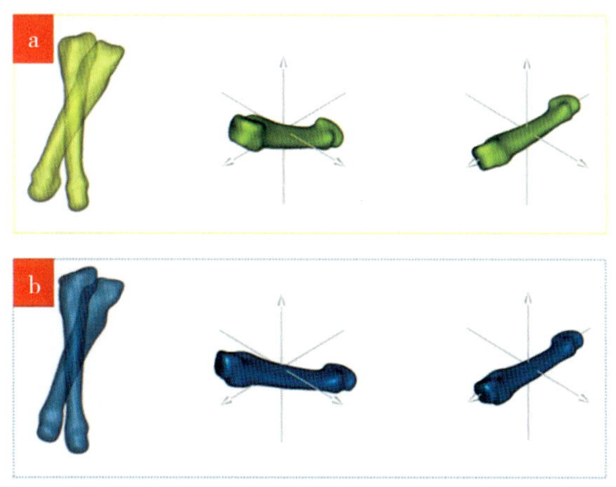

图 16　第四跖骨标准化坐标系

图 a 为摔跤运动员第四跖骨的标准化坐标系；图 b 为排球运动员第四跖骨的标准化坐标系。用 Mimics 重构第四跖骨的三维模型，由“点云”处理（Mimics 中的一个选项）储存为文本文件格式。应用方程（3）进行坐标系标准化，用 Geomagic Studio 进行处理后的“点云”数据封装与摊平。然后，储存三维模型为 STL（标准模板库）文件。最后，导入标准化的第四跖骨三维模型到 Mimics。左图为运用标准化坐标系（SCS）前后的骨对比图，中间图为运用 SCS 之前本体坐标系中的骨骼姿态，而右图为运用 SCS 之后本体坐标系中的骨骼姿态。当设备坐标系转化为骨质心，便可以发现两物体第四跖骨的两种不同的姿态。但在运用 SCS 后，骨的本体坐标轴便转化为骨的惯量主轴，骨骼的姿态方向能统一于坐标系当中。

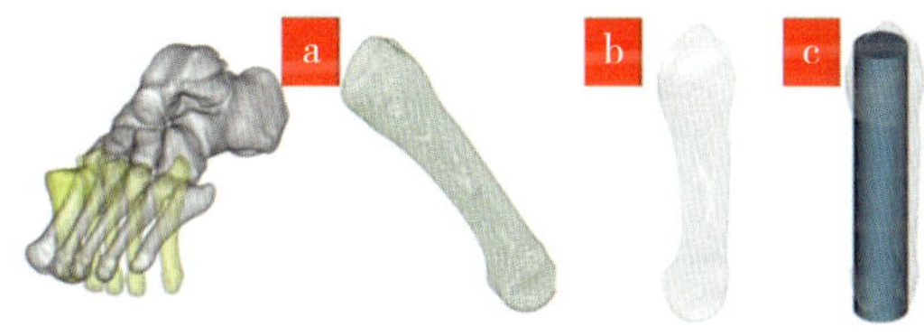

图 17　运用 SCS 后第四跖骨的断层重建

图 a 为运用 SCS 前第四跖骨的断层图像。图 b 为运用 SCS 后第四跖骨的断层图像。图 c 为运用 SCS 后第四跖骨的断层图像与“海平面”。根据第四跖骨的形态学特征，设相对于长惯量主轴（主转动惯量为最小值）的第四跖骨骨组织间距平均值为半径，那么圆柱体与长惯量主轴的中轴将会重合。左图为第一至第五跖骨在 SCS 前后的姿态对比。若圆柱体放置在图 a 中，并非骨断层图像，而是运用 SCS 后的断层重建图像垂直于圆柱中轴（亦即最小惯量的主轴）。受试者的姿态决定圆柱体的非垂直中轴的断层图像。不同的姿态会形成不同的断层图像。在没有 SCS 的情况下，骨表面地图的展开断层边界并无唯一性，但使用 SCS 能形成独特骨表面地图。

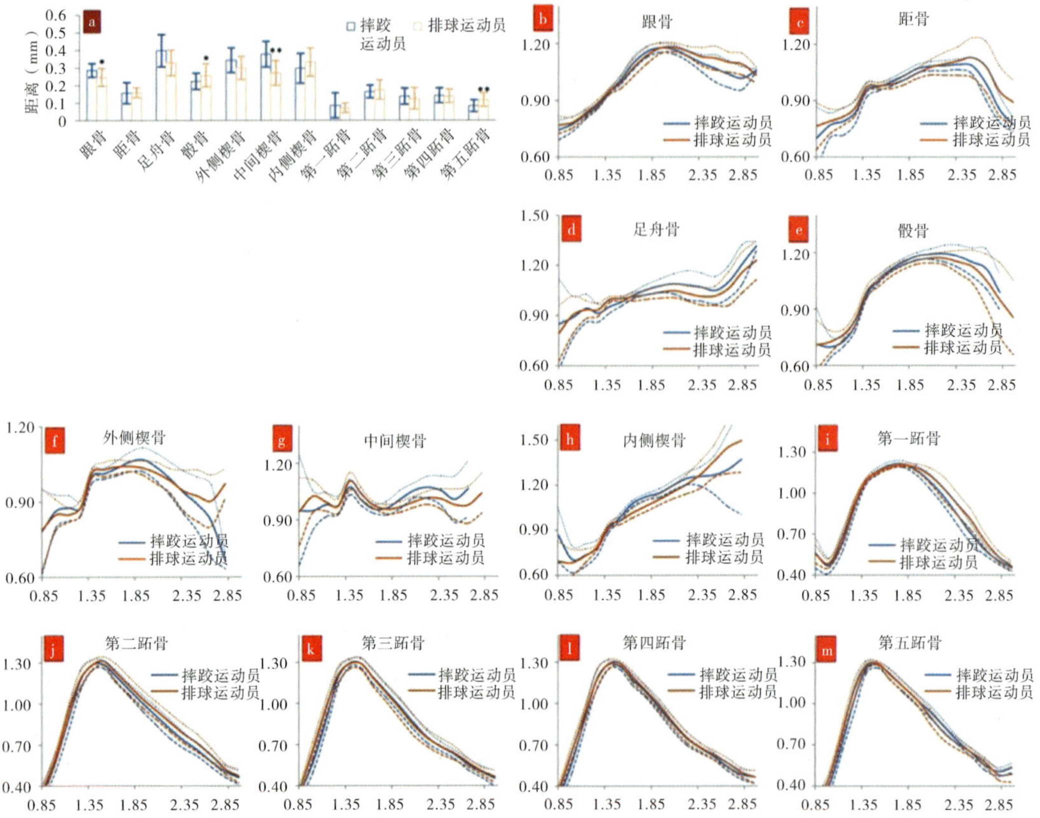

图 14　骨质心与形心高度重合原理的应用

图 a 为密质骨形心和骨形心之间的位置关系；图 b～图 m 为骨组织密度与分布半径的关系；其中 x 轴代表组织密度，y 轴代表组织标准化平均分布半径。数据采集于 192 块摔跤运动员足骨和 192 块排球运动员足骨。$* p<0.05$，$** p<0.01$. 当 $\rho>1.65$ 时，骨组织为密质骨。方程（2）和方程（3）用以计算密质骨质心与形心，方程（4）计算两点间距，方程（5）计算骨组织分布半径。图 a 为密质骨质心与形心间距的结果，质心与形心由骨组织半径进行标准化。方程（6）用于计算相同密度的组织半径，由骨组织半径标准化。见图 b～图 m。

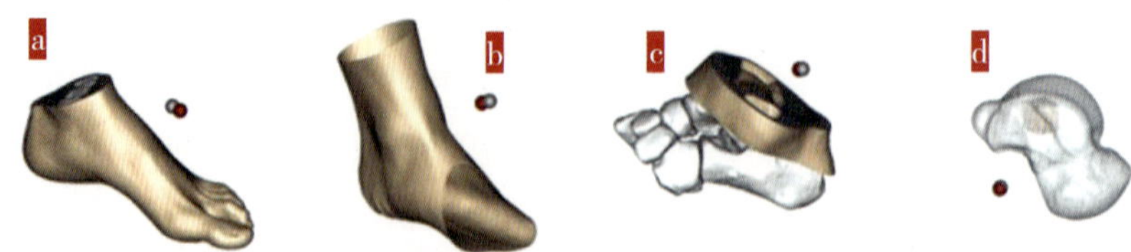

图 15　非骨组织质心与形心

图 a 为足骨质心与形心位置关系；图 b 为踝部皮肤的质心与形心位置关系；图 c 为非骨组织（为一组取于踝关节的断层影像）质心与形心位置关系；图 d 为在距骨形心周围建立单位为 $1cm^3$ ROI 的质心与形心位置关系。灰色小球代表质心位置，红色小球代表形心位置。小球半径为 0.5mm。根据非骨组织密度定义，方程（2）和方程（3）用于计算非骨组织质心和形心。三维模型构建出于 Mimics。

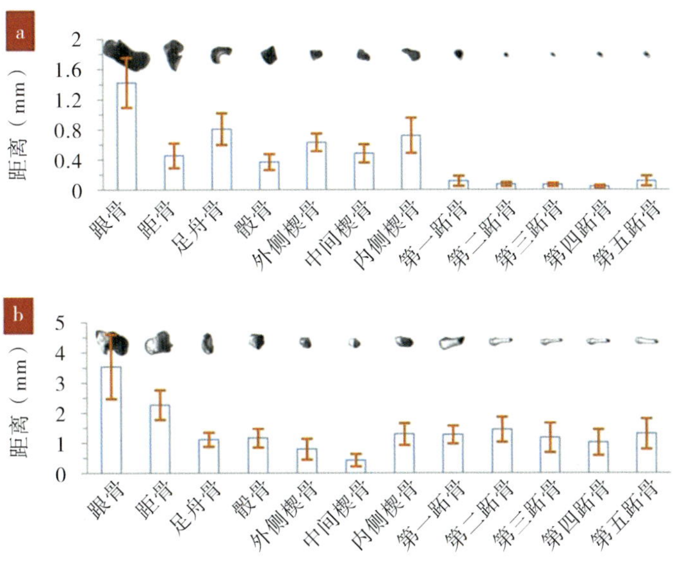

图 12　截面质心与形心之间的关系

图 a 为经过坐标原点的截面的质心与形心之间的位置关系；图 b 为截面形心与骨形心之间的位置关系。当 z 轴的截面体微元位置值约等于骨形心，即 $z_i \approx z_s$，则截面断层经过骨形心。计算骨骼截面质心与形心，然后通过平面距离公式计算两点之间的距离。图 a、图 b 所示为由平面距离公式算出的形心截面与骨形心在 $x-y$ 平面上（x_s，y_s）坐标的间距。

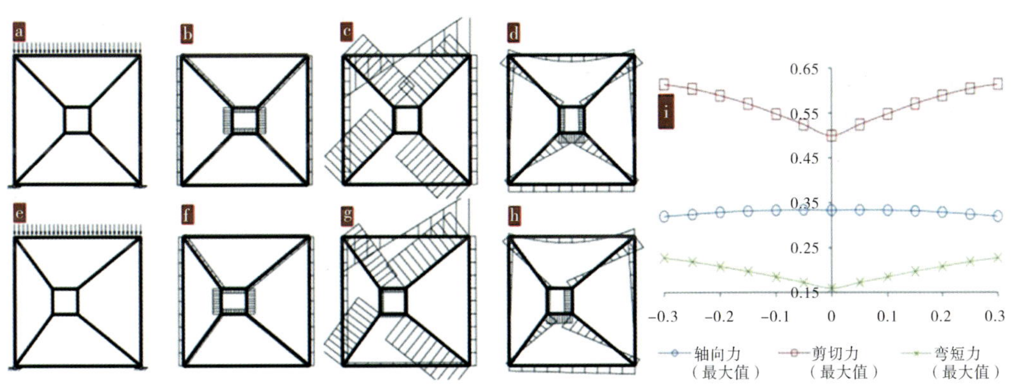

图 13　桁梁的质心与形心

图 a 与图 c 为约束与负荷下的结构：图 3b 和图 3f 为该结构的轴力分布：图 c 与图 g 为该结构剪力分布；图 d 与图 h 为该结构的弯矩分布；图 i 为内正方形位置与强度之间的关系。该结构的支杆及支杆间的连接皆为刚性。内外正方形边长分别为 1 和 0.2。将两个正方形的顶点连接，构成简单的机构性力学模型。使大正方形底部的顶点相交，而上部则取决于分布负荷（体积为 1），小正方形的纵坐标高度重合于大正方形。横坐标范围调节至 ±0.3。利用 SMSolver 软件，得出结果如图 a ~ 图 i 所示。

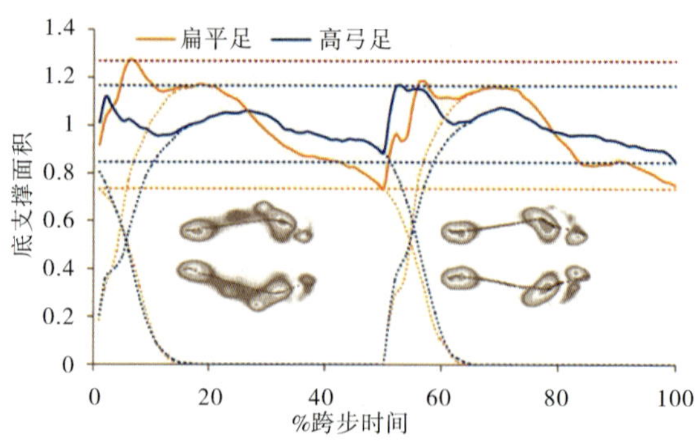

图 10　足底支撑面积和跨步时间的关系

蓝色（深色）虚线表示高弓足者左右足的足底支撑面积，蓝色（深色）实线表示高弓足者足底支撑面积之和，蓝色（深色）水平虚线表示高弓足者足底支撑面积之和的变化范围。红色（浅色）虚线表示扁平足者左右足的足底支撑面积，红色（浅色）实线表示扁平足者足底支撑面积之和，红色（浅色）水平虚线表示扁平足者足底支撑面积之和的变化范围。左右足的反弹力来自于 Zebris FDM 的测试报告，足底支撑面积之和采用 $F_{\mathrm{sum}}(t)=F_{\mathrm{left}}(t)+F_{\mathrm{right}}(t+t_0)$ 得到。根据步态最小作用量原理，$t_0=\frac{1}{2}T$，T 为跨步周期时间。

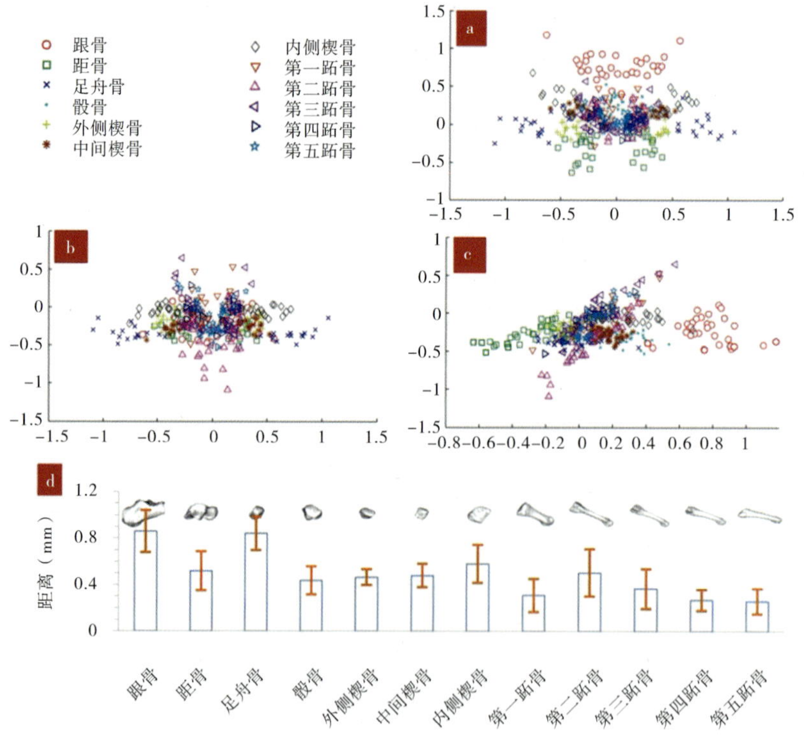

图 11　骨骼质心与形心的位置关系

图 a 为 $x-y$ 平面上的质心与形心之间的位置关系；图 b 为 $x-z$ 平面上的质心与形心之间的位置关系；图 c 为 $y-z$ 平面上的质心与形心之间的位置关系；图 d 为质心与形心的距离；骨骼形心与质心结果源于方程（2）和方程（3）的演算。以质心为原点选择坐标系时，与形心的坐标相关，可推得 $(x_s-x_c,\ y_s-y_c,\ z_s-z_c)$。通过用 $(x_s-x_c,\ y_s-y_c)$，$(y_s-y_c,\ z_s-z_c)$ 和 $(x_s-x_c,\ z_s-z_c)$，384 块关于质心的形心骨骼坐标能够定位于 $x-y$，$y-z$ 及 $x-z$ 平面上。如图 a、图 b 和图 c 所示（单位为 mm）。通过方程（4），能够算出 384 块骨头的形心与质心的间距，得出图 d。

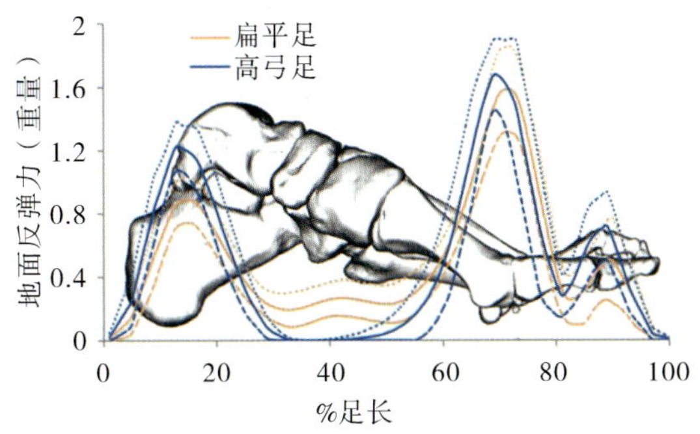

图8　支撑相足部VGRF分布

蓝色（深色）实线表示高弓足者足底VGRF，蓝色（深色）色带表示高弓足者足底VGRF的标准误差线。红色（浅色）实线表示扁平足者足底VGRF，红色（浅色）色带表示扁平足者足底VGRF的标准误差线。地面反弹力根据体重进行标准化（体重标准化为1），跨步周期时间和足长被百分化。

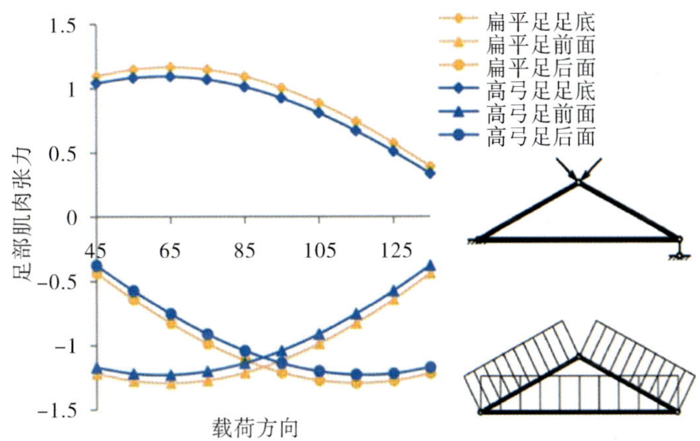

图9　肌群拉力和负重之间的关系

把足弓简化为三角形构架，构架宽度（足长）标准化为1，构架高（足弓高）为足弓指数，集中力大小为1，方向由45°变为135°，力加载在构架顶端。

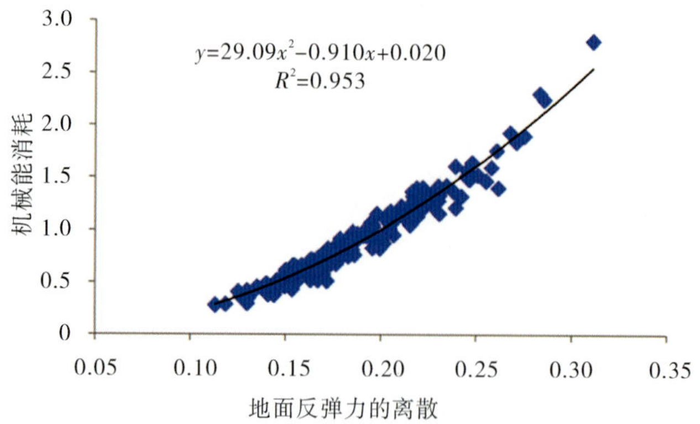

图 6　垂直机械能的消耗

用受试者地面反弹力离散程度的函数来表示垂直机械能的消耗。实曲线是对数据的二次拟合。

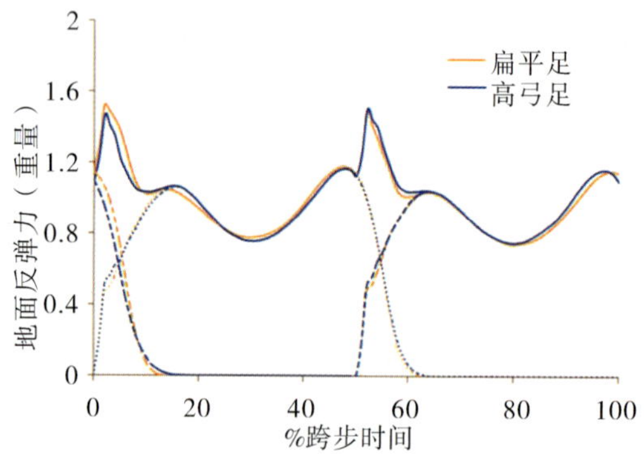

图 7　跨步时间与 VGRF 的关系

蓝色（深色）虚线表示高弓足者左右足的 VGRF，蓝色（深色）实线表示高弓足者 VGRF 合力。红色（浅色）虚线表示扁平足者左右足的 VGRF，红色（浅色）实线表示扁平足者 VGRF 合力。左右足的反弹力来自于 Zebris FDM 的测试报告，合力采用 $F_{sum}(t)=F_{left}(t)+F_{right}(t+t_0)$ 得到。根据步态最小作用量原理，$t_0=\frac{1}{2}T$，T 为跨步周期时间。